UNDERSTANDING
FOLK
RELIGION

D0165351

UNDERSTANDING
FOLK
RELIGION

A CHRISTIAN RESPONSE to POPULAR BELIEFS AND PRACTICES

PAUL G. HIEBERT
R. DANIEL SHAW
TITE TIÉNOU

Baker Books

A Division of Baker Book House Co
Grand Rapids, Michigan 49516

© 1999 by Paul G. Hiebert, R. Daniel Shaw, and Tite Tiénou

Published by Baker Books
a division of Baker Book House Company
P.O. Box 6287, Grand Rapids, MI 49516-6287

Printed in the United States of America

Library of Congress Cataloging-in-Publication Data

Hiebert, Paul G., 1932–
    Understanding folk religion : a Christian response to popular beliefs and practices / Paul Hiebert, R. Daniel Shaw, Tite Tiénou.
       p.   cm.
    Includes bibliographical references and index.
    ISBN 0-8010-2219-3
    1. Christianity and other religions. I. Shaw, R. Daniel (Robert Daniel), 1943–
II. Tiénou, Tite. III. Title.
BR127.H54   1999
251.2dc21   99-046639

For information about academic books, resources for Christian leaders, and all new releases available from Baker Book House, visit our web site:
http://www.bakerbooks.com

To:
Frances, Karen, Marie
Coworkers with us in the Lord's ministry.

CONTENTS

PREFACE

Many books are born out of life experiences. This is one of them. We, the authors, have been involved in church planting ministries around the world, and we have faced similar problems in the lives of many Christians. Paul Hiebert served in South India. He studied Hinduism to communicate the gospel more effectively in rural India, but he found that most villagers knew little more than the rudiments of Hindu theology. He found himself teaching them their theology in order to present Christ as the better way. He also found that much of village religion has little to do with Hinduism. Hinduism stresses *ahimsa*, not taking life, but many of the village ceremonies involved blood ceremonies. Hinduism has high-caste priests, but many of the priests in local rites are from the low castes and untouchables. Hinduism deals with cosmic gods, but village beliefs focus on the many local spirits that reside in trees, rivers, rocks, and hills. He found that new converts to Christianity left the Hindu temples and attended churches, but they still struggled with the questions of spirits, magic, divination, and ancestors. It became increasingly clear that missionaries must not only study Scripture and the formal religions of the people they serve, but also the day-to-day religious beliefs and practices that rule the people's lives if they wanted to communicate the gospel as an answer to all the people's hopes and fears.

Daniel Shaw served as a Bible translator among the Samo in Papua New Guinea. As an International Anthropology consultant for the Summer Institute of Linguistics, he studied the religious beliefs and practices of people in the many small-scale societies of Melanesia to assist translators to communicate God's word effectively in communities in which local beliefs often center around spirits, magic, divination, and ancestors, and are accompanied by ritual and ceremony designed to bring comfort and security. He sought to understand cargo cults with their focus on a local messiah who often led people to their destruction rather than to the salvation they so eagerly sought. He wrestled with translating the cosmic truths of the gospel for people living in highly particularist religious communities into languages where there was no name for an all encompassing creator God. It became clear that translators had to relate closely to people who held to ani-

9

mistic beliefs, and to demonstrate through their own life experience that God's power is stronger and more mighty than the strongest sorcerers and evil spirits.

Tite Tiénou has extensive experience in theological education and ministerial formation in Africa and the United States. He is the founding director of a Bible school in Burkina Faso, and the founding President and Dean of a seminary in Côte d'Ivoire. He taught world religions and African religions for more than a decade in various settings: a Bible school in Burkina Faso, study centers and seminars in Africa, and seminaries in Côte d'Ivoire and the United States.

Some books are matured in classes. This is one of them. We have tested many of the ideas in this book in classes and doctoral seminars on folk religion, folk Islam, folk Hinduism, African Traditional Religions, and religions of the Pacific Islands. We owe much to the many participants in these classes and seminars, who contributed immeasurably to our thinking. We also profited greatly from reading the doctoral dissertations on the subject written by missionaries and church leaders serving around the world. Many of them will recognize the results of class discussions in which they participated. Others will see their works cited in the text. To all of them, we offer our deep thanks for their contributions to our thinking.

Much has been written in recent years on various aspects of folk religions, such as demon possession, spiritual warfare, witchcraft, divination, and power encounters. Most of it has approached the subject taxonomically—looking at the different kinds of spirits, powers, divination, and ancestors found around the world. These studies introduce the reader to the bewildering array of beliefs found in folk religions, but they do not help us understand why faithful Christians persist in turning to traditional practices in times of crisis. For this, we need to understand the reasons why people return to old ways. This book is an attempt to look beneath the surface of taxonomies to examine folk religions as legitimate belief systems that do, in some measure, answer the longing of human hearts. This does not mean we believe them to be true or biblical in nature. It does mean we must take them seriously and provide better answers if we want the old ways to die out.

The purpose of this book is not to present ready answers to the questions folk religions pose. Rather, it is to sensitize Christians to the need to deal with folk religions, and to understand them. It is to challenge Christian leaders to think biblically in responding to them. Most attention is given to understanding the nature of folk religions and the reasons why they persist despite centuries of church censure. Some guidelines for theological responses are offered, but more attention is given to analyzing the questions folk religions seek to answer because most church leaders have more knowledge of biblical truths than of human beliefs and practices.

Every book is based on implicit systems of belief. This one is no exception. It is important to make these explicit so that readers know where the authors are coming from, and to keep readers from expecting more than is intended and faulting the authors for not including materials not promised. The writers are committed evangelicals who believe that God has called all people to follow Jesus Christ. Their theological convictions shape the way they respond to folk religions. The authors are committed to the mission that God is carrying out through his church in the world, and they view mission in certain ways.

First, mission is about people, not programs. It is not projects to be accomplished through human engineering and action. It begins with learning to understand people deeply, identifying with them, and building relationships of love and trust. It is to communicate the gospel to them in ways they understand that can help them to critique their old religious ways, and to think biblically in their everyday lives. Those who expect in this book to find formulas or strategies for quick solutions to the problems raised by folk religions will be disappointed.

Second, mission is about principles, not pragmatic answers. It is easy to try alternative solutions to see which works, but to do so is to reduce missions to problem solving. Christianity is about truth and righteousness, not only in the ends it seeks, but also the means it uses to achieve those ends. The medium is an essential part of the biblical message. There is no easy shortcut to the goals of Christian ministry.

Third, mission has to do with the particular, not only the universal. When God spoke, he spoke to Moses on the Mount, David in the field, and Esther in the palace. He addressed them in their languages and contexts. The gospel is not truth in general. It is truth for people who live in specific places and times, and are caught in particular straits in life. In dealing with folk religions it is important to remember that they are incredibly diverse. Models for analysis, such as the one offered in this book, provide broad guidelines for the study of folk religions, but church leaders and missionaries must move beyond these models to understandings and answers specific to their contexts. There are no standard answers that fit all, or even most, of the cases.

Finally, mission is a process, not a task to complete. It is calling people to faith, discipling them, organizing them into living congregations, encouraging them to do theological reflection in their contexts, and sharing with them the vision of God's mission to the world. It must continue as new fields of ministry are opened, new generations are born, and cultures and societies change. Each generation of Christians in each location must discover for themselves the message of the gospel for themselves and their times and places.

The book is divided into four sections. The first examines theories of religion and develops a model for use in examining folk religions. The second looks at the key questions of folk religions and the answers they give. The third explores the behavioral manifestations that express folk religious beliefs. These two sections approach the study of folk religions phenomenologically to help us understand them in their own terms. The final section examines key biblical principles that Christians can use in dealing with the folk religions around them, and suggests missiological processes for helping Christians move from where they are to where God calls them to be.

Finally, some books have a long gestation period with a large number of people contributing to the whole. This is one of them. A multiauthored book with the authors at different academic institutions puts a special strain on the many who helped in the production and editing of the text. To all these and many more, including our family members who have been patient with our occasional impatience, we are truly grateful. Mere acknowledgment is a woefully inadequate expression of our deep appreciation for all they have contributed, not only to the book, but to our thinking and to our lives.

DEVELOPING AN ANALYTICAL MODEL

Around the world Christian churches face the challenge of folk religions. Missionaries brought formal Christianity encoded in systematic theologies, churches, and institutions such as schools and hospitals. They assumed that traditional religions would die out as the gospel displaced animistic beliefs and practices. Today it is clear that old ways do not die out, but remain largely hidden from public view. Christianity is an overlay, and the two coexist in uneasy tension. People affirm orthodox theologies, but go to witch doctors, shamans, diviners, and healers during the week, often in secret for fear of the condemnation of church leaders. They are baptized in the church and initiated in traditional rites in the forest. There is also a resurgence of folk religions in the West, which contradicts the assumption that religions die as science and secularism gain ground. The questions folk religions raise have less to do with heresy than with syncretism—the mixing of different beliefs and practices in ways that distort the truth and power of the gospel.

This book examines folk religions and provides guidelines for churches to deal with them. Section One develops a missiological model for analyzing folk religions. Sections Two, Three, and Four apply this model in the analysis and Christian response to the questions they raise.

SECTION OUTLINE

Section One lays out the theoretical framework for the book.
Chapter 1: Defines the problem and outlines the process of critical contexualization that is the theoretical basis for the book.
Chapter 2: Examines the nature of religious systems and their relationship to cultures and societies.
Chapter 3: Develops a model for examining religious belief systems.
Chapter 4: Looks at the relationships between folk and formal religions and gives reasons for the rise of split-level Christianity.

1

SPLIT-LEVEL CHRISTIANITY

The central concern of this book is the persistence of a two-tier Christianity around the world despite centuries of instruction and condemnations by missionaries and church leaders. Deeply committed Christians faithfully attend church services and pray to God in times of need, but feel compelled during the week to go to a local shaman for healing, a diviner for guidance, and an exorcist for deliverance from spirit oppression. Sidney Williamson writes,

> Most Christians live on two unreconciled levels. They are members of a church and ascribe to a statement of faith. But below the system of conscious beliefs are deeply embedded traditions and customs implying quite a different interpretation of the universe and the world of spirit from the Christian interpretation. In the crises of life and rites of passage the Church is an alien thing (Williamson 1965, 158).

Regarding the church in Ghana, Kofi Abrefa Busia writes,

> As one watches the daily lives and activities of the people and takes account of the rites connected with marriage, birth, death, widowhood, harvest and installation of traditional offices, one learns that a great deal of the normal communal activities of the converts lie outside their Christian activities, and that for all their influence, the Christian churches are still alien institutions, intruding upon, but not integrated with social institutions (Pobee 1996, 2).

This "split-level" Christianity[1] is found in young churches planted among traditional religionists around the world. It is common in churches in the West. It has sapped the vitality of churches and limited Christianity to a segment of people's lives. How should missionaries

---

1. The term "split-level Christianity" comes from Father Jaime Bulatao, who referred to it in 1962, and later elaborated on the concept in *Split-Level Christianity* (Manila: Ateneo de Manilo, 1992).

and church leaders respond to the persistence of old beliefs and practices long after people have become Christians?

To understand this religious schizophrenia, it is important to understand the history of the modern mission movement that originated largely in the West, which was profoundly shaped by the Age of Exploration and the Enlightenment.

ROOTS OF THE PROBLEM

Like all people, missionaries are shaped by the times in which they live. To understand how Western missionaries in the past century dealt with other 'religions,' it is important to understand how the Enlightenment defined the world in the West after the eighteenth century.

THE MODERN[2] WORLDVIEW

The sixteenth century opened up whole new worlds to European explorers seeking routes to the spices of India. They discovered unknown lands and strange peoples not found on their maps. New questions emerged. Were these creatures of the new worlds humans? Did they have souls that needed to be saved? How did their ways of life relate to those in the West?

One answer to these questions was colonialism. The conquest of lands around the world convinced the people of the West of their own cultural superiority. Western civilization had triumphed. It was the task, therefore, of the West to bring the benefits of this civilization to the world.

A second answer was the Enlightenment separation between 'natural' and 'supernatural' realities. This gave rise to sciences that studied this world and gave naturalistic explanations that had no place for God.

---

2. The terms 'modern' and 'postmodern' are widely used, but there is considerable disagreement on their definitions and the relationship between them. By 'modern' we mean the worldview that emerged in the West after the fifteenth century, culminating in the Enlightenment. Today it is spreading around the world and taking various forms. Its chief characteristics are a focus on materialism as the ultimate reality, on rational positivism and empirical testing as final authority of truth, and on a mechanistic worldview (Berger, Berger, and Kellner 1973; Ellul 1964). The hallmarks of modernity are science and technology. Postmodernity is the contemporary reaction to the hegemony and arrogance of modernity, and calls for the deconstruction of grand narratives, a reaffirmation of the subjective nature of knowledge, and relativism. Some see it as a new stage in history displacing modernity (Rosenau 1992), others as another short-lived reaction to modernity similar to romanticism in the eighteenth century (Berger 1973, Ellul 1964, and Gelner 1992), and others as the last stage in the evolution of modernity (Harvey 1990). We will not address the question of postmodernity, in part because it is largely a Western intellectual phenomenon. We will use the word 'modern' in the general sense with reference to the contemporary worldview built on rationalism, empiricism, science, technology, and market economy.

It also relegated religions to beliefs in the supernatural heavenly realities which were believed to be rooted in faith, not facts. Science was seen as public truth to be studied by all. Religion was a matter of personal choice and private faith. This dualism had no place for this-worldly supernatural realities such as earthly spirits and spirit pos-

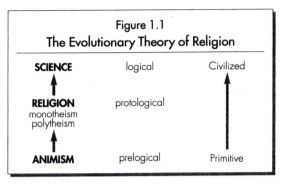

Figure 1.1
The Evolutionary Theory of Religion

SCIENCE	logical	Civilized
RELIGION monotheism polytheism	protological	
ANIMISM	prelogical	Primitive

sessions, witchcraft, living ancestors, and magic, and ridiculed belief in these as fairy tales and sleight of hand.

A third answer was the theory of cultural evolution. If the political solution to the awareness of cultural pluralism created by the age of exploration was colonialism, the intellectual solution was evolutionism, which saw all cultures at different stages of development, some more advanced and others more primitive. Following the lead of A. Comte, cultural evolutionists postulated the evolution of religion from simple animistic beliefs and practices to the complex religions of the present, and attributed this evolution to the growth of human rationality. They divided history into three stages—animistic, metaphysical/theological, and scientific (Figure 1.1).

E. B. Tylor[3] (1913) defined 'animism' as the earliest stage in the evolution of religion, and equated it with belief that this world is inhabited by spirits and powers. He attributed the origins of animistic beliefs to primitive humans reflecting on the nature of death, dreams, and invisible realities, and argued that early humans concluded that people have invisible souls, or 'breath,' which leave the body and wander to distant places. Later, he argued, primitive people extended this notion of spirit to animals, plants, and even inanimate objects. From a belief in spirits, Tylor argued, it is only a small step to belief in the "continuance" of these spirits beyond death in an afterworld, their "embodiment" in objects, their "possession" of living persons, and the existence of powerful "high gods."

James G. Frazer (1922) examined the role of magic in traditional religions and concluded that it is based on belief in impersonal supernat-

---

3. Originally Tylor defined animism as belief in supernatural beings and powers. He divided belief systems into those that affirmed the reality of supernatural beings and forces, and those that denied them. By this definition, Christians are animistic and able to understand and communicate with people of societies that hold such beliefs in ways that atheistic scientists do not share.

ural powers that operate on earth, and two mistaken notions of causality, namely, that of similarity (pouring water produces rain) and contagion (acts performed on one part of a person's body, such as hair clippings, affects the whole being of a person).

Tylor, Frazer, and others argued that animistic beliefs were the products of primitive, prelogical minds. They believed that over time animism evolved into religions (belief in and worship of a high god), which they saw as explanation systems based on early rational reflections. They also argued that as human investigation became more rational and empirical, religions would be replaced by science and "positive objective knowledge."

Evolutionary views of religion deeply influenced Western thought. In the nineteenth and early twentieth centuries, most Europeans and Americans believed that the West was "civilized" and that other people were "primitive." They attributed this difference to the growth of human rationality from prelogical to logical, and used this theory to justify the colonial expansion of Western governments and the spread of science and technology around the world. In this view, religious beliefs associated with magic, earthly spirits, living ancestors, witchcraft, curses, divination, and evil eye were seen as superstitions to be eradicated by the introduction of scientific knowledge. Because such beliefs would die out, there was no need to study or understand them as serious explanation systems.

MISSIONARY WORLDVIEW

Western missionaries were influenced by colonialism, the Enlightenment, and the theory of evolution, often unwittingly. Many believed in progress, and assumed the superiority of Western civilization. They saw it their task to civilize and Christianize the people they served. Charles Taber writes,

> The superiority of Western civilization as the culmination of human development, the attribution of that superiority to the prolonged dominance of Christianity, the duty of Christians to share civilization and the gospel with the "benighted heathen"—these were the chief intellectual currency of their lives (1991, 71).

Belief in progress influenced the way missionaries approached other religions. They studied Hinduism, Islam, Buddhism, and the other high philosophical religions because they saw these as challenges to Christianity. They developed Christian apologetics in response to the abstract philosophical systems of these religions, and debated the superiority of Christianity with their religious leaders. Moreover, missionaries assumed that ordinary Indians were Hindus, Arabs were Muslims, and Chinese were Buddhists. They were often unaware that most ordinary people knew little of the orthodox beliefs and practices of the religions they espoused.

Progress also meant that old animistic beliefs and practices were seen as primitive superstitions and could be ignored. John Pobee observes, "all the historical churches by and large implemented the doctrine of the *tabula rasa*, i.e., the missionary doctrine that there is nothing in the non-Christian culture on which the Christian missionary can build and, therefore, every aspect of the traditional non-Christian culture had to be destroyed before Christianity could be built up" (1982, 168). Consequently, there was little need to study the religions of ordinary people.

The Enlightenment division of reality into two worlds—supernatural and natural—also influenced the Western mission worldview. Most missionaries taught Christianity as the answer to the ultimate and eternal questions of life, and science based on reason as the answer to the problems of this world. They had no place in their worldview for invisible earthly spirits, witchcraft, divination, and magic of this world, and found it hard to take people's beliefs in these seriously.

Missionaries often tried to stamp out animistic 'superstitions,' but they did not go away. Because they were not consciously dealt with, they went underground. Young converts knew they dare not tell the missionary about their old ways lest they incur the outsider's anger. So these ways became part of the new Christians' hidden culture. Christian marriage ceremonies were held in the church, and then the people returned to their homes to celebrate the wedding in traditional ways in private. Amulets were hidden under shirts, and Christians did not admit to Christian doctors that they were also going to the village shaman. The people continued to practice their old ways, but did so in secret to avoid the condemnation of the missionaries. They added Christianity as a new layer of beliefs on top of the old. The result was two-tier Christianity. In the long run, this uneasy coexistence of public Christianity and private "paganism" led to syncretism. Moreover, today these underground beliefs are resurfacing around the world and creating havoc in young churches as well as in the West.

The Enlightenment separation between supernatural and natural realms also led to the secularization of science. God reigned in the heavens and was concerned with eternal matters, such as creation, sin, and salvation. Science, based on natural law, was used to explain and control the events on earth. Medicine and technology gave answers for the problems of everyday life. Many missionaries brought this dualism with them. They brought the Gospel and planted churches. At the same time they established schools and hospitals that taught an essentially secular science. Much of the world adopted the modern science they brought but rejected the gospel, or, like the Western counterparts, created a dualism between religion, which they turned to in times of crisis, and science, which they used to deal with life.

A CHRISTIAN RESPONSE

How should missionaries and church leaders respond to this two-tier Christianity today? Stamping it out with condemnations and disciplinary actions works no better now than before. Ignoring it and hoping it will die out only leads to weak churches and syncretism. Missionaries and church leaders must deal with the problems, realizing that many Christians live with deep inner dissonance between what the church teaches and what they face in their everyday lives. The problems are multifold, and vary from culture to culture. Some Christians must deal with witchcraft, curses, and ancestors. Others face spiritism, demon possession, and divination. Still others face materialism, secularism, and an obsession with health, wealth, and power. How should Christians in general and missionaries in particular deal with these diverse beliefs and practices?

REJECTION OF OLD WAYS

Historically, one common response has been to reject all old customs as pagan. Drums, dances, traditional rituals, sacrifices to spirits, and divination rites were condemned because they were directly or indirectly related to traditional religions, and were stamped out by means of church discipline.

There was some validity in this rejection of old ways because in most traditional cultures no sharp line was drawn between sacred and secular practices. All of life for the people was embedded in religious beliefs. Consequently, to incorporate old ways into church life was to open the door for unintended syncretism. The simple solution was to reject all traditional beliefs and customs.

Such wholesale rejection of old beliefs and customs, however, creates several serious theological and missiological problems. First, it assumes that the cultural forms of Western Christians are themselves Christian. An uncritical rejection of other cultures as pagan is generally tied to an uncritical acceptance of Western Christian expressions as biblical. A second problem is that new beliefs and practices must be introduced to replace the old ones that have been rejected. This importation of practices from outside has led people in many lands to see Christianity as a foreign religion, and has alienated Christians from their own peoples. It is this foreignness and not the offense of the gospel that has often kept people from following Christ. A third problem is that attempts to suppress old customs generally fail. The old ways simply go underground. Often, over time, these resurface in the church and lead to Christopaganism (Yamamori and Taber 1975).

Uncritically Accepting Old Ways

A second historical response to traditional practices was to accept them uncritically, thereby allowing them into the church. The old cultural ways were seen as basically good, and few if any changes were thought to be necessary when people become Christians.

Those who advocated this approach generally had a deep respect for other peoples and their cultures, and recognized the high value people place on their own cultural heritage. They also recognized that the foreignness of the Christian message was one of the major barriers to its acceptance. Consequently, they stressed the communication of the gospel in indigenous forms and called for little or no cultural dislocation.

Such uncritical acceptance of culture overlooks the fact that sin is found not only in individuals but also in the institutions of society and in cultural ideologies. To overlook this is to bar sin at the front door of the church, but to allow it in the back door. New converts are often more aware of the evils in their old ways and the first to call for transformed lives. An uncritical incorporation of old beliefs and practices into the life of the church opens the door to syncretism of all kinds as well as to cultural and philosophical relativism, which destroys all truth and authority.

Critical Contextualization

A third approach, and the one we take in this book, is to deal with old beliefs and practices consciously through a process of 'critical contextualization.' Critical contextualization involves a four-step process (Figure 1.2).

Phenomenological Analysis

The first step in critical contextualization is to study the local culture phenomenologically. Before judging people, it is important to understand their beliefs because it is on the basis of these that they act. It is too easy to judge people before understanding them deeply.

As churches become aware of the need to deal with some area, local church leaders and missionaries should guide the congregations in gathering and analyzing the traditional beliefs associated with the questions at hand. For example, in asking how Christians should bury their dead, local Christians should begin by analyzing their traditional rites: first de-

Figure 1.2
Critical Contextualization

Appropriate Responses:

	Step 1	Step 2	Step 3	Step 4	Result
Religious Beliefs and Behavior in Folk Religions	Phenomenological Analysis	Ontological Reflections	Critical Evaluation	Missiological → Transformations	**Critical Contextualization**

Inappropriate Responses:

Denial and Condemnation of Old Beliefs and Practices ──→ *Syncretism*
Uncritical Acceptance of Old Beliefs and Practices

scribing each song, dance, recitation, and rite that makes up their old ceremony, and then discussing the meaning of each in the overall ritual.

Studying a culture means understanding the categories, assumptions, and logic the people use to construct their world. This requires careful observation and study. Based, in part, on an anthropological model, missionaries have generally lived among a people, learned their language, studied their practices, and asked them questions. They begin with descriptions and categorizations, and then seek to understand these as parts of larger systems of belief and worldviews. In this process missionaries must reserve judgment on the truthfulness of what the people say until they have understood, at least in part, the world in which the people live. This "bracketing," or withholding of judgment, is essential because premature judgments are generally wrong, and because the people will not talk about their deep inner conflicts if the outsiders show incredulity or shock. The purpose here is to understand the old ways, not to judge them.

Having studied the world in which the local people live, missionaries must study their own categories, assumptions, beliefs, and worldview to understand how these shape the way they themselves think. Their views are based not only on biblical truth, but on their cultural assumptions. It is often harder for them to see their own cultural biases than those of other cultures because these biases are what they think with, not what they think about.

These two insider, or "emic,"[4] views of reality help missionaries and

---

4. Emic descriptions are attempts to understand the world not as the missionary or scientist does, but as the native people do. It is based on a distinction made by Kenneth Pike between *emic* (particular, inside, and organized) and *etic* (generalized, outside, and comparative) views of reality (1954).

leaders see the world first as the people and then as they themselves see it, but these do not provide a bridge for communication between cultures, nor a framework to compare cultures. By learning to live deeply in two or more cultures, people learn to construct metacultural grids, or analytical frameworks that are outside any one specific culture. This "etic" view of an outside observer enables bicultural people such as missionaries to translate between cultures and languages, and to compare them.

Emic and etic views of reality should not be divorced from each other (Headland, Pike, and Harris 1990). Missionaries must begin by learning to see the world as the people they serve do. They must also develop metacultural grids for describing and comparing cultures, while, at the same time, constantly returning to emic analysis to make certain they do not misunderstand the particular people they serve. They are participant-observers—as participants they identify with and seek to understand the people they serve, and as observers they study, compare, and evaluate different cultures. Missionaries are culture brokers, seeking to communicate the gospel between specific cultural contexts, helping their sending churches to understand the churches they plant, and the young churches to understand and appreciate the sending churches.

ONTOLOGICAL CRITIQUE

Phenomenology helps outsiders to understand other cultures, and, therefore, to make more informed judgments. It does not provide criteria for making those judgments. To stop with phenomenological analyses is to end with cultural relativism. Cultures are relative to one another in the sense that no one of them can claim to be right. To end up with total cultural relativism, however, is to deny meaningful communication between cultures, tests of truth, or moral judgment of evil. Peter Berger notes that some acts, such as the Nazi gas chambers, are so evil that to refuse to condemn them in absolute terms would offer prima facia evidence "not only of a profound failure in the understanding of judgment, but more profoundly of a fatal impairment of *humanitas*" (1970, 66). In the end, cultural relativism leads to a total disbelief in science, religion, and all systems of human knowledge. Ernest Gelner points out,

> Relativism *does* entail nihilism: if standards are inherently and inescapably expressions of something called culture, and can be nothing else, then no culture can be subjected to a standard, because *(ex hypothesi)* there cannot be a transcultural standard which would stand in judgement over it (Gelner 1992, 49–50).

Christians must go beyond phenomenology to ontological evaluations that test the truth claims of different beliefs and values.[5] They can use two tests of truth: the tests of Scripture and objective reality.

THEOLOGICAL CRITERIA

For Christians, the fundamental test of truth is Scripture which reveals God's view of reality. Consequently, in this step the pastor or missionary leads the church in a study of the Scriptures related to the question at hand. In the example of burial practices, the leader uses the occasion to teach the Christian beliefs about death and resurrection. Here the pastor and missionary play a major role, for this is their area of expertise.

Christians must recognize that they read and interpret Scripture in the categories and logics of their own cultures, but this does not mean that their theologies are totally culturally shaped. The more they read and carefully study Scripture, the more its categories and logic shape their thinking. They must also test for their own cultural biases by studying Scripture with Christians from other communities and cultures, because others often see cultural biases more clearly than individuals do themselves. Such intercultural dialogues help Christians see how their culture has shaped their thinking and their interpretations of Scripture.

There are several ways to study Scripture that can help Christians deal with the problems of split-level Christianity. The first is to do an analysis of the categories, logic, and truths revealed in Scripture itself. This systematic theology helps them develop a biblical worldview and a biblical understanding of reality.

Like all Christian books, this one is based on implicit theological positions. It is important, at the outset, to make these clear. The writers are committed evangelicals who believe that God has called all people to follow Jesus Christ. We take a number of theological doctrines as givens. We accept Scripture as divine revelation, and therefore as fully authoritative. The Bible is our basis for theology, for understanding ultimate nature of reality, and for God's work in creation, history, and eschatology (2 Tim. 3:16).

We believe that Jesus Christ is the center of theology, for it is through him that we definitively know God. Therefore, we must understand the Bible in terms of the person of Christ, who is the fulfillment and supreme manifestation of divine revelation (John 1:1–5, 18; Heb.

---

5. This is not the place for a philosophical discussion of the epistemological and ontological issues involved in judging religious truth, or an apologetic in defense of the truth of Christianity. For further analysis of these issues, see Hiebert 1999.

1:1–5). We take seriously the
incarnation of Jesus Christ,
who was both fully God and
fully human (1 John 1:1–3).
This mystery of God in
human form is the basis of
our salvation. It is also the
analogy we use to under-
stand divine revelation in
human languages, universal

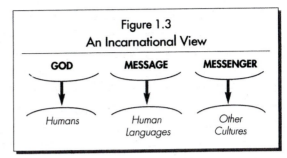

Figure 1.3
An Incarnational View

| GOD | MESSAGE | MESSENGER |
| Humans | Human Languages | Other Cultures |

truth in particular contexts, and the Christian messenger in non-Christian cultures (Figure 1.3). We affirm the reign of Christ over all creation, and the establishment of God's kingdom to be the goal of divine
history. Mission takes place in this broader framework, calling people
to follow Christ and proclaiming the kingdom of God as the culmina-
tion of history.

We assume the continuing active work of the Holy Spirit in the world
today in the lives of all believers and in unbelievers. The Holy Spirit
woos unbelievers to Christ and his kingdom, and convicts them of sin.
The Spirit gives believers the power to live godly lives (Rom. 8:1–17;
Gal. 5:22).

We believe that all humans are sinners in need of salvation and reconciliation with God and with one another. This is possible only
through the death and resurrection of Jesus Christ. The cross and resurrection are central to all Christian understanding of how God works
in the world and how he uses power (1 Cor. 1:18–19). God saves those
who turn in repentance and seek his salvation. This turning, or conversion, involves a change of fundamental allegiance that makes Christ the
Lord in all areas of believers' lives (Rom. 8:1–8). It leads to a life of discipleship that transforms all areas of human life.

We believe the church is the sign and evidence of the kingdom of God
now invading the earth. It is made up of communities of faith that worship, fellowship together, and minister to one another's needs. The
church is also a hermeneutical community. All believers have the right
to study and interpret the Scriptures, but they must do so within believing communities where errors in interpretation can be checked. The
church is also a mission community. It exists to bring to a lost world the
message of God's salvation, and to invite all into his kingdom. Mission
is not a fruit of the church. It is of its essence. Without mission the
church is not the church.

A second approach to the study of Scripture is to use the questions
and methods of history. Biblical theology is essential to understand the
story of creation, fall, redemption, and the restoration of God's reign in

eternity. Here the focus is on the cosmic narrative and how it relates to the histories of churches and biographies of Christians.

Systematic and biblical theologies are essential in seeking biblical answers to the questions Christians face, but they do not provide answers on how to communicate and apply those truths in specific human settings. Missiological theology takes for granted that all humans live in different historical and sociocultural settings, and that the gospel must be made known to them in the particularity of these contexts. Eugene Peterson writes,

> This is the gospel focus: *you* are the man; *you* are the woman. The gospel is never about everybody else; it is always about you, about me. The gospel is never truth in general; it's always a truth in specific. The gospel is never a commentary on ideas or culture or conditions; it's always about actual persons, actual pains, actual troubles, actual sin; you, me; who you are and what you've done; who I am and what I've done (1997, 185).

The question is, how can the gospel be translated between vastly different languages and cultures without losing its meaning? How can people with other worldviews understand its prophetic message?

Missionaries must cross linguistic, cultural, and social boundaries to proclaim the gospel in new settings. They must translate and communicate the Bible in the languages of people in other cultures so that it speaks to them in the particularities of their lives. They must bridge between divine revelation and human contexts, and provide biblical answers to the confusing problems of everyday life. This process of cross-cultural communication means that missionaries, by the very nature of their task, must be theologians. Their central question is: "What is God's Word to humans in this particular situation?"

From these theological assumptions it should be clear that the foundations of this book are based on God's Word, not social and cultural insights. However, the Bible reflects the historical and cultural contexts of authors across the centuries who penned the sixty-six books. Therefore, to understand the biblical concepts, Christians must also understand the cultural manifestations expressed by those authors. It is only then that theological concepts can be understood and applied to new contexts.

REALITY TESTING

The second ontological test is 'reality testing.' All people use empirical verification to test their ideas. One person says there are ten cows in the field, another there are eleven. They count the cows to see who is right. In fact, both may be wrong. Modern science systematizes the use of reality testing, but all cultures have sciences based on observations, rational deductions, and independent verification.

Cross-cultural reality testing forces people to examine both their own and others' understandings of reality. Most people simply assume that the way they look at things is the way things really are, and judge other cultures' views of reality before understanding them. These judgments are based on ethnocentrism, which closes the door to further understanding and communication. Furthermore, ethnocentric judgments keep missionaries from examining their own beliefs and values to determine which of them are based on biblical foundations and which on their cultural beliefs.

As noted earlier, understanding other cultures deeply shatters the belief that one's own culture is right and others wrong, and opens the door for people to move beyond monoculturalism to the development of metacultural grids that enable them, in some measure, to understand different cultures (Hiebert 1999). These grids also enable them to compare and test the truth claims of different cultures.[6]

EVALUATIVE RESPONSE

Returning to the process of critical contextualization, the third step is for churches to evaluate critically their existing beliefs and customs in the light of their new biblical understandings, and to make decisions on the basis of this newfound truth. The gospel is not simply information to be communicated. It is a message to which people must respond. Moreover, it is not enough that the leaders be convinced that change is needed. Leaders may share their convictions and point out the consequences of various decisions, but they must allow the people to participate in the final decisions in evaluating their past customs. If the leaders make these decisions, they must enforce them. People will abide with decisions arrived at corporately, and there will be little likelihood that the customs they reject will go underground.

To involve people in evaluating their own culture in the light of new truths draws upon their strengths. They know their old culture better than the missionary and are in a better position to critique it, once they have biblical instruction. Moreover, their involvement helps them to grow spiritually through learning discernment and applying scriptural teachings to their own lives.

Congregations may respond to old beliefs and practices in any of several ways. They will keep many, for these are not unbiblical. Western Christians, for example, see no problem with eating hamburgers, singing secular songs, wearing business suits, or driving cars. Some prac-

---

6. Questions related to reality testing are complex, and involve hermeneutics, epistemology, and ontology. A discussion of these is beyond the limits of this book. For a further discussion, see Hiebert 1999.

tices will be explicitly rejected as unbecoming for Christians. The reason for such rejection is often not apparent to missionaries or outsiders, who may see little difference between the songs and rites the people reject and those they retain. But the people know the deep, hidden meanings of their old customs and their significance in the culture. At some points the missionary may need to raise questions that the people have overlooked, for they often fail to see clearly their own cultural assumptions.

Sometimes people will modify old beliefs and practices to give them explicit Christian meaning. For example, Charles Wesley used the melodies of popular bar songs but gave them Christian words. Similarly, the early Christians used the style of worship found in the Jewish synagogues, but modified it to fit their beliefs. At times local churches substitute Christian symbols and rites borrowed from Christians in other cultures. Such functional substitutes are often effective, for they minimize the cultural dislocation created by simply removing old customs. People may also create new symbols and rituals to communicate Christian beliefs in forms that are indigenous to their particular culture.

It is important for churches to add rituals that affirm their spiritual heritage. All Christians live between two worlds, cultural and Christian. The addition of such rites as baptism and the Lord's Supper not only provides converts with ways to express their new faith, but also symbolizes their ties to the historical and international church.

Having led the people to analyze their old customs in the light of biblical teaching, the leader or missionary must help them arrange the practices they have chosen into new ways that express the *Christian* meaning of the event. These rites and practices will be Christian for the people are seeking explicitly to express biblical teaching in them. These will also be *indigenous*, for the congregation has created it, using concepts and forms the people understand in their own culture.

A word of caution is needed here. The missionary or leader may not always agree with the choices the people make, but it is important, as far as conscience allows, to accept the decisions of the local Christians, and to recognize that they, too, are led by the Spirit of God. Leaders must grant others the greatest right they reserve for themselves, the right to make mistakes. The church grows stronger by consciously making decisions in the light of Scripture, even when the decisions may not always be the wisest, than when it simply obeys orders given by others.

TRANSFORMATIVE MINISTRIES

The final step in missiology is transformative ministries that help people move from where they are to where God wants them to be. Missionaries and church leaders cannot expect people simply to abandon their old ways and adopt new ones. People can only move from where they are by a process of transformation. This is true for individuals as well as social and cultural systems. In Figure 1.2 we called this *missiological transformation*.

Ministry has to do with the particular, not only the universal. The gospel is truth for people living in specific places and times, and caught in their own dilemmas. In dealing with folk religions it is important to remember that they are incredibly diverse. There are many kinds of witchcraft, divination, spirit possession, ancestor veneration, and magic, and each requires a biblical response that deals with its particular nature. Specific missiological answers must be formulated in specific contexts by the leaders and missionaries involved. This book does not provide ready answers to the many different beliefs and practices of folk religions around the world today. It seeks to provide a conceptual framework whereby Christians can think biblically about folk religions they encounter.

This book is organized around the four steps of critical contextualization. Chapters 2, 3, and 4 develop a model to study religions phenomenologically. This draws heavily on the insights provided by anthropology. In Sections Two and Three, this model is used to examine folk religions in order to understand their beliefs and practices. Only then can missionaries and church leaders provide biblical answers to the questions they seek to answer. The failure to understand folk religions has been a major blind spot in missions, and is, in part, the cause for the split-level Christianity found around the world. Section Four moves beyond phenomenology, and looks at issues associated with the last three steps in the process, namely, ontological critique, evaluative response, and transformative ministries. It offers some brief theological and missiological guidelines for dealing with folk religions, outlines some of the common dangers involved, and suggests steps by which local churches can study Scripture under the guidance of the Holy Spirit, and help their people live as faithful followers of Christ in non-Christian settings.

2

PHENOMENOLOGY OF RELIGION

The first step in a biblical response to popular religiosity is to seek to understand folk religions phenomenologically. They consist of a bewildering array of rites, festivals, beliefs, symbols, texts, practitioners, institutions, buildings, schools, art, music, and processions. Some of these are seen in public, but many are hidden in private life. Unlike in the West, where religion is often a small segment of life, in most of the world it is the core of the culture and touches every area of people's lives. How can one make sense out of this diversity? Here the theories and methods of the human sciences can help missionaries understand folk religions in terms of their own internal logic, and compare and evaluate them.

HUMAN SYSTEMS

Folk religions must be understood in the broader context of religions in general, which, in turn, are part of cultures and societies. There are many approaches in the sciences to the study of humans in general, and religions in particular. Theologians and philosophers study humans primarily in terms of their systems of belief and doctrine. Psychologists look at humans in terms of the inner workings of the individuals, and examine the motivations, conversions, emotions, beliefs, and actions of specific persons. Sociologists look at human relationships that maintain religious beliefs and practices, and at the social, economic, political, and legal dimensions of social systems related to religion. Cultural anthropologists look at religions as systems of beliefs, symbols, behaviors, and worldviews, and at the rituals and practices associated with these. Geographers, biologists, and other natural scientists study how time, space, geography, and human biology affect religious practices. Historians look at changes that take place in

31

religions over time. All build on a common empirical methodology, using reason to organize and analyze human observations, but each of these perspectives brings a different focus and a different set of questions, and each sheds valuable light on the complex nature of religions.

How do these different perspectives relate to each other? Taken by themselves, these piecemeal approaches to the study of humans fail to look at the whole. Human societies, cultures, and individuals cannot be separated in reality. The problem is that, given their finite limitations, human minds cannot comprehend the whole of human reality in one picture. It is necessary, for analytical purposes, to focus on one or another aspect of reality.

REDUCTIONIST APPROACHES TO INTEGRATION

The easiest solution to bring these perspectives together is reductionism. Scholars recognize the insights of other theoretical views, but turn to their discipline for final explanations. Sociologists recognize the importance of cultures, but see them as ideological systems that hold a society together. They do not take seriously people's claims that cultures help them understand the true nature of reality. Psychologists see cultures and societies as the beliefs, fantasies, relationships, and behaviors of individuals, and overlook the corporate nature of human life.

Sociocultural anthropologists take beliefs and activities seriously, but often lose sight of the uniqueness of each individual in a society. These reductionisms undermine a true understanding of the multifaceted nature of religious life.

Another approach to integrating the insights different disciplines have to offer is what Geertz (1965, 97) calls the 'stratigraphic method.' Different models of analysis are stacked in discrete layers. In analyzing humans, scholars peel off layer after layer, each seen as complete and irreducible, revealing another quite different sort of layer beneath. Stripping off the beliefs and practices of culture, they find the structural regularities of social organization. Peeling these off, they find the underlying 'basic' psychological needs that shape individual persons. Beneath these are biological needs—food, shelter, and health—that underlie the whole edifice of human life. This stratigraphic approach leaves scholars with fragmented humans and a subtle reductionism that gives priority to the lower levels.

A SYSTEMS APPROACH TO INTEGRATION

In life, religion is not compartmentalized. To gain a holistic view, it is important to recognize the insights each discipline has to offer and to integrate them in a 'system of systems' model of human realities.[1] Here the validity of studying different dimensions of reality as mico systems is recognized—including physical, biological, psychological, social, cultural, and spiritual systems—but they are seen as parts of an encompassing macro system.[2] The contributions each approach has to offer are seen as complementary.[3] They are like different blueprints of the same building, or different maps of the same city. Each can be studied separately, but ultimately the relationships among these systems must also be examined. For example, physical illness can cause psychological depression and spiritual doubts. On the other hand, spiritual struggles can cause physical illness, psychological anxiety, and social tensions. Causes may arise in any of these systems, but the symptoms are often found throughout the whole. Consequently, when dealing with human ills, it is important to treat the symptoms but also to find root causes. To complete the picture, it is important to keep in mind that religions are always in historical contexts. They are constantly changing through internal and external forces and teleological pulls.

1. This system of systems approach was outlined by Talcott Parsons, Edward Shils, Clyde Kluckhohn, and others in *Toward a General Theory of Action* (1952). Their model consisted of three systems: personal, social, and cultural. To this we have added the biophysical system and the material world, and the spiritual system noted in the Bible. The latter is the one we generally leave out of our everyday analyses of life, and one we must restore to the center of our understanding of human affairs.

A contemporary illustration of a 'system of system's' approach is the recent integration of the U.S. Army, Navy, Air Force, and Marines into one military force in which the four 'systems' remain autonomous, but their actions are coordinated in a single military mission such as the Gulf War.

2. A system is a set of related elements that interact in predictable ways to form a functioning whole.

3. Complementarity is not simply juxtaposing different views of reality. These must be embedded in an overarching blueprint that integrates the others in one overview. Moreover, the different blueprints must not contradict one another in the areas of their overlap. If there are discrepancies, these must be resolved. For example, if one blueprint shows wiring in a wall that does not exist in the structural blueprint, one of them must be wrong.

An example of complementarity is the way anthropologists look at human realities (Headland, Pike, and Harris 1990). On the one hand, they must take what the people claim to see and believe (emic knowledge) seriously, even though they may not believe what the people say. On the other hand, anthropologists examine reality using other questions and methods. To integrate these two approaches in the study of culture, anthropologists must develop a 'metacultural grid'—a position of detachment outside both views that enables them to translate from one view to the other, and to compare and test them for truth. While this model based on comparing different points of view is itself a new perspective, it allows an analysis that is in some sense more 'objective' than observations in either of the other viewpoints alone.

Diachronic (historical) and synchronic (structural) models are also complementary. When we study the history of a people, the structure of their society and culture is peripheral to our vision. When we examine their social and cultural systems, their history is out of focus.

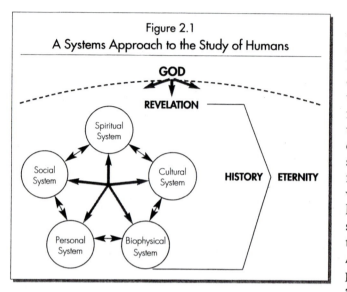

Figure 2.1
A Systems Approach to the Study of Humans

GOD

REVELATION

Spiritual System

Social System

Cultural System

HISTORY ETERNITY

Personal System

Biophysical System

To stop here, however, is to remain captive to a secular Enlightenment view of religion. Central to the study of religions is the reality of spiritual beings and powers. Christians must see that angels and fallen angels play very real roles in the lives of individuals, societies, and cultures in history. Above all, they must place God above all, and see him acting not only directly on people and societies, but also through the other systems (Figure 2.1). God calls individuals to mission. Sometimes he does so directly through visions and dreams, sometimes through social systems such as the church and leaders, sometimes through cultural systems, such as books and sermons, and sometimes through psychological systems, such as inner convictions and sense of calling.

A systems approach avoids the problems of reductionism and linear causality. It recognizes that evil may arise in any of these systems, but the consequences are often found throughout the others. When dealing with human ills, it is important to treat the symptoms but also to find root causes. Similarly, an experience, such as the conversion of an individual to Christ, can affect all the other systems and lead to broad transformations.

A second advantage of a systems view of human life is that change can be introduced at any point and spread to other systems in the larger order. Christians can lead individuals to Christ. They in turn organize churches and formulate theologies that challenge their societies and cultures. Christians may also introduce the gospel through preaching, mass media, medical work, schools, relief work, and agricultural programs. Ultimately, lasting change calls for the transformation of all these systems in the light of God's reign on earth.

Clearly, a complete analysis of humans in all these ways is impossible in any single study. It is important, however, to keep these various approaches in mind and to have an encompassing framework lest the study becomes reductionistic by neglect.

A Systems View of Religion

The first step in applying a system of systems approach to religion is to examine how it operates in each of the human systems: spiritual, cultural, social, psychological, and biophysical. Because each of these systems warrants a whole book, this study is limited to an analysis of the cultural and social nature of folk religions. The second step is to examine how religious expressions in these particular systems interact in the larger system. The focus here is on the interaction between religious manifestations in social and cultural systems. Little attention is given to personal beliefs and practices and how these are shaped by the cultural and social systems in which individuals live. Needless to say, individuals reflect the larger system of which they are a part, and by understanding the religious constraints in a particular society, anthropologists and missionaries can learn much that will assist them in daily relations with individuals in that context.

Religion as a Cultural System

Traditionally, religion has been defined as beliefs in 'supernatural beings and forces,' and the behavior and practices associated with them. In this view, religion stands in contrast to science, which deals with facts regarding the 'natural world' run by impersonal, deterministic natural laws. This definition is fatally flawed. First, it is ethnocentric: it is based on the Western dualism of spirit and matter, mind and brain, supernatural and natural—a dualism that does not exist in most cultures. Most people see the world as full of beings (spirits, ancestors, humans, unborn, animals, plants, and earth spirits) and forces (magic, mana, witchcraft, evil eye, fire, gravity), visible and invisible, that interrelate in everyday life. Second, from a Christian point of view, this dualism is unbiblical. The distinction in Scripture is between God the Creator and his creation, and creation includes angels (good and evil), humans, animals, and nature. Scripture does not divide reality into supernatural and natural realms—into spiritual and natural concerns.

Anthropologists now define 'religion' as beliefs about the ultimate nature of things, as deep feelings and motivations, and as fundamental values and allegiances. This definition provides the big picture of how people perceive reality. In this sense, atheistic Theravada Buddhism, Marxism, and scientism are religions. According to Clifford Geertz, "religion is 1) a system of symbols which acts to 2) establish powerful, pervasive and long-lasting moods and motivations in men by 3) formulating concepts of a general order of existence and 4) clothing these conceptions with such an aura of factualness that 5) the moods and motivations seem uniquely realistic" (Geertz 1979, 79–80).

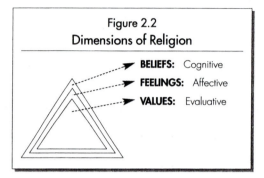

Figure 2.2
Dimensions of Religion

BELIEFS: Cognitive
FEELINGS: Affective
VALUES: Evaluative

We need to examine further some of the elements implicit in this definition.

DIMENSIONS OF RELIGION

Culture consists, in part, of belief systems made up of three interacting dimensions: ideas, feelings, and values. Religion, as an essential component of culture, reflects these same dimensions (Figure 2.2). In Geertz's definition, these are seen in such terms as "concepts of a general order of existence," "powerful, pervasive and long lasting moods," and "motivations."

BELIEFS

Religions have a cognitive dimension. This includes the deep religious beliefs and knowledge shared by the members of a group. For example, Christians speak of God, angels, demons, sin, and salvation. By the latter they mean eternal life with God in heaven. Hindus speak of *devas* [gods], *rakshasas* [demons], *karma* [the cosmic law of good and evil that punishes and rewards gods, humans, and animals, and determines their future lives], *samsara* [the cycle of rebirths], and *moksha* [salvation]. By the latter they mean deliverance from endless life and merger back into the cosmic whole. The Tiv of Nigeria speak of God, ancestors, spirits (good and bad), and life force. They attribute many diseases to witches. Without such shared beliefs, communication and community life are impossible.

Christians must take the religious beliefs of other people seriously, not because they agree with them, but because they want to understand those people in order to effectively share with them the good news of the gospel. Religious beliefs are not merely imaginary stories created by a community to unite its members and keep them in line. Most people maintain that their beliefs are more than useful fictions. For them, beliefs declare the way things really are, and, therefore, are true in an ultimate sense.

As noted in Chapter 1, it is important to understand religious beliefs in terms of people's experiences, assumptions, and logics. A phenomenological description of their world, however, is not enough. It is equally important to compare different religions in order to develop metacultural grids that facilitate understanding between and evaluation of different religions. Such comparisons provide invaluable insights not only into the nature of different religions, but also of the religious longings of the human heart.

FEELINGS

Religions also involve deep feelings—expressions of joy and sorrow, fear and revulsion, and awe and worship. These powerful, pervasive, and long-lasting moods act as a wall, protecting beliefs from attacks from within and without by providing emotional support to their truthfulness. These emotions are expressed in different ways in different cultures. In some religions, the dominant emotions are awe and wonder in the presence of great mystery expressed in high rituals. Others seek peace and calm by means of meditation and mysticism. Still others stress ecstasy, achieved by means of dance, drums, drugs, and self-torture. In short, religions vary greatly in the emotions they value and in the ways these emotions are expressed.

Cross-cultural communicators often overlook the importance of this affective dimension in the lives of ordinary people. Leaders stress the preaching of cognitive truth in church services, and downplay the importance of feelings in worship. They push to get work done and don't see the emotional distress caused by their actions. People often leave the church with their heads full and their hearts empty. Most people make religious decisions on the basis of emotions and experience as much as on rational argument. On the other hand, stressing affectivity alone leaves people with their hearts full and their heads empty. Both cognition and affectivity are vital to religious life.

VALUES

At the heart of most religions is a call for transformed lives based on a moral order that judges people and their actions as right or wrong, righteous or evil, moral or immoral, just or unjust, proper or improper. Underlying this order are fundamental allegiances—the gods that people worship, whether these are deities, group, self, materialism, sex, or power—the values that are at the core of a religion. These allegiances and values are the basis on which people decide what is true and false, and righteous and evil. For instance, in North America it is worse to tell a lie than to hurt people's feelings. In other cultures it is more important to encourage other people, even if it means bending the truth somewhat. In North American Christianity sexual immorality is one of the greatest sins. In South Asia losing one's temper is the worst offense.

Values are the basis for human action. It is possible for people to leave church with their heads and hearts full, but with no change in their lives. Only as people respond to their beliefs and feelings do these become a living religion in their lives. These three dimensions—ideas, feelings, and values—are important in understanding the nature of religion.

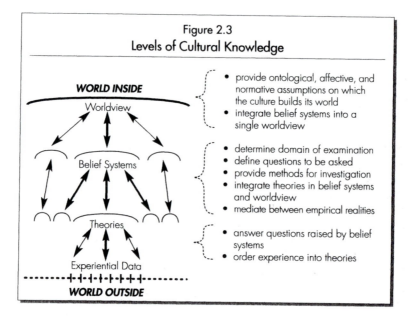

Figure 2.3
Levels of Cultural Knowledge

WORLD INSIDE

Worldview
- provide ontological, affective, and normative assumptions on which the culture builds its world
- integrate belief systems into a single worldview

Belief Systems
- determine domain of examination
- define questions to be asked
- provide methods for investigation
- integrate theories in belief systems and worldview
- mediate between empirical realities

Theories
- answer questions raised by belief systems
- order experience into theories

Experiential Data

WORLD OUTSIDE

LEVELS OF KNOWLEDGE

Having examined the dimensions of religion, we now examine the nature of belief systems and their place in culture as a whole. Larry Laudan provides a helpful model of cultural knowledge (1977, Figure 2.3). He points out that human minds work on several levels of abstraction. Understanding these is crucial to understanding folk religions and their relationship to formal religions.

SIGNS

Human experiences of reality are mediated through words, gestures, drawings, and other signs that link experiences to images in the head. Signs enable people to sort the world into a manageable number of concepts with which they can think. For example, English speakers lump together a great many experiences and call them all 'trees,' 'rocks,' 'cows,' 'ducks,' and so on. Mary Douglas describes the process (1966, 36–37),

As perceivers we select from all the stimuli falling on our senses only those which interest us, and our interests are governed by a pattern-making tendency. . . . In a chaos of shifting impressions, each of us construct a stable world in which objects have recognizable shapes, are located in depth, and have permanence. In perceiving we are building, taking some cues and rejecting others. The most acceptable cues are those which fit most easily into the pattern that is being built up. . . . As time goes on and experiences pile up, we make a greater and greater investment in our systems of labels. So a conservative bias is built in. It gives us confidence. At any time we may have to modify our structure of assumptions to accommodate new experience, but the more consistent experience is with the past, the more confidence we can have in our assumptions . . . by and large anything we take note of is pre-selected and organized in the very act of perceiving.

Signs reduce a great many experiences into a single category so that human minds can grasp them. They are building blocks that enable humans to construct mental worlds of reality as they perceive it. They use these inner worlds to live in the external world and to manipulate it. In their minds they think of their house and drive to it. They mentally picture a purple cow, so they paint their cow purple. In short, experiential data give an outsider an appreciation for the signs and symbols used in a particular religious context.

To understand religion as a cultural system, it is important to study the signs people use to reflect their beliefs, feelings, and values. We must also study how they use these signs, because in doing so we learn to understand the mental worlds of the people who use them. (The nature of religious signs is examined in greater depth in Chapter 9.)

THEORIES

Continuing the discussion of Laudan's levels of cultural knowledge, we move to theories that are limited, low-level explanatory systems that seek to answer specific questions about a narrow range of reality (Figure 2.3). They do so by linking perceptions, concepts, notions of causality, logical comparisons, and the like to form explicit understandings of reality. For example, some people attribute illnesses to viruses and bacteria, others to the anger of ancestors, others to curses, broken taboos, and witchcraft, and still others to fate or bad *karma*. All are logical explanations for reality as perceived by people in a particular context. They are alternative explications for the same set of questions—in this case, "why do people get sick?" Theories themselves may be on different levels of generality, with broader theories subsuming more limited ones.

BELIEF SYSTEMS

Theories, in turn, are embedded in higher level systems of knowledge. Thomas Kuhn (1970) calls these 'paradigms,' Laudan (1977) refers to them as 'research traditions,' and we will label them 'belief systems.' These are bodies of knowledge that emerge in response to key questions and agreed-upon methods to find answers. For example, in the sciences 'physics,' 'chemistry,' 'biology,' 'medicine,' and the other disciplines are belief systems. In theology, systematic theology and biblical theology are distinct belief systems. In everyday American life belief systems include auto mechanics, electrical engineering, cooking, football, classical music, and farming. Belief systems guide thought processes, and enable people to focus on experience and formulate theories to help them solve the problems of life and to pursue their goals. In so doing, belief systems help give meaning to life.

Formal religions, folk religions, and sciences are different belief systems that seek to answer different questions, using different methods, and focusing on different bodies of data. Too often missionaries and church leaders provide answers to the questions of formal religion, but fail to understand that folk religions seek to answer other questions. Consequently, when people are converted, they simply add formal religious beliefs to their existing folk religious beliefs, one set public and the other more private. The result is split-level Christianity. To deal with this uneasy coexistence of two belief systems, it is important that Christian leaders provide answers to the everyday questions of people's lives, questions embedded in folk religions which are rooted in the people's understandings of truth.

WORLDVIEWS

At the highest levels of abstraction, belief systems are reflected in worldviews. Worldviews are the most encompassing frameworks of thought that relate belief systems to one another. They clothe these belief systems with an aura of certainty that this is, in fact, the way reality is. They are the fundamental givens with which people in a community think, not what they think about.

Because worldview assumptions are taken for granted, they are largely unexamined and implicit. They are reinforced by the deepest of feelings, and anyone who challenges them challenges the very foundations of people's lives. As Geertz points out (1979), there is no greater human fear than a loss of a sense of order and meaning. People are willing to die for their beliefs if these make their deaths meaningful.

INTERCONNECTIONS

To understand religion as a cultural system, it is important to study religious symbols, theories, belief systems, and worldviews, and to show the connections among these levels. To begin with, it is important to show the link between explicit beliefs and practices, and the larger belief system in which they are embedded. It is easy to listen to what people say and look at what they do, and to describe their religion in terms of specific beliefs and practices, such as ancestor veneration, witchcraft, magic, or divination. This misses the point that beliefs and doctrines are part of larger belief systems that seek to answer fundamental questions in life. It is important to study the questions, data, and methods that lie behind explicit manifestations of religious life. For ex-

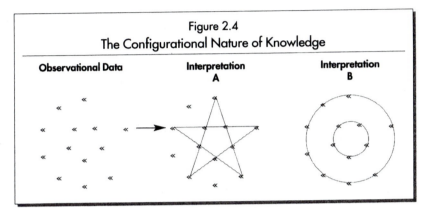

Figure 2.4
The Configurational Nature of Knowledge

Observational Data · Interpretation A · Interpretation B

ample, it is important to know not only why people believe a person is spirit-possessed, but also what they believe about possession in general—what its manifestations are, when and why it occurs, what the possible remedies are, and how it relates to other beliefs. Belief systems legitimate key questions, data, and methods of analysis, which are answered through explicit beliefs.

Next, it is important to show how belief systems are embedded in worldviews, and how they relate to one another. Worldviews provide the fundamental assumptions about the nature of reality and of right and wrong which belief systems use to build their theories. Worldviews also mediate between belief systems when conflicts arise. For example, in the West, the tension between science and religion cannot simply be resolved by reconciling the two on the level of specific theories such as those related to the origins of humankind. Integration can only occur when both are embedded in a single worldview that mediates their disagreements.

CONFIGURATIONS

Interconnection must show not only the linkages between different levels of knowledge. It must take into account the configurational nature of all human knowledge. Knowledge is not the sum of bits of information, but the system of interpretation that links those bits into an explanatory whole. Configurations combine objective facts and subjective interpretations of these facts to account for reality. For example, people look at ten dots or 'facts' (Figure 2.4), but try to give them meaning by organizing them into a larger pattern. Some see a 'star,' others two 'circles.'

Do the stars or circles exist in reality, or are they created by the mind of the beholder? The answer is both. Individual observers interpret the shape of a star or two circles. However, the observers would not see a star or circles if the dots were not placed in a way that could be inter-

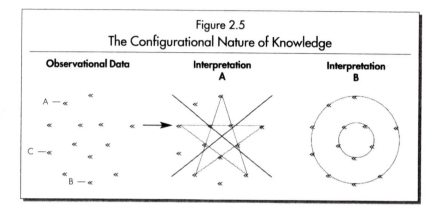

Figure 2.5
The Configurational Nature of Knowledge

preted as the shape of a star or two circles. If the dots were placed randomly on the page, observers would conclude that there is no order in their arrangement. It is the configurational nature of knowledge that gives meaning to uninterpreted experiences by seeing the order or story behind them. Configuration gives to knowledge a coherence and comprehension that make sense out of a bewildering barrage of experiential data entering the mind. It helps people to 'picture' reality.

The configurational nature of knowledge is important in understanding culture change. Normal change occurs in a belief system as new data are added and lines are redrawn to fit the new information. Revolutions, what Kuhn calls 'paradigm shifts,' occur when the existing configuration is rejected because it no longer adequately accounts for the data, and a new configuration is adopted that explains the data better. For example, when there are two interpretations of the same set of dots, the question arises, Which fits the underlying order most closely? To answer this more dots are needed in order to confirm one interpretation and eliminate the other. If further research shows a dot at point A, observers begin to question the interpretation of the dots as a star (Figure 2.5). If further facts emerge at points B and C, observers come to realize that two circles better explain the new information than does a star and begin to look for verifying data at points D and E.

A configurational understanding of the nature of knowledge helps missionaries and Christian leaders understand the nature of Christian conversion. Some people argue that conversion requires a rejection of all the parts of the old religion, for it is made up of the sum of its parts. To include elements from the old in the new is to contaminate the new. If meaning is found in the configuration that orders experience, however, not every fact must be present, or even totally accurate, to see the larger pattern. Partial and approximate data are often adequate to understand what is going on. It is possible, therefore, to use traditional elements in creating Christian responses in specific cultural contexts, but these must explicitly be given new meaning in new Christian belief systems and worldviews.

Section Two of this book examines folk religions as belief systems, and looks at the key questions they seek to answer and some of the many answers given to these questions. Section Three studies the signs, myths, and rituals that give expression to these beliefs.

RELIGION AS A SOCIAL SYSTEM

Folk religions must be studied as social systems made up of real people relating to one another in many and complex ways. Communities of believers organize religious activities. Ancestors must be fed, spirits placated with blood sacrifices, high gods worshiped with fire and incense, and animals and earth accorded respect through offerings. Newborns must be transformed into children, children into adults, adults into married couples, and the aged into ancestors through proper rites. Festivals. rain dances, pilgrimages, and religious fairs must be organized and funded, magic performed to assure good crops, and amulets made to guard brides and grooms from any evil eye that may be in the audience. Institutions, such as monastic orders, schools, and denominational structures, are built, and conferences held. Religious movements arise and challenge existing religious orders. These religious events, like all social activities, have economic, social, political, legal, and ideological dimensions, and to understand these events, we must understand their social dynamics.

Social systems are needed for corporate activities. Roles are defined, resources are gathered, events are planned, power is allocated, and individuals are encouraged or compelled to participate. Just as culture cannot exist without socially instituted forms, so religion—true or false—cannot survive without corporate activities. Social systems are also essential to pass religious beliefs and practices on to the next generations. Inner beliefs that do not find outward expression in social systems cannot be passed on to the young and soon die.

The social nature of folk religions is not the major focus of this book, but some aspects of it, such as leadership, organization, and religious movements will be examined in Section Three. .

RELIGION AS A PERSONAL SYSTEM

A full analysis of folk religions requires a study of the psychological factors involved. What are the mental states and processes of participants during a ritual dance, a funeral, a festival, or a sacrifice of animals or humans? How do people worship their gods in private, and what are the mental processes involved in conversion? Because the focus of this book is on folk religions as part of sociocultural systems, psychological factors will not be covered except as they enter into discussions of the cultural and social systems of folk religions. It is important, however, to keep in mind the importance of religious persons as individuals, and their relationship to the cultural and social systems of which they are a part. While their beliefs and practices are intensely personal, these are also shaped by the beliefs, worldview, and organization of the community in which they are involved.

RELIGION AS SPIRITUAL REALITY

Finally, Christians must take spiritual realities very seriously. God is at work wooing people to himself, and Satan and his followers are trying to blind their minds so that they do not turn to the light. Much of this battle has to do with religious systems. God reveals truth; Satan seeks to blind human minds through slightly twisting truths into false ideologies. God works through the church as a corporate body of believers; Satan uses social institutions such as religious communities, kinship systems, social classes, and nations to keep people from turning to God. What keeps many people from faith is not only false ideologies, but the social structures in which they live which persecute and kill them if they convert.

On the spiritual level, it is important to distinguish between real and unreal, between the truth of God and the deceptions of Satan. Do witches have real power? Do some people have evil eyes that cause others to get sick? Are there earthly spirits living in trees, rocks, and rivers? Can spirits possess humans? Is there magical power in amulets and charms? Here the analysis must move beyond phenomenology and a comparison of different claims of truth, to an ontological critique of these claims. Preliminary missiological answers are explored in Section Four of this book.

We turn now to a study of folk religions as belief systems, and examine the difference between folk and formal religions.

3

ANALYZING BELIEF SYSTEMS

If, as we contend, folk religions are belief systems, how do they differ from and relate to other belief systems, such as formal religions, sciences, music, agriculture, and cooking? To examine these relationships and the problem of split-level Christianity, we need a model that enables us to compare and contrast different types of belief systems.

AN ANALYTICAL MODEL OF BELIEF SYSTEMS

The model we will use in this book has two dimensions of analysis. The horizontal dimension has to do with the fundamental analogies people use in formulating their beliefs; the vertical, with transcendence or scale.

ROOT METAPHORS

Humans use fundamental analogies—what Steven Pepper (1949) calls 'root metaphors'—to provide pictures of the nature and operations of the larger world. People speak of the 'head of state' and 'the arm of the law' as if a nation were a living being. They compare love with flowers, computers with brains, and spirits with shadows.

Two basic analogies are particularly widespread: organic metaphors that see things as living beings in relationship to each other, and mechanical metaphors that see things as inanimate objects that act upon one another like parts in a machine (Figure 3.1).[1] One may be dominant in a given culture, but both are found in all cultures. For example, the modern worldview, which dominates science and the public arena of life, draws on mechanistic themes, but the private sphere of home and religion stresses relationships and the expression of emotions.[2]

---

1. In Western philosophy these are referred to as *personae*, referring to God, spirits, humans, and other personal beings, and *impersonae*, referring to the category of impersonal Absolute.
2. We draw here on Morris Opler's model (1945), which examines worldviews as dynamic tensions between themes and counterthemes, which vary in different social contexts and change over time.

Figure 3.1
Root Metaphors

ORGANIC	MECHANICAL
• like a living being	• like a machine
• life processes	• impersonal forces
• relational	• controlling, formulaic
• ethical in nature	• amoral in nature

ORGANIC METAPHORS

To understand complex phenomena, people often compare them to living beings. In these organic analogies, the elements being examined are thought to be alive in some sense, to undergo processes similar to human life and to relate to each other in ways that are analogous to interpersonal relationships. For example, in describing human civilizations, philosopher Oswald Spengler and historian Arnold Toynbee speak of them as organic entities that are born, grow sick and old, and eventually die. Similarly, traditional religionists see many diseases as caused by evil spirits that are alive, that may be angered, but can then be placated through supplication or the offering of a sacrifice. Christians see their relationship to God in organic terms: God is a person and humans relate to him in ways analogous to human relationships. In the Psalms God is referred to as "shepherd," and "father of orphans and protector of widows." The apostle Paul uses such analogies often in his discussion of the Church as the "body of Christ" (Rom. 12:4–5, 1 Cor. 12:14–30, Eph. 4:25, Col. 3:15).

Organic explanations see the world in terms of living beings in relationship with one another. Like humans and animals, objects such as rocks, trees, and the earth are widely thought to have feelings, thoughts, and wills of their own, and to initiate actions and respond to the actions of others. Organic beings are often thought to love, marry, beget offspring, quarrel, go to war, sleep, eat, persuade, and coerce one another.

Organic metaphors have several characteristics. First, they are thought to have a life of their own, with internal processes such as birth, health, illness, and death. For example, some sociologists speak of the birth, growth, decline, and demise of institutions, and describe them as healthy or sick. They see institutions as actors that choose courses of action and act on their own initiative.

Second, organic metaphors focus on the parts that make up the body, and the function these serve in maintaining the life of the organism. A living creature is not simply an assortment of organs. These organs are linked to each other in complex systems in which each organ performs functions critical to the maintenance of the life of the organism. Furthermore, relationships are dialectic—the action of each organ affects the others. The whole constitutes a homeostatic system in which there is balance and mutual contribution to the well-being of the whole.

Third, organic metaphors are moral in nature. Humans can sin because they are living creatures and accountable for their actions. Gravity, fire, and nuclear energy do not sin, even though they do great damage. Righteousness and immorality have to do with relationships between living beings.

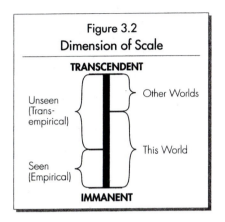

Figure 3.2
Dimension of Scale

MECHANICAL METAPHORS

A second metaphor humans frequently use is that of a machine. In this analogy, things are thought to be inanimate parts of greater mechanical systems, controlled by impersonal forces or impersonal laws of nature. For example, Western sciences see the world as made up of lifeless particles that interact on the basis of forces. When gravity pulls a rock down to earth, it is not because the earth and rock wish to meet—neither earth nor rock has any thought in the matter.

Mechanical entities are essentially deterministic because, like a machine, they are controlled by impersonal laws. If humans know these laws they can manipulate and control the system to their own advantage by using the right formulas. In a sense, they exert godlike control over their own destiny.

Mechanistic realities are basically amoral. Forces are intrinsically neither good nor evil. They can be used for both. As noted earlier, gravity, nuclear energy, and wind do not sin—it is how humans, spirits, and gods use them that is good or evil.

SCALE OF TRANSCENDENCE

The vertical dimension in the analytical model pictured in Figure 3.2 of belief systems is that of *immanence-transcendence*. On the bottom is the empirical world of human senses; on the top, the cosmic realms beyond human experience; in between, the unseen or transempirical realities of this world. These three levels emerge out of the intersection of two distinctions: this world (earth, universe) and other worlds (heavens, hells), and seen (empirical) and unseen (transempirical).

THIS WORLD—SEEN

The first level is the world of immediate human experience—what people see, hear, touch, and taste. All people are aware of this world and develop sciences to explain and control it. They develop theories about 'nature' around them—how to build a house, plant a crop, or sail a canoe. They also have theories of human relationships—how to raise a child, treat a spouse, or deal with a relative. When a Naga from northeast India attributes the death of a deer to an arrow, or a Yoruba wife from West Africa explains cooking in terms of the fire under the pot, they are using scientific explanations based on empirical observations and deductions. Western science, in this sense, is not unique.

THIS WORLD—UNSEEN

The second level has do with beings and forces that cannot be directly seen, but are thought to exist *on this earth.* They include spirits, ghosts, ancestors, demons, and earthly gods and goddesses who live in trees, rivers, hills, and villages. In medieval Europe these beings included trolls, pixies, gnomes, brownies, and fairies, all of which were believed to be real. These spirits do not live in some other world or time, but with humans, animals, and plants in this world and time. Most of them never travel to other worlds such as heavens and hells. Forces on this level include supernatural powers such as mana, evil eye, magic, and witchcraft, all of which we will discuss at length later in this chapter and, indeed, throughout the book.

In many traditional religions there is no sharp distinction between the seen and unseen realities of this world. Spiritual beings and forces play a central part in the lives of the people. They inhabit a parallel world of the shadows. For example, among the Fon of Benin, the royal dynasty reigns in both worlds—the royal ancestors in the spirit world enjoy the same status and wealth as their descendants who are kings in the material world. Birth and death are passage points from one world to the other, and communication between the two worlds is maintained through prayer, sacrifice, and divination. Each world affects the other. Angry or neglected ancestors can injure or kill the living, and placated ancestors can bless them and their kingdom as a whole.

OTHER WORLDS—UNSEEN

Furthest from the immediate world of human experience are other worlds—heavens, hells, purgatories, and other levels of reality that exist outside this world. The Greeks believed in seven heavens and seven hells, with the natural world in between. In this transcendent realm fit African concepts of a high god, and Hindu ideas of Siva and Vishnu. Here is located the Jewish concept of Yahweh, who stands in stark contrast to the Baals and Ashtaroth of the Canaanites, who were deities of this world, of the middle zone. To be sure, Yahweh enters into the affairs of this earth, but his abode is above it. On this level, too, are the transcendent cosmic forces such as the Hindu belief in *karma,* the cosmic moral law, and the Muslim belief in *kismet,* a transcendent power similar to 'fate.'

Figure 3.3
Framework for the Analysis of Religious Systems

Organic Analogy
Based on concepts of living beings relating to other living beings. Stresses life, personality, relationships, functions, health, disease, choice, etc. Relationships are essentially moral in character.

Mechanical Analogy
Based on concepts of impersonal objects controlled by forces. Stresses impersonal, mechanistic, and deterministic nature of events. Forces are essentially amoral in character.

	High Religion Based on Cosmic Beings:	**High Religion Based on Cosmic Forces:**	
Unseen or Supernatural Beyond immediate sense experience. Above natural explanation. Knowledge of this based on inference or on supernatural experiences.	cosmic gods angels demons spirits of other worlds	kismet fate Brahman and karma impersonal cosmic forces	**Other Worldly** Sees entities and events occurring in other worlds and in other times.
	Folk or Low Religion local gods and goddesses ancestors and ghosts spirits demons and evil spirits dead saints	**Magic and Astrology** mana astrological forces charms, amulets, and magical rites evil eye, evil tongue	**This Worldly** Sees entities and events as occurring in this world and universe.
Seen or Empirical Directly observable by the senses. Knowledge based on experimentation and observation.	**Folk Social Science** interaction of living beings such as humans, possibly animals and plants	**Folk Natural Science** interaction of natural objects based on natural forces	

THE MODEL

Combining these two dimensions of metaphor and transcendence produces a grid or matrix for examining and comparing different belief systems (Figure 3.3). The model creates six sectors, two on each level of the immanent-transcendent scale. Each level deals with different ontological entities. At the bottom are the sciences—belief systems in which people use 'natural' explanations to account for empirically perceived phenomena. Natural sciences use mechanical or impersonal analogies, and the social sciences use organic or transactional ones. At the top are what is typically called 'religions'—belief systems that have to do with ultimate cosmic realities—heavenly gods, demons, fate, *karma*, heavens, and hell. The middle level is hard for modern people to understand. It deals with the *transempirical realities of this world*—with magic, evil eye, earthly spirits, ancestors, witchcraft, divination, and the like. The focus of this book is primarily to help missionaries and church leaders understand this 'middle zone.'

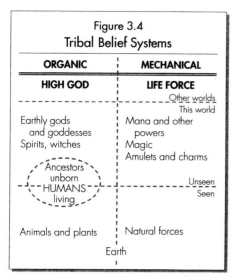

Figure 3.4
Tribal Belief Systems

ORGANIC	MECHANICAL
HIGH GOD	**LIFE FORCE**
	Other worlds
	This world
Earthly gods and goddesses	Mana and other powers
Spirits, witches	Magic
	Amulets and charms
Ancestors *unborn*	
HUMANS	*Unseen*
living	*Seen*
Animals and plants	Natural forces
Earth	

Figure 3.5
Folk Chinese Belief Systems

ORGANIC	MECHANICAL
Jade Emperor (T'ien)	Ming
Gods and goddesses	Yin and Yang
	Other worlds
	This world
Earth gods	Five elements
Sages	Magic
Mythological figures	Feng-shui
Spirits and ghosts	Divination
Ancestors	Palmistry
Animal spirits (totems)	Luck
	Unseen
	Seen
People	Acupuncture
Animals and plants	Matter

It is important to remember that this is an analytical model. In reality the boundaries between the categories are often fuzzy. Organic and mechanical analogies form a horizontal continuum with many shades between the poles. For example, people in the West do not think of plants or cells as being as fully living beings as humans and animals, and young men often talk to their automobiles as if these were alive. Similarly, the boundaries between the vertical dimension of otherworldly and this-worldly transempirical, and between this-worldly transempirical and empirical are fuzzy. Beings and forces also move between levels. Living humans enter the spirit world when they die, fate and *karma* determine the future of people on earth, and heavenly gods take on human form and enter human activities.

To see how this model can help us understand different religious systems, we need to look at a few examples (Figures 3.4, 3.5, 3.6, 3.7). Such a comparison helps us to see some of the systems used to account for and explain human experiences.

THE MODEL ELABORATED

Before applying the model to the study of specific religions, we need to look more closely at the six categories that emerge in the analytical grid, looking first at examples of organic metaphors, and then mechanistic metaphors on each level of transcendence.

ORGANIC METAPHORS

Organic metaphors are common in most religions. A bewildering variety of living beings populate the universe in different religions. Some live on or under the earth, others in the sky and heavens, and others in other universes or planes of reality.

OTHER-WORLDLY BEINGS

Belief in other worlds inhabited by a diversity of beings is widespread. A few illustrations can help us understand this diversity.

HIGH GOD

The concept of a high God—a supreme being who lives in the heavens or sky—is found around the world. He or she is believed to be powerful, the creator of all things, and to have an important role in giving rain, crops, game, children, and success in life. More than two-thirds of tribal religions believe in a creator God, sometimes seen as male, sometimes as female, and sometimes as combining both genders. In sub-Saharan Africa, belief in a creator God is taken for granted by almost everyone. The Masaii call this god "Engai," the Yoruba "Olorun" ["Lord of the Sky"],[3] the Dinka "Nhialic," the Mende "Ngewo," the Ibo "Chukwu," and the Fon "Mawu." His or her name is frequently on people's lips in salutations, blessings, and everyday business.[4]

People often use descriptive names to refer to this supreme being. Common among these are He-Who-Is, He-That-Lives-Above, Ancient-One, Creator, First Father or Mother, Most-High-One, and Most-Mighty-One. He or she is often described as eternal, omniscient, beneficent, omnip-

Figure 3.6
Folk Indian Belief Systems

ORGANIC	MECHANICAL
Brahma, Vishnu, Siva	Brahman
Other high gods	Karma, samsara
Rakshasas, yakshasas	Dharama
other demons	_Other worlds_
	This world
Goddesses of this	Magic
earth	Evil eye
Capricious spirits	Astrology
Ancestors, unborn	Amulets and charms
	Unseen
	Seen
Living humans	Ayurvedic and Unani
Subhuman beings	medicines
Animals and plants	Natural forces

Figure 3.7
Folk Muslim Belief Systems

ORGANIC	MECHANICAL
ALLAH	Quismet
Archangels	
Angels and devils	_Other worlds_
	This world
Jinn	Baraka
Quarina	Magic
Zar	Dhikr
Aisha Quandisha	Astrology
Ancestors, souls of	Evil eye
the dead	Auspicious numbers
	Quran, sacred objects
	Amulets
	Unseen
	Seen
Walis, holy men	Medicines and herbs
Saints, prophets	Natural forces
Humans	
Animals and plants	

---

3. Like most traditional religions, the Yoruba have more than one name for the high God. They also call him Olodumare, and Olofin, and use titles such as Eleda [the Creator], Alaaye [the Living One], and Elemii [Giver and Owner of life].

4. The same is true in the West, where people routinely call on and blame God when accidents, failures, deaths, and other terrible events take place.

otent, and absolutely good. Some people compare the high God to "shining light," "blazing fire," or "a great ancient human." For almost all, this god is the author and guardian of the moral code that exhorts humans to offer god prayers and sacrifices, obey the elders, care for human life, maintain sexual morality, be honest, and care for the sick, weak, aged, and others in need. God rewards morally good action and punishes evil.

This high God, however, is often seen as far removed from humans. Many peoples have stories that the high God was once close to earth, but that some act of greed or folly by people of old caused him or her to depart in anger, leaving humans to fend for themselves. For example, the Ashanti say that a woman pounding grain raised her pounding stick too high and hit God as he sat in the clouds, so he became angry and left people to their own devices. The Ibo of Nigeria say that God became tired of being bothered by every little complaint the people made. People still remember him, but sacrifices to him are rare and prayers are made only in emergencies. In everyday life humans are left to deal with the spirits, ancestors, ghosts, and witches that surround them through the use of gifts, bribes, rituals, magic, and spirit repellents. The Kilibob stories along the north coast of the island of New Guinea have a similar ring (Strelan 1978).

Although the high God is all-knowing, all-powerful, and the final arbiter of right and wrong, in many traditional religions he is not worshiped directly. For the most part he has no priests and no shrines dedicated to him. People may make an offering to him in every sacrifice, but rarely do they offer a sacrifice exclusively to him. He has withdrawn himself from concern with this world and left it to lesser gods, spirits, and humans.

The concept of a high God is also found in most high religions, including Christianity, Judaism, Islam, Hinduism, and Mahayana Buddhism. In many of these so-called high religions, God is the only God, the ultimate reality, the creator of all else, and the all-powerful and righteous. There are no other gods.

In Christian missions, this concept of a high God is often a bridge whereby people come to understand the God of the Bible (Richardson 1981). The message that won the Buganda of East Africa to Christ was the good news that this distant high God is, indeed, interested in human beings. J. V. Taylor writes (1958, 252–253),

> The message which was received and implanted, and upon which the church in Buganda was founded, was primarily news about the transcendent God. "Katonda," the unknown and scarcely heeded Creator, was proclaimed as the focus of all life, who yet lay beyond and above the closed

unity of all existence. This was in itself so catastrophic a concept that, for the majority of hearers, it appeared to be the sum of the new teaching.

LESSER GODS AND GODDESSES

Belief in lesser divinities is common. Most small scale and peasant communities have their own pantheon of deities and spirits that inhabit their land. Many of these spirits are associated with natural phenomena, others are part of the original order of things.

In China the gods constitute an imperial government with rulers, intermediaries, delegated ministers, executioners, spokespersons, attendants, servants, and enemies (Kramer and Wu 1970).

Yu-huang-shang-ti is the high God, above all the others. Under him is San-kuan-ta-ti, the chief in the central administration, and the heads of the departments of education, agriculture, labor, business, medicine, navigation, recreation, casting out evil, controlling plagues, female skill, and birth. Wu-fang-ta-ti, the head of the local administration, presides over the four gods of protection and the ten gods of Hades. Wang-yeh is the commander of the divine armies: the heavenly armies with thirty-six generals, the armies of Hades with seventy-two generals, and five battalions of divine soldiers with five camps on earth (Central, Eastern, Western, Southern, and Northern). Cheng-huang is the chief of police, and under him are police officials, judges, and a police force.

All these are lesser gods (small *g*) and powers (small *p*) with no absolute existence. They live under the rule of higher gods or God. Their cosmic social order serves as a model for human societies.

OTHER-WORLDLY SPIRITS

In addition to gods and goddesses, there are widespread beliefs in other spirit inhabitants of heaven and hell. Common among these are spirits who mediate between the transcendental realm of the sacred and the profane world of humans. Zoroastrianism, Judaism, Christianity, and Islam affirm the presence of different kinds of angels and archangels who serve God and do his bidding. In popular Islam, female angelic beings in heaven provide male Muslims with erotic delight after they die.

Demons are spiritual beings generally thought to be evil in character. In Islam, *shaytns*, *ghls*, and *'ifrts* are demons who assist Iblis or Satan in his rebellion against Allah. In Hinduism *asuras*, *rakshasas* and other demonic adversaries of the gods bring darkness, drought (by withholding the monsoon rains), and death to the righteous. *Asuras* aid humans who perpetuate evil and injustice, and *pantis* assist humans who rob the gods of their cows. In Buddhism, the archfiend is Mara, who is often thought to be an *asura*. He is surrounded by the denizens of hell, with their deformed bodies, hideous faces, and multiple eyes and limbs, who engage in terrifying and malevolent activities.

UNSEEN BEINGS OF THIS WORLD

In addition to these other-worldly beings, most people believe in invisible creatures that inhabit this world. These include earthly spirits that live in communities with humans, plants, and animals, and the surrounding lands. They have different roles, and they often use their powers to maintain the moral order by punishing the wayward and rewarding the good. Some spirits are seen as good, others as evil, but many are good to those who placate them and harm those who incur their anger. They live in certain places on earth, such as rivers, mountains, forests, and oceans, and their power is believed to be limited to their immediate neighborhoods.

GODS AND GODDESSES OF THIS WORLD

Most tribes[5] and peasant communities have their own pantheons of deities and spirits that inhabit their land. Many of these spirits are associated with natural phenomena. Others are part of the original order of things. The Yoruba of Nigeria speak of *orishas* such as Obatala, who makes people rich or poor, Ogun, who gives victory in battle to warriors, and Shango, the god of storms. The Fon of Benin believe that Mawu created three pantheons under herself: the sky pantheon that rules the heavens, the earth pantheon that rules the world, and the nature pantheon that rules thunder, rivers, and illnesses. They also believe in personal gods who play more immediate roles in individual lives.

The Taiwanese worship sea gods (Ma-Tsu and Hsuan-Tien-Shan-Ti) thought to control the dangerous Taiwan Strait, local patron gods (ethnic gods such as Pao-Shen-ta-ti and San-Shan-Kuo-Wang) which they brought from their homelands in mainland China, household gods, the god of health (Wang-Yeh), and the god of commerce (Kuan-Kung). In India, people speak of *murthis, devatas* who form a pantheon of lesser deities in Hinduism, and of local village goddesses who guard it from calamities, but require blood sacrifices to keep them happy.

SPIRITS OF THIS WORLD

People around the world believe in earthbound spirits. These may be ugly spirits of the earth. They may be kind ones that help people, and

---

5. In some parts of the world the term 'tribe' is seen as demeaning because it is seen as 'not modern.' Unfortunately, there is no good word to substitute for it. It has had a long and honored place in anthropological analysis, and tribal societies have provided stable, meaningful life for most people throughout much of human history. Furthermore, the problem is not with the word 'tribe,' but with 'modern.' Any word that stands in contrast to it is automatically seen as primitive and prelogical. We will use tribe, but in a technical sense, as a way of organizing societies that has much integrity, if not more, than modern societies, many of which are now in transition into what analysts are calling postmodern.

attach themselves to people who feed and care for them. They must be appeased if they get angry. Unlike heavenly spirits that descend to earth for periods of time, but live in the heavens, these earthly spirits live on earth just as humans do. The Ashanti *obosom,* Burmese *nats,* Thai *phi, preta* and *jag,* Ifugao *anitos,* Melanesian *totowoho* and *tubula,* Haitian *loas,* Malaysian *roh,* Cebano *agta, calag* and *encanto,* Kachin *ndang* and *jaht ung,* South Indian *ammas,* Japanese *kami,* Korean *kuisin,* Hindu *dayams,* and Muslim *jinn* and *quarina* are a few examples.

THE WORLD OF THE KALABARI OF NIGER DELTA, AFRICA

EARTHBOUND REALITIES

1. Level of the visible, tangible world: *komi kiri*
   - humans, animals, vegetables, inert objects
2. Level of invisible earthbound spirits: *teme*
   - **spirits of every person, plant, animal, and thing**—closely associated with their physical realities
   - **ancestors**—spirits of once-living people who look after the welfare of their lineage descendants and in return expect to be looked after themselves. Deceased heads of a lineage are particularly important and have innate relationships with the living lineage heads, who preside 'in their names' and 'with their strength'
   - **village heroes** *(am'oru)*—who came from a distance and introduced new ways of life and then disappeared into the sky or ground. Their spirits remain to strengthen the village as a whole
   - **water people** *(owuamapu)*—live in fabulous towns under the water decked in coral, gold, and rare cloths. Can materialize as humans, pythons, or rainbows. They are associated with particular creeks, swamps, and mudfalts. They control the weather, supply fish, keep waterways open, and give humans great power and wealth
   - ancestors, village heroes, and water people can displace a person's spirit and so possess him or her

OTHER-WORLDLY REALITIES

3. Heavenly creators: *tamuno*
   - **personal creators**—everyone has a personal creator who joins spirit and body in the womb and guides his or her destiny
4. Heavenly Creator: *opu tanumo*
   - the **Great Creator** who created the entire world out of mud and watches over it so nothing happens against her will
   - she is sometimes refered to as 'in the sky *(so).*' (Horton 1962)

Most tribal religions are full of spirits (see insert on Kalabari spirits). There are nature spirits: spirits of the earth, forest, rocks, mountains, rivers, and sea. There are plant spirits: the Karens of Myanmar say that plants have *la,* and call back the spirit of rice when their crops wilt, and South Sea Islanders ask forgiveness of trees they cut them down for canoes so that the spirits of these trees will not plague them. There are animal spirits: the Native Americans, the Stiens of Cambodia, and the Ainos of Yesso beg pardon of animals when they kill them, and the Kafirs entreat elephants not to tread on them.

Some societies differentiate earthly spirits on the basis of their abode. "Spirits above" are those that dwell in the air and are associated with phenomena such as the sun, moon, clouds, lightning, and thunder; "spirits below" live on the earth, and "spirits underground," such as dwarfs, inhabit an upside down world beneath the soil.

Belief in earthly spirits is also common in peasant societies (see insert on Thai Spirits). Filipino peasants believe in one supreme creator god, *Bathala* who resides in the heavens, and other high deities such as the moon and stars, war gods, and guardians of human souls. They also placate the *anitos,* which are associated with fields and crops, journeys by sea, battle, diseases, and houses. Among these are the *dwende* and *tamawo,* who live in trees, creeks, seas, and rocks. They are not malevolent, but interfere with everyday life by moving things around the house, kidnapping beautiful young women, and causing physical injuries when people bump into them. The most feared earthly spirits are the *aswang,* who attack people and kill them by eating their livers. They include blood-sucking vampires, human-eating were-dogs, corpse-eating ghouls, and viscera-sucking spirits. The last of these appear as beautiful women in the daytime, and strange women in the community are often suspected of being *aswang* in disguise. Wives warn their husbands of such *aswang* to keep them from philandering, and children are warned that *aswang* attack those who cry too much. A strange woman may marry an unsuspecting man to destroy him and his family. At night these viscera-eaters perch on a house and stick a long tongue through the roof to suck out a person's internal organs. Sharp knives, light, loud noises, ashes, salt, vinegar, and spices are used to scare them off. Steep roofs and sharp bamboo staves are designed to make it difficult for the *aswang* to balance on the roof. The *maligno* live in underground tunnels and bring sickness, disharmony, and death to humans (Hobson 1996).

SPIRITS IN THAILAND

Thai beliefs in spirit realities juxtapose Buddhist and Brahmanical beliefs with the indigenous traditional worship of spirits and other supernatural beings. These are found on three levels.

phommalog: the world of the highest gods *(phom)* that includes Brahmanical and Buddhist gods. Made up of four levels.

thewadalog: the world of the lesser gods. Made up of sixteen levels.

manudalog: the world of humans, spirits, and other beings. Made up of eleven levels.

winjan: the soul that lives in the heart of a person and leaves at death to go to heaven *(sawan)* or to hell *(bnarok)*.

khwan: the "free soul," "ego," "morale," "spirit of life," or "soul stuff" of a person. If a person has *khwan* he or she is happy, well, and prosperous. If it leaves the body, the person is frightened and sorrowful. The *tham khwan* ceremonies must be performed to call the *khwan* back if it wanders away.

phi: a large variety of spirits that appear largely at night in patches of dark vegetation. These include ghosts of the dead and astral bodies of the living; nature spirits; and capricious other-worldly spirits who are malicious if not properly propitiated.

phra phum chao thi: spirits that inhabit and control certain geographical locations—guardian spirits that inhabit houses, camps, doors, ladders, stables, forests, fields, and bodies of water.

preta: other spirits who are not particularly dangerous. They are tall with small heads, small mouths, and large stomachs and are always hungry. They are pitied more than feared.

jag: merciless giants that live in Tibet. They fly and require sacrifices.

agricultural spirits: rice goddess, mother earth goddess, subterranean snake *(naga)*, and spirits of the six cardinal directions.

(Cf. Thambia 1970; Attagara 1968; deYoung 1966)

The tin miners in the high Andean plateau of Bolivia placate images of Tio, the devil who controls the rich ore and reveals it only to those who give him offerings. His body, hands, face, and horns are always shaped from ore; his eyes are burned-out bulbs from the miners' torches; his teeth are made of sharpened glass; his hands are stretched out, grasping bottles of alcohol; his mouth is open, stuffed with coca and ready to receive offerings.

The world of popular Islam is densely populated by an array of good and evil earthly spirits that influence human affairs. *Jinn* are proud and rebellious creatures with shadowy bodies, who are linked with the practice of magic, epidemics, and madness (*jinn*-possessed). Women in childbirth, newborn infants, brides, and bridegrooms are in particular danger of being attacked by them. There are male and female, and Muslim, Jewish, Christian, and pagan *jinn*. As a rule *jinn* are invisible, but they can assume animal or human forms, and unwary humans run the risk of marrying them. They love darkness and are afraid of light. To protect oneself against them, one should always say Basmalah ("In the name of God") before eating or undertaking anything important.

Like shadows, spirits appear and disappear at will. They are immaterial, but they have the ability to change their appearance and to manifest themselves to humans in many different forms. In most cases, the power of these spirits is local, extending little beyond the land they cover in their daily travels—often not more than a few miles from their abode. E. Bolaji Idowu points out (1975, 174) that earthly spirits "are ubiquitous; there is no area of the earthly, no object or creature, which has not a spirit of its own or which cannot be inhabited by a spirit."

HALF-DIVINE BEINGS ON EARTH

Between the worlds of sacred and human beings, there are half-divine figures who serve as mediators between the two. Some of these are humans who become gods. In Uganda, the Buganda believe that great persons become *balubaale*. In India, women who committed *suti* by throwing themselves on the funeral pyres of their deceased husbands were often deified and enshrined in their own temples. In China, Chang I, who lived in China during the Han dynasty, was known for healing people through special drugs. Later, during the Sung dynasty, Emperor Hui Tsung elevated him by giving him the title Jade Emperor God and commanding everyone to worship him as a god. Many Taiwanese worship Koxinga (1624–61), who defeated the Dutch and led the settlement of the fertile western plains of Taiwan, and Liau Tien-Ting, a hero during the Japanese occupation during World War II. These symbolize their ethnic identity.

ANKAMMA

Ankamma lived on the Godavari River in South India. Each morning her husband floated across the river to care for the cattle on the other side, using a large earthen pot to buoy himself up because he could not swim. One night in the dark he accidentally picked up an unfired pot. It dissolved in the water and he drowned. In her grief his wife committed suicide. Today she is worshiped as *devata*, or goddess, by women of the Kama caste, for whom she is the model wife.

Some gods are thought to become human. For example, the Pharaoh of Egypt[6] and the Emperor of Japan were thought to be divine. Still other semi-divine beings, such as Dan Gun in Korea, are the descendants of marriages between gods and humans or animals.

Particularly common are the half-human and half-divine founders and protectors of tribal societies, and the focus of their communal worship. Often these beings are seen as culture heroes who taught the people how to live civilized lives—how to build fires, make canoes, plant

---

6. The Pharaoh had to marry his half-sister because she, too, was partly divine and could survive his divine power. Any mortal woman married to him would die from his divine power.

crops, and build houses—tasks on which the group depends for survival. For example, the Tenetehara of Brazil believe that Maira gave them manioc, their staple food, and taught them how to farm. Before then, they hunted game and gathered wild fruit. At first, the manioc planted itself and matured in one day, but Maira's second wife refused to gather it, so Maira cursed the manioc so that it would take a whole winter to grow. Maira also gave the Tenetehara cotton and taught them how to weave hammocks. He stole fire from the vultures and taught his people how to roast meat (Wagley and Galvao 1949, 101–32).

The Kalabari of eastern Niger believe that cultural heroes introduced them to new laws and ways of life. One introduced them to European trade, another to masquerade dancing, another to head-hunting, and another to purification rites. Like ancestors, these heroes once lived with humans, but they were not born into the group. They came from distant places, and instead of dying like ancestors, they disappeared into the sky or ground, and left no descendants behind them (Horton 1962, 200).

Trickster gods are also semi-divine beings. They are not ancestors and not concerned with human well-being, but may accidentally help them. An example is the famous Native American Coyote, who stole the sun, moon, and stars, but didn't know what to do with them, so he put them in the sky. He stole fresh water from the spirits to drink, but spilled it all over the world, creating lakes and rivers. Another example is Iolofath of the Carolina Islands, who was born from a tryst the god Lugeilang had with a woman (Lessa 1966, 57).

Some semi-divine beings are human saints who have particular relationships with sacred beings because of the spiritual lives they live. This is the case of Muslim *fakirs* and *dervishes*, Hindu *sadhus* and *sanyasis*, Buddhist *boddhisatvas*, and Christian saints. People turn to such mediators because these are near, and the people do not fear them. Sacred beings, on the other hand, are often seen as distant and terrifyingly powerful.

ANCESTORS, GHOSTS, UNBORN AND LIVING HUMANS

Another category of earthly spirit beings is humans. The belief that people have invisible spirits is widespread. The Algonquins, Tasmanians, and Quiche described this as "the person's shadow." West Australians and California Indians spoke of it as "breath" or "soul." These souls are commonly believed to leave the body in dreams and trances to visit distant relatives. Dreams are not taken as fictions of the mind, but real experiences of the soul in its wanderings. Consequently, the people take dreams seriously as warnings or as omens of good fortune. On the other hand, if a person is awakened suddenly, the soul does not have enough time to return and is in danger of wandering off. Furthermore, souls may flee the body when alarmed. The Samo of Papua New Guinea use these concepts as a rationale for creating confusion and noise during a raid. Surrounding a forest long house in the early hours of the moonless morning, a group of raiders wait until two of their number quietly enter the house swinging stone clubs. The confusion and noise resulting as people are hit and others are awakened produces a flight response that enables the waiting warriors to shoot arrows through all who attempt to escape. The deaths are understood by the Samo as simply taking bodies that had no spirits. Souls may also be stolen and eaten by other spirits. The losses of one or more souls make people withdrawn, sick, and die. At death this spirit is generally believed to be set free to linger near the tomb, to wander on earth, or to travel to the region of the spirits—the world beyond the grave. For example, the people of New Ireland believe that when a person dies, the spirit remains beside the body until it is buried. After the burial spirits begin the journey to the underworld, Tuna. On the way they must have a ritual bath in a well at Manala on Panaeati Island. After bathing they assume their physical forms again and say farewell to their loved ones. They then disappear and take on spiritual forms that enable them to enter Tuna (Namunu n.d., 94).

Belief in a second soul, a spiritual double or guardian spirit, is widespread. The Yoruba call it *ikeji*. The Muslims call it *quarina*. Doubles accompany people all their lives, and are the cause of much of what happens to them. Many people believe that photographs steal these souls and make them visible, but in so doing they cause the person to get sick and die. Similarly, shadows are often seen as projections of the soul, and must be protected. John Warneck writes regarding the Batik of Sumatra,

> The shadow of man must not fall on a grave or a place where evil spirits dwell, otherwise the spirits will get the owner into their power. A man must not let his shadow fall on other people's food, else the eater will appropriate with the food the man's soul power, and he will pine away (1961, 196).

SPIRITS IN TRADITIONAL KOREAN RELIGION

HIGH WORLD—SKY DEITIES
    Hananim [High God]

sun god	moon god	star god
Buddhist gods	Taoist gods	

MIDDLE WORLD SPIRITS
    Nature spirits

earth spirits	road spirits	fire spirits	wind spirits
tree spirits	stone spirits	animal spirits	agricultural spirits

warrior spirits   disease spirits   gate spirits [Chunsin]
direction spirits [O Fang Chang Koon: East, South, West, North, Up]
mountain spirits [Sansin, Sunghwan Dang]
birth spirits water spirits [Young Wang, dragon, guardians of boats]
luck spirits [snake = Kurumi, Weasel = Chokchebi, spirit = Inup]
house spirits [House tujoo, Sungjoo, Keullip, Cheisuk Jar, Kitchen Spirit]
free lance spirits [Tukeibis, Deusin, Tokkebi]
Human spirits
royal spirits [king spirit, queen spirit, princess spirit]
commander spirits [general spirit, general's wife spirit, other spirits]
lord spirits   madam spirit   bride spirits   haman spirits
miscellaneous spirits [e.g., Sonkaksi = girl who dies before marriage, spirits of people who drown]

UNDERWORLD SPIRITS
Hades gods [Yumma, Ulwang]   demons
(adapted from Kim 1996, 69)

Belief in multiple souls is widespread. The Ga of Ghana believe that a human consists of three entities: the *sumsuma*—the conscious relational self that leaves the body in dreams and soul-wandering; the *kla*—the life force; and the *ghomotfo*—the physical body. At death the *kla* departs, leaving the person to become a *sisa* or ghost. In time the *kla* is reborn in the same tribe, reaffirming the tribe's unity (Burnett 1988, 47–48).

In most societies, humans include the ancestors who are commonly thought to participate in the everyday activities of family life. When one eats it is necessary to share the food with them, and when one goes on a journey they must be informed. They must be given a share of the bride's wealth, harvest, and game taken in a hunt. Ignoring one's ancestors is a sin not only against them, but against the whole extended family, including its cattle, goats, sheep, and crops.[7] The ancestors may get angry and bring misfortune or withhold blessings; and parents, after they die, may bring a curse on their descendants for maltreating them during their last days in this world.

Ancestor spirits are departed elders, and their role must be understood in the light of the high respect accorded elders in many traditional societies. For example, if a person grievously wrongs his parents, it is utterly disrespectful to ask forgiveness of them personally. He must find a respectable elder to take a token of repentance to the parents. A young man must approach a young woman's parents through a respectable mediator. A subject cannot go to a chief or king directly, but has

---

7. Normally, all members of a family must participate in ancestor rites for these to be effective. This puts great pressure on those who become Christian while other family members remain traditionalists.

his case brought through a subchief. Similarly, in approaching God, the greatest and most powerful being, in many societies people must use intermediaries, and the ancestors close to both the living and the Supreme Being are most qualified to function as such (Moyo 1996, 5–6).

Attitudes toward ancestors vary greatly. They are widely regarded with respect and feared as powerful members of the family. Many people carry out elaborate rituals to pacify the ancestors. For example, the Khasis of Assam and the Burmese give money to the dead for their expenses on their journey to the other world so that they do not come back. Others dread ghosts and try to mislead them. Certain Australian bands make widows keep silent for years so that their jealous husbands will not find and harm them. The annual remembrance feasts held in honor of ancestors frequently mingle sentiments of awe, anxiety, and affection.

In much of the world ghosts are seen as the souls of people who have not lived fulfilled lives, or have died tragic deaths. They are thought to exist in a halfway house between the human world and the world of ancestral spirits, and to search for a human body that they can enter and make sick through their nefarious activity.

In many folk religions the people believe that the unborn already exist, awaiting the opportunity to be reborn. Trobriand Islanders believe that unborn spirits live in the lagoons, and when young women carelessly walk through the water, the spirits enter their bodies to be born. Australian Aborigines hold that the spirits live in holes in the earth and jump into the bodies of young women who unsuspectingly walk over them. The Baoule of Côte d'Ivoire believe that the unborn live in a spiritual world called *blolo*, of which little is known.

SEEN BEINGS OF THIS WORLD

The human soul provides the transition from unseen beings to the seen of this world. These include animals, plants, and the earth, which many people believe to be alive. We turn now to a discussion of some of those manifestations.

WITCHES

One belief found around the world is that some humans have witch spirits that they can send out of their bodies on errands or to do harm to others. In some societies, witches are thought to inherit their powers, in others they learn as apprentices to other witches or acquire these powers unknowingly. Among the Azande, for example, witches are thought to be dangerous without their knowing it—their power is automatically activated by their feelings of resentment against others. Some witches publicly acknowledge their practices and are widely feared. Others are falsely accused of being witches.

In many societies, witches are seen as antisocial and as living lives opposite that of normal humans. They stay up at night, have their feet on backward, and fly in the air. They are thought to transform themselves into wolves, rabbits, cats, and other animals; to travel great distances in a moment of time; and to have special ties to owls, snakes, hyenas, and baboons. They are accused of acting in vile self-interest, and of refusing to share what they have with others. In short, the witch epitomizes the exact opposite of what a given culture considers appropriate and normative. Generally, those accused of being witches are old or mentally deranged people, women with no kin to defend them, or those who are antisocial.

SUBHUMANS

Around the world there are beliefs in half-human, half-animal beings and other subhuman beings such as monsters, trolls, and 'little people.' During the Middle Ages, North Europeans had stories of gargantuan humanoids who were embodiments of evil forces. They spoke of *satyr* (half-human and half-beast with goat feet, pointed ears, and shaggy bodies), *pyrs* (hairy woodman), water-sprites, and Grendel of *Beowulf*. After the coming of Christianity, these monsters were seen as the "descendants of Cain" (Jeffrey 1980).

ANIMALS AND PLANTS

Animals and plants are part of everyday life in all societies, but in most societies they are not seen simply as natural beings. Many are believed to have their own spirits that interact with humans and gods. The Eskimo pour fresh water into the mouths of seals they kill, believing that seals long for fresh water and allow themselves to be caught to get a drink of it.

Animals are often seen as sacred: cows and monkeys in India, crocodiles in West Africa, snakes by the Zulu and Masai of East Africa, eagle-hawks by Native Americans, and mantis by the Bushmen of the Kalahari Desert in South Africa. Others are considered to be evil. Tigers, horses, deer, and many other animals are seen as totems related to human social groups; crows, hares, dogs, and pigeons are seen as messengers from the spirit world; turtles, elephants, serpents, fish, and bulls are believed to carry the earth on their backs; and crocodiles, birds, and other animals are believed to be reembodiments of people when they die, or bearers of the dead to heaven or hell. Eclipses are blamed on snakes, wild goats, and other creatures who eat the moon, shake the earth, and cause other disasters to befall their victims.

Plants, too, are active participants in everyday encounters. Cedars, oaks, and ash trees were worshiped in medieval Europe, and rubber trees and stinging nettles are believed to harbor malevolent spirits in parts of Southeast Asia. Forests are widely seen as places where spirits live.

NATURE

Nature itself is often thought to be alive. The sun and moon are widely believed to be powerful spirits that influence human lives. Sky spirits are placated so that they will provide rain for the crops.

Land has special meaning in many traditional societies. Hilltops, rivers, caves, and great rocks are commonly seen as sacred places. The hearth in the home or a wall facing a particular direction is often seen as a shrine.

Land is not a secular commodity that can be bought and sold. It is the symbol of a people's corporate identity. For example, in most tribal societies land belongs to a vast family of whom many are dead, a few are living, and countless more are still unborn. It is the trust and sanctuary of departed ancestors and the heritage of the yet unborn. The living are only temporary caretakers of it.

All these organic metaphors help humans to understand the impact of spiritual beings on their lives. Our organization of them in an analytical model enables us to appreciate people's beliefs and apply that understanding to show how the true God desires to meet their needs and concerns. We turn now to examples of mechanical metaphors as we seek to fill out the analytical model for explaining belief systems.

MECHANICAL METAPHOR

Mechanical metaphors are found on all three levels of the model. We will examine a few of them.

OTHER-WORLDLY FORCES

Like transcendent beings that pervade the cosmos and impact human beings, there are widespread beliefs in other-worldly forces that affect the lives of humans. Some examples follow.

FATE AND FORTUNE

The term 'fate' is used in explanation systems that see ultimate reality as determined by impersonal forces outside this universe. For example, traditional Koreans believed in *woon,* or fortune, which is based on the four pillars and the eight characters that represent the year, month, day, and star that determine a person's life. People go to the fortune teller to seek good fortune and escape calamity on important occasions, such as celebrating the New Year, choosing wedding dates, taking school examinations, or seeking employment. Muslims speak of *kismet* or fate.

People can divine their fate by means of horoscopes, fortune tellers, palmists, and other diviners. Forewarned, they can soften or delay a little the hard blows, abandon hopeless plans, and be alert to opportunities that cross their paths, but they cannot radically change their fate.

COSMIC MORAL ORDER

There is a widespread belief in an impersonal cosmic moral order, which guarantees that good deeds bring about good results—prosperity, long life, many children, and other blessings, and that bad deeds have evil consequences—illness, failure in business, bad marriages, and even death. Closely associated with this belief are the concepts of merit and demerit. In doing good deeds, a person earns merit, which can be accumulated and used to achieve his or her goals. Similarly, evil actions result in demerits, which also accumulate and result in disasters.

In South and Southeast Asia there is a widespread belief in *karma*, the impersonal cosmic moral law that governs the universe, rewarding good deeds and punishing evil ones. A person's present state is prescribed by the deeds done in his or her previous life. This moral force determines the present and future of all beings—gods, spirits, humans, and animals. In Thailand, the doctrine of *karma* is linked to belief in merit and demerit. Unlike sin, which is an offense against other beings such as God, demerit is the natural moral consequence of doing bad deeds. Buddhism outlines five ways for making merit: don't kill any living thing, don't lie, don't steal, don't commit adultery, and don't imbibe any intoxicant. To these the Thai have added a list of behaviors that ensure merit: become a monk, give food to the monks, participate in Buddhist holidays and festivals, give money to a temple, and build a temple. Many commoners encourage their sons to enter the monastery for a period of time to earn merit for the family. The main motivation for young men to become monks when they are about twenty years old is to "pay back their mother's milk" and to assure their parents a good life after death.

The Chinese speak of Tien, sometimes translated as Heaven. For many this refers to the cosmic harmony, moral precepts, or mandate from heaven, which is the mysterious force that directs the welfare and misfortunes of human lives. Tien is sometimes associated with Tao, The Way, and with the concepts of Ying and Yang, the negative and positive poles of natural phenomena. Sometimes it is associated with Li, the universal principle or order underlying all things, the universal law governing all things, the reason behind all things, the highest standard of all things.

EARTHLY TRANSEMPIRICAL FORCES

There are many forces at work in this world, and most peoples do not divide them into the categories transempirical and empirical. Moreover, there is a very fuzzy line between all pervasive cosmic forces that govern the universe, such as fate and *karma*, and specific forces that impact the way human beings live their lives. For analytical purposes, however, it is helpful to distinguish between empirical and transempirical forces.

LIFE FORCE

People around the world believe in many kinds of life force, a spiritual energy field that pervades everything. It is sometimes called "vital essence," "personal magnetism," or "soul-stuff." It is the spiritual, nonmaterial substance of life. Life force is vital for health, wealth, worldly power, and success—in fact, everything that makes life at all worth living. To have it is to be healthy and strong; to lose it is to grow weak and die. It exists in greater concentration in famous men, strong charms, revered fetishes, and powerful gods. Gods, humans (both living and departed), animals, and plants have life only as they have this vital force. Families, lineages, and tribes have corporate vital force and their happiness and prosperity depend on conserving and strengthening it.

In many parts of the world this force cannot be separated from life itself. Placide Tempels points out that the supreme value of the Bantu of Central Africa is *ntu,* the great vital force that lies behind the universe and infuses all existence. It is found in *kintu*—the intelligence that flows through all things, *hantu*—the dimensions of time and space, *bantu*— each human being, and *muntu*—all humanity. *Ntu* is the comprehensive connectional system of life force that underlies every area of life. He writes,

> We can conceive the transcendental notion of 'being' by separating it from its attribute, 'force', but the Bantu cannot. 'Force' in his thought is a necessary element in 'being,' and the concept of 'force' is inseparable from the definition of 'being.' . . . Without the element of 'force,' 'being' cannot be conceived. . . . When we say that 'beings' are differentiated in their essence or nature, Bantu say that 'forces' differ in their essence or nature (Tempels 1959:34–35).

Stephen Neill notes (1961, 133),

> The European thinks in terms of 'being' or 'existence.' The African thinks in terms of 'vital force' or 'energy.' . . . This vital force can be increased or it can be threatened or diminished. When a man's vital force is on the

increase, he is well. If an African is tired, he says 'I am dying,' a phrase which sounds ridiculously exaggerated in European ears, but which to the African is perfectly sensible, as implying the sense of a diminution of vital powers which, unless repaired or checked, will lead in the long run to his decease.

The Bantu universe is not a chaotic tangle of unordered forces blindly struggling with one another, but a system of forces that operate by determinative natural and moral laws. Furthermore, humans can influence or undermine the life force of others. For example, through curses they can attack the life force in others, and cause them to become sick or have accidents. In such a worldview, all misfortunes must be explained in terms of the influence of other humans or spiritual beings. There is no such thing as an accident. On the other hand, a strong vital force gives a man many wives and children, and, in warfare, the tribe with greater vital forces is the victor.[8]

Human vital force also influences the inferior life force of animals, vegetables, and minerals, and, in so doing, affects other humans. Forces can be concentrated at vital centers of a living being. The lion's force is focused in its teeth, and by getting a lion's tooth the hunter adds its force to his own. In the hunt, the struggle is between the forces of the hunter and the prey. The vital force exercised by individuals must be kept in balance and steps taken to guard against other forces that are dangerous to one's own life forces.

The Thai speak of *khwan,* the vital force that gives a person the qualities of completeness and dignity. It can be lost through sickness, stress, crisis, fear, insults, and blows to the head. When this happens, the person feels depressed, frightened, unlucky, absent-minded, and weak. To assure its strength, people perform the Su Khwan Ceremony at important events in life, such as pregnancy, puberty, weddings, illnesses, and when returning to the village after long absences.

Another example of a vital force is the Chinese belief in *feng shui.* At the heart of this is the notion of *qi,* a life-giving cosmic breath that lurks in the natural landscape. Buildings and tombs must be designed and aligned with the terrain for *qi* to accumulate and circulate in them. Closely related to *feng shui* is the *t'ai-chi* (Grand Ultimate) diagram, which incorporates the eight trigrams found in the *I Chang* (The Book of Changes) and is widely used for divination and sealing coffins. The *t'ai-chi* is the energy field at the center of the universe that harmonizes all things.

8. Westerners are often thought to have a greater vital force. That explains their superiority in battle and technology. Modernity has not caused the idea of vital force to disappear.

MANA

Mana is a supernatural force found throughout Melanesia. It is similar to life force in many ways, but broader in scope. It is like a supernatural electricity that influences events in this world. It follows certain laws and those who know them can control it for their own benefit. Robert H. Codrington, a missionary in Melanesia, wrote (1969, 118–20),

> The Melanesian mind is entirely possessed by the belief in a supernatural power or influence, called almost universally *mana*. This is what works to affect everything which is beyond the ordinary power of men, outside the common processes of nature; it is present in the atmosphere of life, attaches itself to persons and things, and is manifested by results which can only be ascribed to its operation.

Beliefs in supernatural power like *mana* are widespread. The !Kung Bushmen believe in *N!ow*, an impersonal, amoral force responsible for the weather. It is released when hunters kill certain animals. The Indonesians speak of *toh*, the people of the West Solomons of *magit* or "soul stuff," the Sioux of *wakanda*, the Crow of *maxpe*, and the Zairians of *elima*. The Fon of Benin speak of *ac*, the force found in varying degrees in all living beings. The Maldovians believe in *fandita*, the positive force that, properly managed, can cure sick people, make crops grow, ensure good fishing catch, and ward off evil spirits, and in *sihuru*, the negative force that causes sickness and misfortune.

Mana, or supernatural force, is found in certain culturally defined places, such as in the body of a great warrior, in certain wild animals, and in strange objects that bring success to their owners. It can be acquired by eating part of such animals or warriors, by fasting and abstaining from sexual relations, and, above all, by proper rituals. It can be stored and concentrated by people who know how to handle it. It can be lost, making a warrior weak and easy to defeat. Mana is often thought to exude from powerful officials for good or for destruction. It is also associated with holy men and women, whose power is as great as their withdrawal into the sacred world, and their humility and poverty. Mana is often found in amulets, magical charms, and fetishes that have inherent power in them, and can protect the owner from disease, accidents, failures, and sorcery. These play an important part in the lives of many people today.

Like electricity, mana can be dangerous to those who do not know how to handle it. A rock or tree full of mana can kill those who touch it. Consequently, where it is found, there are taboos that protect ordinary people by warning them of danger. On the other hand, religious practitioners such as magicians, witches, and shamans know how to control powerful forces without destroying themselves.

One example of impersonal force is the Muslim concept of *baraka*. This is a spiritual force that is said to congeal in certain individuals. It is granted by God to certain persons, and may be transferred by them to other persons or inanimate objects. Ordinary people who come in contact with a person with *baraka* experience beneficial results. When a saint dies, his *baraka* increases and is inherited by persons and places associated with him, especially his tomb, or *kuba*. After his death a saint often becomes the patron and protector of the locality in which he lived. People seeking blessing, especially barren women and the sick, visit his tomb in the hope that power will impact them and bring about a desired result.

MAGIC

Magic is the control of this-worldly supernatural forces, such as *mana*, by the use of proper chants, amulets, and automatically effective rituals.[9] It does not involve supplicating supernatural beings in the hope that they will respond. People believe that saying the right formulaic sounds causes the rain to come, or protects them from diseases or evil spirits. Thus magic is a specific attempt to force a response that will result in changing the status quo.

Early anthropologists saw magic as meaningless, childish fantasies and prelogical thought. We now know that it gives meaning to people's existence by creating a harmonious world in which everything is connected to everything else, and that acts in one part of the world cause changes in other parts. This connectedness is not based on biophysical connections alone, but on assumed spiritual realities underlying the universe.

Sir James George Frazer (1922) noted two laws that underlie magical thinking. The first is the "law of sympathy," or homeopathy—the principle that "like produces like." For example, a shaman pours water to produce rain, and a magician makes a doll resembling his enemy and sticks pins into it, causing the enemy to become ill and die. Similarly, the crowd at a football game leans toward the goal line trying to help

---

9. We reject earlier anthropological theories that magic represents some primitive, prelogical form of thought, alien to our Western understanding. Rather, we see it as a serious belief system that seeks to make sense out of human experience. As Larry Laudan notes, magic, religion, and science are not different ways of knowing. Rather, they start with different questions and assumptions about the nature of reality and causation. This does not mean we accept the ontological truth of magical thinking, but recognize that for many people it is the world as they see it. As we will note later, most people have a tendency toward thinking in 'magical' terms when living their lives.

their team make a touchdown. The second is the "law of contagion," the principle that things which have once been in contact continue ever after to act on each other. For instance, the magician may do magic on a piece of clothing, fingernail clipping, or strand of hair from a victim, causing that person to grow weak or become sick, a wife may secretly perform magic on her husband's food if she suspects that he is having an affair, or a young man may cast a spell on a young woman's scarf to make her fall in love with him. An example of this is the Yoruba sorcerer who said,

> You take the hair of a man's head. You prepare medicine and put it with the hair and put them both in an ant hill. As the ants are circulating about the medicine, so the victim will feel it inside his head, or you may put the medicine and the man's hair under an anvil, and every time the blacksmith strikes the anvil so he will feel it inside his head (Price 1964, 90).

To cure a person suffering from evil magic, someone must perform countermagic that nullifies the original magic, or deflects it back on the performer. Other remedies have no effect against it.

Magic is essentially pragmatic—if something seems to work, then keep on doing it until it no longer does. There is little need to explain why things work, only to know that they do.

Magic is amoral; it can be used for good or for evil. In fact, what is good in the eyes of the one performing the magic may be destructive to the person on the receiving end. Most magic is used to benefit people, particularly when it is practiced by a community. A shaman or medicine man performs rituals for a family, village, or tribe to control the weather, prevent diseases, assure victories in battle over enemies, punish deviants, and bring prosperity. Practiced individually and secretly, however, magic is often used for selfish and evil ends. A man seeks to gain advantage over a neighbor using "waste away" magic. He curses a rival to kill him or casts a love spell on a woman to compel her into an illicit relationship.

EVIL EYE, MOUTH, AND TOUCH

Another widespread belief, particularly in the Near East, Europe, North Africa, and South Asia is that certain people have a malevolent power that causes harm through their sight, speech, or contact. A look, word, or touch can cause a cow to stop giving milk, crops to wither, and people to get headaches, become impotent, and even die. Infants, newlyweds, cows, and ripe crops are particularly susceptible to the evil eye. So too is freshly cooked food. Those who eat it after it has been seen by someone with an evil eye get stomach cramps and fever. In many societies, the evil eye is associated with envy. People who are jealous of others are often accused of harming them by casting a hateful look on them.

An example of evil eye is the Arab belief in *ayn* ("eye"). Some people are believed to consciously seek this power. Others acquire it involuntarily. Those most likely to have it are barren and unmarried women, people with blue or deep-set eyes, or those with misshapen faces. Those in greatest danger of attack are small boys, pregnant women, brides and bridegrooms, and people whose beauty or success make them objects of envy.

Fear that the words or touch of certain people can harm others is less common, but is a part of life in many religious communities.

ASTROLOGY

One widespread belief is that the sun, moon, planets, and stars radiate forces that influence human lives for good and for evil. The precise conjunction of the sun, moon, and planets at the time of a person's birth determines his or her good and ill fortunes at any given moment in life. Consequently, humans must carefully calculate the cycles of the planets to determine auspicious times for weddings, starting new businesses, or going on a journey, and to avoid accidents, failures, and death. The daily publication of horoscopes in newspapers around the world speaks to the widespread belief in astrological forces.

EARTHLY EMPIRICAL FORCES

At the bottom of the analytical model on the mechanical side are beliefs related to physical substances and forces that people can use to both control and protect themselves from the world around them. All people have beliefs about natural forces. Wind, fire, flowing water, human power, and animal traction are some of the forces people seek to guard against and to use for their own purposes. Knowledge of these is the basis for their natural sciences and technologies.

MEDICINES

Most people distinguish between minor, common, and obvious ailments that they can handle themselves, and serious sicknesses that are mysterious, and cannot be cured apart from specialized knowledge and the skills of medical practitioners. Coughs, rheumatism, toothaches, snake and scorpion bites, and even measles are generally treated as unexceptional conditions amenable to treatment with home remedies. More serious illnesses require technical knowledge regarding medicines—natural cures such as leaves, herbs, bark, tree sap, ground-up bones, and manufactured chemicals that prevent or cure diseases, and foster health and success. For example, the Paiute and Shoshone Indians of Nevada used approximately three hundred species of plants for medicinal purposes. Some traditional medicines have been scientifically shown to have curative effects. The pharmacopoeia of South American tribes provided modern medicine with many drugs, such as digitalis, curare, coca, and Peruvian balsam.

Most societies do not differentiate between natural and supernatural explanations for the causes and treatments of illnesses. Medicines are blessed, and chants recited as the medicines are administered. Cures are attributed to the medicines and to the magical powers associated with them. In many societies shamans are in charge of healing rituals. Others, however, have medicine societies made up of specialists who possess the secret rituals and medical knowledge to heal. They deal with severe illnesses, and command great prestige. For instance, the Sia of New Mexico have a Snake Society whose members cure snake bites, a Fire Society whose members treat burns, a Shim Society whose members treat illness caused by ants, and at least six other medicine societies. To join a Zuni medicine society, a person must first be cured from a serious illness, and then pay for an expensive initiation ceremony.

PHYSICAL FORCES

People worldwide know of physical forces. A stone can crack a coconut; a club, a man's head; fire can warm people and burn down their homes; and electromagnetism can run a motor and transmit radio broadcasts around the world. In their fascination with supernatural forces strange to them, Westerners should not forget that all people appeal to natural explanations for much of everyday life.

Having developed and illustrated a model for analyzing belief systems, we now turn to a closer look at the nature of formal and folk religions, and the prominence of the middle zone in the everyday life of most people in order to help "nonbelivers" understand the rationale behind folk religious beliefs and practices.

4

FOLK AND FORMAL RELIGIONS

Having developed a model for analyzing belief systems, it is time to examine the differences between folk and formal religions, and the reasons why they so often coexist in uneasy tension.

THE NATURE OF FORMAL RELIGION

When speaking of "religions" most people think of Christianity, Islam, Buddhism, Hinduism, and other "high" or "universal" religions. These formal religions claim to offer universal cosmic truth about the ultimate nature of reality. For the most part, they are highly institutionalized. They have written texts, defined theologies, temples, prescribed rites, rules, and regulations, and other institutional trappings. They are led by trained religious specialists who constitute an intellectual and spiritual elite set apart from the commoners. These leaders are particularly concerned with philosophical reflections on questions regarding eternal realities.

The centers of orthodoxy for these formal religions are often found in large institutions, old leaders, normative religious texts, written commentaries, schools where young leaders are trained in the accepted beliefs, and large centers of worship and pilgrimage where people come for deep, authentic religious experiences. Robert Redfield refers to these centers of orthodoxy as the 'great tradition' of a religion.

Below these centers of great tradition are the "little traditions," the many local expressions of the religion. These include local temples, churches, mosques, and shrines scattered around the countryside; the prophets, *purohits*, pastors, *mullas*, priests, evangelists, and lay leaders associated with them; the sermons, rituals, classes, and teachings in local congregations; and the religious beliefs and rituals found in the homes of ordinary people.

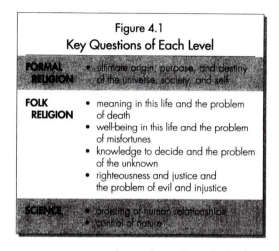

Figure 4.1
Key Questions of Each Level

FORMAL RELIGION	• ultimate origin, purpose, and destiny of the universe, society, and self
FOLK RELIGION	• meaning in this life and the problem of death • well-being in this life and the problem of misfortunes • knowledge to decide and the problem of the unknown • righteousness and justice and the problem of evil and injustice
SCIENCE	• ordering of human relationships • control of nature

There is an ongoing exchange between religious centers and religious beliefs and practices among the common folk. Leaders at the religious centers define religious beliefs for the people, often in high philosophical terms. They are often suspicious of the unorthodox beliefs and practices of leaders and laity in local communities. Local leaders, on the other hand, must deal with the everyday problems of their followers, and have little time or inclination for abstract reflection.

As noted in Chapter 2, belief systems are defined by the questions they ask, the realities they examine, and the methods they use, not by the answers they give. Answers change, but the questions remain much the same over time. One of the main differences between formal and folk religions is the questions they ask (Figure 4.1). Formal religions are concerned with ultimate reality, and issues of truth and logical consistency. For the most part, they seek to answer questions raised on the top level regarding cosmic, other-worldly realities. These central questions have to do with the deepest human concerns, namely, the need to find ontological meaning in life. Formal religions give meaning to life by answering the ultimate questions human face, which have to with the origins, purpose, and destiny of the universe, of a people, and of individual persons.

In their broadest scope, the questions of origin, purpose, and destiny have to do with cosmic realities (including heavens and hells)—what is ultimate truth, how did this world begin, why does it exist, and what is its end? For example, Genesis 1 starts with eternity and God, and the creation of everything else. In Revelation the story of this cosmos ends, and everything reenters eternity.

In this cosmic frame are questions about the origin, purpose, and end of humanity. Where did humans come from, why do they exist, how are they different from animals, and what is their destiny? Answers to these questions provide people meaning through a sense of their identity and history as humans. For example, Genesis 1:26–2:24 describes the creation of humans, and points to their unique identity as creatures created in the image of God.

In much of the world, the chief concern has to do with a particular people. Their central questions are, "How did we as a people originate, what is our unique place in the world, and what is our destiny?" Genesis 12 introduces the story of Israel, and describes its origin and divinely ordained purposes. The story of the people of Israel continues through the Old Testament and culminates with Acts 2, and the birth of the church, the new Israel. Many Christians are still deeply concerned with God's future plans for the Jews and their final destiny as a people. Most peoples have stories that explain their unique place on earth.

Finally, the most immediate questions of ultimate meaning have to do with people as individuals. Their questions are, "Where did I come from, why do I exist, why do certain things happen to me, and what will be my end?" Comparative religious studies show the different answers universal religions give to these root questions.

THE NATURE OF FOLK RELIGION

As the term suggests, 'folk religion' refers to the religious beliefs and practices of the common people. These are astonishingly diverse in their expressions, so generalizations about them must be taken with caution. There are, however, some underlying characteristics that we can explore.

TYPES OF FOLK RELIGION

Folk religions commonly take two forms, depending on the nature of the society in which they are found. Most small kin-based societies are particularistic in nature, and each has its own religion shared by all the members of the community. In large-scale societies, specialization, pluralism, and universalism emerge, and these forces are at work in the area of religion as well.

SMALL KIN-BASED SOCIETIES

In most small kin-based or tribal societies, until recently, there were no high philosophical religions. They are characterized by an egalitarianism and holism that pervade all aspects of life. The shaman gathers or raises his or her food like everyone else, and serves as a healer and spirit mediator on the side. Religions in these societies are particularistic in nature, and differ greatly from one another. Each has its own gods, ancestors, lands, and people. Underlying them, however, are widespread themes and practices that can be compared.

First, for the most part these traditional religions[1] focus their atten-

---

1. Harold Turner refers to these as 'primal' religions because he sees them as early forms of religion. Others refer to them as 'tribal' religions. We will use "traditional religions" to emphasize the traditional nature of these structures and their on going impact in societies around the world.

tion largely on middle-level questions—existential questions the people face in their everyday lives. There are philosophers in these societies who can articulate complex, sophisticated views of the nature of reality and meaning of life,[2] but the common folk are concerned with how to make sure they have good crops, how to explain the sudden death of a healthy young adult, and whether they should raid their enemies and when. Their central concern is success, and for this they need the power of mana, the gods, the spirits, the ancestors, or good fortune, which they can control through rituals, amulets, and offerings. They also need to ward off disaster and evil by utilizing charms, medicines, magic, omens, and by placating the spirits. In these small-scale societies, 'folk religion' is the traditional beliefs and rites of a particular society.

LARGE-SCALE SOCIETIES

A second form of folk religion appears in large, complex peasant and urban societies in which formal religions are found. For example, most Chinese peasants are Buddhists and Confucianists, most Indian peasants are Hindus or Muslims, and many Americans are Christians. Beneath the expressions of formal religion are the many animistic[3] beliefs and practices that continue on in the everyday lives of common people. The result is the mixing of animism and the little traditions of formal religions in various ways—sometimes in conflict with one another and sometimes in uneasy coexistence (Figure 4.2).

From their little traditions, common people learn some of the general doctrines of their formal religious traditions. They gather in local meetings, take part on special occasions in the rituals and practices in the temple, mosque, shrine, or church, and call preachers and priests to take part in family rituals at home. For most of them, however, the local forms of formal religion are only a part of their lives. Ordinarily they are preoccupied with making a living and dealing with the crises of their everyday existence. Because leaders in the formal religions are often concerned with bigger issues, the people turn to local beliefs and practices, such as spirit possession, ancestors, magic, and evil eye, to

---

2. The philosophical systems of traditional societies have been largely ignored in formal studies of religions. Too often scholars have assumed that these societies lack any philosophical sophistication, and can, therefore, be ignored.

3. In the theory of the evolution of religion, the term 'animism' carried notions of pre-logical primitive thought. We reject those connotations and, for lack of a better word, use it to refer to the beliefs and practices associated with the 'middle zone,' with this-worldly supernatural realities such as earthly spirits, magic, evil eye, divination, and the like. In other words, animistic practices make sense if we understand them, even though we may not believe them to be true.

explain and deal with their day-to-day questions. In complex societies, therefore, folk religion often consists of a mixture of formal and animistic beliefs—of high and low religion, or dual religion (Schreiter 1987).

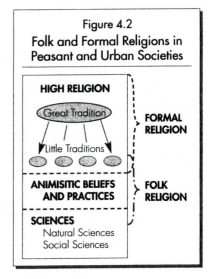

Figure 4.2

Folk and Formal Religions in Peasant and Urban Societies

There is often a tension between formal religious leaders and animistic practitioners. The former strive for religious orthodoxy, and often see animistic practices as a threat to true faith. Consequently, they condemn these practices as heterodox and superstitious. Today, Islamic and Hindu fundamentalists are trying to root out local religious practices in their communities around the world. On the other hand, animistic practices often flourish on the edges of high religious institutions. Worship at Hindu temples focuses on Siva, Vishnu, or other high gods, but under nearby trees one finds local practitioners promising fertility to barren women, cures to people with specific diseases and protection from the evil eye through powerful amulets, and curses to defeat an enemy. Similarly, the shrines of the Virgins of Guadalupe and Majugorje are surrounded by numerous folk beliefs and practices.

Despite the spread of formal or high religions and modernity, folk religious beliefs dominate around the world. In Taiwan 65 percent of all adults are believers in Chinese folk religion (Chiu 1988, 5, cited in Warton 1996, 38). In India most Hindus are folk Hindus; in Arabia, Pakistan, Malaysia, and Indonesia most Muslims are folk Muslims; in China most religious believers are folk Buddhists; and in America many Christians are folk Christians.

QUESTIONS FOLK RELIGIONS ADDRESS

Animistic beliefs address a different set of questions from formal religions. They are more concerned with the existential problems of everyday life and less with ultimate realities. Consequently, they are interested more in issues of power and success than truth and logical consistency. In this book we will examine four human problems that underlie most folk religious beliefs and practices.

THE MEANING OF LIFE AND PROBLEM OF DEATH

The first question has to do with the human desire for a meaningful life and the problems death raises for the living. People seek meaning, not only in a future heaven, but in their lives as lived out here on earth. They are even willing to die if their death gives meaning to their existence. But death challenges the human search for meaning, and if humans cannot account for it satisfactorily, their explanation systems fail. How do people explain the sudden, tragic death of infants or of young adults in their prime?

On the folk religion level, the problem of death often has less to do with what happens to the person who has died than with the pain and meaninglessness that death brings for the living. How can the living deal with the devastation caused by the death of a loved one? A widow cries in anguish, wondering who will take care of her now that her husband has been killed. A young mother weeps because her child has died. A society wrestles with the sudden death of a leader in his prime. To say that these dead are in heaven does not assuage the grief and fear of the bereaved, or solve the crisis of meaning that death brings to a community.

On this level the question is not about "how" death occurred. All people have immediate explanations for it—illness, a blow to the head, a drowning. The real questions are "Why and why now?" and "How will this affect me and my family?" A ladder breaks and a young man falls to his death. His relatives agonize at their loss. Why did it have to be him? Why not the man who climbed up just ahead of him, or the man behind? The people know that old, rotting ladders break, but why did this one break now and why when this man was on it? Those who remain behind must bear the agony and loss of his death, and wonder why this had to happen to them. (The question of the meaning of life and of death is examined in Chapter 5.)

THE GOOD LIFE AND THREAT OF CALAMITY

The second question folk religions seek to answer has to do with the human desire for a good life, and the constant threat of misfortune. People want to live fulfilled and fruitful lives. Many want to have health, good food, and homes, and be surrounded by children and grandchildren. Others want success, wealth, status, or power. All face the threat of failure, barrenness, disease, drought, floods, fires, and a thousand other misfortunes that plague human life. In the West unforeseen misfortunes are called accidents or luck, and hence are unexplainable. But most societies are not content to leave such an important set of questions unanswered, and the answers they give are often stated in terms of ancestors, demons, witches, and local gods, or in terms of magic and astrology. (The answers different folk religions give to questions of success and crisis are examined in Chapter 6.)

GUIDANCE AND THE PROBLEM OF THE UNKNOWN

The third question relates to the human desire to know the past, present, and future in order to decide on a course of action. Despite knowledge of facts, such as that planted seeds will eventually grow and bear fruit, or that travel down this river on a boat will bring one to the neighboring village, the future is not totally predictable. Accidents, misfortunes, the intervention of other persons, and other unknown events can frustrate human planning.

There are many things which, if known, could make people's lives better. The problem is that so much of life is unknown. How can one prevent accidents or guarantee success in the future? How can one make sure that a marriage will be fruitful and happy? How can one avoid traveling on a plane that will crash? In the West these questions are left largely unanswered. In much of the world people seek guidance and ways to discern the unknown, and so to assure themselves of success and avoidance of disasters. (Chapter 7 looks at ways humans have sought to learn the unknown to keep control of their lives.)

MORALITY AND PRESENCE OF EVIL

The final question examined in this book has to do with the human desire for righteousness and justice in life on earth, and the existence of oppression and injustice. Human beings want things to be right, decent, proper, clean, and fair. Without a sense of moral order, meaningful community life is impossible. On the other hand, how do they explain the very real presence of evil on earth? (This question is examined in Chapter 8.)

THE NATURE OF FOLK SCIENCES

Questions on the bottom level have to do with understanding the order of the material world to control it. All people have natural sciences that explain many events in everyday life. People in the Pacific Islands know which kind of tree to cut down and hollow out to make a canoe. They know how to navigate across vast expanses of open ocean to reach a distant island, watching the shape of the waves to direct them to it. All people also have social sciences that tell them how to rear children, choose leaders, organize group activities, and deal with thieves.

Modern sciences have systematically sought to answer questions on the bottom level, and Western Christianity those on the top level. Both have failed to adequately deal with the "middle zone." The result is a dichotomous worldview in which science explains this world, and religion other worlds. This book examines the nature of the middle zone and how people fill it, and recommends Christian responses to the questions it raises.

WORLDVIEW OF FOLK RELIGIONS

Religions, like all belief systems, are embedded in worldviews that provide their cognitive, aesthetic, and moral givens by depicting these as
the unalterable shape of reality and the real conditions of life, and by
invoking deeply felt moral and aesthetic sentiments as experiential evidence for their truth. Clifford Geertz notes,

> In religious belief and practice a group's ethos is rendered intellectually
> reasonable by being shown to represent a way of life ideally adapted to
> the actual state of affairs the world-view describes, while the world-view
> is rendered emotionally convincing by being presented as an image of an
> actual state of affairs peculiarly well-arranged to accommodate such a
> way of life (1979, 79).

While folk religions around the world vary greatly, there are some
worldview themes common to many or most of them.

CORPORATE ANTHROPOCENTRISM

In contrast to high religions, which focus their attention on the cosmic order, folk religions are human-centered. Humans—ancestors, the
living, and the unborn—are seen not only as actors in the universe, but
as the center of existence. The common life they share as a family, a lineage or clan, and a society must be preserved by supplicating, coercing,
or bribing the surrounding gods and powerful but capricious spirits
who share in the same vital force and who are important not in their
own right, but because of their involvement in the lives of human beings. Russell Staples writes,

> [T]he primal world-view is local rather than universal. . . . [T]hey are
> closed systems of thought focused upon local deities and spirits, which
> sustain relationships almost exclusively with a specific group of people.
> In a contradistinction both the God and the man of the first chapters of
> Genesis have universal significance. God is the creator, and Adam is the
> father, of all humankind. The universality of these chapters disturbs pri-
> mal patterns of thought to the core (1982, 71).

Mary Douglas writes,

> The cosmos is turned in, as it were, on man. Its transforming energy is
> threaded onto the lives of individuals so that nothing happens in the way
> of storms, sickness, blights or droughts except in virtue of these personal
> links. So the universe is man-centered in the sense that it must be inter-
> preted in reference to humans (1966, 85).

In most cases this anthropocentrism focuses on corporate human existence. The individual is important only as he or she is a member of a group—a lineage, clan, or community. Only members of that group are fully human. Others are subhuman, and it is not stealing to take from them or to kill them. Furthermore, the living are important only because they contribute to the stream of life that flows from the ancestors to the yet unborn.

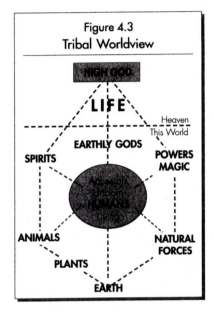

Figure 4.3
Tribal Worldview

THE SPIRIT WORLD

In many folk religions, humans live in a world surrounded by spirits, ancestors, witchcraft, curses, magic, and other supernatural beings and forces, many of which are hostile to human beings (Figure 4.3). Regarding the Semai of Malaysia, C. A. Robarchek writes,

Nearly every entity and activity, no matter how seemingly innocuous, carries the potential for injury, illness, and death. The most mundane activities—gardening, hunting, fishing, eating, even playing—are enveloped in taboos and circumscribed by ritual in a vain attempt to avoid precipitating the dangers that threaten from all sides. Even children playing with those most harmless creatures, dragonflies and butterflies, may provoke an attack by *Ngku*, a thunder "spirit" who strikes with wind, torrential rain, flood, and landslides (1989, 912).

In such worlds, everything is interconnected. Unlike modern thinking in which things (animals, humans, villages), specializations (doctors, lawyers, mechanics), and domains of life (economic, social, political, religious) are differentiated and seen as mutually independent, traditional religions view all things and events as interdependent. Laurenti Magesa notes,

Every creature has been endowed by God with its own force of life, its own power to sustain life. Because of the common divine origin of this power, however, all creatures are connected with each other in the sense that each one influences the other for good or bad. Nothing moves in this universe of forces without influencing other forces by its movement. The world of forces is held like a spider's web of which no single thread can be caused to vibrate without shaking the whole network (1997, 46).

Physical forces are thought to be interwoven with the lives of people, and the mind is believed to influence the external material world. There is no sharp boundary between the internal and external worlds.

In such a world nothing happens by accident. Denis Masson notes, "Two events cannot happen simultaneously and still be independent of each other. . . . There is no hazard or chance; probability does not exist. There has to be a cause for every event" (Hill and Arensen 1995, 123). Because most events of life are explained in relational terms, people spend much of their time trying to appease and coerce the gods, spirits, ancestors, and other people with offerings and bribes to gain their help and turn aside their anger. People handle what they can control in the natural world through their science, but turn to folk religion to deal with that which is beyond their control. Generally speaking, the greater the areas of uncertainty in people's lives, the greater the number of spirits and deities in the village, each dealing with one set of problems. Ordinary problems of life they take to small shrines, where they placate the local spirits with small offerings. Big problems they take to the powerful spirits who reside in big and distant shrines, and require costly rituals and possibly blood or human sacrifices. Major community problems call for involvement by the whole group, village, or region, and are held annually or in times of great crisis. Rites are performed to placate and control the gods, ancestors, and spirits, who can do great damage. Their favor can be gained by gifts and offerings, their anger tempered by blood sacrifices. Therefore, there is often little sympathy for people when things go wrong. They are considered stupid. They didn't do what they should have to prevent misfortune.

Given this view of the world, it is not surprising that new converts often see Christ as a more powerful spirit that they can control through proper rites. It is hard to exchange an old god who can be seen and controlled and who demonstrates power on demand for a transcendent God who cares for humans and seeks them out!

HOLISM

The interconnectedness of all things leads to a holistic view of life. Folk religions, particularly those in small-scale societies, are not religions in the Western sense of the word. They absorb the whole of life. They underlie every aspect of life: family, law, politics, land ownership, agriculture, technology, food, and entertainment. These elements are not autonomous, but complement each other. For example, in India the direction one places one's head at night is religiously important—the gods live in the North and East, and, as a proverb says, only water buffalo sleep with their feet sticking in the faces of the gods.

PARTICULARISM

Folk religions are particularist in nature. Their frame of reference is the local community, not cosmic order and universal truth. For example, time in most folk religions is episodic, discontinuous, and particularistic. There is no absolute "clock," no universal time scale. Nor is time a "thing" or commodity as it is in the modern world. Time has multiple forms and is coordinated in different ways, each having a different duration and quality. There is mythical time, historical time, ritual time, agricultural time, seasonal time, solar time, lunar time, and rest time. Moreover, in contrast to the concern of high religions for eternal time, folk religions focus on the now, not some distant past or future.

Land and space, too, are local. People are tied to their gods and to their land. They recognize that other people have their own gods, ancestors, and land, and in battle each group calls upon its gods and ancestors for help. The gods gave them their land, and that is where their ancestors now reside. The land gives them food, and to eat of its fruits is to gain one's identity with it and with others in the society. The land is also inhabited by earthly spirits who exercise their power in the mountains, streams, or forests where they live. In battles, victories and defeats are attributed to the power and territorial control of these spiritual rulers.[4] The victor does not try to convert the defeated, for it is impossible for others to adopt their gods without becoming a part of the blood of the community and of its land.

This focus on particularity is seen in everyday events. When the chief shows up at a modern hospital, the Western doctor expects him to stand in line like everyone else. The people expect him to go to the head of the line because he is more important than they. The missionary doctor charges everyone the same for medicines. Local people expect the rich to pay more for the same treatment. The particulars of each case must be taken into account to determine how each person should act.

EXISTENTIALISM[5]

As noted earlier, folk religions are concerned primarily with existential questions—questions having to do with here and now, and with the living not the dead. The central questions people ask have to do with

4. For instance, the Philistines and other tribes thought Israel's God was the God of the hills, because that is where the Israelites lived (Judg. 2:3; 1 Kings 20:23–28). In contrast to this animistic worldview, Yahweh declared himself not to be a territorial god, but the God of the universe, and writers of Scripture attribute Israel's defeats not to the superior power of other gods, but to God's judgment on his own people. This is a view totally foreign to an animistic worldview, where a people's god must always help them to win.

5. Existentialism here is used in its general sense and does not refer to a particular philosophical school.

success and failure, and with power and knowledge needed to control life. The primary concerns are diseases, promotions, money problems, jobs, husbands' debauchery, divorce, deviation of children, exams, selection of spouses for marriage, and deciding times to begin new ventures or take different moves.

To achieve their everyday goals, most people are pragmatic. They turn to several mutually contradictory systems simultaneously with the hopes that one will work. A person many go to the magician in the morning for a protective amulet, to the Western-style allopathic doctor in the afternoon for a penicillin shot, and to the witch doctor that night to drive away any witches that might be preying on him.

POWER AND PRAGMATISM

Folk religions are not interested in an academic understanding of metaphysics and truth, but in procuring a good, meaningful life and guarding against evils that disturb it. They are not based on contemplation and rational speculation, although critical reason and logic underlie them, but on practical results. People are not interested in logical consistency or what is ultimately and ontologically real. They are like people who wiggle the wires and shake the TV or computer when these do not work.

The test of folk religions is that they work, at least sufficiently well, to convince the adherents. Western secular analysts explain the successes of folk religions in terms of coincidence and psychological suggestion, but to the practitioner, supernatural beings and powers are very real because they work. When diagnoses and remedies fail, people do not question their explanation system, but the diagnosis or remedy. Did the magician say the words incorrectly? Did the shaman leave out an essential ingredient in the medicine? To guarantee success, people and practitioners alike take many precautions. They go through every word in the formula to make sure none is omitted. They use mysterious and archaic tongues, for these seem to work the best. From this perspective, their action is perfectly logical, for what matters is not 'truth' but an operational pragmatism.

Given this worldview, it makes sense for patients to use several, seemingly contradictory, remedies to solve their problems. When they are sick, they may go to the witch doctor, the magician, and the diviner, and also to the mission doctor who uses Western medicine. They do not care which medical system might heal them. They are only interested in getting well by any means possible.

In folk religions the focus is on power—the ability to make things happen. People see themselves engaged in constant struggles with spirits, other humans, and supernatural and natural forces that surround them. In such a world, everything can be explained in terms of competing powers and power encounters in which the stronger dominate the weaker. There are no such things as accidents. In the hunt, the struggle is between the forces of the hunter and the prey. In human life, all misfortunes and deaths must be explained in terms of curses, evil eyes, and jealousies. Mary Douglas illustrates this pragmatism.

> To ask an Azande whether the poison oracle is a person or a thing is to ask a kind of nonsensical question which he would never pause to ask himself. The fact that he addresses the poison oracle in words does not imply any confusion whatever in his mind between things and persons. It merely means that he is not striving for intellectual consistency and that in this field symbolic action seems appropriate (1966, 89).

In a sense, the poison oracle acts like the computer expert who uses words and symbols to program a computer. He knows that the computer does not 'understand' words, but it does respond to them in predictable ways.

It is not surprising that many people become Christians to acquire more power. They believe that their prayers will protect them from their enemies, and that saying a prayer before a meal will guard them from poison someone may have placed in the food. Jacob Loewen points out that some Wanana Christians from Panama believe that Christianity gives them new, more powerful words they can use to harm their enemies. In prayer meetings they sit in front of their rivals so that when they turn and kneel, the rivals are in front of them. They then say 're-demp-tion,' 'sal-va-tion,' and other powerful Christian words to make that person sick or weak.

ORALITY

Folk religions store and transmit their information orally; they are highly immediate, personal, and relational. Words are spoken in the context of specific relationships, and they die as soon as they have been said. Communication is a flux of immediate encounters between humans and other beings, and is full of emotions and personal interests. Beliefs and practices are passed down by shamans and other religious practitioners to their apprentices. There are few sacred texts like those found in the high religions, and few commentaries to make the meaning of those scriptures clear to ordinary people. There is little institutionalization of either leadership or of religious organizations.

Sounds point to the invisible and speak of mystery. In the jungle, the hunter hears the tiger before he sees it; the mother hears a noise at night and is warned of an enemy attack. It is not surprising, therefore, that sounds lead people to believe in spirits, ancestors, gods, and other beings they cannot see. Sight, conversely, carries little sense of mystery and leaves little room for what is not seen.

In folk religions sounds are widely thought to be powerful and sacred. To say them is to cause things to happen. W. J. Ong notes (1969, 637), "Sound signals the present use of power, since sound must be in active production in order to exist at all." The right sounds can cause rain to fall. Other sounds, such as drumming and shouting, protect people from evil spirits. Hence, sounds are often central to magic.

TRANSFORMATION AND TRANSPORTATION

In the animistic worldview there is no watertight distinction between humans and animals, or between animate and inanimate existence. Moreover, things may not be what they appear to be.

SAMO SHAMAN SOUL FLIGHT

Individuals especially designated by the ancestors assist their fellow human beings. They are *kogooa oosoo*, 'ancestor people,' either female or male, who have a special spirit imparted by the ancestors. This spirit serves to mediate between human beings and their ancestors. In this capacity, a shaman's spirit flies to the ancestral abode, where it communes with the ancestors in order to enable the shaman to understand what is happening in the human context and interpret it for kinsmen. This celestial communication takes a form of glossolalia that often sounds like bird calls and can be heard by anyone in attendance at the gathering. Returning to the medium's body, the repossessed spirit begins to sing the message it received from the ancestor. The audience responds, singing what they hear phrase by phrase. This sets up an antiphonal song between medium and audience, and reinforces the message in the minds of all who participate.

Mediums can use the wanderings of their spirit to benefit human beings in many ways. On one occasion, the brothers of a man who had died sought a medium's services to find a shotgun he had used. During an all-night ceremony, the medium was informed of the problem, and on the way back to his body the medium's spirit passed over the forest in the vicinity of the dead man's hunting activity and saw the lost gun under a sleeping platform in a particular bush house. This information was passed on to the brothers during the song, and they went to the house the next day and retrieved the gun. (Shaw 1996, 101–2)

A hunter goes to the forest, shoots a wild animal, and discovers he has killed a human being. A farmer takes his cutlass and hacks what he thinks is a branch that needs to be removed, only to discover he has cut his own arm.

In this world, transformation, or 'lycanthropy,' is common. People are believed to turn themselves into wolves, rabbits, or tigers. If someone shoots them with an arrow, they return the next day as humans with similar wounds on their bodies. Evil spirits take the form of humans, animals, and plants, animals turn out to be gods in disguise, and the mana of a warrior is transferred to those who eat his body.

One common form of transformation is spontaneous combustion. Objects, animals, and even people are thought to suddenly burst into flames and be consumed. This indicates that they are no ordinary things or beings. Return to life after death is another common belief associated with transformation.

Another characteristic of this world is transportation. Shamans are believed in their trances to travel long distances in an instant to harm an enemy village, or to enter the world of the spirits and fight with them to retrieve the souls that have been stolen or wandered away during sleep. Some people are believed capable of traveling great distances in their spirits while in trances or sleep, and to see things ordinary people cannot see.

FEAR AND SECURITY

A final worldview theme that runs through nearly all folk religious belief systems is near constant fear and the need for security. In a world full of spirits, witchcraft, sorcery, black magic, curses, bad omens, broken taboos, angry ancestors, human enemies, and false accusations of many kinds, life is rarely carefree and secure. Regarding the Semai, Robarchek writes, "The forest world surrounding these encapsulated communities is a world of unremitting hostility and anger, a world filled with malevolent beings and forces, nearly all of which are aggressively hostile to human beings" (1989, 912). S. D. Porteus notes,

> Devils haunt to seize the unwary; their malevolent magic shadows [a person's] waking moments. He believes that medicine men know how to make themselves invisible so that they may cut out his kidney fat, and then sew him up and rub his tongue with a magic stone to induce forgetfulness, and thereafter he is a living corpse devoted to death (Neill 1961, 137).

Crops fail, game vanishes, plagues decimate the village, sudden death takes the young and strong, enemies attack at night, and rivals seek one's life. Life in most traditional societies is precarious and fear is common.

Life for common folk, however, is not all fear. People find security in their kinship groups and joy in their community gatherings. They turn to ancestors and gods for help and to magic and divination to protect them from surrounding dangers.

FOLK RELIGIONS AND CHRISTIAN MISSION

How have Western Christian missionaries responded to folk religious beliefs and practices? They led people to faith and salvation in Christ. They prayed for the sick and dispensed modern medicine. They warned people of the power of Satan and the judgment of hell. Nevertheless, in many parts of the world, people who become Christians continue to turn to shamans, diviners, medicine men, witch doctors, and magicians to deal with their everyday problems of life. Why has this split-level Christianity emerged? The analytical model used here helps us not only to understand animistic worldviews and the worldview that Western missionaries often bring with them, but also the very nature of the missionary task.

CATHOLIC MISSIONS

The Catholic mission movement began when Columbus discovered the New World. Augustinian, Jesuit, and Dominican friars accompanied the Spanish explorers, and sought to convert the people they encountered to the Christian faith. For example, Ferdinand Magellan arrived in the Philippines in 1521 and claimed the islands for Spain. A week later he baptized the king, queen, and entire population of Cebu.

Catholic missionaries took evil spirits seriously, and tried to stamp out all practices associated with them. In many cases, the people clothed their old religious beliefs and practices in Christian dress. For example, in Brazil, the African *orisha* brought over by slaves were given the names of Christian saints, and the people kept their old beliefs and practices but hid these from the Catholic priests. In other parts of the world, the same mixture of pagan and Christian beliefs and rites occurred. The result was a 'split-level Christianity' which allowed the same person to hold two religious systems at the same time (Bulatao 1992, 22). Many common folk were Catholics by sincere confession and church attendance, but animists in everyday practice. Both systems were considered right and were understood as situationally relevant—Catholicism for church and life cycle rites, and folk practices outside church settings. The peoples' strong indigenous beliefs ran parallel to their public accommodation to the new religion brought by their conquerors. Common folk were often aware of the inconsistency of this accommodation, but felt little guilt until the church leaders appeared. When the split was made public, they felt a loss of face or shame (Hobson 1996). However, pragmatism prevailed and the high religion/low religion dualism continues today.

PROTESTANT MISSIONS

The modern Protestant movement began in the eighteenth century when modernity and the Enlightenment had captured the minds of people in the West. Underlying these movements was a major worldview shift. The medieval European world-view, shaped in large part by Christianity based on a Hebrew view of reality, made a distinction between God and the world, between Creator and creation. Angels, demons, and spirits were very

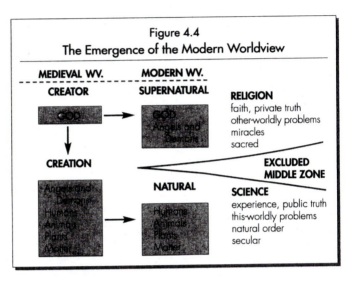

Figure 4.4
The Emergence of the Modern Worldview

MEDIEVAL WV.   MODERN WV.

CREATOR   SUPERNATURAL   **RELIGION**
faith, private truth
other-worldly problems
miracles
sacred

CREATION   **EXCLUDED MIDDLE ZONE**

NATURAL   **SCIENCE**
experience, public truth
this-worldly problems
natural order
secular

much a part of this worldview (Figure 4.4). After the tenth century, the Greek worldview was reintroduced through the Crusades and the universities in Spain. It made a sharp distinction between spirit and matter, mind and body. In this worldview, spirits, such as angels and demons, exist in the realm of the supernatural, and humans and other material beings in the natural world, which is governed by natural laws.

ENLIGHTENMENT THINKING

Belief in the middle level—in this-worldly spirits, magic, witchcraft, and evil eye—began to die out in the nineteenth century with the spread of Enlightenment thinking based on Platonic dualism and science based on materialistic naturalism. The result was the secularization of science and the mystification of religion. Science dealt with the empirical world using mechanistic analogies, leaving religion to handle the other-worldly matters, often in terms of organic analogies. Science was based on the certitudes of sense experience, experimentation, and proof. Religion was based on faith rooted in personal opinions, visions, and inner feelings. Science sought order in natural laws. Religion was brought in to deal with miracles and exceptions to the natural order— but these decreased as scientific knowledge expanded. The middle zone of fairies, trolls, gnomes, other earthly spirits, magic, evil eye, and other supernatural forces were rejected as 'fairy tales'—as fiction and illusion. In time, even God and the supernatural realm were discarded as unnecessary hypotheses by secular Western scholars. The result was Western materialistic monism, and a deep faith that science, based on facts and reason, would enable enlightened humans to construct a utopian world.[6]

Protestant missionaries, like other Westerners, were deeply influenced by this Enlightenment worldview. They retained their faith in God and the domain of the supernatural, but they also placed great value on science and reason. They built churches to focus on religious matters, and schools and hospitals in which they explained nature and disease in naturalistic terms. When people spoke of the fear of evil spirits, the missionaries often denied the existence of these spirits rather than claim the power of Christ over them. The result was that in many parts of the world Western Christian missions became a major secularizing force.

SPLIT-LEVEL CHRISTIANITY

Converts to Protestantism are caught between their traditional beliefs in the spirit world, and the naturalism of Enlightenment thought. Some reject their old beliefs in favor of modern science, but as one scholar at the University of the Philippines put it, "I do not believe in ghosts, but I am afraid of them" (Bulatao 1992, 52). Other converts maintain a split-level Christianity. They profess faith in Christ for their salvation, but live out their everyday lives using traditional practices because they do not find effective answers in the church to meet their problems of illness, misfortune, and fear of spirits (Figure 4.5). Many reject Western medicine because it treats diseases as purely biological problems and does not address the social and spiritual dimensions of illness. For them, healing has to include all dimensions of the patient's life.[7]

Still other converts are "scared Christians" who believe deeply that all the spirit beings and practices of their old religion are evil and demonic, and have to be rejected, but who have no Christian ways to guard themselves against attacks (Hobson 1996). Knowing that the missionaries do not believe in earth-bound spirits, and being given no biblical answers to their everyday questions, the people continue their old ways, but hide them from the missionaries and their leaders. In church they deal with formal Christian doctrines, looking at Christianity as a high religion. In private they continue to practice many of their

---

6. The Enlightenment took a mechanistic view of reality, and ran into problems when it sought to apply this to the study of human beings. Many scientists reduced humans to biochemical machines shaped by psychosocial forces. But this denied human choice and reduced ideas, including science itself, to electron flows in the brain.

7. Anthony Allen, physician, psychiatrist, and theologian, argues that the gospel call to healing ministries has been left by the West to medical professionals because of its uninformed acceptance of the Cartesian split between mind and body, between spirit and matter (Williams 1996, 15).

traditional ways, appropriating beliefs and practices associated with animism.

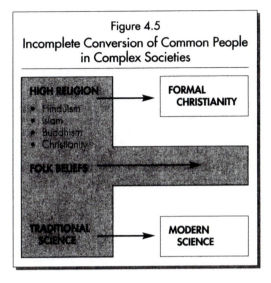

Figure 4.5
Incomplete Conversion of Common People in Complex Societies

Today young churches around the world struggle with the resurgence of old folk religious beliefs that threaten to destroy the churches, and to render Christian faith marginal to the everyday lives of the people. For their part, many missionaries assumed that as people became Christians, their new faith would displace their old animistic beliefs. In recent years, the charismatic movement has focused attention on questions of the middle level. The answers they offer, however, are often not tied closely to an encompassing theology that deals with higher-, middle-, and lower-level questions.

In part, this book is an attempt to help missionaries steeped in modernity understand and deal with the problems of folk religion. On theological grounds they may deny the existence of earthly spirits and magical forces, in contrast to angels and demons which are described in Scripture, but many of the people they serve believe in these deeply. If missionaries try to stamp out these beliefs and practices, they will go underground. If they accept these uncritically, they run the danger of turning the gospel into Christo-paganism—a form of Christian animism that denies the truth of the gospel as expressed in Scripture. Missionaries must understand the beliefs and practices of people who hold to traditional belief systems and the questions to which these are answers. Only then can they provide better Christian answers and deal with the old ways.

It is important to note that a Christian response to folk religions is not to stamp them out. Christianity at the beginning was a folk movement, a gathering of ordinary sinners who turned to Christ. The heart of the gospel is not abstract philosophical systems, complex institutions, or large programs. It is people, common people. As soon as the church becomes a haven for the powerful, educated, high-ranking elite, it ceases to be the church. Eugene Peterson writes,

Much of the anger towards the church and most disappointments in the church are because of failed expectations. We expect a disciplined army of committed men and women who courageously lay siege to the world's powers; instead we find some people who are more concerned with getting rid of the crabgrass in their lawns. . . . We expect to meet minds that are informed and shaped by the great truths and rhythms of scripture, and find persons whose intellectual energy is barely sufficient to get them from the comics to the sport page. At such times it is more important to examine and change our expectations than to change the church, for the church is not what we organize but what God gives (1996, 72).

It is important that missionaries and church leaders not make people into professional Christians, but transform churches into living communities where the gospel is heard and applied to all of life. The Christian answer to folk religions is to bring them under the lordship of Christ so that he can transform people in their everyday lives. Christianity does deal with heaven and eternity, but it also answers the questions traditional folk religions raise. Its answers, however, must be rooted in a biblical, not an animistic, worldview.

We turn, in the next four chapters, to look at four key questions central to folk religious belief systems and at some of the many answers given to these questions.

FOLK RELIGIOUS BELIEFS

All religions are rooted in deep beliefs about the nature of reality. This is also true of folk religions. When Western scholars and missionaries first encountered traditional religions around the world, they branded these as illogical superstitions because they did not pass the tests of formal Western logic. They assumed that people would leave their old beliefs when they saw the superiority of reason. Secular scholars went further. They saw Christianity, Islam, Hinduism, Buddhism, and other formal religions as proto-logical because they did not meet the empirical tests of science.

The chapters in this section examine the logical foundations of folk religions, and seek to show that they help people make sense of the existential crises of their everyday lives. These religions do so by answering the key existential questions all humans must face. Four of these are studied. The first is finding meaning in this life and explaining the devastation death leaves behind for those who remain alive. The second is defining the good life and accounting for the crises that are very much a part of human experience, including sickness, barrenness, drought, floods, earthquakes, and failures. The third is planning and controlling one's life and overcoming the problem of the unknown. The fourth is longing for justice and morality, and accounting for the presence of evil and oppression as a daily experience. After seeking to understand the answers given by traditional religions, we suggest guidelines for biblically informed Christian responses to these questions.

SECTION OUTLINE

Section Two examines folk religious beliefs, particularly as these relate to four central questions people seek to answer, and offers Christian responses to these questions. The approach is phenomenological—to try to understand the world as the people see it without passing judgment on their beliefs.

Chapter 5: How do people find meaning in life on earth, and how do they explain death?

Chapter 6: How do people try to get a good life, and how do they deal with misfortune?

Chapter 7: How do people seek to discern the unknown in order to plan their lives?

Chapter 8: How do people maintain a moral order, and how do they deal with disorder and sin?

5

THE MEANING OF
LIFE AND DEATH

Is there meaning in human lives, or are people animals who die meaningless deaths? If there is no meaning, there is no need for them to give
themselves to others or to live moral lives. Clifford Geertz points out
that the search for meaning is a fundamental human craving, and that
meaninglessness is worse than death (Geertz 1979). Many people have
gone willingly to their deaths for the sake of their beliefs.

In formal religions, meaning is given by answering questions of ultimate reality—what are the cosmic origins, nature, purpose, and end of
the universe, humankind, and the individual? Folk religions give people
a sense of meaning by answering the existential questions of everyday
life, and by providing the living a sense of place and worth in their society and world.

THE MEANING OF LIFE

All humans seek to make sense out of their lives. Two types of explanation are widely given: synchronic ones that help explain who humans
are—the nature and structure of their being; and diachronic ones that
tell where people came from and where they are going—the stories of
their lives. Taken together these provide a bifocal view that helps people
make sense of their lives as they live in a wide array of cultural contexts
and belief systems around the world. Both synchronic and diachronic
approaches need to be examined to see how folk religions give meaning
to humans in their everyday lives.

SYNCHRONIC MEANINGS

Synchronic explanations give people a sense of meaning by showing
them that their lives are structured and orderly. Disorder and chaos are
commonly associated with meaninglessness, for if there is no order,

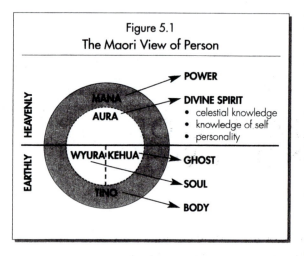

Figure 5.1
The Maori View of Person

things have no explanation. Synchronic meaning is given to life in five ways: (1) showing people who they are, (2) charting the progression of their lives, (3) assigning them a community to which they belong, (4) providing them a home in the world, and (5) giving worth to what they do and have.

MEANING IN BEING

Who am I? Most folk religions answer this question, in part, by giving people a sense of their theological identity—a definition of what it means ultimately to be human. This identity assigns them great worth, and sets them apart from animals and other earthly creatures. For example, each Alaskan tribe identifies itself as "the Human Beings." *Tlingit* means "the people." *Yup'ik* and *Sugpiaq* mean even more: "the real People." Regarding their beliefs, Michael Oleksa writes,

> When the world was made, or more importantly, when the first human beings appeared, they were given their own way to live appropriately, in harmony with the forces, spirits, and creatures with whom they share the cosmos. The beginning of each child's education is marked by this sense of self and collective identity. We are the human beings. We are the *real* people. *Our* ways are the ways human beings were from all eternity meant to follow. Any deviation—due to forgetfulness or carelessness—threatens to bring imbalance, and therefore catastrophe to the universe. To forget is to perish (1987, 8).

Folk theologies define humans, in part, by describing their component parts. Like many people around the world, the Maoris of New Zealand believe that people are made up of two components—a spirit that goes to the heavens at death, and a body that belongs to the material world. The Maoris divide these two parts into segments (Figure 5.1). The *aura* or divine spirit is self-aware and capable of celestial knowledge. It shapes a person's personality, and survives in the other world after death. The *aura* is surrounded by *mana*, a shield of supernatural power that the person can create by rituals or acquire from people who have much of it. On earth a person also has a *wyura* or soul, and a *tino* or body. In death the *wyura* leaves the body and becomes a ghost or *kehua*, roaming the earth seeking food and shelter.

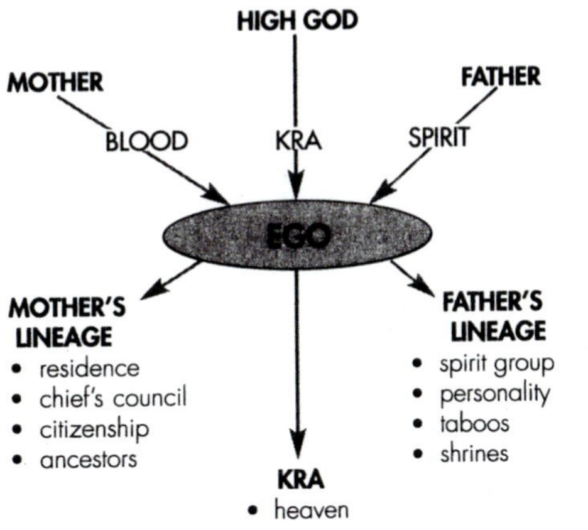

The Ashanti of Ghana believe that humans have three souls (Rattray 1923, 140ff.; Figure 5.2). From their mother they get their *mogya*, or blood and natural life. In earthly matters, therefore, they belong to their mothers' matrilineage, which gives them their land, residence, citizenship, and earth-bound ancestors. They live with their matrilineal kin, and are ruled by its chief and his council. From their fathers they get their *ntoro*, or spiritual substance that gives them character, genius, temper, and personality. They belong to his spirit group, worship at his patrilineage shrines, and observe his spiritual taboos. From the high God each person receives an *okra*, or divine spirit, that is their conscience. Such theological understandings of humans give the Maori and Ashanti a sense of their special worth by showing them that they are more than animals.[1]

Figure 5.2
The Ashanti View of Person

Scripture clearly establishes the identity of humans in their being—in the fact that they are created in the image of God. That image was tarnished by the fall in the Garden of Eden, and the whole of Scripture can be viewed as God's re-creation of his image in human beings.

MEANING IN BECOMING

Meaning for individuals, in part, has to do with the progression of their lives. They start as infants—as nobodies, without titles or achievements. They become full humans—fathers and mothers, warriors, businesswomen, priests, presidents, and many other persons of importance. They end life as respected elders and honored saints.

Most societies divide the progression of life into stages, and mark transitions by rituals. These "life cycle rites" transform persons from

---

1. Ironically, the modern theory of evolution reduces humans to animals and values the survival of the fittest. Violence is justified for the sake of survival. There is no moral basis in the theory for the preservation of human life, care for the poor and weak, and altruistic love for others. Ethnic cleansing and wars are evidence that the successful win by power.

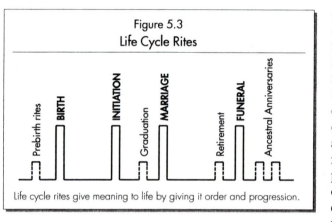

Figure 5.3
Life Cycle Rites

Prebirth rites · BIRTH · INITIATION · Graduation · MARRIAGE · Retirement · FUNERAL · Ancestral Anniversaries

Life cycle rites give meaning to life by giving it order and progression.

one level of identity to another, and, in so doing, give them a growing sense of worth and importance (Figure 5.3). The unborn become children, children become young adults, young adults marry and become parents, parents become elders, and elders become ancestors. The main rites celebrated in many societies around the world include birth, initiation, marriage, and funerals, but there are many others specific to different societies. For example, in the West baptisms, graduation ceremonies, and retirement parties mark transitions from one stage in life to another.

BIRTH RITES

Why are humans here? To be human requires an answer to this question. In the West, animals are simply born and plants grow from seeds. No explanations for their presence as individuals need be given because animals and plants do not have purposeful lives. To explain human births, on the other hand, is to turn newborn creatures into humans, and so to give meaning to them.

One question associated with birth the world over is "where do we come from?" The answers often given rise to 'origin myths.' The Samo of Papua New Guinea believe that an ancestral spirit enters a baby's body at birth, thereby giving it life. The term *kogooaiya*, 'to get an ancestral spirit,' is used for births. The Aborigines of Australia believe that the spirits of the unborn live in holes in the earth. When a young woman carelessly walks over one of these, one of the spirits jumps into her body to be born. Moreover, the unborn spirits reside in particular geographic territories. By way of analogy, Americans might think of the spirits living in Minnesota as Minnesota spirits and those in Wisconsin as Wisconsin spirits. If a Minnesota woman is traveling in Wisconsin when she becomes pregnant, it is obvious that her child is a Wisconsinite. Consequently, the same family may have different territorial 'spirits' in it, somewhat in the way modern children obtain citizenship from the nation in which they are born, and one family may have children with different passports.

The Baoule of Côte d'Ivoire believe that there are three possible origins to babies. They may be strangers who come from the spirit world without any prior involvement in the family; they may be reincarnations of an ancestor (children are examined to see if they resemble any ancestor); and they may be gifts from God or from the genii of the forest due to the request of parents or the kindness of the spirits. Parents must determine at birth which type of child they have in order to treat it properly when it becomes sick.

A second question is when a person becomes human. Normally this occurs when the baby is given a name. A nameless child is not fully human—it is not a he or she but an "it." To give it a name is to turn the baby into a member of the society. Many people wait to give a name until they are sure the life will remain. Among the Samo a child is not considered fully human until she or he has teeth and can walk and talk. This takes about three years, allowing family members time to determine which ancestor has returned to energize this life. Once determined, the child is given that ancestor's name and joins the household as a functioning member (Shaw 1990, 81).

In most societies, names are not arbitrary labels. Frequently they are selected to reflect or create the personality of the child. Native Americans give names to their children that both reflect their budding personalities and are hoped to shape them—Eagle, Lovely, Warrior. Among the Eskimo, to call a person's name is to call his or her spirit. Consequently, the living do not mention the dead by name for that will call back their spirit. The Akamba of Kenya name their children after the seasons, time of day, and other circumstances surrounding the birth. One father named his three sons after the morning, afternoon, and evening. Another named his son Mutisya—postponed—because his birth was delayed, and caused the father to be late for work.

A third question at birth has to do with paternity, for this often determines the child's place in the community. There is seldom any question who the mother is, but the identity of the father is not always clear. This must be established socially for the child to have an identity in the community. In polyandrous societies the father must be chosen from among the husbands, and a ritual of paternity conducted. Among the Todas of South India, the first husband can claim the child by putting a small bow and arrow in a nearby tree. If he does not, the second husband can claim the child. This continues on down the line until a father is assigned. Among the Mukamba of East Africa, the mother is asked by the midwife, "Can I give this child to you to suckle?" If the mother answers yes, she declares that the child is the legitimate offspring of her husband. If she says no, the child is assumed to be illegitimate by either adultery or incest. Legitimate children are incorporated into the society with celebration, but the lot of illegitimate children is one of rejection and derision.

Another custom of paternal legitimation is called "couvad," and is found among such widely scattered peoples as the Aino of northern Japan, the Caribs of South America, and in parts of China, India, and Spain. In this custom, the father goes to bed after the delivery of his child, and the mother returns to work. This not only helps the man to recover from the ordeal, but also enables him to lay claim to the child. In some cultures the rite is also performed to protect the vulnerable mother from evil spirits, who are tricked into attacking the husband in the delivery hut.

INITIATION RITES

All societies must determine when children become adults. Most have initiation rites to mark this transition. These rites are often associated with puberty and sexual maturity, but not necessarily so. What is important is that the young are now incorporated as full members in the society. The rites vary greatly according to gender. For example, the Samo rarely initiate males before they are in their late teens or early twenties, whereas females are often considerably younger.

One major function of initiation rites is to transform children into adults. Boys become men, girls become women, outsiders become members of the community, and strangers are brought into fellowship with the gods. Without initiation, they remained 'boys' and 'girls' all their lives.[2] For example, among the Marakwet of East Africa, women who are not initiated by circumcision are estranged outsiders. Only initiates have a right to contribute to and participate in community life, to own property, and to vote or be voted for. It is the old women who have suffered in past initiations who are often the firmest holders of traditional customs. Their attitude is often, "it will do her good, didn't I go through it, why shouldn't she, it will make a woman out of her."

A second major function of initiation rituals is to educate initiates in the responsibilities of adult life. Young women are taught how to be good wives and mothers, men to be good husbands and fathers. There is instruction on how to relate to people of the opposite sex, and above all the need to be faithful to spouses. Throughout life, old men and women oversee the behavior of younger married couples to see that they do not violate their society's norms.

---

2. J. M. Whiting and his associates (1958) studied fifty-six societies and found that there is a clear correlation between harsh male puberty rites and patrilineal social organization. It appears that a boy who has an initial prolonged dependence on his mother needs to be removed from her influence. The severe initiation rites act to "cut the apron strings" and remove the boy from his mother and the women's world where he grew up.

A third function is to incorporate the initiates into the community of adults. They are transformed from passive to active members of the society, and entrusted with preserving social traditions. To belong to one's ethnic group and to be identified with it carries certain obligations, and the newly initiated are expected to carry these out.

Changes in social status are often associated with the giving of new names. For example, in the Old Testament Abram ("Exalted Father") became Abraham ("Father of a Multitude," Gen. 17:5) when God made a covenant with him, Sarai became Sarah ("Princess") to show her importance in the covenant, and Jacob ("May He be at the Heals") became Israel ("One Who Strives with God and Prevails," Gen. 32:28). Similarly, Hindu and Muslim converts to Christianity often take biblical names after their baptisms. Likewise, when children are initiated, their transformation into adulthood is often marked by the acquisition of a new name.

MARRIAGE RITES

All societies must regulate sexual relationships and establish primary social groups. The most fundamental way to accomplish this is through the rite of marriage and the establishment of families. Marriages may be simple affairs in which a man and a woman publicly declare their wedding in a court or church. In many societies they are seen as family alliances, arranged by family heads to cement social relationships between different kinship groups. The success or failure of a marriage is of concern not only to the couple involved, but to others as well—hence in many cultures the wedding rituals are elaborate and involve large segments of the society.

In South India, in a traditional wedding, the two kinship groups are introduced to each other in the *edrkolu* ceremony on the first night, and the bride's parents wash the feet of the groom, showing him their respect. During the following days the couple is married, taken to visit the gods, paraded around the village for all to see, and finally taken to their new home.

Marriages, like other rituals, serve many functions. They provide entertainment and excitement, which breaks the monotony of everyday life; they provide group support and recognition for the participants at the time of their achievement; they are public announcements informing everyone about the changes in the status of the bride and groom so that the people can make appropriate adjustments in their behavior toward the couple; and they help the married couple to learn and psychologically adjust to their new roles.

In most societies, marriage is more than a social matter. It involves the ancestors, spirits, and clan gods. In high religions, marriage is often

seen as a sacrament. In other words, marriages made on earth are recorded in heaven, and to divorce is to break not only a social bond, but
to shatter the cosmic order as well. Destroying a marriage brings down
the wrath of the gods and causes disaster in the lives of those involved.

FUNERALS

All societies must deal with the trauma created by death and neutral-
ize the dangers associated with it. Death is not simply a personal matter. It must be socially recognized and handled, and this is done
through funeral rites.

Death rites serve several important functions. First, they give meaning to life by recognizing the challenge of death and ritualizing people's
response to it. The chaos created by death is replaced by a new order.
No society discards the bodies of the dead on waste heaps. To do so is
to reduce humans to mere animals. Only the bodies of enemies and
paupers are disposed of without ritual. The remains of infants and children are given small funerals; those who are 'fully human,' such as
kings and queens, presidents, heroes and great persons, are handled
with considerable ritual and pomp, showing what a human being ideally should be.

Second, funerals ritualize the separation of the living from the departed. They set apart a time for mourning, demonstrations of sorrow,
and processing grief. Friends and extended family members gather to
pay respect to the deceased, and hold a wake, because it is unthinkable
to leave the corpse alone. One reason for this is the belief that witches
might eat the soul of the departed.

A third function is to reorder the social relationships of the living
that the death has disrupted, and to reallocate the duties and resources
of the dead to the living. The death of an adult, particularly one with
major roles in the society, often entails elaborate rites in which roles
and wealth are redistributed. The burial of infants, on the other hand,
is often a private family matter for they have no important roles in the
community.

A fourth function is to transform the dead into ancestors and assign
them new roles in the community. There are two major attitudes about
the dead: they leave the society to live in another world, or they remain
active members in their society. In the former, the return of the dead is
regarded as undesirable because they disrupt the social order and daily
routine of life. In such cultures the dead are likely to be greatly feared,
and an elaborate system of beliefs and rituals is constructed to separate
them from the living. In the latter, ancestors remain a part of everyday
life. For example, the Chinese believe that ancestors live in the family
house and bring good or bad fortune to the living. Homes have ances-

tral shrines with tables listing the names and ancestors of the family. Observances are led by the eldest son, who offers prayers, incense, food, and drink offerings. Special rites are observed at New Year and the anniversary of the death of the person. Daughters marry out of the family, and if there is no son to make offerings to them, the parents may become homeless 'hungry ghosts.'

Other ancestors become malignant spirits. In much of the world ghosts are seen as the souls of people who have not lived fulfilled lives or who have died tragic deaths. They are thought to exist in a halfway house between the human world and the world of ancestral spirits, and to search for a human body which they can enter and make sick through their nefarious activity. The Shona of Zimbabwe believe in the *ngozi*, the spirit of vengeance of a family member who died aggrieved or was murdered. It returns to kill relatives of the person responsible for the death until the crime has been confessed and compensation made to the members of the family of the deceased. A family that feels it has been sinned against can call one of its deceased members to come as a *ngozi* to kill members of the other family until they admit their sin and pay compensation (Moyo 1996, 39). In India *bhuta* are the ghosts of those who die untimely and troubled deaths, such as mothers dying during childbirth, sailors drowning at sea, and those who are murdered; *preta* are spirits of children who die in infancy or are born deformed; *pishacha* are the malevolent spirits of men who are mad, dissolute, violent, misers, or jealous lovers; and *churel* are spirits of unhappy widows and childless wives (Kakar 1982, 56).

Funerals may also be related to anniversary rites that maintain the memory of the dead among the living, and solicit their help. These ancestral rites may continue for many years, particularly in the case of important people. For example, in China ancestors are remembered on the first, third, seventh, thirteenth, seventeenth, twenty-third, twenty-seventh, and thirty-third anniversary of an individual's death. Funeral anniversaries also assure the living that they will be remembered when they pass on, not cast aside and forgotten. To live after death is to live on in the memories of one's children and grandchildren, and in the society. This is seen in the great tombs, portraits, and histories that enshrine the memories of great and honored people such as kings and queens.

OTHER RITES

Many other rituals mark the transitions of life in different societies: graduations, retirement, entering new age grades, acquiring new ranks as a warrior, and even divorce. All these rites help make sense of life by showing how it is ordered—how people progress through life. A profound social meaninglessness sets in when life cycle rites are abandoned—when people start living together without marriages, when bodies are thrown away with no ceremonies, and when no one notices when someone is promoted or retired.

MEANING IN BELONGING

Much meaning in life is found in belonging to groups. To be human is to be connected to a community. This is captured in the Kiswahili phrase, *wa kwetu*, meaning "one who is from my home, family, and tribe." The Dangomba of Ghana use the term *mabia*, "my mother's child," to introduce themselves to others in their society. An Igbo proverb says, "kinship is strength." In the West people say, "blood is thicker than water." In much of the world people would not say *cogito ergo sum*, "I think, therefore I am," but *cognatus ergo sum*, "I belong, therefore I exist." No worse fate can befall one than to be removed from fellowship of the community and treated as an outsider or a nobody.

LINKAGE

People in many societies see themselves not as separate, autonomous individuals, but as intimately interconnected nodes in large webs of kinship. The same blood, the same life, which they received from their first ancestor, runs through the veins of all. Individuals are important only because they are linked with others in families, clans, and tribes. Their well-being is dependent on the group's well-being, and their life has meaning only as it is shared. The most important obligations of the people, especially the leaders, is to protect and nourish this life. To be an autonomous individual is to be as good as dead. This sense of corporate identity is expressed among the Yoruba of Nigeria. Lowery-Palmer (1980, 63) writes,

> Man is not created to be alone. He is created to be a being-in-relation. The whole existence from birth to death is organically embodied in a series of associations, and life appears to have its full value only in those close ties. Those close ties include extended family members, the clan and village, the various societies and organizations in the community together with the close ties to the ancestors and gods who are interested in the day-to-day life of a man . . . [T]he basic need of the Yoruba individual is that of attachment to other human beings.

An example of this sense of linkage is found among the Yoruba of Nigeria who believe that all persons and things are part of a great net of relationships that are manifestations of an underlying power which unifies all creation. One form of this power is human thought which, it is believed, can by its wishes and emotions affect other persons. Conse-

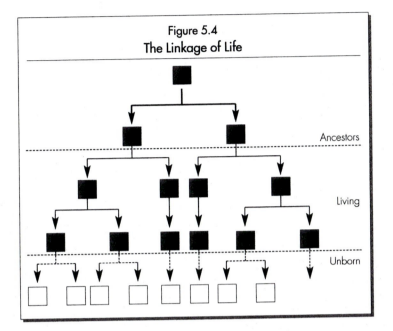

Figure 5.4
The Linkage of Life

Ancestors

Living

Unborn

quently, individuals are concerned about how others think about them. Well-being is dependent not only on how others act toward you, but also what they think about you. Moreover, because all life is a visible expression of the same power, humans, plants, animals, and spirits are seen as a continuum of beings, differing only in the amounts of their power.

Central to this corporate view of life is the concept of 'linkage' or connectedness. Life is not seen as divided into discrete units. It is an unending stream that flows from parent to child, and from generation to generation (Figure 5.4). The tie between parent and child is seen as much more than biological. It is primarily social and spiritual. Not only do children receive their bodies from their parents. They get their personalities, their social identities, and their spirits from this flow of life from parent to child. Consequently, the righteousness of the parents brings blessings to their children, and the sins of the parents bring punishment on their children and children's children (cf. Exod. 20:5–6). In Enlightenment thought, with its stress on the autonomous free individual, each person and generation begins anew, and each person should be judged by her or his own actions. Not so in most other societies, where good and evil are attributed to the life or 'blood' that runs through whole families and clans.

Linkage gives rise to a group of people who can trace their descent from a common ancestor. They all share his or her 'blood' or life. Many

believe that life is passed on from father to child. The result is patrilineal lineages and clans—people who can trace their descent to a common ancestor through the male line. Some attribute life to the mother,
and form matrilineal lineages and clans. Both see the stream of life as
greater than the life of any individual. Imagine for a moment that all the
people with the name Smith believe they share in the same life, and
what is important is not the life of any one of them, but the continuity
and growth of the Smith clan in the future. Any Smith could ask other
Smiths for help and expect to receive it, even though they had never
met. Moreover, any Smith may be asked to die for the prosperity of the
community which embodies Smith life.[3]

The concept of linkage provides people with a sense of meaning by
giving them a clear identity and security. They are not individuals who
happen to live in families—they exist only as they exist in families,
clans, and communities. These groups give birth to people, raise them,
marry them, give them land, help raise their children, feed them when
they have no food, transform them into ancestors, and immortalize
them by remembering them when they are gone.

THE WHOLE COMMUNITY

Linkage gives rise to kinship communities made up of the ancestors,
the living, and the unborn, who are linked together by biological, psychological, social, and spiritual ties (Figure 5.4). People cannot separate themselves from their children, grandchildren, and great-grand-
children—living or unborn, or from their parents, grandparents and
great-grandparents—living or deceased. The whole family must always
remain together. As children grow up, they eat, live, play, and work together with their fathers and mothers, grandfathers and grandmothers,
nephews and nieces, and neighbors and friends. They have many parents, for all their aunts and uncles are mothers and fathers. They have
many brothers and sisters, for these include cousins who share the
same blood. Each person has a communal responsibility for the behavior of every other member. One cannot conceive of a happy life apart
from the family. Riana, a Luo of Kenya said, "The good life is with and
among people, your own people" (Kirwen 1987, 76).

In such communities, perpetuating the family is of central importance. If there are no children, the ancestors are forgotten, the family
dies out and therefore becomes nonexistent. This emphasis on membership in a greater family provides people with a strong sense of iden-

---

3. Many find it hard to think of dying for the well-being of the family or clan, but not
of dying for the defense of the state. This shift from identity and loyalty in kinship groups
to nation-states is one of the hallmarks of modernity.

tity. Including the ancestors provides a sense of stability and continuity, and the awareness of the unborn assures that the family—all its members, past, present, and future—will continue on.

TOTEMISM

In some societies, the concept of linkage not only joins humans into lineages, clans, and communities, or even all people into one human family, it also links human spirits to those of animals and plants. Just as humans are divided into different groups, so, too, animals and plants are separated into different species (Tigers, Deer, Eagles). In totemic societies, each human lineage is thought to be linked to a particular species of animals, and sometimes to plants as well. One common myth is that the first ancestor had three children (Figure 5.5). The first child was a human and became the founder of the Tiger Clan; the second, an animal and progenitor of all tigers; and the third, a plant and the ancestor to all tiger-lilies. Consequently, human lineages and clans are connected to clans of animals and plants in a web of life that includes all of nature.

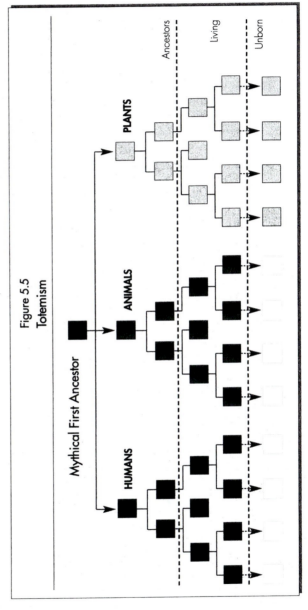

Figure 5.5
Totemism

People of a clan do not normally eat their own totemic animal or plant. Rather, they must ensure that these multiply so that people of other clans have food. They only kill and eat their totemic animal or plant in special rituals whereby, W. R. Robertson Smith argues (1889), they identify with their animals in a communion sacrifice and establish relationships in both this and the other worlds.

Totemism gives meaning to human life by locating it in a larger theology of ecology. Underlying this view of the world is the belief that human, animal, and plant life are linked together in one interdependent world. All nature, therefore, takes on religious significance and religion encourages the careful treatment of nature. Such ecological concerns draw attention to another synchronic approach to life, namely, that centered around the importance of place—a concept that extends from one's home to the universe.

MEANING IN HAVING A HOME

Meaning in life is found in knowing where one is—*in having a home*. The physical world is where humans reside. Their real world is the one in which they mentally live, and which is relevant and meaningful to them. In many parts of the world this sense of place is associated with the notion of "sacred" space—a place in the cosmic order of things—and is sanctified by the gods. Outside this is the "profane" world beyond which is the chaos of the unknown.

Many traditional religions see the world as one dynamic whole, linked together by a vital or life force and inhabited by people, ancestors, spirits, animals, mountains, and rivers, which are constantly interacting with one another. For most of the world's people, religion is not simply a segment of life, as it is in Western cultures. Rather, it is at the heart of all life, and affects everything one does: how one eats, who one marries, how one plants seed, and where one is buried.

GOD, LAND, AND PEOPLE

Central to the concept of sacred space is a people's view of their land.[4] Some spaces are sacred places that link humans to the gods and the cosmos, and that model reality. For example, the Alaskan Indians build their houses according to a fixed blueprint, for these are their sacred "homes." The ground is leveled, a basement is dug, and a dome-shaped roof of driftwood and sod with a smokehole in the center is erected according to the traditional mode.

Each procedure is done in the same sequence, for the work is not only a matter of providing housing for a family group. It is the re-creation of the

---

4. The modern view of land is that it is a secular commodity that can be bought and sold at will. Graveyards are relocated, church buildings converted into restaurants and shops. This is part of the secularization of worldview.

world, each house being a microcosm, a replicate universe. The design never changes, for the shape of the world does not change. At certain times of the year, activities are appropriate inside the dwelling; at other times, the same activities are appropriate only outside the house. The cycles are fixed, the rhythms eternal. And the human beings must behave in harmony with the flow of the cosmos (Oleksa 1987, 8–9).

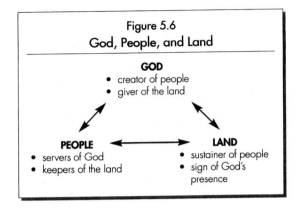

Figure 5.6
God, People, and Land

GOD
- creator of people
- giver of the land

PEOPLE
- servers of God
- keepers of the land

LAND
- sustainer of people
- sign of God's presence

For the Achilpas, the Australian desert is "their world." Numbakula created their ancestor and erected a pole up which he climbed into the sky. The pole represents the center of the world, the cosmic axis. Around it the land became habitable and was transformed into the "world." Wherever the people move, they take the pole with them. When the sacred pole of one band broke, the people were distraught. They wandered haphazardly for a time because their world had collapsed, and finally sat down on the ground and allowed themselves to perish (Eliade 1976, 20).

For the Israelites, the sacred space was the Holy Land given to them by God. At the center was Jerusalem, and the foundation stones of the temple represented the foundation of the world. This was the place closest to heaven and the center of the geographical world. For the Jew, to journey to Jerusalem was to go to the center of the world, to the fountain of reality, and to the place of blessing par excellence.

In most traditional societies, the land is not owned in a modern sense of that word. People know that they have the right to use land as individuals, but they can never own it. It belongs to their lineage and tribe, and is a gift from their god. An Ashanti saying from Ghana goes, "The farm is mine, but the soil belongs to the stool." The royal stool was a wooden seat that represented the authority and power of the chief, and incorporated the soul of the nation. It stood for what the dead and the living could own together.

This identification of people with their gods and their land makes the living the temporary possessors of a heritage that is destined to be passed on to generations yet unborn (Figure 5.6). Land belongs to the people's gods who gave it to them. It belongs to the ancestors who are buried in it and make it sacred. It is an ancestral trust—the most valuable heritage of the whole community. It belongs to the living who eat the food it produces, which becomes a part of them. It belongs to the unborn who will live on it one day. A traditional ruler in Ghana once said, "Land belongs to a vast family of whom many are dead, a few are living and a countless host is still unborn."

CAMP, VILLAGE, CITY

Places where people reside are often seen as sacred and truly 'home.' Here they gain significance, security and support, order and harmony, and life itself. Here they socialize and become part of the community. Those who do not help to build the community receive little help at their burials.

Camps, villages, and cities must be founded—they do not simply emerge out of the chaos of profane space. There is often the myth of a founder who inaugurated the alliance among the gods, earth, and people. In many cases a ritual center must be established. In India, a village is begun by dedicating a Navel Stone—a rock-lined hole in the ground. This marks its "birth," and is the site for all important village rites that bring prosperity to the community. The center of Rome, too, was a hole representing the navel of the earth, the point of communication between the terrestrial world and the lower regions.

The center of a residential community is often marked with a shrine or temple built in the likeness of the universe. For example, the temple of Angkor in Cambodia symbolizes Mountain Meru, and its five towers stand for the five peaks of the sacred mountain. Around it are subordinate shrines representing the astrological constellations. As devotees circle the temple in the prescribed direction, they pass through each stage of the solar cycle, and so traverse time as well as space. At times the center is represented by a palace. The center of Bangkok, "the celestial royal city," is the palace of the king who is the *cakravartin,* the creator and sustainer of the cosmos. The Chinese saw the world as a rectangle with China in the middle surrounded by four barbarian nations. Towns were built as quadrangles with gates on each side, and a palace at the center where the sovereign was to rule his domain with justice and peace.

A residential community is also defined by its boundaries. The immediate ritual boundaries are the camp fences, village walls, and city fortifications. The distant ones are the borders of the community, including its fields and forests. These are important in maintaining the prosperity of the community and defending it against spirits and powers from the barbaric world beyond. For example, during the village protection rite in south Indian villages, a water buffalo, purchased by contributions from every home in the village, is slaughtered. Members of the community then carry the severed head in procession around the ritual boundaries of the village, cracking coconuts and burying balls of bloody rice to erect sacred barriers against intruders seeking to harm them, or to steal the power they generate in the ritual. This also placates the goddesses of smallpox, cholera, and plague, who see the evidence of sacrifice and pass on to less protected villages.[5]

The residences and fields of a community belong to the human domain, and are made safe and fertile through sacrifices and proper care. By contrast, forest and bush land are often seen as untamed and inhabited by dangerous beings. Paths that go beyond the community are often seen as dangerous, and must be guarded by spirit shrines and magical incantations. For example, the Samo build a house in the middle of a large garden in order to put some distance between themselves and the spirits that inhabit the forest.

Many people believe that heaven is a traditional village where life goes on as before. Moreover, there is an ongoing relationship between earthly and heavenly villages. Among the Akan of Ghana each married person on earth has a spouse in heaven as well as one on earth, and he or she must spend time each week with the spirit spouse. It is also important to be buried in one's natal village for that is connected to heaven.

Finally, land is important for it encodes the oral theology of the people told in local myths. This tree was planted by the founding ancestor of the tribe, that hill is where the local god lives, the river marks the people's victory over an advancing enemy. Raja Rao points out that every Indian village has its *stala-purana*.

There is no village in India, however mean, that has not a rich *stala-purana*, or legendary history, of its own. Some god or godlike hero has passed by the village—Rama might have rested under this pipal-tree, Sita might have dried her clothes, after her bath, on this yellow stone, or the Mahatma himself, on one of his many pilgrimages through the country, might have slept in this hut, the low one, by the village gate. In this way the past mingles with the present, and the gods mingle with men (1967, vii).

HOUSE

Houses, too, are often seen as sacred—as more than secular places in which people reside. They are not objects or "machines in which to

---

5. Village rites require that every family contribute to a sacrifice. Christians who refuse are often beaten and ostracized, not because they worship Christ, but because they refuse to perform their caste obligations in the rituals, such as beating big drums or carrying the gods on procession.

live," but "homes" in a religious sense. For example, a Dyak house symbolically re-creates the cosmogonic myth that the world came into being as the result of a battle between Mahatala, the supreme being, and the primordial Water Snake. The foundations represent the snake, the roof the mountain on which Mahatala is enthroned. The central pole in the Mongolian tent represents the pillar holding up the sky, and the opening in the roof is the "window of heaven" by which humans communicate with the gods. The sacred lodges of the Sioux represented the universe. The roof symbolized the dome of the sky, the floor represented the earth, the four walls pointed to the four directions of cosmic space. In other words, the cosmos is represented in symbolic form in the buildings in which people live.

MEANING IN DOING

Meaning in life is also found in what people as individuals do with their lives. One person becomes a chief, another a shaman, another a great mother, a model husband or wife, a brave warrior, a great hunter, a scientist, an astronaut, a Nobel Prize winner, or a witch. In strong, group-oriented societies, people are valued according to their ascribed status in the community, and individuals are honored for the contributions they make to the community as a whole. In individualistic societies, people find meaning primarily in their personal achievements, which often die with them.

MEANING IN POSSESSIONS

Finally, people often find meaning in having possessions. To be wealthy is honored in most societies. The Masai of Kenya value their cows. Indian money lenders count their gold. Arabs take pride in horses and camels. In North America consumerism has become a folk religion (Fox and Lears 1983; Kavanau 1986). Shopping has become a religious experience for many Americans, providing meaning to life. Buying a suit gives a person a sense of purpose and well-being for a few weeks, a new car for a few months.

We turn now from synchronic to diachronic answers to the question of meaning in life.

DIACHRONIC MEANINGS

A second major way humans find meaning is through the stories of their lives (Figure 5.7). A textbook on human biology is invaluable to a doctor trying to deal with illnesses, but ultimately meaning in human lives has to do with biographies and histories that impose an orderly, purposeful drama or plot on the jumble of human happenings. There are many levels of stories. We will examine three: personal stories—or biographies; the story of a people; and the cosmic drama that encompasses everything.

BIOGRAPHY

People find immediate existential meaning in the everyday stories of their lives. But do these stories make sense? Religions sometimes explain personal conditions by attributing these to fate, curses, or witchcraft. At times

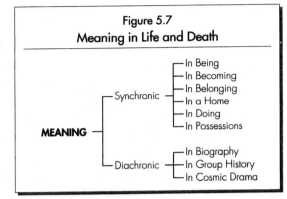

Figure 5.7
Meaning in Life and Death

they give meaning to individual lives by placing them in a moral universe. Humans are not simply amoral animals. They live in a world in which there is right and wrong, and their lives contribute to good or evil. This helps explain why some are poor and others rich, some strong and others crippled, and some become great and others wicked.

In South India, for example, ordinary people have a toolbox of explanation systems from which they choose one or another to explain the events in their lives. Immediate fortunes and misfortunes are commonly accounted for in terms of magic, sorcery, and astrological influences. The larger picture of life is attributed to *tala vrata*—their fate. This is written on the forehead of every person, and can be read by diviners who have the power to discern invisible writing. Hinduism offers people yet another explanation for their lives. This is the concept of *dharma* or righteousness and duty—the belief that the cosmos is ruled by the moral law of *karma*, and that all beings are rewarded according to their deeds, good and evil. Since moral balance is rarely achieved in this life, people, gods, and animals must be reborn after death in other forms to reap the rewards and punishments of their previous lives. Because Hindus believe that all life is one, good humans can become gods, and gods who sin are reborn as ants. By attributing moral significance to human actions, transmigration explains why bad things happen to good people—in their past lives they did something evil. They alone must bear the blame for their present misfortunes. Life with its sufferings, illness, even death is meaningful and can be endured because it is part of a moral universe.

GROUP STORY

Personal stories take on greater meaning when they become part of the larger stories of a community of people. For example, Genesis 12 marks the beginning of the people of Israel. Thereafter, Israelites found

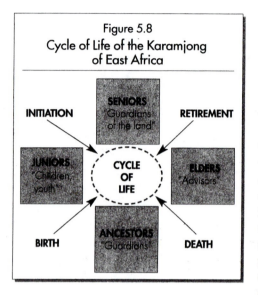

Figure 5.8
Cycle of Life of the Karamjong
of East Africa

INITIATION

SENIORS
"Guardians
of the land"

RETIREMENT

JUNIORS
"Children,
youth"

CYCLE
OF
LIFE

ELDERS
"Advisors"

BIRTH

ANCESTORS
"Guardians"

DEATH

their identity in belonging to a particular tribe, and, above all, to God's chosen people. They told and retold the stories of great individuals, such as Abraham, Moses, Deborah, and David, whose lives gave shape to their nation.

Some religions link individuals to the community through the belief that humans are part of a great cycle of life. For example, the Karamjong of East Africa believe that there are four generations of people: the children, the adults, the retired, and the ancestors (Figure 5.8). In time each generation moves up. Children become adults, adults retire, the aged die, and ancestors are reborn as children. A person is his or her great-great-grandfather/mother, and his or her own great-great-grandson/daughter! Together, these four generations form one great community that bridges between this world and the other world.

How Things Began

Long ago Onyakopon lived on the earth near us. A certain old woman used to pound her fufu yams, and the pestle would constantly knock up against Onyakopon [the high God]. So he said to the old woman, "Why do you always do so to me? Because of what you are doing I am going to take myself off up to the sky." And he did so. Since the people could no longer approach Onyakopon, the old woman told her children to bring all the mortars they could find and pile them up one on top of another until they reached Onyakopon. They did, but needed one more to reach him. She said, "take one out from the bottom and put it on the top to make them reach." So her children removed one and all rolled and fell to the ground, and many died. (Rattray 1923, 20–21)

The story of a group's origins and history is often recorded in myths. Many of these tell of events in the distant past, before the beginning of time and space. The opening of such myths often signals that important information is about to be communicated: "long, long ago before anything existed. . . ," "before the ancestors were. . . ," or "once upon a time . . ." Other myths tell of important events in the history of the community. For example, the Samo only tell myths when incidents in the com-

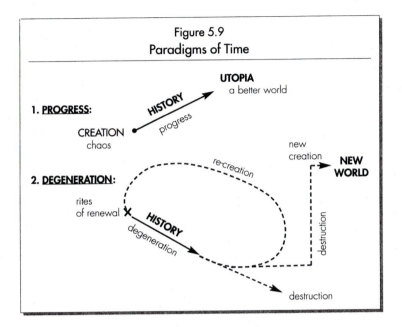

Figure 5.9
Paradigms of Time

munity or natural disasters, such as a flood, precipitate the need for special explanation. When a flash flood destroyed a sago stand some years ago, they recounted the flood myth during an all-night ceremony, and everyone understood the cause and meaning of this calamity.

With the rise of nation-states, people began to define their corporate identities not so much in terms of ethnicity as nationality. Nations have their own heroes, rituals, and myths that show people their place in the world. The emergence of the global world is forcing people to think of their identity in terms of their place in the whole of human history. The theory of evolution is an example of a myth seeking to explain the history of humankind.

COSMIC STORY

Ultimately, meaning is to be found in the cosmic story: the 'big' story about the beginning, meaning, and ending of all things. Cosmic myths vary greatly from society to society. Two common ones are those of progress and degeneration (Figure 5.9). The first of these tells of a creation that begins in disorder and ends in utopia as order is created out of chaos. Examples of this are the theories of evolution, capitalism, and democracy in the West. The second sees a perfect world degenerating through the growth of evil, violence, and sin, and culminating in collapse and death, followed by a new world. For example, the Ghost Dance myths of the North American Indians predicted a period of de-

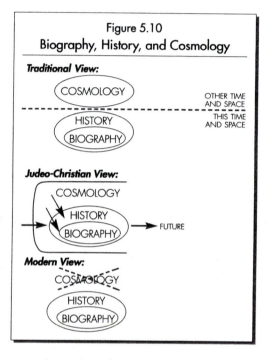

Figure 5.10
Biography, History, and Cosmology

Traditional View:

COSMOLOGY — OTHER TIME AND SPACE

HISTORY — THIS TIME AND SPACE
BIOGRAPHY

Judeo-Christian View:

COSMOLOGY
HISTORY
BIOGRAPHY → FUTURE

Modern View:

COSMOLOGY
HISTORY
BIOGRAPHY

struction (settlers invading the land) and a restoration of the golden age of the past. In Hinduism the world is constantly degenerating, and is propped up by periodic incarnations of one or another of the gods seeking to renew it. In Marxism the injustices of capitalism will spread until the people rise up and destroy it through revolution. (These cosmic stories are examined in more detail in Chapter 10.)

CONNECTION BETWEEN STORIES

How do these three types of stories relate to one another? Biographies are clearly part of the story of a society, and take meaning from this connection. Throughout history individuals have found meaning in being part of the history of their people or of some great movement. In the past, a Tshimshian warrior willingly let himself be killed if his death could prevent a feud between his clan and other clans. His sacrifice was told in the stories of great warriors. Marxists like Che Guevera threw themselves into battle for the sake of their cause, oblivious to the dangers they faced. American soldiers are expected to die to preserve their country, and the stories of great heroes are told in textbooks and biographies.

The relationship between the stories of individuals and societies, and cosmic meta narratives are more complex. Eliade points out (1975, 135) that in most societies, these are disconnected (Figure 5.10). Cosmic myths tell the stories of the heavens. Human stories narrate events on earth. In such cases, biographies and human histories are disconnected from the primordial era and have little meaning in themselves. They are transient and passing. The great lasting and meaningful stories have to do with the gods, angels, and demons of other times and places.

Eliade argues that for the Israelites, biography and history were embedded in the center of cosmology. Genesis 1 starts with God in eternity, and links the origins of creation to him. It, therefore, is meaningful. Moreover, God constantly interacts with those on earth, particularly with his chosen people, thereby rendering their histories meaningful. If their history as the people of Israel took on meaning, so, too, did their personal lives as Israelites. They were not isolated individuals who lived and died meaningless deaths. They were part of a much bigger story being worked out by God. He called them as individuals to do tasks he assigned them. This person was called to be the mother of Samuel, that person to be King David. He punished them to pull them back to the paths of righteousness. He saved them when they cried unto him in their troubles. They found meaning in the fact that they were God's chosen people.

Early Christians had a similar view of history, but extended it to all humans. They were a part of the church which is Christ's body, and the church was the outpost of the kingdom of God now invading the earth, and a foretaste of the time when Christ would rule over the whole universe. Many of them went triumphantly to their deaths because they saw their lives as part of the story being written by God.

Finally, Eliade points out that modern humans have tried to get rid of cosmology.

> Modern nonreligious man assumes a new existential situation; he regards himself solely as the subject and agent of history, and he refuses to appeal to transcendence. In other words, he accepts no model for humanity outside the human condition as it can be seen in the various historical situations. Man *makes himself*, and he only makes himself completely in proportion as he desacralizes himself and the world. He will become himself only when he is totally demysticized. He will not be truly free until he has killed the last god (1959, 203).

Lacking a cosmology, modern scholars are seeking to reconstruct all of history in hopes that when every piece is in place the picture will emerge and give meaning to the whole. But, Eliade argues, history without cosmology is ultimately meaningless.

GIVING MEANING TO DEATH

To make sense of human lives, humans must give meaning to death, the great reality that challenges all systems of meaning. If they cannot do so, their explanations of life fail. Folk and formal religions answer different sets of questions related to death. Formal religions explain where the dead have ultimately gone. Folk religions deal with the questions of death that confront the living. First, they must explain the cause of death to give it meaning. To say it is an 'accident' is to render it meaningless. Eddie Arthur points out,

Death is not seen as a natural or accidental event, but rather something which is caused by the active intervention of someone who, for one reason or another, is badly disposed toward the deceased. So the greatest felt need is not forgiveness, or to find meaning in life as in the West, but rather to find protection from those who would cause harm. This protection is to be had from diviners who suggest rituals and charms that can ward off evil (1995, 143).

Second, they must answer the questions facing those left behind. "Why did this happen to us?" Who will care for us in our old age now that our son has died?" "How can we communicate with the dead?" The answers to these questions have to do with this world and the present.

LIFE AFTER DEATH

Formal religions focus on what happens to people after death. Folk religions answer the question of death by seeking to maintain relationships with the dead. Most hold that human spirits exist beyond death, and continue to live in their old community with living humans, spirits, animals, and nature. These spirits need to be fed and cared for to keep them healthy and happy. For example, Chinese folk beliefs speak of three 'souls.'[6] These separate at the death of an adult: one resides in the ancestral tablet erected to his or her memory, the second remains in the coffin, and the third departs to the spirit region to undergo its merited punishment (Harrell 1979). According to the Chinese, humans also have in them positive and negative forces—*yin* and *yang*. If the deceased is not cared for after death, the *yin* (the evil force) is dominant and the condition of the ancestor is wretched and desolate. If the dead soul is properly provided for by living relatives, their *yang* thrives. The departed need clothes, food, a place to live and work, money, and entertainment. If the living do not provide these, they become Hungry Ghosts. Therefore the living burn paper houses complete with paper maids, paper money, and paper televisions and computers so that the ancestors may live in comfort. It is a great sin and an unforgivable breach of filial piety to fail to periodically offer incense and food sacrifices to one's deceased parents. Failure to give them homage is believed to result in disasters and misfortune for the living.

The finality of separation at death is often blunted by belief in visitations by the deceased. Many Filipinos believe that the soul of a dead person returns to visit his or her family. This may occur three days after the death, but may be delayed until months after the funeral. The visit

6. In Chinese folk beliefs the most serious candidates for the number of 'souls' is two, ten twelve, three, and one. The most commonly held beliefs relate to three souls (Harrell 1979).

comes in the form of a dream or sensory experience, such as an unusual sound or scent. Sometimes it takes the form of a ghost *(multo)* that can be seen. At other times, living family members fall into trances, and the spirit of the departed speaks through them, giving detailed information and instructions regarding life in the world beyond. Thereafter the visits become increasingly rare.

ANCESTORS

A second explanation that mitigates the pain and meaninglessness of death is that the departed become ancestors who continue to live in another world, but whose relationship to the living on earth does not cease at death. Ancestors are vitally interested in the well-being of the family to which they gave life. They help those who care for them, and punish those who bring disgrace and harm to their kinsmen. In turn, the living must care for the ancestors by revering them on special occasions.

Forefathers
Listen more often to things rather than beings.
Hear the fire's voice,
Hear the voice of water,
In the wind hear the sobbing of the trees,
It is our forefathers breathing.
The dead are not gone forever,
They are in the paling shadows
And in the darkening shadows,
The dead are not beneath the ground,
They are in the rustling tree,
In the murmuring wood,
In the still water,
In the flowing water,
In the lonely place, in the crowd;
The dead are not dead
Listen more often to things rather than beings.
Hear the fire's voice.
Hear the voice of water.
In the wind hear the sobbing of the trees.
It is the breathing of our forefathers
Who are not gone, not beneath the ground,
Not dead.
The dead are not gone forever.
They are in a woman's breast,
A child's crying, a glowing ember
The dead are not beneath the earth,
They are in the flickering fire,

In the weeping plant, the groaning rock,
The wooded place, the home.
The dead are not dead . . .
—Birago Diop, poet from Senegal
(Quoted from *An African Treasury*,
by Langston Hughes. [New York:
Pyramid Books, 1961], 174)

Ancestors are revered for several reasons. First, they are the founders of the family, and, therefore, have a natural interest in caring for it. They have ancient knowledge not known by the living. A young person may say, "My parents, grandparents, and ancestors know more about life than I. They are wiser in terms of experience, and I can go to them for advice." This sounds strange to Westerners, who focus on the independence of each individual. However, in traditional societies the relationships of parent and child, and of grandparent and grandchild, are very strong, and there is great respect for progenitors. This sense of genealogical descent carries with it a strong sense of belonging to a historical movement that began with the ancestors and runs through the living to the yet unborn. All belong to the group.

Second, all humans face the question of what follows death, and ancestors have experienced it. They know the spirit world hidden from the living. Because they exist beyond death, they see the spirits, witches, and ghosts that plague humans, and are able to protect the living from them. Hence, the living seek their help by means of dreams, visions, diviners, and necromancers.[7]

Third, great ancestors are remembered for their power and achievements. The accomplishments of the living never equal those of the founders of society; the great warrior who delivered them from destruction; the hero who brought culture to the people; or the kings who built the pyramids and whose achievements are repeated in myths and folk tales. The Israelites remembered Abraham, Isaac, and Jacob for their accomplishments, and referred to God as the "God of our fathers" (Exod. 3:16; 1 Chron. 29:18). Ancestors are also referred to in the New Testament (Mark 12:26; Acts 3:13; 7:32), providing the Jewish people with a heritage and identity rooted in their founding fathers, lands, and histories. Whenever the Jews were in trouble, they retold the stories of the patriarchs and how God had delivered them from Egypt and made them a chosen nation.

Fourth, for the most part, ancestors are thought to have the well-being of the family at heart. They are its guardians. They protect those

---

7. This fascination of life after death has led, in the United States, to the study of 'near-death' experiences starting with Elisabeth Kübler-Ross's early study.

who are loyal to them and give them food and drink. They reward family members who bring honor and prosperity to the community. They bring fertility to family members and their land, and victory in battles with others. They also punish relatives and friends on earth who neglect them or live wayward lives. The fear of ancestors serves as a powerful force in maintaining moral standards in family life.

Finally, ancestors are often seen as intermediaries between God and humans. Families and clans relate to God mainly through their departed elders. One does not turn to the departed elders of families with whom one has no blood relationships.

To live beyond death means to be remembered and revered by one's descendants. In many cultures the big void means "to be forgotten." Most ancestors are remembered for three or four generations as their stories are told and their shrines venerated. In time they are forgotten and merge into the general category 'Ancestors,' which includes all who have gone before. Lineages are collapsed by leaving out unimportant ancestors in order to keep them manageable.[8] Only a few heroes, particularly the founders of a people, are remembered for many generations

Not all the dead become ancestors. Some leave no descendants to keep their memory alive, and some are so insignificant in life that no account needs to be taken of them. Some suffer untimely or tragic deaths and become malevolent spirits that take out their discontentment on the living. Their bodies may be cremated and the ashes scattered to prevent them from returning to plague the living.

Ancestors provide people with a cosmic view of reality and their place in it. The living are not alone in a harsh, impersonal world. They belong to large families and are surrounded by powerful ancestors. They will continue on in the memories of their people. In this they find security and a sense of history. What they do is not for themselves, but for the group, which is much larger than themselves. Belief in ancestors also comforts the living, for those who die remain among them as the living dead. Given all this, it should not surprise us that in many societies ancestors are venerated.

It is important to use the term 'veneration' when referring to services rendered to ancestors before they are understood. The term includes the ideas of respect and of worship. Too often outsiders label all ancestor rites as 'worship' because they do not understand them. They need to reserve judgment until they know how the people themselves view the practices. Only then is it wise to pass judgment on whether these rit-

8. For example, compare Gen. 5:3–32 with Luke 3:36–37, or 1 Chron. 1:28–6:30 with Matt. 1:2–15. In the New Testament only the lineal descendants leading to Jesus are remembered.

uals are worship or only respect. The Scriptures are clear. People are to respect their parents. This is the first of the Ten Commandments dealing with social matters, and the only one with a promise attached to it (Exod. 20:12; Lev. 19:3). Yet, the living are *not* to worship their deceased parents. Unfortunately, in their effort to destroy ancestor worship, missionaries have often failed to substitute Christian rituals showing respect to parents, so Christianity is widely seen as a religion that ignores the ancestors and rebels against parents.

CHRISTIAN RESPONSE

How should Christians respond to beliefs and practices that give people a sense of meaning in life and death? If they simply condemn the ways of others as pagan and introduce their own ways, or even their understanding of biblical ways (which are always filtered through a cultural bias), the people will reject Christianity as irrelevant or become Christians for other reasons and continue their old customs in secret.

NEW MEANING IN LIFE

What is the biblical response that answers the longings of human hearts to live meaningful lives on earth? Scripture shows people who they are as human beings by providing them a sense of identity, a community of believers, a home in the world and in heaven, and work that is meaningful because it is done for God.

A NEW IDENTITY IN CHRIST

It is important in proclaiming the gospel to emphasize the fact that each person is created in the image of God, and therefore has present and eternal worth. If Christians begin by emphasizing people's sins and sinfulness, they lose sight of God's original intentions in creating humans, and have little to offer in terms of the purpose of life here and now. Moreover, Christians are then tempted to come as outsiders with an attitude of superiority—as those who are saved seeking to rescue those who are lost. It is important to see people *as God sees them*, as having great worth. It is equally important to identify with them as fellow sinners, and to invite them to a new life as children of God—important, perfect, beautiful. Leslie Newbigin writes, "The real point of contact between Christian and non-Christian is not in the religion of the non-Christian, but in his humanity" (1958, 65). Only then will Christians avoid the spiritual arrogance and colonialism that too often have characterized missions. Bosch notes, "We are not the 'haves', the *beati possidentes*, standing over against spiritual 'have nots,' the *massa dam-*

nata. We are all recipients of the same mercy, sharing in the same mystery" (Bosch 1991, 484).

Next, missionaries and Christian leaders must teach converts that now they are "In Christ People."[9] Union with Christ is an indispensable part of their new identity. They are Christians, not for intellectual, emotional, or external reasons, but because of their union with God. They have a real participation in the divine nature, the very image of Christ drawn upon their souls (Stott 1991, 38).[10] For them, Christ is not only a great teacher, He is the living Lord and Savior who now is in and with them. Because of this union, they have a new status as sons and daughters of God, with all the privileges this entails. They are now members of his body. Nothing else can give people so great a sense of worth and meaning in their everyday life as this.

A New Christian Maturity
When all my labors and trials are o're,
and I am safe on that beautiful shore,
Just to be near the dear Lord I adore,
will through the ages be glory for me.
Oh that will be, glory for me, when by His
grace I shall look on his face,
That will be glory for me.
—Hymn: Charles H. Gabriel

As seen earlier, meaning is found in the growth of a person into full adulthood and maturity, and this growth is often marked by life cycle rites that make public the beliefs people have about the destiny of human lives. It is important that Christians develop rituals that express their deepest beliefs about the dignity of every human being and the importance of marriage and the family. Especially, they need a theology of godly dying and funerals to give meaning to death by showing that it is not the end, but the transition for Christians into the presence of God. The modern denial of death runs counter to the teachings of the church throughout history that made much of death and gave it meaning through sermons and hymns.

Missionaries from the West are in danger of undervaluing the importance of rituals in life, of rejecting traditional rites because they believe these to be pagan, and of introducing practices that are foreign to the

---

9. Paul makes a great deal of our new identity as *en Christo* people in Ephesians.

10. John Stott notes that the expressions 'in Christ,' 'in the Lord,' and 'in him' occur 164 times in the letters of Paul. He quotes James Stewart: "The heart of Paul's religion is union with Christ. This more than any other conception . . . is the key which unlocks the secrets of his soul" (1991, 38).

people. Rites that are truly Christian but expressed in the cultural symbols and idioms of the people need to be encouraged. When these rites are held in public so that all can see, they become powerful witnesses to the joy and hope of the gospel. (The need for Christian life cycle rites is examined in Chapter 11.)

A NEW COMMUNITY IN CHRIST

Christian leaders need to build strong churches that are new communities of God's people. Followers of Christ now belong to a new *ecclesia*—a new family, a new community. For many people this is good news, for they cannot conceive of meaning apart from belonging to a people linked by common ties of blood and kinship.

How did believers look at the church in the New Testament? There were numerous clubs and corporations in the Greco-Roman society, which the first Christians could have emulated. Believers, however, used the term *koinonia* to describe their gathering. They used metaphors such as children of one family, parts of the same body, citizens of the same colony (Phil. 3:20). In all these metaphors, the church is more than a gathering of individuals, because the autonomous individual is not a whole person. A whole person is a person-in-community.

The church is a covenant community of living believers. Too often people from the West see churches as religious crowds that entertain believers or as clubs that keep believers in faith and busy until they are raised to heaven by death. Or they organize churches as corporations— formally organized institutions with defined roles and contractual relationships. To introduce these patterns is to offer a poor substitute for what the people already have in lineages, villages and whole societies. More important, Western-style churches are rarely true communities in the biblical sense of the term.

The church is also a people who share a new life and blood. It is a new kindred, a new family. From a human point of view, the church is a community like other human communities, a living reality fleshed out in human relationships and experiences of life. From God's perspective, it is a unique kind of body because it is a community of the Spirit—a gathering in which God is at work (Phil. 1:1–11). Membership is not based on similar characteristics or shared interests, but on a new birth. Christians find meaning in this life by belonging to a new family, a new race, a gathering of those who share the same Lord and Spirit, and who devote themselves to one another's well-being (Acts 2:42). In such kindred communities, members must learn to live together in harmony— to sacrifice their personal interests, where need be, for the sake of the common good. They minister to one another, work together, play together, and turn to one another for help and comfort.

However, the church ultimately does not exist for the well-being of its members. C. Norman Kraus points out that the goal of Christianity is not "the self-sufficient individual secure in his victory through Christ enjoying his own private experience of spiritual gifts and emotional satisfaction" (Kraus 1974, 56). Membership in the church is not based on relationships between members, but on their relationship to the same Lord. Moreover, the church does not even exist for itself. The church exists because of and for Jesus Christ. It is his body, his family, his colony. Its primary purpose is to worship him, and to carry out the mission on earth, which he gives it to do. Stanley Hauerwas and W. H. Willimon write,

> Christian community . . . is not primarily about togetherness. It is about the way of Jesus Christ with those whom he calls to himself. It is about disciplining our wants and needs in congruence with a true story, which gives us the resources to lead truthful lives. In living out the story together, togetherness happens, but only as a by-product of the main project of trying to be faithful to Jesus (Hauerwas and Willimon 1991, 78).

The church is also the beachhead of God's kingdom on earth. By being something the world is not and can never be, it is a sign to the world of God's presence and rule on earth.

> The confessing church seeks the *visible* church, a place, clearly visible to the world, in which people are faithful to their promises, love their enemies, tell the truth, honor the poor, suffer for righteousness, and thereby testify to the amazing community-creating power of God (Hauerwas and Willimon 1991, 46).

A NEW HOME ON EARTH

African American spirituals and other Western folk music point out how important having a home and land is to ordinary people.[11] These feelings are shared by most people around the world. In response, Christians must proclaim that this world is their home, and that it is God's world—God created it and continues to rule over it. People need sacred places where they are reminded of God's presence among them, and Christians should have a special space, such as a church, retreat center, or family worship centers, where believers go to meet God. Similarly, pilgrimages to memorial sites can be powerful spiritual symbols in the lives of ordinary folk. There is a danger, however, for people from animistic backgrounds to see these sites in magical terms. It is

---

11. We need recall only a few titles to see this: "This world is not my home," "I'm going home on the morning train," and "Lead me gently home."

this space and this time that are powerful in themselves. It is vital to instruct Christians that these places and times are not important in themselves. They are reminders of the need to get away from the cares of this world and to enter the presence of God. On the other hand, without sacred times and places, humans are in danger of making everything secular.

For Christians, however, homes on earth are only foretastes of their eternal homes in heaven. Churches are not permanent abodes, but temporary camps of God's people ministering in a broken world.

Missionaries must also have a theology of ecology—of the earth and its creatures, and human responsibility to care for them. People are not souls temporarily indwelling bodies. They are body-souls. Their material being is intrinsic to who they are. Moreover, the earth is not "background scenery" that God made simply for the benefit of humans, and which they can dispose of as they wish. James Nash points out, "The traditional idea that the earth or even the universe, was created solely for humans is . . . sinfully arrogant, biologically naive, cosmologically silly, and therefore theologically indefensible" (Stevens 1997, 3). Creation is God's cathedral, and it itself will one day be set free (Rom. 8:19).[12]

A New Gifting in Christ

Proclaimers of the gospel need to affirm the fact that God has called his people to specific ministries, and has given them all the gifts they need to carry out their ministries. All Christians are needed to form a true community, and each gift contributes to the whole. Paul makes much of this in his exhortations to the church (1 Cor. 12, Eph. 4:1–16). No one, no matter the gift or status, can say to another they are of less worth or unnecessary. In the church there should be no marginal people. All are needed in ministering to a broken and lost world.

New Christians must be encouraged to bring their respective gifts into the service of Christ, and the church must open doors for them to do so. Humility and serving one another in the congregation must be encouraged. Christians must fight against the fallen human tendencies to create hierarchies and to see some people as better than others. The church must work to equalize the rich and powerful with their weak, poor, and marginalized sisters and brothers. If churches live as communities of God's reign on earth, they will attract many to it, particularly

---

12. As modern people, we have interpreted Gen. 1:28 as "rule over" the earth. We have seen our relationship to nature as one of battle and conquest. The result has been a devastating destruction of the earth. A better translation is to "care for," or "garden" the earth.

those who are rejected and marginalized. Does this mean Christians turn away from the rich and powerful? Certainly not. But they, too, must come as repentant sinners, and their wealth and power give them no advantage in salvation.

A NEW VIEW OF POSSESSIONS

Finally, Christians need to see themselves as stewards of creation. Land, air, water, food, and other resources of the earth belong to God, who gives them to humans freely for the well-being of all people. It is in the sharing of these resources with those in need that people find meaning, not in hoarding them. The old belief that wealth is important for self-indulgence and status needs to give way to the Christian joy of giving so that others may live full lives.

A NEW MEANING IN DIVINE HISTORY

Proclaimers of the gospel must show people the meaning of their lives by showing them how their lives are part of God's cosmic story. Their lives are important in the life of the church, and the church is a manifestation of the kingdom of God that is now invading the earth. This is, indeed, good news for people who feel oppressed and rejected.

A COSMIC STORY

In the Bible, human history is embedded in cosmology. It begins with God creating the universe and ends with God reestablishing his reign over it. Unlike most cosmic stories, the Bible ties human history directly to the bigger story of God and eternity. It looks to a perfect future, and offers hope to humans mired in the trials of everyday life.

Too often in preaching and teaching Christians from the West stress theological details, and do not focus on the big picture in which all else makes sense. Christians need to know the whole of the cosmic drama that begins with the creation and fall, centers around Christ's birth, life, and death, and culminates in Christ's return to establish his rule over creation. An example of this is Trevor McIlwaine's new approach to tribal evangelism, which he calls "Building on Firm Foundations" (1991). In it people are taught the whole of the Bible story before they are invited to become followers of Jesus Christ. This approach has been very successful in establishing new churches that are solidly based on biblical teachings.

As Wolfhart Pannenberg points out, the biblical drama makes sense because Christians know the ending. God has triumphed, and will establish on the new earth and in heaven his kingdom in which righteousness, peace, and justice will reign. All of this is essential to a biblical worldview.

A HUMAN HISTORY

Scripture places human history in the middle of the cosmic story. It begins with creation and culminates in Christ's return. In between, history is the record of human sin and God's salvation, of the triumph of love over hate, justice over oppression, peace over violence, and of God over those who rebel against him. The story is one of God's constant involvement in human affairs. In the Old Testament, the prophets and psalmists tell and retell the story of God's deliverance from Egypt, and call on the people to turn back to God. The same history is told in the New Testament by Philip and Paul to show that that story finds its fulfillment in Jesus Christ of Nazareth. It is he that the prophets spoke about.

It is important that the church provide people with a sense of their new identity, both as members of their community and as members in the body of Christ, by telling the story of God's work in the church. David Scotchmer found that the Maya in Central America do not see the church as an invasion from the West, but as their rediscovery of their identity as Mayans in a modern world. For them evangelicalism both affirms their identity as Mayans over against the Catholic peasants, and their place in the broader world in which they now find themselves (Scotchmer 1989).

It is also important to remind people of their own church's history, and of the way it fits into the larger history of the global church—past, present, and future. This history must include not only the work of the missionaries, but also the many untold stories of local evangelists and pastors who often suffered great persecution and suffering in remote places. Throughout church history, it is they who have truly planted the church in their villages and towns. A church with historical amnesia does not know who it really is.

PERSONAL BIOGRAPHY

Finally, it is important to help Christians see their personal biographies as meaningful stories, because these are part of the history of the church and of eternity. Ordinary people seek meaning in the dreariness of their everyday lives. Christians need to offer them better answers than those they find in their traditional religious ways. The church can give them meaning through a new identity in Christ, a new community in the church, a new home, and a new calling in life. It offers them meaning in the stories of their lives by linking these to God's redemptive history and to the cosmic triumph and reign of God over all creation. Their lives are now intertwined with sacred history. They are valued by God. This, indeed, is good news. Public testimonies of God's work in the lives of his people encourage them, and remind them that they are under his care.

NEW MEANING IN DEATH

Just as Christians gain a new and greater appreciation for life based on an understanding of Scripture, so they also gain new perspectives on death. Christians should encourage people to see a new meaning in death as their loved ones meet Christ and fulfill their salvation. Death for believers is not final. It is a transformation from life in the fallen world into the perfect world of eternity.

This central message of Christ's victory over death, and the hope of eternal life with him must be a central message in Christian funerals. Death surfaces deep human anxieties and longings that are buried under the flood of daily activities of life, and, therefore, is a critical time for ministering to people who are now open to hear the gospel. This is a time when young Christians must be instructed in the foundations of their faith, and sustained as they bear the staggering weight of grief and loss. As Zahniser notes,

> [Funerals] help the shock of bereavement contribute to a deepening of faith and trust in God. In times of death, sorrow may become unbearable and the foundations of life shake and crumble; believers must negotiate the rough currents of bafflement and pain that wash away the signposts of meaning that once seemed immovable. Funerals make death tangible and real. They give closure to the event. They enable the bereaved to own their pain and accept the inevitability of death (1997, 99).

Death is a time to remind believers that God is no stranger to pain and death, and that he defeated its power and sting (1 Cor. 15:20–57).

Funerals are also public testimonies to the message of the gospel. In most societies, they are public events seen by insiders and outsiders alike. In traditional societies, Christian funerals have often been powerful testimonies to the great hope Christians have, a hope often lacking in traditional religions. The triumphant expectations surrounding the deaths of Christians and missionaries have opened the doors of evangelism to many people.

The triumph of Christ over death can also be proclaimed through telling the stories of saints and martyrs who have gone before. They are models of the victory of Christian faith over death. They are in that great cloud of witnesses in heaven encouraging believers facing death.

A THEOLOGY OF ANCESTORS

A theology of death must deal with the question of ancestors. In much of the world this is one of the central questions facing new believers, and holding people back from faith. The question is not a new one. In the sixteenth century, Jesuit missionaries in China led by Mateo

Ricci decided that burning incense and bowing at the funeral showed community respect, not worship of the dead. The Dominicans under Jean-Baptist Morales objected, claiming that these practices were indeed worship. In 1645 Pope Innocent X condemned ancestral rites and forbade their use. The Jesuits, under Martin, sent letters to convince the pope of the rightness of their evaluation, and in 1656 Alexander VII reversed the earlier decree and approved the rites. The Dominicans petitioned and in 1669 Clement IX said the rites had to be judged in each cultural setting.

Protestant missionaries have experienced the same disagreements. How should beliefs and practices associated with ancestor veneration be handled? This question has two parts: (1) how should Christians relate to their biological ancestors—those who gave them physical and cultural life? (2) and how should they deal with their spiritual ancestors—those who passed the faith on to them? Before answering these questions, the church needs a biblical theology of the dead and the unborn, and of the difference between respect, which the Bible enjoins people to do, and worship, which it forbids.

BIOLOGICAL ANCESTORS

Is the linkage of parents to children biological, psychological, social, or theological? What does Scripture mean when it says that in Adam all died, and in Christ believers are made alive? It is clear that the tie between parents and children is much more than biological. In the Old Testament, for example, the sins of Achan led to the slaughter of his children. On the other hand, the blessings of godly parents are passed on to "a thousand generations." This may help Christians understand how Christ could bring salvation to humans by becoming part of the one bloodline that connects them all.

The family has a central place in God's intentions for human societies, and Christians must affirm family ties. The church needs to develop beliefs and rituals that strengthen families against the onslaught of individualism. Children should be taught to honor their parents and elders. Because of a fear of ancestor worship, missionaries often overreact, and are seen by the people as breaking family responsibilities and respect.

The question remains, what should Christians do about their biological and cultural ancestors? Asian theologians have wrestled with a Christian response (Ro 1985), and many have concluded that practices such as burning spirit money, offering incense, holding joss sticks, and bowing before the deceased are unscriptural and should be discarded. On the other hand, they stress that Christians should look for ways to express their love and respect for their parents and their family. They should attend the funerals of non-Christian relatives, talk about the deceased, listen to family members, and help in the arrangements, as conscience allows. Some East Asian churches conduct Christian memorial services on the anniversaries of the death of a relative (Lim 1984). The focus is on the worship of God, and thanking God for the life of the ancestor, particularly if he or she was a Christian. Some use flowers instead of sacrifices and incense, and give memorial gifts to Christian ministries instead of burning paper for the ancestor. Above all, Asian churches should openly discuss how they can model Christian family loyalties and love to non-Christians without compromising their understanding of Scripture.

African theologians face another set of questions. There the deceased are not deified, nor do they leave earth and go to some other-worldly abode. Rather, they remain as living members of the community, and must be invited to participate in its ritual activities. Libations are poured onto the ground to invite them to join the living in the activity, the ancestors are informed of the proceedings in a welcome address, and prayers are offered to the gods requesting their blessing. Kwame Bediako points out that in these rites there is that which is idolatrous, and that which can be reinterpreted in communicating the Christian gospel (1995). African churches and theologians need to develop a clear theology of ancestors which affirms the importance in the family, but heeds the biblical injunctions against worshiping or consulting the dead (Deut. 18:11; Isa. 8:19). Christians have the Holy Spirit to guide them, so they no longer need to turn to ancestors for guidance and protection.

A theology of ancestors must also be rooted in a theology of how God is at work in making his message known to the people before the coming of the missionaries. There are many stories of people who have had visions or dreams of someone bringing them God's word, and who have been the first to convert when the missionary arrived.

Veneration of ancestors also raises the question in the minds of those wanting to turn to Christ—what happens to their ancestors who died before Christ was made known to them? Rather than a harsh condemnation of the dead, proclaimers of the gospel should take a pastoral approach by encouraging the living to follow Christ, and to commit their ancestors to God knowing that his judgments are totally loving and just. Seekers can also be encouraged by pointing out that had their ancestors known, they would have encouraged their children to follow Christ.

SPIRITUAL ANCESTORS

The Scriptures speak of spiritual ancestors (Heb. 12:1), and the communion of the saints. Too often Westerners stress biological or cultural genealogies, and forget that great cloud of witnesses whose faithful witness down through the centuries made it possible for people to hear the gospel. Seeking to avoid saint worship, Protestants have often failed to look to the heroes of faith as examples for their own lives and as encouragements to pass faith on to their children. Furthermore, following the lead of more egalitarian societies, the church can be seen as made up of saints who have gone before, the living and the unborn. This is a particularly powerful message of hope in many parts of the world.

The question of spiritual ancestors raises a difficult question in some parts of the world. Some African theologians argue that Christ can be portrayed as an ancestor, or a departed elder, because he stands as the intermediary between God and humanity. In their societies, people never go for help to elders with whom they have no blood relationship, and many see Jesus as the intermediary for the Jews or for the whites. They say that Christ must also be presented as the people's ancestor—as the most senior of the departed elders, the apex of the pyramid of all intermediaries, above whom there is only God. Christ is seen then as the universal ancestor. His blood makes all persons blood relatives, and he must be seen as a 'brother' ancestor (Moyo 1996, 43). Other African theologians argue that because ancestors are only humans, Christians cannot speak of Christ as First Ancestor (Bediako 1995, 216–23). Here again, careful reflection is needed to develop a solid, biblically based theology of spiritual ancestors. These issues will surface throughout the remainder of the book. In Chapter 14 some approaches are discussed that allow proclaimers of the gospel to work with local Christians and churches as, together, they seek a relevant theology for their particular contexts.

6

HUMAN WELL-BEING
AND MISFORTUNE

We turn now to the second central question folk religions seek to answer. How can people get a good life, and how should they deal with the misfortunes that threaten their well-being? On the level of folk religion, the central concern is for well-being on earth, not eternal life in heaven, and many beliefs and activities are designed to gain blessings here and now.

All people seek a good life, even though they define this differently. Some want health and wealth, others status and honor, others many children and grandchildren to care for them when they are old, and others God's approval and eternal life. Yet, hard as people work to gain a good life, their best efforts do not guarantee success. In everyday life, they face diseases, physical ailments, loneliness, business failures, money problems, anxieties in gambling, losses in real estate investments, a husband's debauchery, divorce, wayward children, exams, decisions to move the grave of an ancestor, and other calamities—seen and unforeseen—which threaten to destroy their efforts. How can they assure themselves of prosperity, and safeguard themselves against such misfortunes?

EXPLANATION SYSTEMS

When striving for a good life, and when misfortunes occur, most people do not stand by in despair and do nothing. They strive to ensure success and overcome crises. The first step is to find the right belief system to explain the situation. Most cultures have a 'toolbox' of different belief systems that they use to explain what is going on. In the West people believe hard work and careful planning leads to prosperity. They attribute mental depression to biological causes and use medication to control it, decide it is a psychological problem and go to a psychologist,

133

or see it as a spiritual problem and turn to a pastor for help. In Osaka, Japan, people go to the Ishikiri Shrine for healing, the Hozan-ji Shrine for business success, the Ikoma Waterfalls for power and purity, and the figures of the Buddha for help in this life.

The selection of an explanation system is both a personal and a community decision. A wife suffering from an illness blames the second wife of putting a curse on her. The second wife denies this, and blames the first wife for angering the ancestors by not feeding them each evening. Their husband sides with his first wife, and blames the second for putting secret medicines in her food. Other families in the community gossip that this family is plagued by a cantankerous spirit that needs to be exorcised. Experts are called in to help clarify the cause. The final diagnosis is based only in part on what really happened, because this is not always clear. It is also based on the social politics in the family and community. Well-being and misfortunes are not private, personal affairs. They are public social events that must be dealt with by the community.

What explanation systems do people use in seeking good fortune and avoiding disasters? For analytical purposes we will look at ways people seek to ensure a good life, and then at ways they try to avoid misfortune. The two, however, are closely tied. Spirit possession, magic, and medicines are seen, at times, as beneficial, and, at times, as harmful. The same is true of witchcraft, which is used to produce rains and give success in battle, or to harm a rival.

GENERATING FORTUNE

People use many means to generate well-being. They know that they must carefully plant and weed crops, hunt game, and work, but they also know that these efforts do not guarantee success. Factors such as droughts, plagues, fires, and sudden deaths undermine their best human efforts. They need to guard against these unknown and unforeseen events, so they supplicate gods, spirits, and ancestors to get their blessings, and manipulate supernatural powers to gain protection and prosperity. A few ways people use to assure their well-being are examined here.

BLESSINGS AND OATHS

Beliefs in the power of blessings to bring good fortune and curses to cause misfortune are worldwide. Blessings are a felt need in the daily lives of common folk throughout the Middle East and Africa. They are conferred on a family when a son is born, when circumcision is practiced, and when a marriage is arranged. Buddhist monks in Thailand bless a new house to drive away evil spirits and bring prosperity. In traditional religion in Korea *(moo-kyo)*, people seek the 'three blessings' of long life, possession of wealth, and peace and harmony in the family.

Closely associated with blessings are curses. These are imprecations calling evil upon offenders and enemies to prevent them from harming those pronouncing the curses. The Lugbara of East Africa differentiate between bad deeds, which are dealt with by humans, and sin, which is punished by God and the ancestors. The latter include quarreling with or harming one's senior kinsmen, committing adultery with close kinswomen, or feuding. These incur the wrath of God, who sends his curse *(nyoka)* on the offenders and cuts them off from the people (Taylor 1963, 172). Because *nyoka* is God's word, it is forever. The world of Filipinos pivots on the concepts of *gaba* (the curse of the gods) and *panalagin* (their blessing). Curses are earned whenever a person violates the laws of the gods, such as showing disrespect for one's parents, acting cruelly to a buffalo, or wasting rice.

Blessing and cursing are attributes of authority. A father, mother, mother's brother, village head, and king can bless or curse. Generally speaking, a son cannot curse his father, nor a subject his ruler, for it would not work if he tried. Particularly powerful are the curses of parents and of husbands. Edward Westermarck cites a Moorish proverb, "the woman who is cursed by her husband is like her who is cursed by her father" (1926, 61). Similarly the blessing or curse of a holy man has great power. The curses of women who are unclean are thought to be particularly dangerous, and should be avoided. Hence men avoid menstruating women, stay away from anything having to do with childbirth, and remain remote from female influence.

Oaths are conditional curses directed toward oneself. They are generally taken to prove one's own innocence against accusations. In them appeals are made to spiritual beings or powers to act if the person is, in fact, guilty. Muslims swear by anything that has *baraka*, such as Allah, the Quran, a saint, or an angel. The Jews swore by God's throne, heaven, earth, or one's head (Matt. 5:34–36). Oaths are also taken to declare loyalties. The Mau Mau fighters in Kenya took oaths of secrecy to protect their members, and oath-taking ceremonies were held during the first elections in Kenya (Van Rheenen 1991, 227). In most societies blessings, curses, and oaths are not seen as mere expressions of good will or anger, but as words having power inherent in them to bring about their fulfillment.

Blessings and curses are important in the Bible, but were seen in a very different light. In the Old Testament blessings were attributed ultimately to God, not to the power of a magical formula. Moreover, God's blessing was seen as the source of all good things. It created order in which human affairs prospered. The fertility of women, livestock, and fields was promised to those who kept God's covenant and observed his precepts (Deut. 28:1–14). When God's blessing was withdrawn and his curse unleashed there was barrenness, pestilence, and confusion (Deut 28:15–24). Blessings and curses were based on the covenant relationship God had with his people: blessings were given for faithfulness, and curses for unfaithfulness. People prospered when they lived in conformity to the holiness of God, and perished when they deviated from it.

BARAKA

One belief in supernatural blessing is *baraka,* which is found in Muslim societies. *Baraka* is the presence of divine favor. It is a mysterious and wonderful power, a blessing from God granted to certain people, places, and things that endows them with grace, divine blessing and mercy, power for leadership, and protection. Orthodox beliefs attribute *baraka* directly to Allah, and deny that it can be transferred to others. Folk Muslims, on the other hand, see it as a magical power that can be created by ritual and manipulated for human benefit. It is found in mountains, seas, sun, moon, stars, animals (particularly horses), certain plants, and magical squares. It is associated with brides and bridegrooms, mothers of twins and triplets, and children in general. It is sensitive to pollution and destruction by uncleanness caused by breaking religious laws. It can be transmitted. Anything that touches something with *baraka* may get *baraka.* Heirlooms and treasures transmit good fortune, and when these change hands, so does the good luck they bring. *Baraka* is also used to explain a marvelously good fortune. It is self-validating in the minds of the people, for when it works it attracts followers and earns more success.

Baraka is strong in two groups of people. The first are descendants of the Prophet Muhammad. Muhammad himself is widely believed to have had *baraka.* This enabled him to perform miracles. The second group is "saints," or holy men, who acquire it by withdrawing from the world and gaining reputations for piety and learning. These saints use their power for curing and blessing. Their power remains around their tombs, where their followers gather annually to commemorate their deaths and to partake in their power. The veneration of saints spread rapidly across North Africa and India in the fifteenth century, and was a major factor in the spread of Islam in these areas. Muslim ascetics or *marabouts* settled near villages, and become known as miracle workers. Their whitewashed tombs became sacred shrines for their followers.

In the New Testament, too, God was the source of blessing (Matt. 25:34; Acts 3:25–26; Heb. 6:7–8, 12–15; 1 Peter 3:9). Paul reminded his readers, however, that blessings were not ends in themselves, but means to holy and blameless lives—lives without shame or blame in the community (Eph. 1:3–4). He also noted that Christ was the one who bore the curse of sin that was upon us (Gal. 3:8–9). The New Testament instructs us not to take oaths, because everything comes from God and because Christians should speak the truth without invoking oaths (Matt. 5:33–37; James 5:12).

MERIT

Another set of religious beliefs associated with the improvement of present and future well-being is that of 'merit' and 'merit making.' These concepts are found in most Asian religions, particularly folk Hinduism and folk Buddhism.

Central to the Hindu worldview is the idea of *karma*, the mysterious moral law or energy that rules the universe. It judges the accumulated merits and demerits of a person's previous lives, and determines his or her present and future lives. The consequences of one's past cannot be changed by the gods or by repentance, but people can do meritorious deeds to improve their future lives, such as building a temple and donating the idol, giving alms to religious mendicants, meditating, and living moral lives.

The notion of merit (*punya* or *kusala*) and merit making is a fundamental belief of Buddhists everywhere. It finds its fullest expression in folk Buddhism. A person's present wealth, physical beauty, and social prestige are seen as rewards for past meritorious actions, and suffering, poverty, ugliness, and lack of prestige are due to past demerits (*akusala*). Good deeds include giving gifts, living moral lives, meditating, and showing respect to elders. The merit of a gift depends on what is given, how it is given (with respect and good intention), and to whom it is given. Making regular offerings of food and robes to the monks, building a monastery, or having a son join the monastic order are of particular merit. Merit can also be given to others to earn their well-being or to pay off their demerits. A housewife who gives food to a monk earns merit not only for herself, but also for her family. Children can transfer merit to their deceased kinsmen to improve their conditions where they are now, and to offer them food and clothing so that they will not suffer.

In the Middle Ages beliefs in merit played an increasingly significant role in Western Christianity, until the Reformation debate arose over the relationship among works, faith, and salvation. The Reformers reasserted the primacy of grace and rejected all reliance on any kind of merit.

MAGIC

As noted in Chapter 3, magic is the use of supernatural forces to control events in life. Normally, Christians think of magic as bad because

South Indian Mantras

Om, oh birth-less Garavara, having seen me, let all evil spirits and planetary forces be deflected. Em ksham, shaum, svaha.

[to ward off the effects of poison after a snake has bitten a person]

it is condemned in Scripture. Most people see it as a good and useful means to accomplish their desires. Like common experiential knowledge, magic is thought to have practical, utilitarian value relating to the problems of everyday life. It frequently fills in where technical knowledge fails. Bronislaw Malinowski (1954) observes that the Trobriand Islanders off the northeast coast of New Guinea work their gardens, prepare for war, and initiate trading expeditions, but they also constantly use charms and spells to increase the effectiveness of their pursuit and protect themselves from potential dangers. They know that their best human efforts often fail because of events beyond their control—droughts, insects, plagues, surprise attacks, and other unforeseen occurrences. They use magic to control these events, which their folk science could not control. Similarly, in the West, people faced with diseases that cannot be cured by doctors and medicines often turn to magical cures. Most magic is associated with the desire for well-being, and offers hope to people when situations are beyond their immediate control.

In South Indian villages, there are several types of magic. *Mantras*, or sacred chants believed to have magical and spiritual efficacy, are used to ward off dangers and to cure those who are afflicted. There are *mantras* to cure most physical diseases, barrenness, and snake bites, and to protect people from accidents, fires, and other dangers. There are *mantras* that generate power which the performer can use to produce good crops, or to harm or kill an enemy. *Mantras* control spiritual forces that permeate the world. Many consist of a command reinforced with powerful sounds *Om, kshaum, hreem,* and *svaha* have no meaning in themselves as words, but are sounds that empower the command and make it work. The most powerful of all sounds is *om,* which is the condensation of all that has ever been said and will ever be said. The universe is the unpacking of this sound.

A second type of magic is *yantras* or powerful symbols (Figure 6.1), which utilize powerful visual symbols. These may be written on paper and tied to the body, inscribed on copper and encased in silver amulets, or penned on paper and boiled in water which is then drunk. Like *mantras*, they are used to heal sickness, cure snake bites, exorcise spirits, heal scorpion stings, guard against the evil eye, induce easy birth, produce virility in men and pregnancy in women, cure aches, and drive off body pain. Some induce passionate love, and others bring plagues on wayward husbands. Still others guard the wearer against all dangers in general.

Most magic practiced by a community is performed for the common good. There is magic to bring about rain, victory in battle, and success in group ventures. Individuals, too, use magic to be successful in farming, to pass business or school examinations, to win football games, and to build houses that assure strong, prosperous families. As we will see later, magic can also be used to harm or destroy others. Magic in this form is usually personal and private. The contrast of good or evil usage is, of course, culturally defined and depends on the perspective of the definer. Those against whom destructive magic is used would not consider it good.

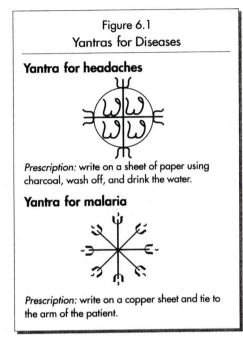

Figure 6.1
Yantras for Diseases

Yantra for headaches

Prescription: write on a sheet of paper using charcoal, wash off, and drink the water.

Yantra for malaria

Prescription: write on a copper sheet and tie to the arm of the patient.

OTHER POWERS

There are many other types of power that people use to gain good fortune. Two of them are examined here.

GEOMANCY

Qi is a force in the Chinese philosophy of space known as geomancy or *feng shui*. It is the life-giving cosmic breath often associated with dragons that live in the natural landscape. Many folk Chinese believe that all persons are linked to nature, and that their well-being depends on their living in harmony with it. Misfortune is attributed to the lack of a happy alignment with the surrounding terrain. To determine the best location for houses, temples, and graves, the people use diviners who discern the influence of rivers, lakes, mountains, and airs, and advise people where to arrange their homes and graves to gain the best results. There are no moral implications in the practice of *feng shui*.

A contemporary example is the practice of *feng shui* in Hong Kong. There, banks that have a view of the harbor are thought to guard their wealth because the harbor represents a larger purse. The headquarters of the Hongkong Bank is said to have fabulous *feng shui*. The tower of its rival, the Bank of China, has little of it. "Its two spires jut up brashly over the skyline, [the *feng shui* men feel] like fingers mocking the gods; the triangular patterning of its walls ensure fierce internal conflict; and . . . the people at the top of the Bank of China building may be powerful, but they are lonely and have bad digestion" (Economist 1995, 91). In an office, a bright and open environment prevents bad *qi* from festering in dark quarters.

LUCK

There is widespread belief in luck or good fortune. Some people are born with it. Others acquire it through fortuitous actions. It may be found in certain objects, such as strange-shaped rocks and bright feathers, which bring good fortune to their owners. It can be lost if people are not careful. Belief in luck is widespread in Chinese communities. Certain days and months are auspicious. Others are dangerous. References to death are certain to bring bad luck.

Many baseball players believe in luck, and to obtain it keep good luck fetishes, such as old baseball hides, old bats, coins, crucifixes, and bobby pins—ordinary objects that have acquired power by connection to an exceptionally hot batting or pitching streak. A player in a slump may find an odd stone just before beginning a hitting streak, and attribute his improved performance to the influence of the new object. Other players associate luck with certain rituals. "After hitting two home runs in a game, infielder Jim Davenport of the San Francisco Giants discovered that he had missed a buttonhole while dressing for the game. For the remainder of his career he left the same button undone" (Gmelch 1989, 299). George Gmelch notes,

> On each pitching day for the first three months of a winning season, Dennis Grossini, a pitcher on a Detroit Tiger farm team, arose from bed at exactly 10 A.M. At 1 P.M. he went to the nearest restaurant for two glasses of iced tea and a tuna fish sandwich. Although the afternoon was free, he changed into the sweat shirt and supporter he wore during his last winning game, and one hour before the game he chewed a wad of Beech-Nut chewing tobacco. During the game he touched his letters (the team name on his uniform) after each pitch and straightened his cap after each ball. Before the start of each inning he replaced the pitcher's rosin bag next to the spot where it was the inning before. And after every inning in which he gave up a run he would wash his hands (1989, 295).

Belief in luck is commonly found where people face uncertainty and risk. Gamblers often refer to it. During World War II, American soldiers used good luck charms (crosses, Bibles, rabbits' feet, medals) to protect themselves, and carried out fixed "rituals" much as ballplayers preparing for a game. All these are attempts to explain and control one's fortune.

DEALING WITH MISFORTUNE

All humans have explanation systems which they use to gain good fortune. Many of these are also used to explain and deal with the calamities of life. These explanations of adversity are based either on the organic or mechanical metaphors laid out in the analytical model, but most involve the following process:

	CHOOSE A BELIEF	DIAGNOSE THE	SELECT A
ADVERSITY→	SYSTEM TO →	CAUSE USING→	REMEDY AND
	EXPLAIN IT	THIS SYSTEM	APPLY IT

Most folk religious practices dealing with misfortunes can be understood in the light of this formula.

TYPES OF ADVERSITY

All people face crises in their lives on earth, but what is defined as a crisis varies considerably from culture to culture. There are, however, many common themes.

UNTIMELY BIRTHS AND DEATHS

Many misfortunes have to do with abnormal events. People widely believe that there is a 'normal' state of the world which is taken for granted, and which is not questioned. Still births, drownings, death before marriage, and other experiences are widely feared.

Having twins is unusual and must be explained. The normal human birth is one child at a time. Two people should not be exactly the same. Two is also viewed as an overabundance of fertility, and it is difficult for a mother to breast feed both at the same time, so one or both lack adequate nourishment. Moreover, twins confuse the classification of elder and younger siblings, because two people are trying to occupy the same position (see Jacob and Esau, Gen. 25:23–26). To resolve this dilemma of too many, the Bushmen of the Kalahari Desert used to put one or both of the twins to death, because two were believed to bring misfortune. Twins born in the royal family of the Ashanti were killed because there could only be one heir to sit on the Golden Stool, the supreme insignia of royalty (Rattray 1923, 66–73). Among the Nyakyusa, not only are twins dangerous, so are their parents and siblings. Monica Wilson writes (1957, 152),

The parents of twins and twins themselves are *abipasya*, the fearful ones, felt to be very dangerous to their relatives and immediate neighbors, and to cattle, causing them to suffer from diarrhoea or purging, and swollen legs, if any contact takes place. Therefore, the parents are segregated and an elaborate ritual is performed.

In some societies twins are seen as sacred. The families of common-ers among the Ashanti of Ghana gave twins special roles in society if they were the same sex. Girls became potential wives to the chief, and boys his elephant-tale switchers at the court. Among the Nuer of the Sudan, twins were symbolically identified with birds (because birds have several eggs), and called "people of the above." The Ndembu of Kenya build twinship shrines in front of the family's house. In other so-cieties, twins are encouraged to become shamans. If the twins are male and female, they are often thought to have lived together in the womb, and so must be married in life.

Untimely and unusual deaths are also seen as tragic. A mother who dies with her infant in childbirth, a woman who dies without children, or a man who dies unmarried is calamitous in any society. In many so-cieties, the people fear that the spirits of the deceased will remain in the community, plaguing the living out of jealousy—the mother harming women who deliver healthy children, the barren woman pestering preg-nant women, and the unmarried man bothering young grooms. Societ-ies have ways to prevent this. In South India, among some castes a young man who dies before marriage is wedded to a banana tree, a sym-bol of fertility, before his funeral is conducted.

Deaths that occur during hunting, fishing, or battles are also disas-trous, particularly if the bodies cannot be recovered and given a proper burial, or if they are taken and eaten by the enemy or wild animals. In some societies all human deaths are blamed on enemies, who are thought to use sorcery, magic, spirits, and curses.[1] Family members must gather and store the bones of the deceased, and at an appropriate time, often years later, they grind and eat the bones to inspire and em-power them when they attack the enemy camp to take revenge. Suicides are particularly calamitous, because they are seen as attacks against the family and community. Frequently those who commit suicide are denied normal burial ceremonies, and are buried away from the community.

Finally, deaths caused by supernatural means, such as witchcraft, curses, broken taboos, angry ancestors, and the like, are particularly tragic because they are intentionally caused by others and because they cannot be cured by medicines.[2]

1. For an excellent description of this worldview, see Mark Ritchie, *The Spirit of the Rainforest.*
2. Thanatomania is the modern medical term used to describe those who die not from any organic disease but from mental trauma. There are clinically documented cases where no modern medical treatment was effective.

NATURAL CALAMITIES

Natural calamities, threaten the prosperous life. Earthquakes, droughts, famines, floods, fires, typhoons, and lightning can undo in a moment a community's efforts to create a good life for all. Frequently, these disasters evoke elaborate rituals designed to end their devastation and protect the people from their harm.

Figure 6.2
Diseases in an Indian Village

- hot diseases (fevers)
- boils and cuts
- bad tempers
- bad luck
- robbed repeatedly
- spirit possession

- cold diseases (chills)
- mental diseases
- quarrelsome families
- frequent accidents
- going broke
- aches and pains

DISEASES

People in all societies face disease. Each society defines symptoms and causes in different ways, and prescribes suitable treatments. Westerners think of cholera, diphtheria, malaria, and dysentery, and blame them on microorganisms. Traditional South Indian villagers speak of 'hot' and 'cold' diseases (Figure 6.2). Hot diseases produce high fevers, and are caused by experiencing too much hot in life—eating too many hot foods (hot spices, meat, eggs, alcohol, tea, unrefined sugar, heavy cereals, foreign foods such as ice cream—generally cheaper foods), having too many hot relationships (quarrels, squandering one's semen particularly in extramarital affairs, high-stress jobs), and doing hot activities (hard labor that causes sweating, hyperactivity). To cure hot diseases, the patient must eat cool foods, maintain cool relationships, and rest.

Cold diseases, which are caused by too much cold food (dairy products, wheat flour, sugar, some fruits—generally more expensive foods that only wealthier high-caste people can afford to eat regularly), cold relationships (store one's semen), and inactivity, must be cured by adding heat to the patient's life. Bad tempers, too, are a plague. A gathering may be peaceful, but when such people arrive, the disease soon spreads to the whole group.

FAILURES

Failures, are a threat to the good life. People work hard on their crops, but the fields are barren. Businessmen know, that despite their best efforts, many things can go wrong, so they perform rites to avoid failure. Young men and women need help in wooing their beloved, and want to avoid rejection, so they slip love potions into their beloved's food, or use love magic to cause those persons to love them. Gamblers try many means, such as gambling magic or astrology charts, to beat the odds and win. Students turn to charms to 'beat the jinx' and be successful in their exams.

WARS AND RAIDS

Life in many societies is plagued by endless raids and battles with enemy peoples. The quietness of cultivating the crops can be broken in an instant when warriors waylay an unsuspecting community. Magic, amulets, spirits, and medicines are needed by those who attack to prevent their attack from being discovered, and to protect them in battle, and by those attacked, to thwart the attack and save themselves.

SAMO MEN PROTECT WOMEN

Preparing gardens involves the entire community. Women clear the dense under-growth while men cut out the small trees. When cleared the site resembles a neatly kept park under the canopy of tall trees. New Plantain or pitpit shoots are brought to the garden and stacked for planting. Prior to planting, however, men must perform the appropriate rituals in order to protect the plants as well as encourage growth and an abundant harvest.

Using digging sticks women make the proper-sized hole and plant the shoots five to six feet apart throughout the cleared area. Watching over all this, men take turns guarding the periphery of the site with their every-present weapons [confirming the Samo aphorism, 'men protect while women produce']. . . . This protective activity allows men to gather an assortment of lizards, snakes, frogs, an occasional marsupial, and all kinds of birds and rodents . . . which contribute to the common evening meal. (Shaw 1996, 81–82)

DIAGNOSING A CAUSE AND SELECTING THE REMEDY

Once a misfortune has been noted, a belief system is chosen to explain the misfortune and select a remedy. People often turn first to simple, immediate explanations and home remedies. If these do not work, they turn to technical experts in the field—to diviners, shamans, witch doctors, herbalists, doctors, psychiatrists, or priests. It is helpful to use the analytical grid outlined earlier to examine some of the causes and corresponding remedies common in folk religion, looking first at those that use organic analogies.

ORGANIC EXPLANATIONS
AND REMEDIES FOR MISFORTUNE

Evil in all its forms—illness, calamity, drought, accident, and so on— is often thought to be caused by deities, ancestors, spirits, or other humans, rather than by impersonal forces, natural causes, or chance. In this view, ritual words and actions are believed to have power to alter the power different beings have on individuals and society. Misfortunes are blamed on broken relationships, and there are many relationships that can go wrong in a folk

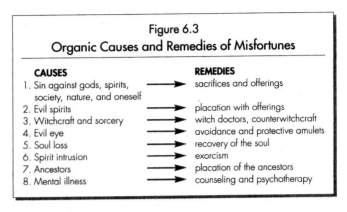

Figure 6.3
Organic Causes and Remedies of Misfortunes

CAUSES		REMEDIES
1. Sin against gods, spirits, society, nature, and oneself	→	sacrifices and offerings
2. Evil spirits	→	placation with offerings
3. Witchcraft and sorcery	→	witch doctors, counterwitchcraft
4. Evil eye	→	avoidance and protective amulets
5. Soul loss	→	recovery of the soul
6. Spirit intrusion	→	exorcism
7. Ancestors	→	placation of the ancestors
8. Mental illness	→	counseling and psychotherapy

worldview (Figure 6.3). It is important to understand these systems as serious beliefs on the part of the people before biblical answers can be given to human misfortunes. Here we examine some of the misfortunes attributed to organic causes.

SIN AND RECONCILIATION

Misfortunes are often attributed to sin. At root, sin is a violation of a relationship between an individual or community and the gods, ancestors, spirits, humans, animals and plants, or the earth. Sin may be individual. A person may offend the gods or other beings and suffer the consequences and experience a sense of personal guilt. Sin may also be corporate. The community may forget to offer sacrifices to the gods, may neglect to placate local spirits with food and drink, or offend the ancestors by abandoning the traditional ways they have handed down. The group as a whole then suffers the consequences and experiences a sense of shame. The sufferings and misfortunes caused by gods and ancestors are not evil. They are punishments aimed at correcting immoral behavior or at restoring a balance disrupted by sin. The offenders must repent and perform the rites necessary to assuage the anger of those offended, and thereby restore normal relationships.

The remedy for violated relationships is reconciliation, the restoration of balance or culturally defined relationship with those who have been sinned against. Reconciliation is commonly associated with terms such as 'redemption,' 'atonement,' 'expiation,' and 'propitiation.' (The concepts of sin and reconciliation will be examined in more detail in Chapter 8.)

SPIRIT ATTACK

Many people see the world as a hostile and dangerous place, full of malevolent spirits and forces that are aggressively hostile to humans.

Seemingly innocuous objects and activities carry the potential for injury, illness, and death. Even mundane activities, such as gardening, fishing, hunting, and eating, are enveloped with taboos and circumscribed with rituals to prevent dangers that threaten from all sides. Children playing with dragonflies and butterflies may provoke an attack by a Thunder Spirit who strikes with wind, torrential rain, and floods. For example, the Semai of Malaysia believe in *mara*, spirits that eat humans.

> They may attack directly, like the forest spirits that shoot with their blowpipes, like the ground spirit that twists and shrivels limbs, or like the wind spirit that accompanies thunder to blow down houses and crush people with falling trees. Assuming material form, it may be the tiger crouching in ambush along a forest trail, or the attack may be more insidious, like the waterfall spirit that causes tuberculosis by placing some object in the body of a person whose "soul" it wants to marry, causing the victim to waste away and die. Whatever their modality, *mara* are omnipresent and unequivocally malevolent, preying on human beings because it is their very nature to do so. One must be constantly alert and cautious to avoid any action that would precipitate the danger that always lurks without (Robarchek 1989, 912).

The Dinka of southern Sudan believe that sky divinities possess people, causing illness. The possessed runs around violently, falls on the ground, leaps with bursts of frenzied movements, and sings unintelligible songs. A priest addresses the victim, trying to learn the spirit's name so he can placate it and cause it to leave.

People try in many ways to protect themselves from spirit attacks. They wear talismans around their necks, burn incense to fumigate the patient, or drink special medicines. They paint signs on walls, and erect stones on roads leading into villages as spirit repellents. In South India women draw *muggus*—designs using unending white lines made of rice flour—in front of doorways to prevent spirits from entering and attacking people. Evil spirits are believed to be fascinated by white lines—wanting to see where they lead. Seeing a *muggu* they run along the lines all day, and do not enter the house. Gypsy women in the same region wear mirrors sewn into their clothes, convinced that evil spirits will see themselves in the mirrors and frighten themselves off.

In parts of China, people believe that spirits like to go in straight lines, so the people build curves into their bridges so that the spirits will fall off into the river. For the same reason, people do not build houses where the front door faces an oncoming street, lest evil spirits coming down the street enter the house.

Most cultures have rituals of exorcism to free people believed to be attacked and possessed by spirits. These rites are normally performed by shamans who are the masters of the spirit world. The exorcist drives out evil spirits by reciting magical spells, praying, and entreating or commanding them to leave; using sweat-baths, cathartics, or emetics to flush them out of the body; singing songs to lure them away; tempting them to evacuate the body by laying out a sumptuous meal for them; or beating or building a fire under the patient; or placing foul-smelling, overripe fruit nearby so that the spirits will want to leave.

DIAGNOSING THE CAUSE OF AN ILLNESS

Magara, a young woman in the highlands of Papua New Guinea, became ill a few weeks into her pregnancy. At first her husband and relatives used ordinary folk remedies to try to cure her. A command that the illness depart was blown into sweet-smelling leaves, and she ate them. Her body was rubbed with stinging nettles and mud so that her pains would leave when the welts subsided and the mud dried. But Magara did not get well. Ombo began to speculate that the illness was due to a powerful new charm he had acquired from Europeans and hidden in the bed, so he removed it, but there was no improvement.

Next Ombo destroyed his spirit house because he had not been diligent in feeding the *nokondisi* that lived there. His father suggested that the angry spirit was taking revenge on Magara. By destroying the house, the spirit had to retreat to the forest where it could do no harm.

When Magara did not get well, Ombo's older brother speculated that a malevolent ghost might be behind the illness. Fumai then recounted a dream he had had the night before in which the ghost of Ombo's great-grandmother was sitting in the forest near memorials raised for the ancestors. She covered herself with ashes and wailed loudly because no one had killed a pig in her honor at the last ancestral rites. The next day, Ombo killed a pig, and offered sweet potatoes and taro where the ghost had been "seen." Magara improved and was able to return to her work in her garden.

A month later Magara became ill again. Ombo was now convinced his wife was being attacked by a sorcerer. He called a magical specialist who tried to pull the pain from her body and cast it onto the ground. The specialist then announced his conclusions—illness by black magic. To counter it, the specialist had Ombo prepare a bundle containing pork and plants with magical properties, which he hung in the rafters of the house. The specialist locked Ombo and Magara inside the house, and walked round and round the house reciting spells and whirling a special plant around his head. With a great struggle he was pulling an unknown object away from the unknown sorcerer. He instructed Magara to open the bundle. Inside with the meat were a spider and a piece of string. The specialist said the spider was his assistant who had taken the string from the sorcerer's house. The sorcerer was thought to be an angry suitor who had cut a bit of Magara's necklace string to use as sorcery when she married Ombo. The community considered her cured. When her child was born prematurely, and died two days later, no one saw any connection between this death and her illness.

(Adapted from Philip L. Newman, "Sorcery, Religion and Man," With permission from *Natural History Magazine* [February 1962]. Copyright the American Museum of Natural History [1962].)

WITCHCRAFT AND SORCERY

Belief in witchcraft is almost universal in human societies.[3] In most societies it is seen as doing both good and evil. In public rites, it is used to make rain, ripen the harvest, procure peace, protect family members from attack, and ensure victory in battle. For example, in Tanzania the Nyakyusa believe that the hidden personal power called *itonga* can be used to protect members of the community from external attack, and to punish those who do not cooperate (Eliade 1976, 59–60). Among the Azande of Sudan, witchcraft is involved in every activity, including agriculture, fishing, hunting, domestic life, and living in community (Evans-Pritchard 1937). In medieval Europe some witches were thought to descend into hell to fight evil spirits and bring back to earth the goods stolen by evil sorcerers, namely, cattle, wheat, and other fruits of the earth. If they did not act, the crops failed.[4] Spectacular successes are often attributed to such power.

In private, witches prey on others, sucking the victims' blood or eating their livers, hearts, or other vital organs, thereby causing a 'waste away' disease. In some groups in West Africa, all deaths, except those of the very old, are considered unnatural, and an "assassin" witch must be found when someone dies. Pallbearers ask the corpse to reveal to them the guilty party, and it pushes them to the right person, who is often surprised and denies the accusation. But the corpse does not lie,

---

3. There is considerable discussion about the relationship between witchcraft and sorcery. Many equate the two. Others differentiate between them—witches inherit their power, sorcerers intentionally seek it. Witches use psycho-psychical power while sorcerers use magical techniques to call on spirits. Witches draw on unconscious powers and sorcerers on conscious powers. For our purposes we will treat sorcery as a type of simple witchcraft found worldwide. Other types are the witchcraft of late medieval Europe, and the pagan revival of the twentieth century. People in different cultures have their own classifications of witches. For example the Lubedu of East Africa distinguish between the wanton evil of the night-witch and the intentional destructive acts of the day-witch .

4. A modern example is water witching, which seeks to discover underground water by means of forked twigs. The practice is used in Europe and was brought to North America in the seventeenth century (Hyman and Vogt 1967).

and the person must eventually accept responsibility and admit the evil act. No further punishment is needed, however (Hill 1996, 331).

In most societies witchcraft and sorcery are among the greatest fears people have. These beliefs have taken their toll literally in blood. Witches are widely seen as antisocial, evil, and malevolent beings, living lives opposite that of normal human beings. They are thought to travel great distances in a moment of time, render themselves invisible, kill at a distance, and master demons. They have special ties to owls, snakes, hyenas, and baboons; are believed to transform themselves into wolves, rabbits, horses, toads, and other animals; and are accused of going to secret night meetings riding on hares, cats, and other animals. They are accused of acting in vile self-interest, and of refusing to share what they have with others. In medieval Europe, witches were accused of consorting with demons, and were believed to stay up at night, have their feet on backward, and fly in the air. In pre-Christian Romania they were believed to turn three somersaults when they returned home to recover their human bodies (Eliade 1976, 79). Among the Kurds, Tibetans, Eskimo, Malgaches, Ngadju Dyaks, Australians, and Europeans they are accused of holding ritual orgies. In short, the witch epitomizes the exact opposite of what a given culture considers normal and normative.

Witches are widely believed to have great power, which they can use against others. They can inject foreign bodies into a victim, causing illness. They enter a person and 'eat' inner organs, causing illness and even death. Spirits often leave their bodies and take the form of a bird, bat, or other animal commonly associated with the night. Bolaji Idowu writes,

> Their main purpose is to work havoc on other human beings; and the operation is the operation of spirits upon spirits, that is, it is the ethereal bodies of the victims that are attacked, extracted, and devoured; and this is what is meant when it is said that witches have sucked the entire blood of the victim. Thus, in the case of witches or their victims, spirits meet spirits, spirits operate on spirits, while the actual human bodies lie 'asleep' in their homes (1975, 176).

The power witches exercise is not that of outside spirits or of impersonal mana. It is the unconscious human psychic power of the individual—what the Adioukrou of Cote d'Ivoire call *agn*. Harriet Hill notes, "It can be considered neutral in the same way that intellectual power, physical power, and emotional power are accepted as neutral" (1996, 337). It is commonly associated with jealousy, hatred, and envy, and the cure is often seen as confession, renunciation, and recommitment to rightful living.

People who believe in witchcraft attribute to it almost every social and personal evil. Barren women, people whose children die at birth, women with irregular menstrual flow, accident victims, traders who suffer losses, office workers who fail to get promotions, a political candidate who fails to get elected, a student who fails examinations, a person who notices scratches on his or her body, a hunter or fisherman who fails to bring home meat, a farmer with bad crop yields, a football team that consistently loses matches—all suspect witches as the cause of their misfortune. Even those who are most successful in their business or profession constantly fear being bewitched by envious relatives or friends (Offiong 1991, 78). It is idle to begin with the question whether witches exist. Observers from cultures that do not believe in witches may hold whatever theory they want, but to many people witchcraft is an urgent reality.[5]

WITCHCRAFT AMONG THE TEWERA

When the Tewera men were in the Amphletts on an overseas voyage, they went for a night to a small sandbank near by to obtain sea-birds eggs. The canoe was not well beached. It floated off in the night, the support of the outrigger boom smashed, and the outrigger boom and canoe sank separately. Fortunately, both were washed on a sandbar within swimming distance. Every man blamed the flying witches. They charm so that we sleep like the dead and do not ground our canoe. They say, "you go to sea" and the canoe goes. Some of them blamed their own women of Tewera, declaring that their habits were vile. Some blamed the women of Gumasila, who were jealous, presumably, of their taking birds' eggs from an island near Gumasila. (R. F. Fortune, "Sorcerers of Dobu," in *Witchcraft and Sorcery*, ed. Max Marwick [New York: Penguin Books, 1987], 102–7)

Witchcraft is often found in societies in which people explain everything in terms of human actions. They do not believe in "accidents," "chance," or "natural causes." They know that the man cut his leg because his ax bounced off the wood and hit it, but their question is why this happened to this man on this occasion when he had been chopping wood for years without an accident. In these societies, every misfortune as well as death is blamed on some person, and that person is believed to cause it by means of magic or witchcraft. They often believe that modern technology is the result of Western witchcraft. If asked why their witches cannot make cars and airplanes, they answer that their witches actually have this technology, but keep these goods for their exclusive use in their invisible world (Masson 1995, 125).

---

5. See Young 1986, p. 67; Kato 1975, p. 22; and E. Bolaji Idowu 1975, 175–76.

Witchcraft is also common in small, tight-knit societies experiencing severe stress such as drought, attacks by their enemies, and the confrontations with modernity (Mukund 1988). In such situations, people are not allowed to criticize one another for fear that it will weaken the solidarity of the group. Consequently, the normal hostilities that emerge between people living together in close relationships are forced underground, further building up stress in the society. At some point this hidden anger bursts out when someone accuses someone else of being a witch and causing all the problems (Kranft 1985). Others join in and the accused is expelled or killed. For a time the stress is reduced, but it soon builds up again, leading to another round of witch trials. This social scape-goating explains, in part, the cyclical nature of fear and accusation in these societies. It also helps explain the persistence of witchcraft trials in Europe during the Middle Ages, and in New England in the sixteenth century when people were surrounded by fear of outside dangers. This form of witchcraft is particularly devastating because it victimizes the poor, marginalized, and strangers.

A particularly evil form of witchcraft is the Satanist movement in the West. Satanic cults appeared in the early seventh century in Europe, and have continued up to today (Moody 1989, 247–53). Unlike the modern Wicca movement that claims to perform witchcraft for good, Satanists gather in secret to oppose Christ, exalt the Prince of Darkness, and gain control over the mysterious forces operating around them by means of ritual and nonritual magic that parody Christian rites.

Means of dealing with attacks by witches vary greatly. One common cure is to go to a witch doctor or diviner, who can detect the source and provide people with witchcraft protection by means of powerful rituals, medicines, and charms. Often, more powerful witches are sought out to deflect the evil power back on the opposing witch. In difficult cases, counter witchcraft may be used to destroy the witch. Sometimes accused witches are killed, and sometimes they are so feared that they are left alone, for they can detect and harm those who seek to kill them.

Witches, too, can be cured. Among the Azande of Sudan, no physical action is taken.

> The witches need only to have their identity and power exposed and they are half cured. "Open confession is good for the soul." After confessing to witchcraft and restoring the soul of the victim, the witch is cleansed with various remedies prescribed by the doctors and sometimes she has to sacrifice an animal (Parrinder 1958, 188).

Most societies have effective antiwitchcraft defenses. A person who suspects witchcraft may consult the diviner or witch doctor. He or she may resort to law and accuse the suspected witch before the elders, but this is not altogether satisfactory. This hardens the animosities in the case, and the court is likely to dismiss the case as idle gossip. Moreover, the witch may counter using even stronger powers. The better course of action is to use witch repellents and other protective measures to ward off the powers of a witch. Camouflaging the village can protect it from night-flying witches. Other defenses include using medicine to circle the village in order to defend strategic entrances such as gates and doors, driving away traitors in the community, and ingesting special food and drugs to protect the intended victims from harm. If a successful attack occurs, the person or community must take strong antiwitchcraft remedies to counter its dangerous powers.

Belief in witchcraft serves a number of religious and social purposes. It provides people with an explanation system that answers the question of why bad things happen to them—the cause of misfortune. They blame their misfortunes on antisocial people and on enemies outside the society. Witchcraft provides a means of affirming group boundaries and exercising social control. Evans-Pritchard (1937, 50) notes that in group-oriented societies it is a means of social sanction that forces people to conform to the social norms and deters deviance from the group. People fear that if they are different, contentious, or conspicuously successful they will excite the envy of others and be accused of being witches.

Witchcraft is also a socially structured way to handle interpersonal hostilities. It provides a channel by which people can deal with hatred, frustration, jealousy, and guilt, and use socially acceptable opportunities for aggression, vengeance, and gaining prestige and attention. It relieves people's anxieties by allowing them to express fear of another person's malicious intent, and to break off relationships that have become intolerable—something that is common in small, tight-knit societies. It gives expression to hidden anger that arises in such societies, with no culturally accepted ways to be resolved. When a man hates his neighbor, he can accuse him of witchcraft if the crops fail. It also keeps the over-ambitious and overpowerful from becoming too strong, for these are most likely to be accused of acquiring their powers by forbidden means.

WITCHCRAFT IN JAVA

In the 1970s a disaster struck a village and nearly all the paddy fields were ruined by unexpected rain. One field was able to produce rice (because it was planted earlier). The villagers performed a special feast to ask for blessing and show solidarity and reconciliation. The whole village is seen as one family and all must support each other. The man with the good field did not show up, and was accused of being a witch. He had to perform a special feast and a wayang puppet show to restore the village solidarity. (Koentjaraningrat, *Kebudayaan Jawa.* Seri Ethnografie Indonesia [Jakarta: Balai Pustaka, 1984], 413ff.)

Finally, witchcraft allows social misfits to find a legitimate place in society. They are often branded as witches because of their deviant behavior, and, in time, pride themselves on this role, which gives them great power and respect. At times witchcraft is also a manifestation of personality disorders such as depression and deep feelings of guilt.

Although witchcraft serves these functions, it is a destructive force. Hill points out,

> Living in a world believed to be full of witchcraft is a fearful experience. There is the possibility of being wrongly accused and, consequently, alienated from society. There is the possibility of committing heinous acts without intending to do so. There is the trauma of determining who caused each unnatural death or illness, resulting in an atmosphere of suspicion. Any extraordinary event is charged with supernatural significance (1996, 328).

Mary Douglas notes that among the Lele of Congo "witchcraft is also an aggravator of all hostilities and fears, an obstacle to peaceful cooperation" (1963, 141). In most cases, witchcraft beliefs generate greater tensions than they allay. In these situations witchcraft is socially pathological. Geoffrey Parrinder concludes,

> [Witchcraft beliefs] resolve certain conflicts or problems: but I did not say that this is a good solution. The aggression invited by witchcraft beliefs is as harmful as anything a society can produce in the way of disruptive practices; the relief offered by witch-hunting and witch-punishing is no more than temporary and their capacity to ally anxieties no more illusory: for if witchcraft beliefs resolve certain fears and tensions, they also produce others (Parrinder 1958, 275).

When people live in fear of being accused of being a witch, and of antagonizing others who might secretly be witches, these fears lead to antagonism and hatred, which undermine community harmony. In such circumstances the gospel of reconciliation in Christ is good news indeed.

EVIL EYE, EVIL MOUTH, AND EVIL TOUCH

Belief in the evil eye is similar to belief in witchcraft. Both hold that certain humans have invisible powers that can cause harm to others, often at a great distance. Most often these powers are thought to be located in the eyes, and people with evil eyes can harm whatever they see. When such people look at cooked food, those who eat it could become sick. When they gaze on an infant, a pregnant mother, or a bride, these become ill and may die. When they stare at ripe crops, the grain falls to the ground.

To protect themselves from the evil eye, people eat their food apart from others, no one calls attention to newborn infants, mothers give babies hideous names so as not to attract attention to them, pregnant mothers stay in isolation, and brides wear bright-colored charms that attract the first sight of those with an evil eye and ward off the evil power. Farmers put up decoys that attract the attention of passersby and draws out their strength. In India if several sons die in infancy, the next may be given a girl's name and clothes, and raised as a daughter. Only when the child is older, about four or five, is it safe to transform it into a boy because the evil eye can no longer harm him.

Less common is the belief that certain people have an evil mouth with which they can curse others, or that they have an evil touch that causes others to become sick or die. Those plagued by these powers must be treated by a shaman who are able to cure people. To prevent future damage, the teeth of those with an evil mouth may be knocked out, and contact with those having an evil touch is avoided.

SOUL LOSS

Another explanation for diseases and other misfortunes is soul loss—the belief that one or more of a person's souls can wander away. Often this occurs at night when souls normally wander from the body. Sometimes they lose their way and do not return before the person awakes. If people are aroused suddenly, their souls may not have enough time to return, and the people feel sick and confused. Souls can also be stolen, causing people to become sick.

A long separation of a soul from the body is harmful to a person's health. The remedy is to have the shaman enter the spirit world in a trance, find the soul, and bring it back, or to use magic to keep the soul from departing. Among the Samo of Papua New Guinea,

> mothers still attach charms and rattles to the string bag in which a baby spends most of its time. These encourage the spirit which might leave temporarily (as when dreaming) to return to the right child. This ritual is usually accompanied by a whispered spell on the baby's behalf. Should the spirit not return, parents rationalize that it was not well attached and preferred to be back among the ancestors while its spiritless body quickly dies (Shaw 1996, 97).

ANCESTORS

Angry ancestors are blamed for illnesses and other disasters. If ancestors are not fed and entertained, they become discontent and cause trouble for the living to remind them to care for their forebears. Regarding African traditional religions Mikulencak writes,

> Belief in a spirit world composed of dead ancestors also strongly influences how Africans regard health care. Traditional Africans believe the spirits of the dead possess great power and force. They constantly observe the living to make sure the traditional ways are followed. If the spirits are displeased, they show their anger by causing illness, or other calamities to befall the living. Their power helps to maintain the hold that traditional ways have over many Africans. Fear of disaster prevents people from rebelling against age-old social structures. That's why there is often much resistance on the part of traditional Africans to the scientific ways of Western medicine (Mikulencak 1987, 358).

To prevent misfortunes, the living must keep the ancestors happy through daily offerings of food, drink, and clothing, and through special offerings to those who are offended due to neglect.

People who die unfortunate deaths are frequently thought to return as ghosts to plague the living: a woman who died barren or a mother who died in childbirth harasses expectant mothers, a miser pesters prospering merchants, a murdered person torments his or her killer. There are many rites to ward of the attack of ghosts or to send disgruntled spirits to the other world.

MENTAL ILLNESSES

Many societies attribute aberrant behavior to mental illnesses. Some pathologies are culture-specific. The Polar Eskimo manifest hysterical flight *(piblokto)* by throwing off their clothes and running out into the winter cold; the Ojibwa Indians experienced *windigo*, characterized by cannibalistic fantasies; Central Asian and Siberian groups are plagued by *latah*, or "arctic hysteria," involving purposeless imitation of others and breaking the rules of modesty; and Malaysians and Indonesians run *amok*, a temporary homicidal violence (LeVine 1973, 29).

In the West mental patients are sent to psychiatrists for counseling and medical treatment. In many societies, people with abnormal personalities are thought to have the gifts of healing and of dealing with the spirits, and, therefore, are candidates to be shamans who heal rather than needing to be healed.

MECHANICAL EXPLANATIONS AND REMEDIES FOR MISFORTUNE

People explain everyday misfortunes in organic terms or use mechanical explanations (Figure 6.4). Beliefs in impersonal spiritual forces such as *mana* is widespread. John Mbiti writes,

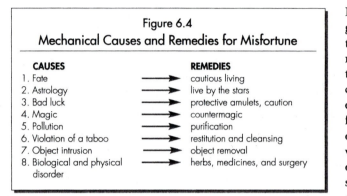

Figure 6.4
Mechanical Causes and Remedies for Misfortune

CAUSES		REMEDIES
1. Fate	→	cautious living
2. Astrology	→	live by the stars
3. Bad luck	→	protective amulets, caution
4. Magic	→	countermagic
5. Pollution	→	purification
6. Violation of a taboo	→	restitution and cleansing
7. Object intrusion	→	object removal
8. Biological and physical disorder	→	herbs, medicines, and surgery

Every African who has grown up in the traditional environment will, no doubt, know something about this mystical power which often is experienced, or manifests itself, in the form of magic, divination, witchcraft and mysterious phenomena that seem to defy even immediate scientific explanations (1969, 194).

FATE

One widespread belief is that the fortunes of human lives are ultimately predetermined by 'fate,' and that people can do nothing to change it. In parts of Asia this is called head writing, the belief that one's whole life is written on one's forehead, which diviners can read. In Arabia, Muslims speak of *qismet,* the cosmic force like fate that shapes a person's fortune.

There are many stories of how humans try to overcome their fate, but fail. One Persian story has to do with a prince. At his birth, the court diviner read his fate, and announced that on his wedding day a great bull would come from the desert and kill him. His father had twenty years to prepare for that day. The king had a great wall built with a massive door. He stationed troops and canon in front of the temple where the wedding would be held. The day came and the prince was married. True to the prophecy, a great bull came charging in from the desert and crashed through the door, but he was killed by the troops and fell in a pool of his own blood. The prince came to see this enemy whom he had defeated, but he slipped in the blood and fell on the bull's horn and died. The moral is, people can delay fate, but they can never avert it.

ASTROLOGY

There is a widespread belief, particularly in Asia, that a person's present fortune is determined by the influences of the cycles of the sun, moon, and planets. This is a system of time in which human lives are seen as microcosms of the greater universe, and each person's time of birth determines his or her fate. It presents a highly ordered and predictable universe in which all human experiences take on meaning.

The use of planets and stars to account for human events was common in ancient Greece. It spread to India, Europe, and North America.

Eurasian astrology relates two different systems: that of the heavens and that of human destinies, both individual and collective. The primary determinant of human fortunes is the zodiac, the twelve constellations through which the planets circulate. These revolve through the twelve houses that represent the key elements of life, such as wealth, health, marriage, death, parents, sons, honors, and friends. The combinations of these determine the hour-by-hour fortune of every person's life in relationship to these elements. Astrology represents a highly complex and symbolically deep conceptual scaffolding that offers people a meaningful view of their universe and gives them an understanding of their place in it.

The rapid spread of astrology in the modern world is due, in part, to the fact that it provides people with a sense of their identity in reaction to the normlessness of modern society. In the United States Hollywood stars and American politicians use astrology to guide their decisions. In 1968 one hundred papers in the United States included horoscopes, in 1980 1200 out of 1,750 newspapers did so (Truzzi 1989, 405–6). Astrological charts are now a regular part of many Yellow Pages. (Astrology is examined at greater depth in Chapter 7.)

BAD LUCK

People in many cultures explain the fortunes of life in terms of good and bad luck. Some believe that bad luck is a disease. Everyone has misfortunes or accidents now and then, but some people seem to be plagued with them. Their house burns down, and their cows die for no apparent cause.

Belief in bad luck is widespread in China. Certain days and seasons are inauspicious, and people must be particularly careful during them. Certain numbers, too, bring bad luck, so people avoid using them in house numbers. Houses in Alhambra (a suburb of Los Angeles with a burgeoning Chinese population) with the number "4" in the address don't sell. Some real estate agents have petitioned the city for new addresses in order to sell a house.

BAD MAGIC

Belief in the use of magic for evil purposes is worldwide. A person may use magic to destroy an enemy, weaken a rival, or cause stomach indigestion in a husband who has been unfaithful. More powerful magic can cause death and bring disasters to whole communities. However, only when it is used in the face of social disapproval does magic become evil. Magicians may gain great honor, but they are always in danger of being accused by their rivals of misusing their power in secret.

The cure for bad magic is countermagic. Medicines, sacrifices, exorcisms, and object removal will not work. The cure must belong to the same explanation system as the cause of misfortune (Figure 6.4). Some magicians are known for their ability to cure those plagued with bad magic, or to prevent it from affecting them. An example is a Muslim saint in South India known throughout the region for countering deadly snake bites caused by magic. When people inform him of a snake bite, he chants a chant that forces the snake to return and symbolically suck out the poison it has injected into its victim. If this is not sufficient, he performs high power magic guaranteed to work, but every time he uses this, he believes his own life span is shortened.

POLLUTION

Concepts of purity and pollution play important roles in many cultures in explaining the fortunes of life. Certain events, such as giving birth, initiation, death, and adultery are defiling, and people must take care not to defile others during their time of pollution. Certain animals and plants may be considered dirty and cannot be eaten. (We will examine concepts of purity and pollution in Chapter 8.)

VIOLATION OF A TABOO

Taboos are mechanical prohibitions or restrictions associated with sacred or defiled objects, such as idols, offerings, and ritual oil. To mishandle or disrespect them is to bring down calamities upon oneself. For example, in precolonial Hawaii, the king was so full of *mana* that his possessions and whatever he touched became dangerous to the ordinary people. Allen Tippett notes that new Christians in the Solomon Islands cut down a banyan tree which was thought to contain much *mana*, and when they did not die, the non-Christians concluded that the Christians had more powerful *mana* that enabled them to overcome the power of the tree (Tippett 1967, 100–102). In the Old Testament, people were forbidden to touch the ark, and when one did, he brought down God's judgment (2 Sam. 2:2).

Taboos are often associated with certain times in life. Young mothers and menstruating women are often isolated as unclean for a time. Warriors may have to avoid sexual intercourse and strong drink before battles.

OBJECT INTRUSION

One widespread explanation for illness found particularly in inner and Eastern Asia and among Native Americans is object intrusion. Pieces of bone, stick, or stone, hair balls, and other objects are thought to be placed in a person's body by witches, hostile shamans, or enemies. Patients must be taken to a shaman who first diagnoses where the object came from, and then finds out everything about the past history of the patient and the community. The shaman then conducts seances in which everyone is encouraged to discuss their grudges against the patient and the patient's grievances against them. Then, surrounded by high expectations, the shaman removes the object by rubbing and kneading the patient's body, gesturing over the diseased area, or directly sucking out the evil object and spitting it out, showing it to all to convince them and the patient of the effectiveness of the healing. The healing has to do not only with the physical symptoms, but also with social tensions in the community.

TABOOS ASSOCIATED WITH BIRTH IN TAIWAN

A pregnant woman must not eat ginger—or she will give birth to a baby with eye disease or with eleven fingers.

A pregnant woman must not watch a puppet show—or the child will be born as a puppet with soft bones.

A pregnant woman must not step over a rope dragging an ox—or her pregnancy will be extended twelve months.

Two pregnant women must not sleep on the same bed—or one or both will face disaster.

A pregnant woman must not stare at the moon through the mist—or she will lack blood in her brain or miscarry.

A pregnant woman must not watch people digging a well—or it will not provide water.

A pregnant woman must not cut things with scissors—or she will offend the fetus god and bear a child without ears.

A pregnant woman must not put the bathtub outside in July—or she will offend the evil spirits and incur misfortunes.

A pregnant woman must not see the eclipse of the moon—or the child will be disabled.

Never say "monkey" to a baby—or it will grow up weak and thin, or die prematurely.

Never feed a baby meat, beans, eggs, or fermented foods—or it will have ulcers, bad teeth, or foul breath, or be difficult to raise.

BIOLOGICAL AND PHYSICAL DISORDER

Finally, all societies recognize biological and physical disorders. An ax slips and cuts a man's foot; boiling water scalds a woman's hand. The people know that they must treat the wound with medicines of various sorts, and bind it so it will not bleed.

In the West, the primary question raised is what causes the disease and how can it be cured. Diseases and ill health are attributed to germs, viruses, hormonal imbalances, physical injuries, and other impersonal causes. In much of the world, the question of the immediate cause of the illness is secondary. The underlying question is why—why did it happen to me, and why now.

DIAGNOSIS AND REMEDY

Once people attribute misfortune to a particular system of explanation, they turn to experts in that system—medicine men, doctors, shamans, herbalists, priests, or psychiatrists—to diagnose the cause and select a remedy. As Staples points out,

> It is essential to find out who has caused the difficulty and why it has been brought about. Only after this is known can proper restorative measures be undertaken. If a deity or ancestor has been neglected or offended, than a sacrifice must be prescribed; if one has been "bewitched" by a sorcerer, then recourse must be had to counteracting ritual action or medicine. Of course, it is recognized by the primal person that there are physical aspects of illness, and the importance of dealing with these is not missed, but this dimension of illness remains a somewhat second-order concern (1982, 71).

Only after the cause is known can proper restorative measures be undertaken. If this ancestor has been neglected or offended, then this sacrifice must be prescribed; if that deity is angry, that gift must be offered; if someone has used harmful magic, protective magic must be performed.

This process of diagnosis and prescribing a remedy is seen in the way Indian villagers respond to their illnesses. When someone becomes ill, the first step is to diagnose the cause—is it due to sin and wrongdoing, spirit possession, a curse, eating hot foods, offending an ancestor, bad luck, or what? If the problem is minor, people generally go first to a person who knows home remedies. If these services fail, they go to practitioners who use more powerful solutions. The saint prays to one or more gods, and because the gods know the cause, he need ask no questions. Moreover, he does his ministry as a service to God, so he charges no fees. Those who are cured, however, give him gifts according to their means to thank the gods and to make sure the gods help them the next time around. The shaman, too, asks no questions. He goes into a trance and his spirit enters the spirit world where it finds and recovers the person's spirit that has wandered away, or battles the evil spirit causing the illness. The magician uses powerful *mantras* and *yantras* to cure the patient after diagnosing the cause of the sickness—a curse, black magic, violation of a taboo, or bad stars. These, too, do their service as an offering to the gods and charge no fees, but accept gifts healed patients give to the gods in thanks.

The medical doctor uses either Ayyurvedic (Hindu homeopathic medical system), or Unnani (Arabic medical system) to diagnose and cure the patient. He charges high fees because of his great knowledge, but he gives a guarantee. Patients pay nothing if they are not healed. Home remedies are prescribed by folk healers, commonly thought to be quacks by professional healers. They ask many questions because they do not know

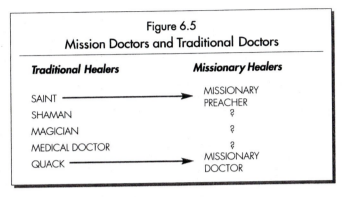

Figure 6.5
Mission Doctors and Traditional Doctors

Traditional Healers	Missionary Healers
SAINT ⟶	MISSIONARY PREACHER
SHAMAN	?
MAGICIAN	?
MEDICAL DOCTOR	?
QUACK ⟶	MISSIONARY DOCTOR

how to diagnose illnesses by technical methods; charge low fees because they have little specialized knowledge; and give no guarantee. The patient must pay for the medicine before receiving it, and there is no refund if it does not work.

Given this view of the world, it should not surprise us that when the first mission doctors (practicing Western allopathic medicine) came, the villagers saw them as quacks (Figure 6.5). These foreign doctors kept asking questions[6] (why should a patient go to the doctor if the patient knew what was wrong?), and gave no guarantees. In mission hospitals, patients had to pay for the medicines whether these cured them or not. In the opinion of village Indians, the most important function of the healer is to pronounce the prognosis and declare with an aura of conviction a sure cure—"He will recover." For them, healing is not a technical skill, but a supernatural encounter. Modern doctors, however, express only their opinion, and do not speak with the authority of the supernatural power. This brings us to a discussion of the missiological implications of understanding these "middle zone" issues of human well being and misfortune.

CHRISTIAN RESPONSE

How should Christians respond to human desires for a good life and for protection from misfortunes? This is a question young churches face around the world, but it is also a pastoral question facing ministers in the West.

---

6. Russell Staples tells of a Rhodesian villager who complained after going to a missionary doctor, "How can he help? All he did was to ask me questions" (1982, 70). He believed a proper doctor would have 'divined' the source and prescribed an appropriate remedy—an appropriate ritual plus some medicine, and not wasted time asking seemingly irrelevant questions.

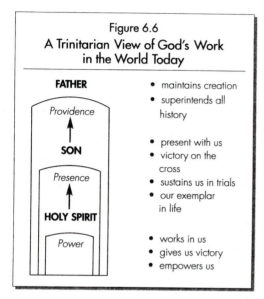

Figure 6.6
**A Trinitarian View of God's Work
in the World Today**

FATHER	• maintains creation
Providence	• superintends all history
SON	• present with us • victory on the cross • sustains us in trials • our exemplar in life
Presence	
HOLY SPIRIT	• works in us • gives us victory • empowers us
Power	

GENERAL PRINCIPLES

It is important to minister to people in their crises, but Christians need to keep in mind biblical principles that guide their responses. Otherwise, Christian prayers and rites will be seen as a more powerful magic, or as better ways to bribe God.

THEOLOGICAL PRINCIPLES

We need to think through the theological principles involved in ministries of healing, protection, and provision. These include a trinitarian view of God, a biblical view of the nature and causes of well-being and misfortune, and a theology of suffering and deliverance.

A TRINITARIAN VIEW OF GOD

First, Christians must root their response to well-being and crisis in a trinitarian view of God (Figure 6.6). This affirms the providence of God as the practical outworking of creation. Throughout the Scriptures, it is clear that God is sovereign over the ebb and flow of history and of human lives. From creation to final judgment God is in control. This does not deny humans the freedom to make choices. It does mean, however, that in the end God directs the overall course of human history according to his purposes.

For the early Christians, the ongoing involvement of God in world history and personal biography was a living reality. This awareness guided their lives and sustained them in times of suffering, persecution, and martyrdom. It also gave them answers to the problems of daily life. Too often today Christians depend on the power of science and medicine, and neglect prayer and dependence on God's working in their lives.

The providence of God affirms God's love for all peoples. He sends rain and harvest, life and health. He created everything good, and he seeks the good of all people. He cares in particular ways for his children, who have given him the permission to work in their lives. He does not leave his people to fend for themselves in a world of chance and happenstance, nor does he delegate ordinary human affairs to angels and saints.

It is important to stress the fact that God does answer the prayers of his people for their ultimate good. He does heal, provide, and deliver. At times, however, he uses sickness, suffering, and trials for their good (Rom. 8:28). Even his judgment is an effort to draw people into righteousness for their own well-being. God is the God of all of life: of sickness, failure, oppression, and death (1 Cor. 4:10–13; 2 Tim. 3:13; 1 Peter 4:12–18). Christians do not always feel God's hand in theirs in times of trial, but in retrospect they often see that God was closest to them during those times. No matter what happens, Christians know that God works all things out for the good of those who love him (Rom. 8:28).

Second, in this bigger frame, Christians need to experience the presence of the living Christ in them. As humans, we live in a world suffering the consequences of the fall. Plagues, famines, wars, and sickness are part of human experience (Rom. 8:19–23). The good news is that in all of these experiences, Christ is with us (Matt. 28:7). This presence manifests itself first in our salvation—Christ saved us and is saving us from the power and judgment of sin. It is seen in the fact that the Father answers prayer because Christ pleads for us (John 14–15), and Christ himself provides us grace and strength to live with weaknesses, insults, hardships, persecutions, and calamities (2 Cor. 12:10). It is seen in the hope of our future resurrection, a resurrection that will deliver us from the crises of life on earth.

Third, Christians must teach that in the care of the Father and presence of Christ they can experience the power of the Holy Spirit. This power was demonstrated in the life of Christ and in the early church in signs and wonders that pointed to the kingdom of God invading the earth, but as the writers of the New Testament point out, these external demonstrations are secondary to the power of the Holy Spirit in Christians leading them to salvation and victorious life in Christ. In missions we often see the power of the Holy Spirit working to convict people of their sins and woo them to faith in Christ. Paul connects *pneuma* (Spirit) and *dunamis* (power) in contexts that deal with the missionary preaching of the apostles. He wrote, "our gospel came to you not only simply with word, but also with power, with the Holy Spirit and with deep conviction. . . . in spite of severe suffering, you welcomed the message with the joy given by the Holy Spirit" (1 Thess. 1:5–6). God often demonstrates his power in extraordinary ways to seekers and young believers who need such signs to confirm their faith. As Christians mature in faith, however, they should depend less on visible signs to sustain their faith, and more on the study of Scripture and a personal walk with God.

The activities of the Father, Son, and Holy Spirit are not three separate works. They are the work of one God. If we overlook the whole work of God on earth and focus only on our own immediate well-being, we are in danger of distorting the gospel.

A BIBLICAL PERSPECTIVE ON WELL-BEING AND MISFORTUNE

Christians need a biblical definition of well-being. Health in Scripture is defined, not in terms of personal well-being, but in terms of *shalom*, which is translated into English using such terms as completeness, soundness, peace, well-being, health, prosperity, and salvation. It begins when we are reconciled to God and our enemies. It manifests itself in our mutual submission to one another in the church and our self-sacrificing service to others in need. Its fruit is physical, psychological, and social health. Daniel Fountain points out, "God's plan for the world is this: that all persons everywhere, in every nation, know God's saving health and be delivered from disobedience, disruption, despair, disease and all that would destroy our wholeness" (1989, 221). To focus on personal well-being and prosperity rather than on *shalom* is to preach a gospel that treats the symptoms but does not cure the illness.

While recognizing that God seeks wholeness, healing, peace, and justice on earth, Christians must be mindful that full delivery is only after death when they receive a new body. For Christians, death is the final release, for we do not want to live forever in our present world, even in perfect health and prosperity.

A THEOLOGY OF SUFFERING

Finally, Christians need a theology of suffering, illness, and pain. These consequences of sin cannot be divorced from one another. The process of aging and death is at work in humans from the moment of their conception. The side effects of this are sickness and bodily suffering. Christians living in a fallen world experience these consequences of sin. Paul refers to colleagues who were not healed (Phil. 2:26–27; 2 Tim. 4:20). Job was sick but God used his suffering to bring him to a more mature and deeper faith (Job 42:5–6).[7]

Christians can also expect hardship, poverty, and persecution because they follow Christ (1 Cor. 4:10–13; 2 Tim. 3:12; 1 Peter 4:12–18). They are called to take up their cross and follow Christ (Matt. 10:38–39; 16:24–26), which often leads to suffering and death, as Christ warned.

---

7. The real question is not "Why do bad things happen to good people?" It is "Why does so much good happen to us sinners?" Why do we continue to have life, sunshine, rain, friends, happy moments, healthful days, and food at all, given that we are rebels against God who gives these to us? With this view we give thanks for the many blessings we do receive and do not deserve, rather than blaming God for the troubles we bring upon ourselves.

Our human tendency is to see suffering and death as totally bad. It is true that in heaven these will no longer exist, but in a sinful world God can use even these to his divine purposes and to human benefit. For the early Christians, more often than not, following Christ meant suffering, sickness, and death, rather than health, prosperity, and long life. Unfortunately, many Christians have bought into the Western cultural emphasis on personal health and prosperity as ultimate ends in themselves. As a result, Western people tend to focus on themselves while millions around the world are dying of poverty, oppression, and violence.

God can use crises to lead his own to Christian maturity. Many people testify to the fact that it was in times of sickness and suffering, when they were most vulnerable, that they were drawn to Christ and learned important lessons of faith. These are times when people realize their own vulnerability and their dependence on God. Health and prosperity often breed a sense of self-reliance that keeps believers from growing spiritually. Unfortunately, a theology that rejects sickness and suffering fits well into our modern age with its denial of death and emphasis on positive thinking.[8]

MINISTRY PRINCIPLES

Biblical principles should guide Christians in the ways they minister to those in need. These need to reflect the corporate, public, and holistic nature of the majority of the world's societies.

HEALING COMMUNITIES

Shalom finds its expression in the church as a healing community. At the heart of the ministry of the church is a pastoral heart. Individually (the pastor) and collectively (the flock), the church needs to demonstrate a love of people and a willingness to share in their struggles and to help bear their burdens. Believers are admonished to "look after orphans and widows" (James 1:27). A church must be concerned with the everyday needs of human life and should minister to these needs in both personal and corporate ways.

Human crises are rarely purely personal matters. Illness, spirit possession, and job losses affect the family, and drought, crop failures, and plagues affect the whole community. What happens to the individual happens to the group, and whatever happens to the group happens to the individual. Ministry must respond not only to the needs of particular individuals, but also restore good relationships within the community. For this reason, prayers for healing often are a testimony of the care and power of God to the whole community.

8. See Ernest Becker, *Denial of Death* (New York: Free Press, 1973).

Christian ministry should take place in the context of the church as a caring community. Often the problem of misfortune is not the suffering itself, but that people must bear it alone. Crisis, Christians must learn, can be a time when the community of faith gathers around those who are suffering and helps bear the burdens and illness of life through prayer, love, and encouragement. Mansell Pattison (1989) found that for many who seek prayer for healing, the important thing was not that they were physically healed (many were not), but that they felt the support of others in their times of difficulty. Western churches can learn much about the therapeutic effects of a community that cares about people from group-oriented societies around the world.

Ministries to those in crisis can take many forms. Special times of prayer can be set aside in certain services for those in need. Christians can minister to their neighbors, and churches can organize medical, educational, agricultural, and other ministries to help people live better lives. Care must be taken, however, not to promise that all the needy will be healed or prosper. The expectations of modern Christians are frequently too low with regard to what God will do, but the church must be ready to minister to those whom God does not choose to deliver.

HOLISTIC MINISTRY

We need to minister holistically, responding to people's biophysical, psychological, social, and spiritual needs, for these are intertwined. Missionaries from the West must begin by transforming their own segmented worldview with its dualism of supernatural and natural explanations; salvation by faith and healing by science; spiritual ministries and social concern. In much of the world, people make no distinction between natural and supernatural explanations, and see healing as involving both material and spiritual transformations. They often reject Western medicine and agricultural science because they see these simply as techniques unrelated to spiritual realities. It is important, then, to demonstrate the fullness of God's salvation both here on earth and in the world to come.

It is important to differentiate between 'disease,' which refers to a malfunctioning of biological and psychological processes, and 'illness,' which refers to the psychosocial experience and cultural meaning surrounding disease. All illnesses and misfortunes are dealt with in the context of cultural systems that define their nature and remedy, and social systems made up of interpersonal interactions. Illness, responses to it, individuals experiencing it and treating it, and the social institutions related to it are all systematically interconnected (Kleinman 1980). Ministry to those who are ill must, therefore, deal not only with physical and psychological disorders, but also with the sociocultural networks involved in health care. It is here that the local congregation can become involved as a healing community.

A differentiation also needs to be made between the immediate symptoms and the underlying causes of the misfortune. Social stress can cause biological illness, and while it is important to treat the biological symptoms, until the underlying cause is recognized and dealt with, there is no true healing of the person. Similarly, living in sin can cause physical, psychological, and social problems. These problems will not go away until people repent and turn from their sins. Dealing with underlying causes often enables Christians to challenge the people's animistic beliefs of causality.

In holistic ministries it is important not to separate ministries into medical, educational, and spiritual activities, and to assign the former to scientific specialists, and the latter to ministers. Doctors, teachers, and agricultural workers need to make prayer and other religious practices a natural part of their work, demonstrating to the public that they see all material measures as blessed by God. Showing how belief in Christ pervades and integrates all parts of life is crucial for an effective, holistic ministry.

TEACHING MINISTRY

A third vital ministry is teaching. In times of crisis, people are open to new ideas, and proper instruction enables them to cope in appropriate ways. Many people are open to the gospel when they are sick and find no healing in their old ways. Others look for new answers when their old explanations fail. It is important at such times to present Christ as the answer, but to do so without manipulation. It is our task to point people to Jesus. When people turn to him, it is he who is the answer to the longings of their hearts.

Leaders must begin by ministering to people according to their specific needs. This is particularly important in reaching out to people who have never heard of Christ and who need signs demonstrating to them his reality and power. Such ministries, however, are preevangelism, and Christians must use these occasions to declare to the people the great news of God's salvation from sin.

Diseases, failures, losses, and other disasters are also occasions for teaching people biblical truths regarding the nature and causes of misfortunes and afflictions. Many people attribute all misfortunes to spiritual or human causes. They need to be taught scientific explanations to help them understand the nature of diseases, but these explanations must be included in a broader biblical understanding of the ways God works in his creation. Misfortunes are opportunities for open dialogue, and for helping people to deal with their problems in Christian ways.

PRAYER MINISTRY

Finally, we need to pray boldly for God's help and not fear the outcome. Too often Westerners are afraid to publicly ask God for healing and deliverance. There is often a fear that people will not be healed or crises averted, and this will lead them to reject God. However, God does not need to be defended. We are called to point people to him, and he will work in the lives of those who turn to him. Prayer is not getting God to do what humans want, but to teach them what God wants and to give God permission to work in their lives.

TRANSFORMING WORLDVIEWS

Christians must move beyond immediate ministries to the long and difficult task of transforming people's animistic worldviews into biblical ones. If we simply work within traditional explanation systems, there is a real danger that the gospel will be transformed into Christo-paganism—animism with a Christian veneer. New Christians often see Christian prayers as magic formulas, Bible verses as amulets, and preachers as magicians more powerful than their old ones. Christianity is perceived as powerful witchcraft and spiritism, but the fear of witchcraft and spirits remains. People's ideas about well-being, misfortune, and evil must be transformed by biblical teaching as much as their understanding of the nature of God.

We see an example of this worldview transformation in the Old Testament. There God started with the beliefs Abram had when he was called, but then began the long transformation of the worldview of the Israelites in preparation for the coming of Christ. God condemned the belief and practice of magic (Exod. 9:11), witchcraft (1 Sam. 15:23; Gal. 5:20), divination (Deut. 18:10), fetishism (Exod. 20:3–6), and shamanism (Lev. 20:6) practiced by the tribes surrounding Israel. He made it clear that the other gods are not gods at all (2 Kgs. 19:18; Isa. 44:6–20; Gal. 4:8). He taught them that their sufferings were not due to the power of pagan gods and spirits, but to his desire to draw them back to himself.

To transform animistic worldviews, missionaries must understand the underlying beliefs in spirits, magic, divination, and witchcraft. Too often outsiders see these as figments of people's imaginations that need to be eradicated through the introduction of science and Christianity. Missionaries cannot simply ignore or condemn these beliefs without explanation, because if they do so, the people will continue their old ways covertly. Christians must take these beliefs seriously—not because they are true, but because these are the beliefs that the people have about reality, and they will not simply die out when confronted with other beliefs. In South Africa, an estimated four-fifths of the people regularly consult traditional healers (Economist 1995, 86).

While seeking to understand the explanation systems of other cultures, missionaries must not equate these beliefs with ontological truth. Not every spirit named in another culture is, in fact, a real spirit. Some are guises of Satan and his hosts; others, such as the Spirit of Small Pox and the Spirit of Lightning, are better explained in scientific terms; and still others are cultural phantasies.

Westerners must also examine their own views of causality and test them in the light of Scripture. They must abandon the dualism that divides their world into supernatural and natural realities, and relegates spiritual problems to religion, and natural ones to science. Pattison writes,

> The naturalistic system of the world of the west, rooted in the rationalism of latter day humanism, provides proximate and limited explanations of isolated fragments of human life. It fails to provide western mankind with a cohesive picture of human life. Further, without ontological grounding it does not provide a rationale, nor purpose, nor meaning to life (1989, 264).

Western science and its construction of reality fails to answer deeper questions of human existence.

In rejecting the modern dualism, Westerners must not reject the knowledge modern medicine makes available, nor should they adopt an animistic worldview with its constant fear of spirits, shades, witchcraft, and magic. The Bible offers a third alternative to modern secularism and animism. It rejects the secularism of the modern worldview. It challenges the magical worldview that dominates folk religions. It calls people to entrust themselves to the care of the God of righteousness and love. The gospel offers them much more than health and success on earth. It gives them *shalom* in the fullest sense of the word.

SPECIFIC MINISTRIES

Building on these general principles, missionaries and church leaders need to develop specific ministries that are biblically based and culturally sensitive.

HEALING MINISTRIES

How should missionaries deal with sickness and healing from a Christian perspective? The Bible is clear regarding human misfortunes. Ultimately they are caused by sin (1 Cor. 11:30; Mark 2:1–12; James 5:14–16). Sometimes illness is sent by God as a remedial discipline to draw people to himself and to help them to grow spiritually (Acts 9:1–18; 1 Cor. 11:30–32). Sometimes they are caused by demonic influences (Matt. 12:22–24; Mark 9:14–29; Luke 13:10–16), but they are permitted by God to bring people back to himself (1 Cor. 5:5; 1 Tim. 1:20). The Bible is also clear on the role of healing in the church and mission. God in Christ has taken on himself the sins and diseases of all humanity (Matt. 8:17). He can and does heal miraculously (Acts 14:8–10). He also heals through Christians' care for others (Col. 4:14; 1 Tim. 5:23; Luke 10:34–35). God does not heal everyone (Gal. 4:13; Phil. 2:25–30). Some of the reasons for this are to show God's glory (John 9:11), to test the believer's faith (Job), to prepare his people for ministry (Heb. 5:11; Isa. 53:4–5; 1 Peter 2:24), and to guide them (Gal. 4:13). Those who do not pray or pray amiss—for carnal, selfish reasons—may not expect healing (Matt. 17:14–21), nor can those who continue to live in known sin without repentance and cleansing (James 4:3). God's highest purpose for human beings is righteousness and purity, not simply physical healing.

Christians are also warned that there are counterfeit healings (Matt. 24:24; Exod. 7:11, 22; Rev. 16:14; 19:20). God heals as a sign of what his kingdom is like. That kingdom has not yet come in its fullness; consequently, Christians are not always healed. Rather, God on key occasions does heal to show us what the kingdom will be like when it comes in its fullness. He often shows his power in the lives of those exploring faith in him. This is demonstrated in conversions of people in traditional religions around the world.

Missionary approaches to healing must be holistic. On the one hand, scientific medicine should be used to its full extent because this demonstrates the ways God works in his creation. On the other hand, illnesses are caused by and affect not only the body, but also the psyche and spirit of those who are sick, and all their social relationships are affected. Pattison points out (1989, 276) that our modern approaches to misfortune have been segmented, isolated, naturalistic, and individualistic. This atomization and particularization have led to the fragmentation of healing, which not only separates body, mind, and spirit, but also leads to numerous medical specializations. The crisis in modern medicine is reflected in the fact that medical sciences deal primarily with the body, and do not provide a belief system to live by.[9] Doctors cannot heal a person in the full sense of the term. The healer must not only heal the body, but restore broken relationships, and thus help to reintegrate patients into their communities.

Christian missionaries should pray earnestly and publicly for the sick, minister to them, and do medical work as part of ministry. They cannot simply ignore the sick, and say to them that healing is not a part of our ministry. It is of Christian character to minister to people out of love for

---

9. This explains in large part the explosion of alternative and New Age medical treatments in the West. Most of these seek to recover a holistic approach to treating diseases.

Christ who first loved us. Ministry reflects the character of Christ and his followers, and should be done not simply to instill faith. We must recognize that many who are healed will never become Christians.

DEALING WITH SPIRIT POSSESSION

When encountering spirit possession, missionaries must be prepared to pray to God to deliver the victims. For those raised in the West, this often means rethinking their understanding of demonic realities in light of Scripture. Biblically, it is clear that demons are real and that they plague people, but they must submit to the authority of Christ.

The first step in dealing with people who appear to be oppressed by demons is discernment. We must not confuse phenomenology with ontology. Some who appear to be possessed, in fact, may be subconsciously or consciously seeking attention. This is often the case when the exorcism seems to be temporary and the victims return repeatedly for more exorcisms. Other cases involve mental illness. To seek to exorcise these patients often makes their condition worse. Still other cases of demonic oppression are real, and must be dealt with as such. One thing is clear: Satan is a master of deceit and wants humans to fear him even when he isn't there. In diagnosing cases that appear to be possession, it is good to involve a team, such as a doctor, counselor, and minister. Exorcism should not be the first approach to a problem, but come only after ruling out other biophysical causes (Augsberger 1986, 307).

Discernment of demonic oppression is difficult because of the complexity of the human personality and human tendencies to self-deception. People who are psychologically ill frequently suffer from delusions of being demon-possessed. Those who are truly demonized do not commonly refer to that fact.

The second step in dealing with demon possession is to be prepared before practicing an exorcism. Missionaries must examine their personal attitudes and relationship to Christ. Deliverance ministries should never be done merely out of curiosity or experiment. Demons know the hidden sins and inner secrets of the counselor (Act 19:13–16). Complete honesty and openness is needed, and a right heart before God. Unconfessed sin, resentment, and an unforgiving spirit block ministry.

Conversely, the possessed person must want deliverance if it is to be successful. God does not deliver people against their will. Moreover, care must be taken to avoid undue emotional involvement, and to maintain as much objectivity as possible. Because such ministries are already subjective and lend themselves readily to excesses and sensationalism, missionaries should not enter such ministry triumphantly.

Third, exorcisms must be surrounded by prayer for protection, discernment, and ministry. We are powerless, it is God who must drive out the spirits. Consequently, we should speak primarily to God, not with the spirits. Some Christian leaders simply order the spirits to depart under the authority of Christ. We must always remember that evil spirits are liars, and we cannot trust their word. It is not important for us to know the name of the spirit to cast it out.

We must avoid all magical tendencies in the deliverance process. It is not dependent on the use of special words or right gestures. The deliverance is by Christ and the Holy Spirit, not by our actions. Jesus, for example, simply rebuked the spirits (Matt. 4:24; 8:16–17; 9:32–33; 12:22; 15:21–28; 17:14–18; etc.). We must also avoid the sensationalism commonly associated with healing and exorcism ministries. Deliverance is most effective when it involves a holistic pastoral ministry that leads the delivered to faith and maturity in Christ.

Deliverance ministries should not focus on the exorcism itself, but on proclaiming Christ. Jesus' exorcism of spirits and healing of the sick took place as part of his ministry. He did not seek out the possessed, but when people came he ministered to them. His central purpose was to declare the coming of the kingdom of God in salvation, righteousness, peace, and justice. When the people wanted miracles and not his message, Jesus ceased doing them.

In dealing with possession, it is important to treat it "matter-of-factly." We must recognize the reality of possession, but not go looking for it. Nor should we fear demon possession. Those demonized are to be pitied more than feared. In the New Testament they are lumped together with the sick. The real opposition to God's work comes not from them, but from those who rationally and consciously choose to oppose Christ either because they choose to follow Satan and evil, or they are self-possessed (2 Tim. 4:1).

It is important to recognize that the battle between righteousness and evil, God and Satan, is real and serious. We know, however, that when we are in Christ, Satan and demons have no power over us other than what God permits. Satan seeks to tempt us, cause us to fear, and delude us. Christians are to stand firm against his attacks (Eph. 6:10–18).

Following the deliverance it is important to incorporate those who are delivered into a Christian community of support and instruction that does not stigmatize them. This requires months of follow-up ministry by mature Christians.

DEALING WITH WITCHCRAFT

Witchcraft has been a serious problem for the church from its beginning. It was widespread in the Roman Empire, and penalties against it were severe during the Constantinian era. During the early Middle Ages simple witchcraft and natural magic were treated with relative leniency. Church leaders assumed that these practices would die out as people became more founded in their Christian faith. The persistence of witchcraft led the church to suppress it by trial and execution during the Inquisition. It was imported to America by the colonists, who experienced a witch craze in the early seventeenth century—hundreds of people were burned at the stake. In part, this persistence of witchcraft for more than a thousand years in Europe was due to the fact that the church simply tried to stamp it out, and did not try to understand it and provide a better biblical response to the human needs that gave it birth.

Today, witchcraft is one of the great problems facing young churches around the world. Even in Christian churches there is a widespread belief in the power of witchcraft and the fear of being bewitched. Christian rituals are often seen as new and more powerful protection against the attacks of one's enemies and those who may be jealous. How should we respond to this persistent problem?

First, it is important to take witchcraft seriously, and to minister to those who believe they are bewitched. This must not be ignored, nor should it be treated as merely superstition. It is very real in the minds of those who believe in witchcraft. To deny its reality only drives these beliefs underground. Missionaries need to show believers that the power of God is greater than any other power they face, and that he can deliver them from curses. In the process, those who are relieved of oppression must be incorporated into communities of believers who can help them take a stand against it.

In the village where I lived from 1984 to 1986, the lay preacher, George, has been married four times. Each time his wife arrived fat and fertile, but after a few years left skinny and sterile. Only two children resulted from all this, and one of those died at the age of five. Why? George's mother, a regular in the church choir, was a witch and killed her grandchildren by witchcraft. She confessed and was put under church discipline for six months. But the problem continued. Now she has died, but her daughter carries on in her place. George says the Bible has nothing to say about witchcraft. (Hill 1996, 323)

Second, missionaries must speak out against the evil that witchcraft can create (Deut. 18:10). It is not something that can be accommodated in the church. David Bosch notes that there is no Satan figure in the tribes of sub-Saharan Africa—no demonic being who is totally evil. The closest personification of evil for them is the witch.

Third, missionaries must recognize that many are falsely accused of being witches. In such cases it is important that we defend and support those who are innocent of the charges, and call to account those making the accusations. During the Salem witch trials, most of the accused were old widows and young girls who had no one to defend them; most of whom declared their faith in Christ until their deaths. Few powerful leaders in the colonies were ever accused, though they were often less pious than those who died.

Fourth, missionaries must form the church as a body of love and community. Church members should forgive and reincorporate individuals who fall. The church must develop methods to deal with the suppressed hostility that spawns and sustains witchcraft. Witchcraft is found most often in tight-knit societies facing external dangers. In such groups people cannot vent their anger for fear of destroying the unity of the group and making it vulnerable to outside threats. Consequently, jealousies and hatreds go underground and fester. Ultimately the hostility explodes and someone accuses another person of witchcraft; the pent-up anger is vented on these hapless individuals.

To avoid the build-up of jealousy and hatred in church communities, it is important that the leaders provide ways for these feelings to be expressed and dealt with in culturally appropriate ways. Reconciliation must take place. In frontier America this often occurred during revival meetings when people 'set things right' with God and with one another—people who had not spoken to each other for years cried and embraced in Christian forgiveness and love. Many African Independent Churches address the problem by using rituals that encourage church members to confess their sins of hatred, jealousy, witchcraft, and magic, and to offer them cleansing and forgiveness. As one African said, where there is jealousy, envy, and hatred, there is witchcraft (Hill 1996, 337). When these are removed, love and fellowship in the church is renewed.

Finally, we must deal with the worldview that underlies beliefs in witchcraft. We will examine this in detail in Chapter 14.

We turn now to examine the third question folk religions seek to answer, namely, the need for knowledge and direction in an uncertain world.

7

GUIDANCE AND
THE UNKNOWN

What would humans want to know if they could know the unknown? The answer, of course, varies with the society in which the people asking the question reside. But in general, this is a question all humans ask. What would happen if we could know beforehand the rise and fall of stock market prices, the winners of horse races, or the accident we might have if we go on a journey? We are only a few minutes away from being rich and avoiding terrible accidents. What if we knew what would happen if we marry this person or that one, or take this job or that one? Answering these questions would allow informed decisions that would affect people's whole lives. But how can we know the future, the present, or the past in order to make good decisions regarding life?

THE SEARCH FOR GUIDANCE

Humans in all societies make plans to avoid dangers and gain success, but everyone faces many unknowns. Unexpected occurrences, unforeseen difficulties, and unknown dangers thwart the best plans, particularly in societies where spirits are seen as capricious, deaths are frequent, and life is viewed as precarious. Modern science helps people gain control over more of their lives, but it cannot predict the future, prevent misfortunes, or fully uncover the past. Everyone struggles with unknowns in decision making. What job should I take? What is happening to friends we do not see? Who stole my wallet? How can I remember what I forgot? These and a thousand other questions about the unknown plague our everyday lives.

SEEKING GUIDANCE

How can people know the unknown and use that knowledge to control the future? People around the world have devised an astonishing number of ways to discern the unknown. Practitioners cast bones, read tea leaves, and throw pebbles. Palmists read the lines in a person's hand. Stock analysts use complex formulas to predict the market. Baseball coaches use statistics to increase success in their games. How do missionaries make sense of all these beliefs and behaviors? We will examine a few of these practices based on the relational and mechanistic metaphors developed in Chapter 3 and used throughout the book.

Discerning the unknown is often a public activity. The community conducts public rituals in which it calls on shamans, astrologers, soothsayers, and other diviners to reveal the unknown for the sake of public good. More often, divination is a private affair. Individuals go to specialists or use home diagnostic techniques to gain information they need to plan their lives.

People place importance on the diviner's ability to diagnose correctly. In some cases, he or she is approached by those seeking guidance, and asked to "divine" the reason for the visit. If successful, the practitioner is allowed to continue; if not, the clients go elsewhere. Generally, the practitioners have a thorough knowledge of local events, local maladies, and remedies, and use leading questions and tentative answers to draw out the expectations of the clients. In many cases the revelation is ambiguous, and people compete to gain public acceptance of interpretations that favor them.

ORGANIC METHODS FOR OBTAINING GUIDANCE

People around the world seek hidden knowledge from gods, spirits, ancestors, and other beings, who are believed to know the unknown. The organic methods people use to obtain guidance vary greatly from culture to culture, but some common patterns emerge.

OATHS AND CONDITIONAL CURSES

People in many societies use oaths to reveal the unknown. Those suspected of an offense are required to take an oath to their innocence. Oaths contain two elements: an affirmation or promise, and an appeal to a spiritual authority to judge and punish falsehoods. The belief is that if people lie, the gods or ancestors will punish them with illness, bad fortune, or even death. Conditional curses are opposite of oaths. They are judgments pronounced on those accused of doing wrong. After a curse is pronounced, the community waits to see if judgment takes place. If it does, the people are convinced that the accused are guilty, for if they are not guilty it has no power over them.

NECROMANCY

Necromancy involves rites to gain information from the dead. Communication with the dead is common in many African religions. Adelowo writes,

The Yoruba and the Africans at large believe that their deceased ones, particularly those who died at a ripe age, can be seen in dreams and trances, and that they can vouchsafe information or explanation or issue instructions on any issues or problems about which the family is in a serious dilemma. They can also relay messages through other persons or through certain cults to their kith and kin on earth. Along the road, in streets and in solitude or during the dead of night, it is believed that the deceased can appear to a person either to issue guidance, instruction, aid or solution or to molest (1987, 79).

Among the Sisala of northern Ghana, three men carry the dead body of a deceased relative on their shoulders at the funeral, believing that as they wander around the crowded funeral, the body will point out the dead person's killer (Mendosa 1989, 279).

In Judaism and Christianity, trafficking with the dead was condemned in the law (Lev. 19:31; 20:6), the prophets (Isa. 8:19–20), and the historical books (1 Chron. 10:13, Deut. 18). Despite this condemnation, Israelites continued to turn to the dead for guidance (Ezek. 21:21; Zech. 10:2). The most famous instance in the Bible is Saul and the medium of Endor (1 Sam. 28:1–25).

PRESENTIMENTS

Some people are believed to have the power to discern the unseen through feelings or presentiments. These practitioners observe body actions, such as sneezing, twitching, and hiccuping, which they interpret as predictions of rainfall, bad luck, drought, or some other coming event. Temne diviners in Ghana are believed to have 'four eyes.' Besides the normal eyes they are born with, they have two invisible eyes that give them a piercing supernatural vision of three other worlds: the world of spirits, the world of the dead, and the world of witches. They use these eyes to find witches, diagnose illnesses, and interact with the spirits. The Yoruba believe that what happens to a person is predestined, so a diviner forecasts their future by his inner sight and shows them how to improve on it. He uses sixteen palm nuts to see the future, and recites oracle poems to the client. Clients must interpret and apply one or more of these poems to their own situation. They often choose a course of action, and ask the diviner to cast the nuts again to see if they will be successful (Ray 1976, 108–9).

PROPHECIES

Prophets, seers, fortune tellers, and other announcers of divine messages are found in most religions. Unlike diviners, who use various mechanisms to determine the unknown, serve the society, and wait on their clients to initiate action, prophets speak revealed messages directly.

For instance, in the past, the Nuer prophets of Sudan and Ethiopia attracted large followings and initiated large-scale action above the village level. They organized cattle raids against their neighbors, the Dinka, performed rituals to stop epidemics, and led resistance movements against the Arab slavers and British colonial powers. One of these was Ngundeng, who lived for weeks alone in the bush, refusing food and falling into trances. He summoned the people and instructed them to build a high earth mound on which they performed their rituals to destroy the Arab slavers raiding the land (Ray 1976, 111).

Not all prophets are genuine prophets—there is always the danger that they are frauds. Many cultures have tests to determine whether a prophet is a true or false prophet. This is seen in the Old Testament, where the people are constantly warned against following false prophets (Mic. 3:5–7, Jer. 14:14, 26:9–10, Ezek. 13:1–9).

DREAMS, VISIONS, TRANCES

Around the world, people believe that dreams can reveal hidden information about the spiritual realm that is not accesible by other means. Often the person's spirit or shadow is thought to leave the body temporarily and enter the spirit world, and bring back a message. Visions and trances induced by mind-transforming drugs are widely seen as sources of privileged information.

Native Americans have long attached great importance to visions. Young men of the Plains and Woodland tribes went on vision quests to lonely spots to acquire supernatural knowledge and power. They sought for a guardian spirit to guide them throughout their lives. This search was aided by the use of drugs, purgatives, self-torture, fasting, staying awake for days, and dancing until they dropped. Buffalo, elk, bear, eagle, sparrow hawk, or other animal spirits with supernatural powers appeared to the expectant seeker, taught him a sacred song, and instructed him just how he should dress in battle. If he later violated these instructions he would lose the guardian's protection and suffer dire calamities. With successive visions a warrior made a "medicine bundle" containing pipes, tobacco, corn, and certain bird feathers.

The messages in dreams and visions are often vague and strange, and must be interpreted by specialists and religious leaders. Prophets are often said to have received their message in a dream, and the interpretation of that dream becomes a key element in the teachings of their followers. Dreams are also associated with shamans, healers, and other spiritual practitioners (Curley 1974).

SPIRIT POSSESSION

As noted in Chapter 6, spirit possession may be avoided as harmful. Often, however, it is sought because of the rewards it brings. Possession bridges the gulf between humans and gods, spirits and ancestors, giving humans a deep sense of their presence and involvement in human lives.

Shamans are often believed to acquire their knowledge from divining spirits or from ancestors. A Ndembu of northwest Zambia becomes a shaman after he becomes seriously ill through the affliction of the spirit of Kayong'u. After a diviner has diagnosed this as the cause of his illness, the man is kept in isolation, and washed with water and medicines. At dawn, as drums begin to beat, he is seized by violent spasms of shaking, a sign that Kayong'u has possessed him. His body is marked with red clay and he bites off the head of a chicken. The elders then test to see if he has the skills of divination. Using a basket full of various objects, he must identify the spiritual and human agents responsible for past misfortunes and deaths in the community. Because the diviner blames most calamities on the sin of broken relationships, he is seen not only as a healer of illnesses, but also a defender of morality (Ray 1976, 105–6).

SAMO SPIRIT TRAVEL

Samo shamans serve their kinsmen in times of distress by falling into a trance which allows their spirit to fly to the ancestral abode where it communes with the ancestors. Inasmuch as ancestors understand the plight of being human because they were there once, they can pass helpful information to the shaman who can return to the human context and interpret it for kinsmen. The celestial communication takes a form of glossolalia that often sounds like bird calls and vocalizations that are normally beyond the range of human vocal apparatus. These sounds can be heard by anyone at a gathering and signal to all present that the shaman is, indeed, speaking with the ancestors. Later, returning to the medium's body, the repossessed spirit begins to sing the message it received from the ancestors so that all present might understand what was said. When ordinary people hear the song, they gather around the shaman in order to catch every phrase which they then repeat in order to reinforce the message. This interpretation process, then, takes the form of an antiphonal choir, the medium singing a phrase and the entire audience repeating it. Everyone present understands and can then act on the content of the message. For this reason the Samo call these events 'ancestral spirit singing.' (Shaw 1996, 101)

The Yoruba mediums of Nigeria forecast the future while under possession. Pierre Verger (1969) tells of a woman whose children died one after the other, a few days after birth. One day she began to gesture uncontrollably, and fell stiffly on the ground in front of Ogun's temple. The elders said Ogun had chosen her, so she began the process of initiation. Three weeks later, she appeared at the festival of Ogun, ready to

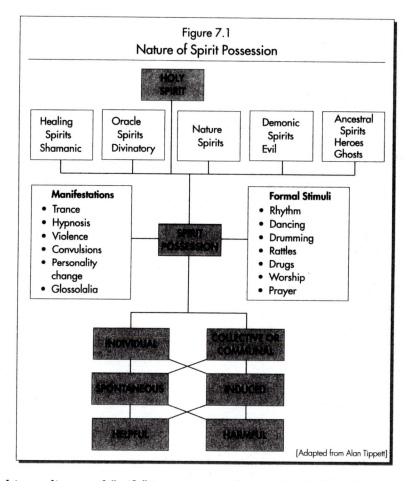

Figure 7.1
Nature of Spirit Possession

[Adapted from Alan Tippett]

be his medium and "wife" in service to the people of the village. Spirit possession is also sought to gain personal ecstasy. This is the case for voodoo in Haiti and the Zar cult in South Iran.

Alan Tippett devised a helpful taxonomy of spirits thought to possess people. They fall roughly into five groups (Figure 7.1): (1) healing spirits that possess shamans, (2) divinatory spirits that speak through oracles, (3) ancestral spirits, (4) nature spirits, and (5) evil spirits. To this we must add a separate category, that of the Holy Spirit who serves as the highest spiritual manifestation and represents the Godhead throughout the universe.

Possession sometimes leads to lethargy, trances, and sleep. More often it produces ecstasy, personality changes, glossolalia, and abnormal speech behavior. It is commonly found among expectant people in a social context where possession is regularly awaited at certain times

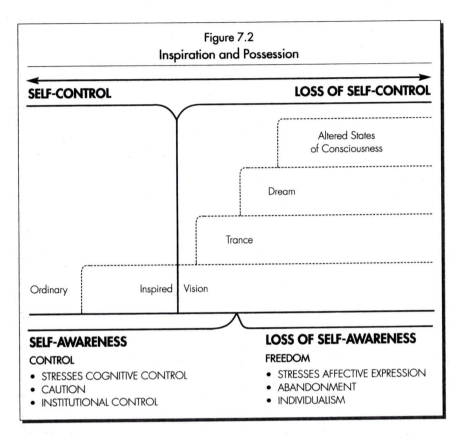

Figure 7.2
Inspiration and Possession

and conditions. People induce it by dancing, hand-clapping, chanting and taking drugs. Sometimes possession is individual, but often it is collective.

There are degrees of possession (Figure 7.2). On the one end is inspiration, in which the person retains self-awareness and control of the body and mind, but experiences strong mental clarity and emotional stimulation. At some point along the movement to the other pole, people lose control over their body movements, but remain conscious of their activities. Some shake, others manifest glossolalia or spirit writing, and others dance or run. The next step is to lose consciousness, while continuing bodily activities. Such people often show great strength, speak in altered voices, and manifest strange behavior.

An example of unconscious behavior occurred in a South Indian hamlet when the elders decided to move their huts from the swampy mosquito-ridden valley to a hill nearby. Before they could do so, however, they had to ask the goddess of the village *(grama devata)* if she was willing to move. Each night they staged a dance to hear her response.

On the eleventh night, one of the men became possessed and began to run around. Several men tried to restrain him, but he dragged them to the hill and pointed to a spot, saying in a high-pitched voice that this was where the goddess wanted to live. This confirmed the elders' choice, and the village moved to the high ground.

In dealing with possession, it is important to differentiate among three types of phenomena. First, there are genuine cases of spirit possession. Second, some believed to be possessed are better treated as psychopathological cases. Third, there are spurious cases in which people simulate possession for their own purposes.

GLOSSOLALIA

The term glossolalia is the anglicized compound of two Greek words—*glossa* meaning tongue, and *lalia* meaning speech. In English it has come to mean the use of human vocalization attributed to divine or spirit beings. It is found among powerful leaders in formal religions, and serves to validate their authority. It is also found in folk religion among the ordinary people who feel overwhelmed by the burdens of life. In many societies it provides the people with a sense of the immediacy of their ancestors and gods during public rituals.

The phenomena are found worldwide and throughout history. The Mari documents of the first millennium B.C. refer to oracles known as *muhhum*, who used music and alcohol to induce ecstatic states to reveal the unknown. In Egypt, Herodotus refers to the cult of Isis in which worshipers inflicted wounds on their bodies and spoke in incomprehensible sounds (Bunn 1973, 40). The Canaanite prophets used ecstatic frenzy and self-flagellation to get messages from the Baals. The Greeks turned to oracles and sibyls who spoke in strange languages that were then interpreted by a priest.[1] Today the *kahin* of Arabia serve as seers, communicating messages from the *jinn; dervishes* seek personal communications with Allah by slowly reciting his names and passages from the Quran, and then speeding up until a state of possession is reached; and shamans in inner and East Asia receive messages from the spirits.

Alan Tippett distinguishes between pseudoglossolalia, in which a person pretends to speak in tongues, and genuine glossolalia. He divides the latter into four phenomenological types based on the nature of the sounds (Figure 7.1).[2] The first is sacerdotal language. Here coherent sentences are spoken interjected with ancient sacred words. This is used by Eskimo, Dyak, Malaysian, and Indonesian shamans, Indian vil-

---

1. See Aeschylus in *Agamemnon*. Oracles were common in the mystery religions that arose in the first century B.C.
2. Tippett's taxonomy is based on the one suggested by May 1956.

lage priests who chant Sanskrit mantras they do not understand, and Haitian priests who use vestiges of African languages. The second are animal sounds, like those of leopards, boars, wolves, dogs, birds, and snakes such as python cults. This is common in totemic societies such as the Chukchee and Ainut. The third are unintelligible sounds such as groans (medicine men of South America and Australia), fragments of words, and alliterative sounds which are frequently repeated (Arctic region, North Borneo, Central Africa, and Micronesia). Esoteric spirit speech is common in Polynesia, East Malaysia, and inner and East Asia. The fourth type of glossolalia consists of coherent foreign languages not consciously known to the speaker, although he or she may have had some contact with them. Instances of this are documented in pagan as well as Christian settings.

Another type of spirit speaking appeared in the late nineteenth century in some Midwest American churches with sleeping preachers. They laid down on a couch and fell asleep; church elders then placed them behind the pulpit, where they preached long and powerful messages; finally the elders laid them back down. After a time, they awoke and claimed to be totally oblivious of the event. The fact that these sermons were not the conscious thoughts of humans added weight to the ordinary believers that this message was, indeed, from God.

MECHANICAL METHODS OF OBTAINING GUIDANCE

Mechanistic methods to discern the future and discover unknowns are diverse and widespread. We can only examine a few general types.

DIVINATION

The term 'divination' refers to a broad range of mechanical practices designed to show diviners the unknown (Figure 7.3). These include tossing sticks, looking at the reflection of candles in amber drops, gazing into crystal balls, reading tarot cards, looking at chicken entrails, and watching ripples on water.

Divination plays a fundamental role in the beliefs of many societies. For example, the Naskapi of the Peninsula of Labrador clean and dry animal bones, particularly the shoulder blades of a caribou, and hold them over hot coals for a short time, causing cracks and burned spots. These are then read by a diviner to answer important questions such as where men should hunt for game or where the community should set up camp. Scapulimancy of this sort was also practiced in North America, India, and Europe.

In Taiwan, common people go to temples to find answers to questions related to their job, illness, marriage, change of residence, school examination, prosperity, disaster, child delivery, death, and fate in

| | Figure 7.3 |
	Types of Divination
AEROMANCY	• observing the ripples in water
ALECTRYOMANCY	• observing rosters in a circle
ANGANG	• seeing a person or animal on a journey
ASTRAGALOMANCY	• casting bones to see how they fall
AUGURY	• watching the flight of birds
BENGE	• giving poison to chickens to see if they die
BOTANOMANCY	• watching how leaves blow
GEOMANCY	• reading cracks in dried mud
HARUSPICATION	• reading the entrails of sacrificed animals
KLEROMANCY	• casting lots (Judg. 20; Josh. 7; 1 Sam. 10:13, 23–46)
LITHOMANCY	• reading rock formations
NECROMANCY	• communicating with the dead (1 Sam. 28:7ff.; Isa. 8:19)
NUMEROLOGY	• observing combinations of numbers
OLEOMANCY	• reading pebbles thrown on the sand
ONEIROMANCY	• interpreting dreams
PALMISTRY	• reading the lines in a person's hand

[These are only a few of the many different kinds of divination]

general. They consult a diviner, who discerns the cause and prescribes a remedy.

Many South African peoples use axes to reveal the unknown. The ax is laid on the ground and held by the diviner at the head. The ax is then moved gently forwards and backwards while the diviner poses questions. The answer is given by the ax's refusal to move in response to the pressure of the diviner's hand. The diviner taps it with his knuckles, thereby releasing it, and he then asks another question. Other diviners gaze into glass mirrors until they see the spirit or reflection of people who are witches. The Azande of Sudan use poison oracles before they undertake any important venture. Poison is fed to two small domestic fowls. From their behavior and sometimes death, the Azande receive answers they place before the oracle.

CASTING LOTS

There are many variations on casting lots to learn the unknown. Buddhist priests throw sticks, West African diviners cast cowrie shells and bones, and Arab Muslims cast lots to know the will of Allah when they divide land in the distribution of an inheritance.

Like other forms of divination, casting lots often involves complex interpretations of observed events. In South India, a barren wife goes to the temple to discern the cause of and a remedy for her malady. She brings an equal number of white and red flowers in a sack. A nearby child is asked to draw a flower from the sack. If it is red, the wife knows that her barrenness is temporary and that she will have a child in due time. If it is white, she knows she has a serious problem. The child is then asked to draw again. If the flower is red, the diagnosis is that she must go to a medical doctor and she will be cured. If it is white, a doctor cannot help her. The child then draws a third flower. If it is red, the wife has offended the gods and must offer them a large sacrifice to be cured. If it is white, there is nothing she can do about her barrenness. But some doubt remains—after three straight white flowers, is the test true or is this pure coincidence? The child draws a fourth time. If the flower is red, the test is true. If it is white, the test is false and the whole process must be repeated again. In most divination there is a measure of ambiguity in the interpretation of the results, and the answers often offer hope to those who have lost hope. But the clients in the end must fit the answers to their own situations.

OMENS

Omens are supernatural messages or portents heard by chance that have some bearing on people's daily lives—premonitions presaging future blessings or warnings of potential dangers. Often they must be interpreted by specialists. Publicly omens are sought to warn the people of earthquakes, eclipses, comets, and wars. Privately they help people to determine which marriage will be good, what day for travel is auspicious, and when to start a business to assure its success.

Omens are often associated with animal behavior. In ornithomancy, diviners watch the flight of birds and interpret their direction of flight, formation and numbers, cry, and position relative to the observer. For example, the Samoans observed birds before setting out on a war party. If they saw an owl, a heron, or a kingfisher flying ahead, this signified victory, but if they were flying the opposite direction, the planned attack was postponed.

Reading the entrails of slain animals (haruspices) is also widespread. It is widely believed that sacrificial animals go to the gods, who foretell the approach of specific events, favorable or foreboding, by means of the form, color, and presence or absence of specific parts of the viscera.

Other signs of the future are associated with the sky, such as eclipses, comets, falling stars, lightning, and thunder. Running and rippling water, too, are widely used to learn the unknown, as are casting sticks, seeds, and dice. Earthquakes, droughts, and aberrations of nature (animals with two heads or five feet) are often considered ominous and viewed with great horror. Reading the lines in the hand, watching leaves fall, noting the auspicious and inauspicious signs on wedding days—these and many other ways are used to foretell the future.

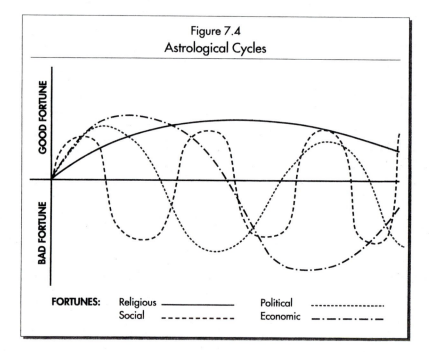

Figure 7.4
Astrological Cycles

GOOD FORTUNE

BAD FORTUNE

FORTUNES: Religious ——————   Political ·················
             Social - - - - - - -   Economic —·—·—·—·—

Another mode of divination is taking omens from sacred texts. Practitioners randomly select passages from the Quran, Bible, or other book, and apply these to the client's situation.

ASTROLOGY

Astrology is the belief that human lives are influenced by the positions of the planets in the heavens, and that each person's time of birth shapes his or her fate throughout life. Each of the stellar bodies influences a specific area of life. For example, one governs a person's economic affairs, another political influence, a third social status, and a fourth religious well-being. Each of these cycles from good to bad, but the length of the cycles is different from one to another. A person's economic cycle may be two weeks, the political cycle three, the social five, and the religious six (Figure 7.4). Each moment, then, is a combination of these. This Tuesday, a person's economic and political cycles may be positive, but the social and religious cycles negative. To start a business venture on Tuesday is good, but Tuesday is not the day to visit distant relatives.

The practice of astrology is particularly popular in South Asia. Annually the local priest determines the yield of crops for the next year and the general health of the village. Individuals come for him to study horoscopes to determine suitable marriages, to choose the proper day and time to start building a new house, to set a day when business ventures and travel are good, and to guide them in decisions that involve uncertainties and risks. The most important event in a person's life is marriage. The marriage date must be chosen so that the cycles of the bride and groom are optimal. Given the many overlapping cycles, it is almost impossible to find a time when all of them are strongly positive. The astrologer must, therefore, find a time that is at least satisfactory in the major areas of life.

ORDEALS

Ordeals are painful and often life-threatening tests that persons suspected of misdeeds may be forced to undergo to test their innocence or guilt. Some such tests are dipping a hand into hot oil, swallowing poison, or having a red-hot knife blade pressed against some part of the body.

The Sisala of northern Ghana use the scorpion ordeal to divine petty thefts or other minor offenses. A husband will use it to find out which of his wives has secretly robbed the compound granary. The suspects are lined up and the scorpion is allowed to crawl over their arms. A sting is both the proof and punishment. Sisala accused of wrongdoing say, "If I am guilty, let a snake bite me." Snake bites are seen as punishments sent by the ancestors (Mendosa 1989, 280).

In one society in the South Sea Islands the suspects in a murder or theft are taken to the river and at a signal their heads are pushed under the water. The first person to come up for air is obviously guilty. The Fon of Benin place a red-hot machete on the tongue of the accused to see if he blisters, take a seed from a pot of boiling oil to see if it burns his hand, or places a pepper under the eyelid to see whether tears form.

USES OF GUIDANCE

Divination, dreams, omens, astrology, and prophecies provide answers, and release anxiety in a world of questions; where illnesses are unchecked by modern medicine, where wells or water holes can go dry, and where crops are at the mercy of the elements. Mendosa found among the Sisala of northern Ghana that the primary reasons people went to diviners were: illness (38%), marriage (12%), going on a journey (12%), childbirth (4%), barrenness (3%), death (1%), and to see the future, settle conflicts, and general troubles (4%) (1989, 284). In some ways seeking guidance is not much different from the models stock brokers use to predict the market, or the statistical formulas engineers, manufacturers, and baseball coaches use to make their decisions. These provide concrete ways to calculate the likelihood of future and unknown events.

Worldwide, divination is used for a great many reasons. Only a few are examined here.

1. *To diagnose causes of misfortune, disease, and death.* As noted in Chapter 6, there are many causes of misfortune, such as ghosts, spirits, ancestors, gods, witchcraft, fate, bad luck, and bad stars. Many people turn to divination, dreams, omens, and methods to determine which of these is responsible for their specific illness, calamity, or failure.

2. *To determine courses of action.* People live in an uncertain world, and must make important decisions involving many unknown factors. They must select spouses not knowing what kind of person each candidate will be years later. Warriors in a village must decide what time is the best to attack their enemies, merchants when it is most auspicious to take a business trip, and farmers the propitious time to plant their crops. The Samo of Papua New Guinea seek the guidance of recently deceased kinsmen to obtain information these ancestors may not have been able to pass on while still alive. This is done through an all-night 'spirit sing' where a medium communicates with the spirit of the individual to obtain the necessary information.

3. *To avoid danger.* How can humans avoid future problems such as impending disasters? Can transempirical beings and powers help in this process? Astrological charts are examined to determine times that are inauspicious for new business ventures or building government buildings. Omens are natural signs that warn of impending events.[3] For example, in China, if a person dies in a house, it may be plagued by the ghost, and is an inauspicious place in which to live. In Indian villages, if an ox in the house of a bride or groom dies the day before the wedding, or either of them sees a wolf, jackal, or snake on the way to the marriage, it is called off because these are signs that it is a bad marriage.

4. *To determine guilt or innocence.* Establishing guilt in most societies is not simply a matter for courts of law. In most kinship and peasant cultures the guilty party is often flushed out by means of gossip and other socially approved forms of negative sanctions. Often ordeals, curses, and tests of truth are used to provide the people with supernatural ways of determining whether a person is guilty or innocent. At other times, astrologers, necromancers, and diviners determine the guilty party.

5. *To select someone for office.* Guidance is often sought to assist a society to select someone for office. People in Western cultures assume that the best way to select leaders is by popular vote,

3. See, for example, Broster 1947.

but they often know little about those they elect or what these leaders will be like after a number of years in office. Other societies seek guidance from the unseen world in making such choices. An example in the New Testament is the selection of Matathias as the replacement for Judas by means of casting lots (Acts 1:26). In America, in the nineteenth century, some Protestant churches selected their pastors from among those nominated by having them choose a hymnal in which were placed paper strips—the person drawing the long strip was believed to be God's choice for the church.

6. *To find lost persons or objects.* One common problem is that people lose track of one another and of objects. Hunters in the forest are lost, and weapons misplaced. Special knowledge is needed to find them. For example, on one occasion a group of Samo brothers was unable to locate a shotgun. During a seance the spirit of the deceased was asked to tell where the gun was located. The next day the brothers went to the indicated bush house and found the gun under a particular log (Shaw 1996, 102). In folk Catholicism Saint Anthony is the patron saint who helps people find lost objects.

7. *To gain supernatural knowledge.* Supernatural means are used to obtain special secret knowledge or *gnosis*. In many cultures, hidden knowledge is highly valued because the most powerful and effective knowledge is secret. Often such knowledge is controlled by secret societies, chiefs and ritual specialists, diviners, blacksmiths, and hunters. Those who have it are believed to have special powers that they can use to gain success, but they are often suspected of using it illicitly for their own individual ends at the expense of other members of the community. This opposition between secret and open knowledge reinforces the hierarchical social order, which ranks chiefs over commoners, old over young, men above women, and secret society initiates above noninitiates. An example of this in the early Christian church was the threat of gnosticism. Paul tried to show that all believers are one in Christ and through him we all have access to the Creator who made human beings, knows them and wants them, to know and have fellowship with him (Gal. 3:26–29).

CHRISTIAN RESPONSE

How should Christians respond to the problem of the unknown, and the human desire to know? What answers do the Scriptures give regarding the way God guides human lives? When new converts ask when they should go to hunt for much needed game—should they go tomorrow or the next day, and should they go north or east—how should missionaries respond? If we ask them where they got game last time, or tell them to take their chances, we inform them we have no religious answers. They will go back to their practitioners who cast bones and tell them to go tomorrow and to go east. Christians must provide better answers to the real questions people ask about life.

Before looking at biblical principles regarding God's guidance, a few preliminary remarks are in order. First, Christians as leaders must model for the people concrete ways of seeking to know God's will. We need a theology of guidance that informs human actions, but theology alone is not enough. It must be made real in everyday life. Like other spiritual disciplines, learning to know God's guidance is as much a matter of mentoring as instructing.

Second, we must keep in mind that God speaks to humans in understandable ways. In cultures where people take dreams seriously, he can and does use dreams. In cultures where manifestations of power are seen as God's actions, God shows himself in extraordinary ways. We must be careful not to restrict God's communication to ways familiar to us.

Third, the way God leads his people changes as they grow in Christian maturity. To seekers in traditional societies, he often shows himself in miraculous healings, deliverance from evil spirits, and visions. Who has not at some time 'put out a fleece' or used sortilage—opening their Bibles and pointing a finger to find a verse for the day. As faith grows, Christians rely more on daily communion with God through reading Scripture, prayer, and counsel from God's saints than on miracles and divine interventions. This maturity is part of the guidance question. People should be encouraged to start with their questions and we must recognize their need for extraordinary signs to lead them. Gradually, as they grow in spiritual maturity, they may no longer need miracles to confirm their faith. Rather, they come to walk with God daily in the normal interaction of spiritual companionship.

Fourth, discernment is at the heart of divine guidance. Not all methods of discernment are open to Christians. Scripture forbids necromancy (speaking with the dead; Isa. 8:19–20), astrology (Isa. 47:13), divination (Deut. 18:10–12), and idolomancy (consulting idols; 1 Sam. 19:13; Ezek. 21:21). Moreover, not all dreams, visions, inner voices, or prophecies are true. Scripture warns against false prophets and diviners (Mic. 3:5–7, Jer. 14:14, 26:9–10, Ezek. 13:1–9), fortune tellers (Isa. 47:13), and sorcerers (Acts 8:11). What is needed, then, is a theology of guidance which can assist Christians as they deal with the realities of life.

MISCONCEPTIONS REGARDING DIVINE GUIDANCE

A theology of God's guidance must not only affirm what Christians believe based on Scripture, but challenge the misconceptions that come out of their cultures. This is true not only of new believers and churches, but also for established Christians and churches that uncritically bring in the beliefs of their cultural environments. Before developing a theology of guidance, we need to consider some widespread misconceptions.

One common misconception is that humans must guess God's will. Many Christians have the mistaken notion that they must somehow find God's will for their lives, and if they don't; they fail and are out of God's will for life. One version of this is a literalistic application of Psalm 32:8, which speaks of God guiding us with his eye: this view urges us to keep looking up at God to make sure we see whether he looks in another direction. But we often find we must look down to avoid the holes in the road ahead, and in doing so, miss God's glance. Scripture makes it clear; however God does not expect Christians to guess his will. He wants us to *know* his will, and is ready to make it known to us if we are willing to listen and obey.

The second misconception is that God will show his will to those who trust him as one option among many to be seriously considered. God does not do this. First, he asks Christians to make up their minds whether they will do his will when he reveals it. Only when they are committed to doing so does he show the way. In metaphorical terms, when humans place their faith in God, they join God's army and give up their right to make decisions on their own. The only question is to obey orders when these are given. It is God's responsibility to reveal his will, which he will surely do.

A third misconception is that God has one perfect plan for his children, and if they stray from God's will for their lives, they must settle for God's second, third, or fourth best. So Christians seek the perfect marriage partner, the perfect job, the perfect life, and in so doing miss out on a relationship with the planner. Life should flow out of relationship with God, to know him and love him forever. If the plan is the focus, it is doomed. From Scripture, however, it is clear that God begins with believers where they are, and has his plan for their lives whenever they turn themselves over to his leading. This does not mean that past losses are undone. It means that Christians can be sure that they are living in God's will for them now.

A fourth misconception is far more ingrained in us as fallen humans, and one that is harder to root out, namely, a magical approach to divine guidance. We already know what we want, and in our prayers we simply ask God to grant us what we want. Prayer, here, is not submission to God's will, but an attempt to control God's actions. Scripture is clear: we are to seek to know God's will, whatever that is, in order that we may do it. Prayer is also giving God permission to use us to answer the requests we place before him.

A final misconception is that God is a wise parent making all decisions for his children who are called to unquestioningly obey his guidance. There is a tendency to want God to tell us what to do. This robs Christians of the greatest gift God has given, the freedom to relate to him as adults. Philip Yancey writes,

> He desires not so much to run our lives as to have us, in full control of our lives, offer them to him in obedience and service. . . . There is no short cut, no magic. . . . There is only the possibility of a lifetime search for intimacy with God . . . [God] wants love and a lasting commitment to take him seriously, everyday, regardless (1983, 25, 27).

It is interesting that Jesus in his parables spoke of stewards, not accountants. There is an important difference. Accountants are human calculating machines who keep track of every cent to make sure it is properly recorded. They do not make decisions regarding investments based on risk and return. Stewards, on the other hand, are given resources and entrusted with using them for the gain of the master. They have many options open to them, and must make wise decisions. God calls Christians to be stewards. He has provided gifts, and sound minds to use them. He gives wisdom when asked, but allows freedom to use these gifts for his glory. When asked, he guards against wasting these gifts, and he helps believers grow to maturity by empowering them to use what he has given in ways that provide meaning and purpose in a multitude of culturally appropriate ways. Too often missionaries have had an accounting rather than a stewardship approach when they give resources to young churches.

A THEOLOGY OF DIVINE GUIDANCE

God does want believers to know his will, not guess it! How, then, does he reveal it? We need to answer this question both on a general level—living life under the guidance of God, and on a specific level—what Christians should do in a particular situation.

GENERAL PRINCIPLES OF GUIDANCE

God reveals his purposes in broad strokes. He has given his Word (the Scriptures) as the guide and norm by which Christians should live. God has communicated clearly his will about righteousness, love, humility, and peace. These principles need to be manifest in Christian decision making. God has provided a community of faith—other believers—to share in relationships and give advice. Above all, the church itself must become a community that seeks to follow God's leading, and helps its members in concrete ways to know God's will for them. This can be done through special times for prayer and discernment by the church or groups of individuals, by listening to leaders gifted with understanding the times and testing their messages against Scripture, and by making decisions and asking God to close the door if these are not according to his will.

God opens and closes doors through circumstances that may change human plans and provide serendipitous opportunities to serve God. Similarly, closed doors may be God's way of moving people in another direction. God has created us with minds and hearts to seek his will, and when we do, he speaks in a quiet voice of conviction and certainty. Yancey notes, "[H]e guides in subtle ways, by feeding ideas into our minds, speaking through a nagging sensation of dissatisfaction, inspiring us to choose better than we otherwise would have done, bringing to the surface hidden dangers of temptations" (1983, 27). Christians need to give these general principles serious consideration as ways in which God speaks to his children. Before acting, however, we need to pray that if the course of action chosen is not what God wants, that he make that plain. Christians can then proceed with clear consciences and conviction, knowing that God can and will lead them.

SPECIFIC PRINCIPLES OF GUIDANCE

As noted earlier in this chapter, the question of guidance on the level of folk religion has mostly to do with making specific decisions in everyday life. Therefore, what should missionaries say when new converts want to know when and where to go hunting? Without answers, people will assume Christianity is irrelevant, and will return to their old ways of divination, which provide them definite immediate answers.

Outsiders must assist new converts in discerning concrete ways of seeking God's guidance. They should be taught to search Scripture and pray, to seek the advice of brothers and sisters in the faith, and to seek for signs of God's guidance. This may be given through convictions, advice, and events that confirm their convictions.

There is much discussion today about receiving personal revelations: prophecies, words of knowledge, visions, dreams, speaking in tongues, demonstrations of power, casting of lots, and sleeping preachers. Keep in mind that God does use these different ways in different contexts, and Christians can respond to God's leading, however it comes. On the other hand, Satan imitates all these ways. There are false prophecies, visions, tongues, and dreams. Satan heals the sick and raises people from the dead. We must remember that there is no visible phenomenon that guarantees that the message given is from God, no matter how self-authenticating it seems to be. John Wesley notes that "Great religious experiences are themselves no sign of their validity or that necessarily they are from God" (1959, 127). The only thing that Satan does not mimic is worship of God and righteousness in living. The issue is one of discernment by the leaders of the church gathered in prayer and the study of Scripture and seeking together to hear the Word of the Lord. The issue is also one of priorities, the prior will of God for those who live holy, obedient lives of service to him. God's will is that his people serve him. But his ultimate concern is their relationship with him. Out of relationship with him and spiritual growth comes guidance.

CHALLENGING OLD WAYS

New converts often bring with them their traditional ways of seeking guidance. In most societies, diviners, prophets, and other intermediaries deal with impersonal transcendent powers and with lesser deities and spirits who are believed to have more direct contact with humans and their problems. Rarely do diviners seek guidance from the high God who is believed to deal with cosmic realities and is not interested in the day-to-day events of human lives.

The importation of these old worldviews is a serious problem for Christians in young churches around the world today. New believers often continue their old practices, but substitute Christian symbols in place of their traditional ones. These new forms, however, are still associated with old meanings. The Bible is not read for understanding, but as a way to divine a course of action. The cross is seen as an omen and used to ward off spirits and other dangers. Christian discipling must not only offer young Christians new ways to find guidance, but also challenge their old worldviews. Christian faith calls for direct relationship with God himself. There should be no intermediaries. Scripture exhorts believers to avoid magical approaches to guidance, and encourages them to seek God's leading.

Syncretism occurs not only in young churches. Many traditional diviners and healers use "in Jesus' name" at the beginning or end of their rites, and keep Bibles handy and recite words of Jesus to their clients.[4] They do not see themselves as witnesses to Christ, however, but as mediators between the unseen world of spiritual beings and forces, and Jesus (Etuk 1984). Because they claim guidance in the name of Jesus, many Christians are attracted to their services. An example of this is

---

4. A similar pattern is seen in folk Islam, where local diviners use chapters and verses from the Quran in their rites (Adelowo 1987).

Subba Rao in South India, who claims to have had a direct vision of Jesus and who is reported to have healed thousands afflicted with leprosy, tuberculosis, hepatitis, skin diseases, epilepsy, and cobra-bites in the name of Jesus. He also casts out demons. Subba Rao denies that Jesus is God, but claims that he is the great guru that can help humans to be reabsorbed into God through the process of meditation, renunciation of the world and self, and service to others (Baago 1968). Many of the independent movements that emerge on the edges of Christianity tend to mix Christian beliefs and old ways.[5]

Churches in the West face another danger. They are deeply influenced by the engineering mentality of their world, and believe that if they know how things work and do the right things, they can control the future and uncover the past. Consequently, planning, budgeting, measuring, evaluating and replanning often constitute the heart of church business meetings. The same can be said of many Western Christians who believe they can control their lives with science. Like Christians everywhere, Westerners need to learn again dependence on God, and a need to seek his leading, and not to trust their own efforts.

5. For an excellent discussion of this in Africa, see Sundkler 1961.

8

RIGHT AND WRONG

The three questions examined so far have to do with explanations of reality. In much of the world, religion has as much or more to do with questions of moral order, right and wrong, righteousness and sin, holiness and defilement. What, for example, is the ideal person? How should humans relate to gods, spirits, ancestors, and nature? What are the proper relations between old and young, men and women, and rich and poor? How should people relate to kinsmen, neighbors, strangers, and enemies?[1]

All societies must have a sense of moral order to survive. Without a differentiation between good and evil, relationships in human communities are impossible. Similarly, all societies have a sense of cosmic order that organizes the world in ways their people consider right. This raises critical questions: What is the basis for beliefs in good and evil, and in purity and pollution, and what is the relationship between these two concepts of order? For common folk, right and wrong is not a philosophical question to be answered in abstract terms. It is an existential reality in which they live their lives. Like the psalmist, they wonder why the wicked prosper and the righteous suffer. As Laurenti Magesa points out (1997), many folk religious beliefs focus on maintaining moral order in everyday life.

The legitimacy of the moral order is sometimes rooted in transcendent beings, such as gods, ancestors, and other beings, in cosmic moral principles, or in laws of just rewards, and other impersonal forces. The relationship between organic and structural moral orders is complex, and varies from religion to religion. We will examine first organic and mechanistic views of moral order, and then the relationship between them will be discussed

1. After the Enlightenment, science, and to a great extent, systematic theology, sought objective truth and did so by divorcing thinking from feelings and values. Morality and character formation have become increasingly marginalized in modern thought and, unfortunately, in much of Christian theology. There are few courses on moral character and lifestyle.

RIGHTEOUSNESS AND SIN

In much of the world, morality is defined in terms of right relation-ships. All humans struggle to maintain good relations with other hu-mans, gods, spirits, ancestors, animals, plants, and nature. Behind this is a sense of moral etiquette or order that defines what is good and evil in terms of relationships between beings—what is fair and unfair, just and unjust, generous and greedy, loving and hateful. Anything that strengthens good relationships is righteous, such as generosity, loyalty, hospitality, and honesty. Sin is anything that violates or dis-turbs these relationships, such as hatred, jealousy, disobedience, and selfishness.

Relational concepts of morality are often found in societies that em-phasize the group over the individual. In many kin-based societies, it is not evil to plunder, harm, or kill people from other groups. This helps Westerners understand the nation-states in Africa, where government officials plunder state funds for the benefit of their own tribe.

Different cultures define morality differently, but to exist all of them must have a sense of what constitutes good, right, and just rela-tionships. All, too, must explain the existence of evil, wrong, injustice, and falsehood. There are several views of morality which we need to examine.

HOLINESS AND SIN

Not only do concepts of righteousness and sin vary greatly from so-ciety to society, their cultural assumptions are manifest in a myriad of ways. It is important here to distinguish between natural precepts that regulate nature, social norms and sins that reflect cultural expectations, and theological sins that reflect religious beliefs.

NATURAL NORMS AND SINS

In many societies, the world is one moral universe in which humans, ancestors, unborn, gods, spirits, animals, and nature interact in one web of relationships in which every being and thing is related to every other. All life originates from and shares in natural life, and therefore the very fabric of nature is sacred. Russell Staples writes,

> The good life is the life that is lived in harmony with the moral order of reality. To offend against that order is to bring calamity not only upon oneself, but also upon the whole community. The evil forces of reality must be restrained and rendered impotent, and the beneficent forces must be supported and kept well disposed to the community. The means by which this may be accomplished is religious ritual (1982, 71).

Humans are central on earth, but they must live in harmony with the world around them. If the natural order is disturbed, it is humans who suffer most.

Sin, in this view, is to violate the earth and nature. It is to kill animals without giving them thanks for sacrificing themselves for human sustenance, to plow the earth and cut down trees without asking their pardon for the pain these cause, and to slaughter more game than is needed for life.

SOCIAL NORMS AND SINS

All societies have their own definitions of social sin, and act to restore balance or eliminate inappropriate behavior when people go beyond what is culturally tolerated. Most societies see offenses as violations against their own members. These may include bodily injury, anger, theft, killing, lying, disrespect, lack of generosity, antisocial behavior, and not sharing. Each society also has its "cardinal sins." For example, in the American church, sexual sins are considered worst, whereas in India, the greatest sin is anger and the loss of one's temper. Particular sins are also associated with particular ages, sexes, roles, or social strata, and punishment is generally carried out by socially approved leaders.

Social norms vary greatly from society to society. Robert Spencer argues, however, that the Ten Commandments in the Old Testament outline basic principles all societies must practice to survive. "Thou shalt not kill"—no society can permit uncontrolled killing, though each defines "murder" and what is justified as killing in its own cultural way. "Thou shalt not steal"—all societies must regulate the ownership of property. "Thou shalt not commit adultery"—all societies must regulate sexual relationships. "Thou shalt not covet"—all societies must control greed and avarice, and foster sharing and some sense of equity. Thus all societies have a sense of moral rectitude and law.

Strongly individualistic societies focus on the rights of the individual, and ethics is defined largely in terms of interpersonal relationships and keeping the 'laws of the land.' Sin is to harm another and harmony is restored when relationships are mended; or sin is to break community laws and offenders must pay the necessary price to restore justice. A system of jurisprudence that contrasts criminal and civil law maintains this dual sense of justice. In either case, the offender has a feeling of personal guilt.

Other societies see the group as the most important human reality. People are seen as whole and right only as they live in harmony and peace in communities. In this view, good is what sustains life and community. It is expressed in hospitality in which people share the gift and power of life with others in the group. Evil is anything that destroys life and community. Above all it is greed, the antonym of hospitality and sociability. For example, the highest values of the Kalenjin in Kenya are *sobondo* (well-being and social harmony) and *teegisto* (respect). People are complete only as they are in right relationship to the ancestors and local spirits around them, to one another in community, and to the world of nature in which they live. This wholeness, being complete and rightly ordered, relates to all spheres of life and includes spiritual, moral, mental, and physical harmony and health. Wrongdoing is often seen as contagious. When an individual breaks the rules, the evil spreads to close kinsmen, family, clan, and people. But it may be arrested and removed at any stage by appropriate rituals (Cox 1994).

In a relational view of morality, sin is socially defined. At root, evil is breaking relations with others in the spiritual, social, or natural community. People sin against other humans in their group by offenses such as bodily injury, anger, theft, killing, and lying. This is in contrast to sins against their community through disrespect, lack of generosity, and antisocial behavior. They sin against ancestors through insubordination, against local spirits and animals by neglect, and against the earth by indifference. Sin not only deprives individuals and the community of peace, happiness, wellness, and prosperity, it also disrupts the social harmony.

One of the greatest sins in group-oriented societies is failure to care for parents and ancestors, who, as punishment, may bring misfortune or withhold blessings on the family. Ignoring the ancestors is a sin that brings misfortune on the whole extended family, including their cattle, goats and sheep, and crops in the field (Moyo 1996, 39). Incest, too, defiles the community, and affects all creation. Rains are withheld as judgment, and severe droughts occur.

Murder is a great offense against a group. The Shona believe that the *ngozi*, the spirits of family members who died aggrieved or were murdered, return and kill relatives of the individual responsible until the crime has been confessed and compensation made to the family of the deceased. A family that feels it has been sinned against can call the spirit of one of its ancestors to come as a *ngozi* and punish the members of the other family until they acknowledge their sin and make compensation. The fundamental good is maintaining the harmony and well-being of the group. Sin is to undermine the community—family, clan, society.

In traditional African societies the maintenance of the moral order is the responsibility of the elders and ancestors. They are seen as stronger, and can claim the allegiance of the younger. All must submit to God, but ancestors are the intermediaries between God and living humans. Magesa notes,

The ancestors are the protectors of the society as well as its most feared direct critics and source of punishment. Above all, they are the direct watch-dogs of the moral behavior of the individual, the family, the clan and the entire society with which they are associated. No serious misbehavior or anti-life attitude among their descendants, in thought, word and deed, escapes their gaze (1997, 48).

In societies with a strong group sense, the violation of relational norms leads to a sense of shame on the part of individuals and groups, because they have failed their community. A woman caught in adultery is ashamed because she has brought dishonor to her family, and her family is ashamed because they raised a daughter who would do this evil. Shame is a human reaction to other people's criticism and gossip, and an acute personal chagrin at one's failure to live up to the obligations and expectations of others. In communal societies, self-respect is vital to a person's identity and place in society, and must be maintained by choosing what is socially defined as right and wrong.

In this view of morality, salvation is restoration of right relationships among all members of the community—living and living dead. When the community sins, repentance, forgiveness, and reconciliation must involve all members of the community and not just individuals.

THEOLOGICAL NORMS AND SINS

In many societies, humans are seen as part of cosmic communities that include ancestors, the unborn, gods, spirits, animals, and nature. This leads to a theological view of good and evil in which righteousness and sin are ultimately defined not in social but in religious terms—as living in obedience and disobedience to the will and commands of God. In this view, sin not only breaks human relationships, it violates the cosmic order created by God. For example, many in the West, with its strong emphasis on individualism, consider marriage a contract between two people which either side can break—it is strictly a personal relationship. In socially oriented societies, marriage is an alliance made between two kinship groups, and divorce rips apart the very fabric of the society. In other societies, theological issues underlie ideas of marriage. In these societies marriages are thought to be made in heaven, and divorce is a cosmic fracturing of fundamental relationships that threaten to destroy the harmony of the entire universe. For them, marriage is a sacrament, not simply a social edict or personal contract. An example of this sacramental view of relationships is found among the Masaii of Kenya. When a young man gives cows to his bride's father, he is not only expressing appreciation for the right to marry the woman, nor is he only doing what his ancestors have done through the ages before him. Rather he is affirming the moral order that he should exchange gift for gift, an order given to the people by God himself.

Violation of divine commands often leads to a sense of fear. Salvation, in this context, is reconciliation with God and restoration of the cosmic moral order. Often this involves sacrifices and rites of submission to the divine commands.

SOCIAL AND THEOLOGICAL OFFENSES

Social and theological sins are often intertwined. Some norms are basically social in nature. They are the ways the society does things. Violating them is a misdemeanor or a crime.

A CLASSIFICATION OF SINS IN JAPAN
DURING THE ENGI PERIOD

These are a few of the sins listed in the seventy volumes of *The Liturgy of Great Exorcism and Purification.*

> *Heavenly Sins:* (sins against the cosmic order)
> *ahanachi:* to break down the divisions between rice fields.
> *mizoume:* to break the water path of the rice fields.
> *hihanachi:* to break the wooden water-pipes in the rice fields.
> *shikimaki:* to sow seed over plants where someone else's seed has already been sown.
> *kushisaki:* to usurp the rice fields of others.
> *tikihagi:* to flay a sacred horse alive.
> *sakahagi:* to flay a horse while it is lying upside down.
> *kusohi:* to urinate or defecate at a sacred place.
> *Earthly Sins:* (sins against the community)
> *ikihadatachi:* to murder or injure a person.
> *shihadatachi:* to desecrate the body of the dead.
> *shirabito:* to be an albino.
> *kokumi:* to be a hunchbacked person.
> *onogahaha okaseru tsumi:* sexual intercourse with one's mother.
> *onoga ko okaseru tsumi:* sexual intercourse with one's daughter.
> *onoga ko okaseru tsume:* sexual intercourse with a woman and her daughter.
> *ko to haha okaseru tsumi:* sexual intercourse with a woman and her mother.
> *kemono okaseru tsumi:* sexual intercourse with an animal.
> *hau mushi no tsumi:* to be stung by an insect.
> *takatsu kami no wazawai:* to be struck by lightning
> *kemono taoshi majimono suru tsumi:* to put a curse on someone by burying an animal in the ground.
> —Minoru Hayashi

Other norms are rooted in religious sanctions, and their violation is seen as sin. Still others link the two. This is often true in societies with a strong sense of group that see life in religious terms. Divine commands are used to legitimate certain social laws, such as those prohibiting adultery, murder, and theft. On the other hand, religions rarely address other social sins such as not mowing one's lawn regularly, bad manners, and driving on the right side of the road. Learning to know which domains are covered by religious constraints and which are not is an important area of investigation in cross-cultural communication.

In examining social and theological sins, it is useful to distinguish between personal sin and corporate sin. The former is a violation by an individual against the gods or others in the society, and in which the individual is solely to blame. The result is a sense of personal guilt, and normally the individual suffers the consequences. Corporate sin is the violation of a person or the group against the gods and ancestors in which the whole group shares the blame and suffers the consequences.

COMMANDS AND DISOBEDIENCE

A second organic view of morality is rooted in authority. Gods, ancestors, kings, chiefs, and others in authority issue commands that those under them must obey, and enforce these laws through councils, courts, police, and other judicial means. Laws in this view are created, and reflect the character and desires of those who rule. Wrong is seen as disobedience, rebellion, and treason. An example of this view of law is found in the Old Testament, where the law was given by God (Exod. 20–23) as a manifestation of his being, and was administered by his appointed representatives (Exod. 24). As we will see later, this view of law as the commands of cosmic or social authorities differs sharply from the view of law as a transcendent, impersonal moral order.

SACRIFICE AND RECONCILIATION

Having discussed how the moral fabric of society can be torn by the evil of broken relationships and disobeyed commands, how can it be mended? How are righteousness, justice, and *shalom* restored? One answer found worldwide is sacrifice. This may be a blood sacrifice: goat, chicken, ox or even a human being. It may be a gift, such as grain, incense, money, or a child. Such sacrifices are often seen as restoring broken relationships and reestablishing a moral order.

Sacrifice is a broad category that takes on different meanings in different contexts. These meanings draw on different metaphors to portray how relationships are restored. We will examine a few of these.

HOMAGE

One meaning of sacrifice is homage. The key analogy is the gift a subordinate gives to a superior—a vassal to the king, a son to his father. The sacrifice here is a symbol of allegiance, praise, and thanksgiving to superiors—to gods, spirits, ancestors, humans, or nature—as a plea for their help and protection. People offer the firstfruits of their harvest, the prize portion of the hunt, or the first sip of water as libation to the gods and ancestors, thereby acknowledging their blessings.

Homage is often paid to gods and ancestors to gain their good will and blessing. For example, the Nuer of Sudan sacrifice oxen during the rains to win the favor of the gods, and to expiate sin and purify the people. Other societies in the area offer sacrifices and prayer for success in hunting and fishing. Sacrifices may be offered to placate powerful, capricious spirits and demons who have power over the well-being of humans. Homage is often paid to placate angry gods and spirits who are believed to cause sickness and death. Offerings are also made to God on behalf of the sick, the barren, and those in distress to assure his favor.

In this analogy sin is insubordination, rebellion, and arrogance. It is to elevate oneself to a level of equality, and to break the relationship of submission.

In the West, with its focus on individualism, egalitarianism, and fear of obligation, people have a difficult time thinking in terms of submission and homage. Asking repeatedly for another's help is seen as begging. In many societies vertical patron-client relationships are seen as the ideal. Patrons are responsible for the total welfare of their clients. In turn, clients give their full loyalty and support to their patrons. The clients' requests for help from their patron are not begging or demeaning, but a normal activity of the relationship.[2] Furthermore, these relationships are not contractual. There is no calculation in which equal goods and services are exchanged. The vassal pays homage; the lord grants blessings. The vassal gains security; the lord gains honor. In some ways this is like the relationship between parents and children in a home.

GIFT-GIVING

A second analogy in offering sacrifices is the mutual exchange of gifts to maintain intimate relationships. Gift-giving is found in all societies. It not only symbolizes relationships between individuals and groups, but creates and reinforces them. To refuse a gift is commonly seen as a hostile act. Aylward Shorter writes,

---

2. In a sense Westerners understand this. They do not hesitate to ask constantly for God's help through prayer, and do not see it as begging.

A gift signifies the giver. It is a part of the giver as it were, placed in the hands of the receiver. The receiver, conversely, is obligated by the gift, placed in the giver's debt. Gifts have the peculiar power of creating what they signify. Refusal of a gift is the refusal of a relationship, perhaps a declaration of war. The symbolism of gift is especially powerful when it concerns food and drink, the ritual feast, by which giver and receiver nourish their life-processes by the same means (1985, 65).

Anthony Gittins points out that gift-giving is often associated with obligations in which the donor, in the act of receiving, is forging a spiritual bond with the receiver. He points out, "A huge portion of goods and services in such a social context [exchanging of gifts] may be seen as 'things-to-be-given-away-and-received-and-repaid,' rather alien to a 'Western' understanding of goods and services as 'things-to-be-acquired-and-retained-and-increased'" (1993, 82). This building of relationships can be seen in the giving of Christmas presents, invitations to meals, and exchange of sisters as brides.

Gifts generally imply some sort of reciprocity. The exchanges need not be of the same kind. People give the gods the firstfruits of their harvest and expect a good crop in return. A merchant gives a priest food, and, in exchange, gains status. Sin in this analogy is the refusal to exchange gifts, a sign that there is no desire for a relationship. Sacrifice is the restoration of relationships symbolized by the giving of gifts.

Some examples of sacrifice as gift are the pouring of a libation on the ground in Africa, the burial of goods in China, Egypt, and Fiji, and the gifts to the gods in Fiji when men construct a new war canoe. The Fijian chief was required to offer sacrifices to a tree before cutting it down, and at all stages of making the canoe. When it was launched, a human (captive warrior or woman) was sacrificed for each of its planks (sometimes as many as one hundred). The canoe was 'rolled' into the ocean on the bodies of the victims and banana stocks. The gods, seeing these gifts, returned protection, success in war, and honor to the chief who had so honored them.

RESTITUTION

A third analogy for sacrifice is restitution—the punishment or compensation for the suffering and damage caused by the sin. The key idea is that of justice. In sinning, one violates the law, and this causes damages that must be repaid if justice is to be kept. Payment may be restitution to compensate for the loss. For example, a family may give a child to another family for killing one of their members, or a criminal may repay stolen money. Or it may be a sacrifice of abnegation and retribution in which the sinner suffers to offset the suffering caused to those wronged. This is the case in being beaten, imprisoned, enslaved, or dying for one's own sin. Restitution may be placing one's sins on a scapegoat that is sacrificed in one's stead (see Dyak scapegoat).

SCAPEGOAT SACRIFICE OF THE DYAKS OF BORNEO

While the entire population of Anik gathers closer, an elder selects two chickens from the village flock. Checking to make sure both chickens are healthy, he slays one chicken and sprinkles its blood along the shore. The other chicken is tethered alive to one end of the deck of the little boat, with a few grains of rice to keep it docile.

Someone else brings a small lantern, ties it to the opposite end of the deck and lights it. At this point each resident of the village approaches the little boat in turn and places something else, something invisible, upon the deck, midway between the shining lantern and the living chicken.

Ask a Dyak what he has placed between the shining lantern and the living, unblemished chicken, and he will reply, *Dosaku!* (My sin).

When every resident of Anik has placed his or her *dosa* upon the little boat, village elders raise it carefully from the ground and wade out into the river. Then they release the boat into the current. As it drifts downstream, Dyaks watching from the shore grow tense. Elders standing chest-deep in the river hold their breath. If the little boat drifts back to shore, or hits a snag and overturns within sight of their village, the people of Anik will live under a pall of anxiety until the ceremony can be repeated the next year! But if the little boat vanishes around a bend in the river, the entire assembly will raise their arms toward the sky and shout, 'Selamat! Selamat! Selamat!' (We're safe! We're safe!). (*Eternity in Their Hearts* by Don Richardson. Copyright 1981. Regal Books, Ventura, CA 93003. Used by permission.)

Common expressions of remorse and payment for sin include fasting, abstinence from secular activities, and self-affliction. Penitent people crawl on hands and knees to a shrine, sit on a rock in extreme heat or cold, lash themselves with whips, and walk on fire to show remorse. Priests of ancient Mexico called for national fasts to seek forgiveness from the deities. Mohammed recognized two months of fasting when a husband divorces his wife *(zihar)*, and two months when a Muslim unintentionally kills another Muslim. Ahab repented with fasting (1 Kings 21:27–29) and the law called for a fast on the Day of Atonement (Ezra 10:6).

COMMUNION

A fourth analogy for sacrifice is communion. Eating and drinking together not only institutes an intimate relationship, but expresses it as well—they are performative and demonstrative acts at the same time. To refuse to eat and drink together shows a lack of regard for the person offering the gift. It is to refuse friendship. Sin in this analogy is the loss of fellowship. Sacrifice is to eat a common meal together as a sign of the restored relationship. Robertson Smith (1889) saw the common meal in which members of a totemic group ate their sacrificed totem as a communion in which solidarity between the group and its totem was reestablished. In many societies, food is offered to the gods, who are believed to eat it as royal guests at a community feast.

An example of sacrifice as communion is practiced by the Lugbara of East Africa after a person has been healed (Middleton 1960, 88–128). The Lugbara believe that all illnesses are due to breaches of the moral order that anger the ancestors. The oracle priest must reveal the offender, whether a ghost or living person, and perform a ritual to show the ancestors that the moral order has been restored. If the ancestors are satisfied, they help the victim. Then a sheep is slaughtered as a communion offering. Portions of meat are placed on the ancestors' shrines, along with beer, and blood is poured out onto the ancestral stones. The remaining meat is eaten by members of the lineage to show that the moral bonds weakened by the offender's misdeeds have been rebuilt and the solidarity between the living and the ancestors has been restored. In the process, the moral norms of the tribe are reaffirmed.

REGENERATION

A fifth analogy for sacrifice is regeneration or rejuvenation. This analogy focuses on the restoration thought to take place through the process of death and resurrection. The model here is a seed which dies and then is reborn as a plant bearing many seeds. An example of sacrifice as regeneration is the live burial of the Dinka Master of the Fishing Spear. As long as he was strong and well, the people prospered. When he grew old or weak, they diminished. Consequently, when the Master's health failed, he requested a special form of death given by his people, for their own sake, not his. If he were to die an ordinary death, the life of the people in his keeping went with him (Douglas 1966, 67–68). Everyone was expected to rejoice on this occasion because in this sacrifice the Dinka faced and triumphed over death itself.

Similar sacrifices are found in traditional East African societies such as the Banyoro, Shona, Amhara, and others. There, too, the chief or king was the symbol of the vitality and life of the society. When the authority figure grew old, weak, or sick, so, too, did the society. The ruler, therefore had to be ritually killed, and a young virile ruler appointed so that the people might prosper. In this model, sin is a kind of decay or loss of vitality, and sacrifice is the restoration of life through death and resurrection or replacement.

OBLIGATION

A sixth meaning of sacrifice is to create obligations. As Marcel Mauss (1967) points out, in many societies, people give gifts to those higher than them—the head of the family, the chief, the king, the ancestors or God—in order to get some greater benefit in return. Certain sacrifices, such as a child, a slave, an ox, or a piece of land, contain some of the giver's spirit, and to accept them places the receiver under obligation to give something greater in return to the giver. It is a seed which is planted, and which, at some later time, brings back a bountiful harvest. Gifts given to God and ancestors place them in debt to the giver, so they must repay the giver with health, wealth, and success. In some ways, this is like homage, but unlike homage, the giver here gives in self-interest. As Mauss suggests, this may be the most common reason for the offering of sacrifices in traditional societies.

COMMUNICATION

Finally, sacrifice is sometimes seen as communication between worlds. In many cultures, the spirit world is seen as radically different from the human world, and communication between the two is difficult and costly. The Egyptian pharaohs did so by giving messages to slaves, and sending them to the spirit world through sacrifice. When East African chiefs were put to death, often their wives, servants, slaves, some subjects, cattle, and prisoners were killed to accompany them and attend to their needs. Widows in India were encouraged, even forced, to immolate themselves on the funeral pyres of their husbands. In China, food, money, clothes, and, recently, cars and computers are burned to send them to ancestors.

PURITY AND POLLUTION

Concepts of a moral order based on mechanistic notions of purity and pollution are almost universal. They are based on beliefs that there is a right order to all things, and that the violation of that order is evil and defiling. Purity and pollution are closely linked, two sides of the same coin, one positive and the other negative. We will examine pollution first and then notions of purity.

POLLUTION

People in all societies view some objects, acts, and states as pure, and others as polluted. Pollution is commonly associated with ideas of disorder, evil, dirt, defilement, nonbeing, formlessness, and death. What underlies this concept of impurity?

Mary Douglas (1966) points out that people in the West have reduced notions of purity and pollution to matters of physical sanitation and health. Food left on a plate is believed to be contaminated by flies, and pus to have germs that can spread. Westerners argue that the Levitical injunction against eating pigs is due to the fact that they often carry trichinosis.[3] In the West, illness and health are seen as the result of natural causes and effects, and sanitation plays a key role in attempts to break the cycle of disease. This concern with purity and pollution as hygienic rules has led to an obsession with cleanliness. Westerners have different soaps for bodies, teeth, hair, clothes, dishes, windows, floors, rugs, cars, dogs, and many other things.

The notion of pollution in the West, however, runs far deeper than disease. Westerners see a great many other things as 'dirty,' 'polluted,' and 'defiling.' They hate spots on cloths, dishes, and rugs, leaves on the lawn, dirt on cars, and rings in bathtubs, even though these are not intrinsically unsanitary. They refuse to eat food from another person's plate, even if it has not been touched. At restaurants, waiters bring food which is seen as clean for all at the table, but which cannot be served to people at other tables because it is now 'dirty.' What is clean food for one becomes dirty for others once it has been touched. What remains on the plate is no longer food. It is 'garbage' and must be thrown away.

Western notions of cleanliness are based more on a sense of order than of sanitation. Don't eat horse, donkey, monkey, or insects; don't walk on the couch with your shoes on; don't eat mashed potatoes with your fingers; rake the leaves off the grass; sort the laundry to wash it—these practices have little to do with maintaining health. Moreover, these ideas of dirt in Western cultures antedate the discovery of pathogenic organisms.

To understand the concept of pollution found in most cultures requires a definition that avoids the Western linkage of dirt to hygiene. Mary Douglas defines dirt as anything that confuses or contradicts established cultural classifications—in other words, anything that people in a society believe is 'out of order.' Every culture imposes a mental schema or structure of assumptions in the light of which new experiences are interpreted. Dirt is anything that confuses or contradicts the established cultural classifications, in other words, anything that people in a culture believe is out of order. In a broad sense, impurity is any

---

3. The evidence, as Mary Douglas points out (1966, 41–57), is that the Israelites did not avoid pigs for health reasons based on a known disease, although some commentators argue that they did. Rather, she shows that the avoidance of pigs had to do more with the sense of material-moral order that God gave to the people through his injunctions against eating certain kinds of food.

deviance that disrupts the sociocultural or cosmic order, and deviance is taboo because it threatens that order. As Douglas points out, thinking about dirt involves thinking about the nature of order and its relation to disorder, of being to nonbeing, of form to formlessness, and of life to death (Douglas 1966, 5).

A few illustrations from Western cultures help us understand this concept of pollution. Shoes are not dirty in themselves, but it is dirty to place them on the dining table; food is not unsanitary in itself, but it is dirty to leave cooking utensils in bedrooms or food spattered on clothing. It is unclean to leave bathroom articles in living rooms, clothing lying on chairs, and outdoor things indoors. It is messy to wear underwear over outer clothing. In the kitchen drawer, forks should be in the fork bin, spoons in the spoon bin, and knives in the knife bin. Spots on walls and mud on floors make these unclean.

All societies face anomalies that do not fit their cultural classification and thus threaten to destroy it. Peoples' reactions to ambiguous objects, persons, and situations are generally that of revulsion and shock, or laughter and ridicule. First, they treat these anomalies as if they don't exist. If the anomalies cannot be ignored, they classify them as dirt and defilement that must be avoided as impure because these distort the order of things. For instance, people may lend their coats, shirts, or blouses to other people, but not underwear. Fingernails, hair clippings, menstrual blood, and body excreta are associated with people and yet are not a part of them. Most foul language in the West has to do with excrement, vomit, and other body waste. The idea of pollution is a reaction to objects and ideas that confuse or contradict people's cherished classifications. Dirt is anything out of place or out of order, and getting rid of dirt is the process of tidying up the world, and making sure that external categories in the world conform to categories in their minds (Douglas 1966, 35–36).

An example of pollution as evil is found among the Kalenjin of Kenya. They speak of *murwonindo*—dirt or pollution. It is produced by menstruation, contact with a corpse, and breaking taboos that govern relationships between fathers and newborn babies, men and women, sons-in-law and mothers-in-law, and brides and grooms. Some are violations of the social rules. The destructive effects of pollution are automatic. If pollution is ignored, it can bring death to the unclean person. Physical dirt *(simdo)* can be removed by soap and water, but *murwonindo* 'pollution' can only be removed by some type of ritual cleansing. The Kalenjin consider droughts and epidemics as punishment for corporate uncleanness, the result of the sin of the whole community. To cleanse themselves, the people perform the Kapkoros ritual involving the slaughter of a pure, monochrome ram and burning the flesh to send the smoke toward heaven (Cox 1994). Pollution is often seen as contagious. If a man commits murder, rape, theft, or witchcraft, he is defiled, and his pollution affects those related to him, whether they are humans, animals, or material goods.

The concept of pollution runs through the Old Testament. Those who were blind, mutilated, diseased, deformed, or descendants of Aaron (who was blemished) were not allowed to offer sacrifices in the temple (Lev. 21). Nor were those who married a divorced woman or a prostitute, or who had recently touched a dead body (except a near relative). All bodily discharges were considered polluting and had to be disposed of outside the camp (Deut. 23:10–15). Moreover, people were not permitted to plant two kinds of seed in the same field, or weave cloth made of two different materials (Lev. 19:19), because to do so was to breach the order God set for them. It would cause God to reject them and they would lose their battles with their enemies.

If pollution is defiling and dangerous, how can people handle it? One answer is to avoid it. In the Old Testament, a defiled person could not approach the tabernacle or touch other people lest they be polluted. In India, all people are ranked on a hierarchy of purity. People avoid touching those below them for to do so is polluting. Cooked food prepared by lower-caste people can pass on pollution, and must not be eaten. Fruit and nuts are pure as long as they are whole, but if they are cut, they can carry pollution. Saliva is extremely defiling, so a person does not drink or smoke by touching cups or cigarettes with one's mouth. Spoons are defiling, so people use their fingers. This separation of the polluted from the sacred is essential to preserve the sense of order. If the sacred is not hedged in with prohibitions, it is in danger of losing its distinctives and becoming ordinary and secular.

Another way to handle pollution is to ritualize its handling. There are rituals to protect people from defilement. There are also rites of purification, which commonly make use of symbols of purity such as water, beer, and milk; symbols of cleansing such as washing, dusting, and immersing; symbols of refining such as fire; and blood sacrifices to rid a person of religious pollution.

PURITY

Purity is a state of being. If pollution marks disorder and confusion, purity is conformity to the ideal high order that makes life understandable and, therefore, meaningful. It should not be surprising that purity is most evident in highly structured ritual events that set people apart from the semiconfusion of ordinary life. For example, a formal wedding is a rite in which the ideals of marriage are portrayed and affirmed. Everyone wears clean cloths, the bride and groom show deep love for each other, and demonstrate proper respect to their in-laws. Sexual norms, as affirmed by religion and law, are observed. (The importance of rituals in maintaining order and purity are examined in more detail in Chapter 11.)

Concepts of purity are culturally defined. For example, the Kalenjin speak of *libwob* to refer to something that is without a defect. Only men who are *libwob* are permitted to officiate in rituals. They must never have fathered children who subsequently died, their first wives must be alive, their bodies and those of their children and livestock must be whole—lameness or blindness in any of them renders the man defective. The defect is proof that sin has scarred the man. Ritual cleaning can never restore *libwobnatet* once it is lost, even though a person can become 'clean' again (Cox 1997a).

PURITY AND POLLUTION

Purity and pollution stand in tension with each other. In most cultures, to be truly human is to be set apart in one way or another from nature and beasts. It is to have culture—a human order imposed on society. This order may involve wearing clothes, cooking food, building houses, eating with utensils (forks or chopsticks), combing hair, wearing ear rings or nose plugs, painting the body, face, nails, or lips, or a thousand other expressions that distinguish people from animals.

It is impossible, however, for everyone to live in high ideal order all the time. Only the royal, respectable, and rich (those considered most human in a society) come close to doing so, and they are often considered more clean than commoners. Living creates disorder. When people sleep, the beds must be made; when they eat, the dishes must be washed; when they work, their clothes must be laundered; and after they celebrate a wedding, everyone must go home to the everyday tasks of ordinary life. Much of life is lived in a semiordered world where blurred boundaries must be restored, dirt removed, and order shored up to preserve a sense of meaning and humanity. High order, however, can become stifling and oppressive, so people seek freedom, which, in the extreme, leads to chaos and pollution. On the other hand, no one wants to live in disorder, pollution, and chaos, even though such places may provide people a temporary relief from tyranny of high structure. So, through rituals people remove impurities and restore a measure of order.

Purity and pollution form ends of a continuum that ranges from high formal order, cleanliness, and control on one end, to disorder, dirt and uncontrol on the other. In between are degrees of informality and semiorder. To maintain this continuum, and a sense of social and cosmic order, the extremes are set apart and ritualized. Both sacred and profane are states separated from normal life, which is lived in between and may be considered secular.

This tension between purity and pollution, between form and freedom, can be seen in Western eating habits (Figure 8.1). Imagine, as an example of high ideal order, a formal banquet put on by Queen Elizabeth for visiting heads of state. The place is Westminster Hall, which can seat a hundred or more guests. The dress is tuxedos and ballroom gowns. The settings are linen, china, and crystal, and there are as many knives, spoons, and forks as there are culinary functions—one spoon for soup, one for stirring coffee, one for dessert, and so on—none can be used for more than one purpose. The food is high cuisine consisting of several courses, starting with drinks and appetizers, and ending with deserts and different drinks. The service is by uniformed waiters—one per guest.

Few of us are ever invited to such a banquet. Our best is a formal banquet put on by a school, church, or business. The place is a formal dining room, the clothing is dark dress suits and formal gowns, the place settings are cloth, china, crystal, and four or five pieces of cutlery, the food is party best served in two or three courses, and the service is by waiters. This, in turn, contrasts with many rural American homes, where the banquet is the Sunday noon meal prepared and served by a mother, to family members dressed in their Sunday best seated in the dining room. The table is covered with a fine cloth, set with the best family china and silver—usually one fork, spoon, and knife. The main meal is often followed by a dessert.

Few people can live at this formal level all the time. By midweek dinner ordinary people use plastic or pottery plates set on plastic tablecloths and stainless steel utensils, and pass the food around. Lunches are eaten on the run at the kitchen table using paper plates whenever one has time. By Saturday mornings individuals serve themselves, eat in the kitchen or on the porch, and use paper plates or napkins and plastic spoons or fingers. At the beach they eat almost anything, anywhere, and anytime, wearing almost anything. About this time, someone says it is time to stop "living like beasts, and wolfing down food like animals." So Sunday they go back to high ritual order to remind themselves that they are people, and what it is like to be truly human, reflecting on the pastor's sermon over a fine dinner.

Purity and pollution have much in common. Both are set apart from ordinary life, share a sense of the dangerous, and must be treated carefully. The same things may be sacred in one setting and polluting in another. Sacred oaths and curses, Christian rites and satanic rituals, and formal realities and parodies have much in common even though they are opposites in their nature. An example of this is the way humans handle dead bodies. On the one hand, these are often seen as very pol-

Figure 8.1
Ways of Eating

	Type	Place	Dinner Setting	Service	Dress	Food
FORMAL (pure, sacred, honor, human)	**Queen Elizabeth Formal Banquet** [Scheduled, rare for guests]	Westminster Banquet Hall	Silver, one each function, linen tablecloths and napkins, flowers, music	Personal servers in uniforms	Tuxedos and ball room gowns	5–7 courses, appetizers
	Formal Seminary Banquet [Scheduled]	Hotel banquet room, candles, flowers, music	Silver, one each function, linen	Waiters	Dark suits, formal dresses	2–3 courses
	Sunday Family Dinner [Cyclical]	Dining room at home	Silver, plate, linen napkins, cloths	Mother	Sunday best	2–3 courses
INFORMAL (everyday, secular, pragmatic, semi-human)	**Weeknight Dinner** [Cyclical]	Kitchen	Plastic tablecloth, paper napkins, one or two utensils	Pass around	Ordinary clothes	1–2 courses
	Saturday Barbeque [Occasional]	Outside picnic table	Paper or no tablecloth, plastic spoons, fingers, paper napkins	Self-service	Casual and outdoors	1 course, snacks
	Beach Party [Any time]	Sand	Cloth on sand, no chairs, fingers	Self-service	Casual and swimsuits	Cold sandwich, snacks
	O'Hare Airport [Any time]	Standup shelf	Stand, fingers	Self-service	Anything	Fast food
BARBARIC (dirty, taboo, beastly, degrading)	**Prison and con-centration camp**	"Mess" or prison yard	Rusty plates, fingers	Prison guards	Prison garb	Prison fare
	Medieval dungeon	Floor	Food thrown on floor or through window	Prison guard	Rags	Survival slop

luting (Num. 5:2–3), and the living who touch them are defiled. On the other hand, humans cannot throw dead bodies away like garbage. To do so is to turn humans into mere animals.[4] Only the bodies of enemies and paupers (often seen as subhuman) are thrown into mass graves without ceremony. The bodies of real people must be handled with rituals that affirm the dignity of their humanness—the more important the person, the greater the ritual. In funeral ceremonies, the sacred and the polluted are both handled carefully in rituals that remove them both from ordinary life.[5]

Rules for purity and pollution are rules for spiritual etiquette. These assure people that if they do the right things at the right time, they will maintain a life of relative peace and prosperity. Those who deviate from the accepted etiquette run counter to the order that underlies the cosmos. As we will note in Chapter 11, in rituals humans dramatize the high order they affirm as the ideal for the world, and they take the memories of that order back into the semichaos of everyday life.

LAW AND LAWLESSNESS

In contrast to laws made by those in authority, which we looked at earlier, there are widespread beliefs in impersonal cosmic moral laws similar to the laws of nature that transcend even the gods and kings. Gods and kings are good when they keep these laws, and wicked when they break the laws. The concept of law as impersonal and mechanical is generally associated with notions of cosmic order that take on moral connotations. To break the law is to violate the cosmic order, and must be rectified by paying the penalty required by law.

An example of this attribution of morality to impersonal law is seen in the Indian concept of *karma*. This is the cosmic moral law that rewards good and punishes evil. No good deed, whether performed by gods, demons, humans, animals, or insects, can go unrewarded, and no evil goes unpunished for there to be a truly moral universe. Good and evil are defined by duties required by the position in the universe into which one is born *(dharma)*. Washermen do right when they carry out their caste duties without complaint, priests when they carry out the temple rites, untouchables when they remove the village refuse, warriors when they kill enemies (though for others killing is sin), gods

---

4. This is one reason for our human abhorrence of cannibalism, and why cannibalism almost always takes place in highly ritualized contexts.

5. This tension between the sacred and the polluted included in the same rite helps us understand Numbers 5:11–28, where the dust from the tabernacle floor was put in holy water and used as the symbol of the curse, the water of bitterness, on a woman accused of adultery. The sacred would protect her if she were innocent, but the impure would bring pain and cause her womb to drop.

when they maintain the universe, and animals when they do their tasks. When death interrupts unrewarded good deeds, or unpunished evil, god, human, or animal must be reborn in another life to receive just rewards. Only those who at the moment of death have no moral dues are released from the endless cycle of rebirths *(samsara)*. *Karma* is the eternal law that rules all worlds. Gods are good because they normally obey its dictates, and demons are evil because they do many wicked deeds. *Karma* is impersonal. There is no place for mercy, forgiveness, or transfer of penalties from one person to another.

Karma is one example of the broader Indo-European view of laws as overarching mechanistic moral order that transcends all living beings, including the gods. Another is the Roman concept of law that has influenced Western societies with its notion that law must be 'blind' (i.e., unaffected by circumstances), and that it is the ultimate arbiter of right and wrong. Where sin is seen as a violation of a transcendent moral law, the primary feeling associated with wrongdoing is that of guilt. In contrast, as we will see later, where sin is seen as a break in relationships, it leads to a feeling of shame.

BEAUTY AND UGLINESS

Another type of order is beauty, which is associated more with aesthetic pleasure than with cognitive order. Beauty is often associated with sacredness. People use colorful clothing, painted masks, stylish hairdos, earrings, lip plugs, nose bones, body paint, taboos, eye shadow, necklaces, feathery headdresses, and many other ways to express aesthetic pleasure. Music, art, dance, robes, sculptures, and icons are central to most religious rituals. On this level, evil is that which is perceived to be dissonant, disjointed, and ugly.

In Christianity, the Orthodox churches stress beauty as a fundamental and essential category of the spiritual world—what the psalmists refer to as "the beauty of holiness" (Ps. 29:2; 96:9). For them, beauty is not an ephemeral matter having to do only with human senses. Icons, candles, bells, liturgy, frescoes, acapella choirs, incense symbolizing the prayers of the saints, and elaborate rituals reveal God to worshipers and carry their worship to him. These are signs of what lies beyond ordinary senses, an innerness and depth that point the way to God. It was this aesthetic constituent of theology, not the rational, that led to the conversion of Prince Vladimir to Christianity in A.D. 933, and the shaping of the Russian Orthodox Church (Clendenin 1995, 30–46).[6]

---

6. Prince Vladimir's emissaries wrote, "The Greeks led us to the building where they worship their God, and we knew not whether we were in heaven or on earth. For on earth there is no such splendor or such beauty, and we are at a loss to describe it."

Figure 8.2
Models of Morality

RELATIONAL ORDER ◄————————► **NATURAL ORDER**

- -

Organic analogy	Mechanistic analogy
Focus on Righteousness and Sin	Focus on Purity and Pollution
Rightness is proper relationships	Rightness is maintaining the natural
Laws are divine commands and	order
instructions	Laws are the impersonal cosmic principles
Evil is broken relationships	by which the universe is ordered
Remedy is restored relationships	Evil is chaos, the violation of natural order
by means of sacrifice, restitution,	Remedy is restored order by means of
reconciliation	purification, washing, scapegoating,
	burial, and denial

Daniel Clendenin points out that it is hard for Western Protestants to understand this visual orientation of Christianity. They stress verbal theology, which is a scholarly exposition of the texts and is a genre of scientific wisdom, and embellish the sermons with music. In many religions, liturgies, icons, pageantry, and aesthetics are at the center of sacramental worship. These appeal more to intuition and contemplation, which seek to transcend reason.[7]

PURITY AND HOLINESS

What is the relationship between organic views of holiness and sin, and mechanical views of purity and pollution? What does a pure heart have to do with clean hands (Ps. 24:4), or being without blemish with offerings acceptable to God?

People in the modern world reduce purity to hygiene and relegate holiness to religion. Consequently, they see little connection between the two. They find it hard to understand concepts of ritual purity and pollution as dimensions of morality which are found in the Old Testament, as well as in religions around the world. Why should dead bodies, feces, food left on the plate, and menstrual blood be defiling? Why in the Pentateuch is purity linked to holiness? The animals offered as sacrifice had to be whole and without blemish, disease, or injury. Possibly the closest Westerners come to understanding the connection is in handling sacred objects. If they drop the bread or spill the wine during the Lord's Supper, they feel they have not only soiled the floor, but more deeply that they have defiled the holy.

---

7. The iconoclastic debates in the early church reflect the fundamental differences between these two worldviews.

In much of the world purity and holiness are inextricably intertwined, giving expression to and reinforcing one another. A moral universe is characterized by order in nature, society, and the cosmos (Figure 8.2). In most societies, purity and holiness are closely linked. Priests
and sacrifices must be pure and perfect specimens for sacred use.
Maimed priests and lame lambs are an affront to the gods.

Sin and pollution are also associated. To touch a corpse, blood, or
spittle is believed to contaminate a person not only physically but also
morally and spiritually. Sin not only breaks relationships. It makes the
sinner impure. In the Old Testament adultery was both defilement and
sin.[8]

Health and illness are commonly attributed to the moral status of
people and their families. Diviners attribute illnesses to sinful acts and
moral misdeeds. In these cases, confessions and restitution are necessary for health to return. Ray reports that one man confessed he had
pains ever since the day he cursed his nephew, a second said he had
been sick ever since he cheated his kinsmen out of their share in a
cocoa-farm, and a woman who had not yet done bad magic against her
husband said she felt ill ever since she made up her mind to injure him
(Ray 1976, 73–74).

Both purity and righteousness have to do with order: one with order
in nature, and the other with order in relationships between beings.
Pollution and sin both threaten this order by introducing disorder and
chaos. This linkage of righteousness with purity and sin with pollution
provides a sacred canopy under which all life is lived. It sanctions the
moral order and leads to a sacramental view of the world. Inner realities are linked to outer symbols and images. Rituals are visible expressions of social and spiritual facts. In sacramental words, everything
takes on meaning because it has its place in the eternal order.

The fact that Westerners with a rationalistic worldview find it so
hard to see the connection between holiness and cleanliness, sin and
defilement, shows how deep the division is between visible and invisible worlds, between natural and supernatural realities. On the one
hand, Westerners have secularized the view of pollution and reduced it
to a matter of aesthetics, hygiene, or etiquette—the violation of which
leads only to embarrassment and social sanctions such as contempt, ostracism, and gossip. Taboos have been reduced to kitchen, bathroom,
and municipal sanitation, and to physical conditions that have nothing
to do with religion or spiritual states of unworthiness. This secularized

---

8. In the Old Testament, the Israelites often equated holiness with keeping the rules
of purity, and God sent them prophets to remind them that their relationship to him was
more fundamental than keeping mechanical laws of cleanliness.

worldview does not hold that sacred objects, places, and rituals are dangerous to unclean people. Moreover, human relationships have been affected by shifting morality from sacred to secular foundations—from divine order to human social contracts. This new order is maintained by law and force, but it lacks both the moral certitude and the inner transformation necessary to bring righteousness to a society.

In the West this secularization has replaced the term 'morality'—with its sense of universal, public absolutes—with 'values,' which are personal, inner, and relative.[9] The secularization of pollution and 'sin' has led to their separation. No longer is dirt associated with evil, or purity and beauty with holiness. Without reinforcement either of a sense of divine sanction, or of purity and pollution, morality withers and laws must be enforced by force. But while laws may help control evil behavior, they cannot transform human hearts.

CHRISTIAN RESPONSE

What does this study of purity and pollution, holiness and sin have for missionaries? Western missionaries, as we have noted, have a truncated view of sin and holiness, of purity and pollution. They have reduced sin to personal violations of God's laws, and pollution to matters of sanitation and health. They need to recover a biblical view of the awesomeness of holiness and the awfulness of sin. They need to recognize that symbols of purity and beauty are powerful means of giving expression in worship in meaningful ways.

Before examining some of the many implications of an understanding of how right and wrong are expressed in different cultures, it is important to see how these concepts help us understand the Bible, particularly the Old Testament.

PURITY AND HOLINESS IN THE BIBLE

Purity and holiness are central themes in the Bible. Yahweh is both the God of holiness and of purity, and he calls his people to be holy and unblemished. Sin is fundamentally a break in the covenant relationship with God, both personal and corporate. The solution to sin is sacrifice, but what kind of sacrifice? Not all types of sacrifice are acceptable to God.[10]

9. For a discussion of this. see Bloom, 1987.

10. For example, human sacrifices as practiced by the non-Israelites (2 Kings 3:27), and by the Israelites are against God's will (2 Chron. 28:3; Ps. 106:37–38; Isa. 57:5; Jer. 19:5). This, however, is no universal proscription for God asked Abram to sacrifice Isaac, though he provided a substitute, and God sacrificed his Son for our sins. We need a more thorough analysis of the nature of sacrifice in Scripture.

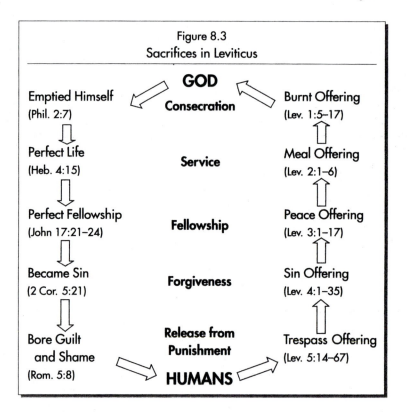

Figure 8.3
Sacrifices in Leviticus

SACRIFICE AND RECONCILIATION

An analysis of the various meanings associated with sacrifices in the Old Testament helps us understand the rich meanings associated with them (Figure 8.3). Scripture portrays a variety of sacrifices and offerings: burnt, meal, peace, sin, and trespass offerings. What does this variety mean? When Israelites went into the presence of the Lord, they had to first offer a trespass offering to atone for their specific sinful deeds. Then they offered the sin offering to expiate their sinful nature. This was followed by the peace offering to restore fellowship with God, the meal offering as service to God, and the incense offering symbolizing homage—the total consecration of the worshiper to God. Only then was the full relationship between humans and God restored.

There is a difficulty here, however. The sacrifices are listed in the opposite order, with the incense offering first and the trespass offering last. Why this reversal? Some argue that before we as sinners can come to God through sacrifice, God himself had first to come to us to open up the way for us to come to God. In his incarnation, Jesus proved himself to be the perfect sacrifice, embodying in his life and death each step in the process of reconciliation. He consecrated himself as the perfect sacrifice (Phil. 2:6–8), offered his life in perfect service, had perfect fellowship with the Father, had no sinful nature, and committed no trespasses. He, therefore, was the worthy sacrifice for sinners.

Human beings, in turn, must have sacrifices that deal with their specific sins and sinful nature before they can enter the presence of God. This is the sacrifice of Christ. In the tabernacle, in the presence of God, the Israelites had to bring their offerings of fellowship, service, and consecration before they could enter the presence of God symbolized in the ark. In the Old Testament the tabernacle was replaced by the temple in Jerusalem, but in the New Testament the temple is replaced by God's people (Acts 7:48–50).[11]

> God cannot be bound to any place, not even the holiest places. God's house, most profoundly, is God's people, especially those who are humble and contrite and faithful, and God remains faithful even when many of them are not (Wiens 1995, 80).

RIGHTEOUSNESS AND LAW

The study of righteousness and purity raises a profound theological question. What is the relationship between righteousness and law? In Hinduism righteousness is defined by cosmic, fixed, impersonal laws *(karma)*, which are like the laws of nature. Even the gods must obey these laws to be holy. In other words, the ultimate reality is not God, but a universal moral law. Christianity begins with God, whose essence is holiness. The moral law was given by God (reflecting his character) to sinful humans as an elementary way to teach them about righteousness. When a true relationship of allegiance and fellowship arises, the law is no longer needed because we do naturally what the law requires. Ultimately, sin is not violation of the law, but disobedience and broken relationship with God. Paul makes this clear when he points out that sin existed before the coming of the law, and that the law was inadequate to bring sinners to salvation and righteousness (Gal. 3–4). Christianity also sees God as a God of love who seeks to save those under the judgment of sin and impurity. It is Christ who demonstrates, in his fully human condition, the nature of righteousness, justice, and holiness.

CONCEPTS OF HOLINESS AND SIN

Given the fact that different cultures define sin differently, how should Christian leaders speak of sin and salvation? As noted earlier,

---

11. For an excellent analysis of the progression in the Bible from Abraham to his global offspring, from Abraham's family to the kingdom of God, and from the tabernacle to the universe is God's temple, see Wiens 1995.

the beginning point is people, particularly their understanding of good and evil and the symbols through which these concepts are expressed. With this awareness, people can then be led to understand the biblical concepts of sin and salvation. All humans have a sense of righteousness and evil. They have standards for the ideal man and woman, husband and wife, parent and child. They often condemn selfishness and greed. Their understandings are not biblical, but they often provide a beginning point for teaching biblical concepts of sin.[12]

Wayne and Sally Dye give us an excellent example of appealing to the people's own norms as a bridge to communicating the gospel message of sin and forgiveness. Wayne writes (1976, 39),

> I tried to translate Jesus' list of sins in Mark 7. As each sin was described, they gave me the local term for it. They named other sins in their cultures.
> "What did your ancestors tell you about these things?" I asked them.
> "Oh, they told us we shouldn't do any of those things."
> "Do you think these were good standards that your ancestors gave you?" They agreed unanimously that they were.
> "Well, do you keep all these rules?"
> "No," they responded sheepishly.
> One leader said, "Definitely not. Who could ever keep them all? We're people of the ground."
> I took this opportunity to explain that God expected them to keep their own standards for what is right, that He was angry because they hadn't. Then I pointed out that it was because they fell short of their own standards that God sent His Son to bear their punishment so that they could be reunited with him.

CULTURALLY AND BIBLICALLY DEFINED SINS

It is important that Christians differentiate between culturally and biblically defined sins. Socially defined sins change as the society changes. The use of lipstick, earrings, and certain fashions were once considered wrong in many American churches. Today these are widely accepted. The danger is the belief that all sin is culturally defined.

Biblical sins are absolute, though their cultural forms may vary and require reinterpretation as cultures change. There are no biblical injunctions regarding which movies to watch, music to listen to, or books to read, so how these issues are handled must be decided on the basis of biblical principles. Laws are frozen to particular cultural forms, but principles are flexible and permit reinterpretation in new cultural contexts.

---

12. It is worth noting that people in many societies around the world understand well the biblical view of purity and holiness, sin and pollution, better than those bringing the message. This is because their cultures parallel those of biblical times, and reflect issues addressed by the biblical authors much better than societies in the West.

Members of a society that converts to Christianity have many social norms that can continue because of the general principles all societies must observe to survive, and because the Bible is silent on most cultural manifestations. Outsiders may find many behaviors unsettling, but they must avoid immediately judging these as all evil. As local Christians learn Scripture, the Holy Spirit prompts them to change practices contrary to biblical teaching. These will be areas of conviction in which God wants them to develop a more Christian lifestyle. Dropping old norms often leads to censure and confrontations with those in the culture who have not become Christians, but these are opportunities for believers to give an "answer for the hope that is within them" (1 Peter 3:15).

SACRIFICES

One bridge for the communication of the biblical concepts pertaining to holiness and purity in different cultures is the concept of sacrifice. Unfortunately, sacrifice has lost its meaning in Western churches, where people speak of Christ's sacrifice but experience little sacrificial living for the sake of the gospel. Many cultures understand that relating to God is no casual, part-time matter, and that true submission to God is costly. Here churches in the West can learn much from churches around the world.

Local beliefs associated with sacrifice can be used as redemptive analogies to help people understand Christ's death for all sinners. An example of this is Don Richardson's account of a chief giving his own child to another in order to stop the feuding which had taken many lives (1978). Beginning with a "Peace Child" understanding of sacrifice was helpful for the Sawi, but they must move beyond this as new believers are instructed that Christ is much more than a Peace Child sacrifice.

Missionaries must also be careful lest the biblical understandings of sacrifice be lost in the communication. Most people perform sacrifices to change the mind of the deity or to placate a deity's anger. It is hard for them to understand that God sacrificed himself for sinners to reconcile them to himself.

THE SEARCH FOR SALVATION

The gospel is not primarily about sin, but about forgiveness from sin and restored fellowship with God and creation. It is the good news of salvation. What does this mean, and how can missionaries communicate this message to ordinary people who are concerned about the problems they face here on earth?

Salvation in Scripture is rooted in the Hebrew concept of *shalom*. Through salvation God restores his creation to what he originally intended before the fall. It begins with forgiveness and reconciliation with God through Christ Jesus, and finds expression in the restoration of harmonious, mutually edifying relationships in the church, and wholeness in the believer. Its final and full manifestation will occur when Christ returns as Lord and establishes his *shalom* throughout all creation.

Salvation in the Bible is not merely a future hope. "It is a real—although at present incomplete—change in the human condition including all its dimensions—spiritual, social, and physical" (Kraus 1987, 172). This includes both the present realities in the life of the church and the believer as well as the eschaton. Salvation is both present and future.

Salvation is also not exclusively a spiritual matter. Unlike the Western worldview, which differentiates between spirit and body, and spiritual and material realities, the biblical worldview presents humans as whole beings in which spiritual, moral, social, mental, and physical attributes are inextricably intertwined. People must understand that salvation involves all of these.

Moreover, salvation is not primarily an individual concern. Unlike Westerners, who see autonomous, free individuals as the fundamental units of human reality and differentiate between personal and social systems, Scripture sees healing and salvation as rooted in the community, and individuals as fully human only as they are part of communities of *shalom,* which are founded upon right relationships with God and reflect his character, namely, righteousness, love, justice, peace, and perfection. These communities seek healing through social justice, provision for the needy—including widows and orphans—and protection of the exploited and oppressed. Above all, they are sent into the world with a divine commission to proclaim that the rule of God is at hand, that Jesus is Lord, and that people should change their ways and live in the light of this new reality and form new communities of followers.

What does this good news of God's salvation mean to those who need (and generally want) salvation? The Bible uses a number of metaphors to describe God's salvation. Each of these casts light on a salvation that can never be fully understood here on earth. Different ones make sense to different people in their varied contexts.

SALVATION FROM THE POWERS OF EVIL

In many traditional societies, the dominant emotion is fear: fear of ancestors, arbitrary spirits, hostile enemies, witchcraft, magic, and invisible forces that plague everyday life. Evil is manifest in demonic oppression, and witchcraft, leading to withdrawal, fear of life, self-hatred, and suicidal tendencies (Mark 1:23–26; 5:2–9). Salvation in these societies consists primarily of being saved from the powers of evil and the problems, hardships, misfortunes, injustices, sicknesses, and death people experience in this world. Van Rheenen writes,

> Sin in animistic contexts is understood to destroy the balance and harmony of life. When harmony is disrupted, people experience suffering and misfortune. The need for salvation becomes apparent to the animist when illness occurs, a wife remains barren, or catastrophe strikes one's business or herds (1991, 297).

In such societies the message of the power of an Almighty God who is loving and just, who protects his people from their enemies, and who drives out the demons that oppress them is indeed Good News.[13] People in these societies need to be assured that their lives are secure in the hands of God who overcomes evil, and has covenanted to care for them,

The danger is that many people see Christianity as a new way to manipulate God to gain personal benefits such as physical healing, bountiful crops, success in business, and harm to rivals and enemies. Their motives remain utilitarian and self-centered. They do not seek God for his own sake and for fellowship with him. This human-centered view of salvation needs to be challenged. People need to discover that the salvation God offers has to do with the restoration of true health and wholeness. This salvation has immediate consequences for people in their everyday lives, for God does care for their needs. They also need to discover the far greater salvation found in Scripture. If they do not, they are in danger of equating salvation with a healthy, prosperous life on earth, and of ignoring the far greater and eternal consequences of reconciliation and fellowship with God.

When communicating in traditional societies, missionaries and ministers must also guard against a split-level Christianity in which people turn to God for salvation from sin, but to local gods, ancestors, and saints to answer the problems of everyday life. In the Old Testament the people of Israel worshiped Yahweh (whom they often saw as high and far removed), but repeatedly turned to local Baals and Ashteroth for help when they were sick and defeated. For many, this was not a rejection of Yahweh. Rather, they turned to God with greater matters, and offered sacrifices to local deities just to make sure these were not offended (2 Kings 17:33). People in traditional societies today need to recognize that as God's children they can go to him directly with the least as well as the greatest of their problems.

---

13. This is the *Christus Victor* view of salvation in which Christ is the conqueror of evil and the restorer of *shalom*. It does not negate the substitutionary or moral views of salvation, but does lead to a more dynamic view of faith.

SALVATION AND SHAME

In strong group-oriented societies, such as Japan and China, people find their identity in belonging to a group. For them, sin is the breaking of relationships and offending the community, and leads to feelings of shame, embarrassment, unworthiness, and remorse. These feelings are often associated with concepts of sin as defilement or uncleanness. Salvation is seen as reconciliation and restoration of good relationships, and cleansing portrayed as washing with water or purging by blood.

These views are dominant in the Old Testament, where sin is the people of Israel breaking God's covenant with them (Exod. 20:24, Kraus 1987, 174ff.), and leads to pollution. Salvation is the renewal of the covenant (Mal. 2:5). In the New Testament Jesus is the King vested with the authority to make a new covenant (Heb. 7:22; 8:6ff.; 9:15) with the church, the "new Israel," based on love and faithfulness, not only his power. In this new community of the Messiah, humans are reconciled to one another (Eph. 2:12–19) as children in the same family (Gal. 3:26), in which the old hostilities are gone, and peace and mutual submission are the norm (Gal. 3:26–29). It is good news indeed when people learn that God is a God of reconciliation, seeking to restore them to fellowship and harmony with himself and one another. In these societies it is important to teach forgiveness, reconciliation, and restored fellowship.

SALVATION FROM JUDGMENT

In individualistic societies with a strong sense of law, sin is violating rules, and leads to feelings of guilt and fear of judgment. Salvation is seen as paying the penalty and being declared just before the law. Here the entry point is to preach the good news that through Christ's sacrifice people are forgiven and they are restored to a right standing before God. This has been the dominant motif in Western theology, which inherited the Roman forensic system of law, and Hebrew tradition of covenant commandments. There is a danger, however. It is easy to see law as an autonomous, overarching code of moral righteousness, and justification as simply paying the penalties meted out by that law. This results in legalism, and places God under the law.[14] In the Bible, laws are God's orders and operate within the broader context of a relationship with him. When people break his laws, they not only disobey his commands, but break relationships with him and no longer offer him alle-

14. Robert Brow argues that Protestants have been heavily shaped by the Roman forensic system of law, which dominates Roman Catholic views of salvation. This view emphasizes legalism over freedom, institution over relationship, judgment over grace, and individual sin over powers of evil.

giance as Lord. The penalty is not a mechanical meting out of justice, but the price of alienation from God.

INJUSTICE AND SUFFERING

What answers do we give to the central question of this chapter, one constantly asked by common people out of their daily experiences: "Why is there injustice and why am I wronged?" It is not enough to say that this will never happen to Christians who truly live by faith, or to thank God because affliction helps people to grow spiritually. Nor can we simply say that in heaven there is no suffering, so people should bear it here on earth. We must provide answers to people's immediate questions, but these answers must be rooted in a biblical understanding of injustice, pain, and suffering.

It is important that local churches be caring, supporting, healing communities. Greater than pain and suffering is the fact that people often must bear these alone. Paul writes, "[God] comforts us in all our troubles, so that we can comfort those in any trouble with the comfort we ourselves have received from God. For just as the sufferings of Christ flow over into our lives, so also through Christ our comfort overflows" (2 Cor. 1:4–5). Christians must bear one another's burdens, for we belong to one body, and when one member suffers, we all suffer. Moreover, in suffering we are drawn together to minister to one another. Philip Yancey writes,

> In my visits to hospitals, I have been impressed by the huge difference between the measure of comfort that can be offered by believers ("We're praying for you") and unbelievers ("Best of luck—we'll keep our fingers crossed'). Today, if I had to answer the question "Where is God when it hurts?" in a single sentence, I would make that sentence another question: "Where is the church when it hurts?" (1990, 254).

In Christian communities, Christians must teach and model a biblical response to injustice and pain. Ultimately, these are not the work of God, but the result of sin. We cannot continue to live as we wish, and expect God to undo the bad consequences of our actions. Even when we live godly lives, we live in a fallen world in which the consequences of sin are rampant. But Christians can confidently proclaim that God truly does understand human pain, for in Christ he suffered and died. God does not abandon his people in their suffering; he is beside them and grants his Spirit to help them bear injustices (Heb. 4:15).

Christians must also teach that God can use suffering for good. This is not to say that pain and injustice are "good," but that they do not have the final say. God is greater even than the power and consequences of evil, and he works all things, good and bad, ultimately to his glory and the good of his people (Rom. 8:28). In many cases, that transformation begins on earth, for through pain Christians are often drawn into a deeper relationship to God, and a greater understanding of themselves. Christians in the West, in particular, need to develop a biblical theology of suffering and the Cross that does not see the avoidance of hardships as the greatest good, but sees God at work around and through all things (Heb. 2:10).

More profoundly, Christians are called to share in the sufferings of Christ (2 Cor. 1:7, Phil. 3:10, 1 Peter 2:21). The full meaning of these passages is hard to understand, but it is clear that suffering gains meaning if Christians see it as part of the "cross" they bear in following Christ. Christ does not always remove their pains, but "he fills them with meaning by absorbing them into his own suffering. We are helping to accomplish God's redemptive purposes in the world as co-participants with him in the battle to expel evil from this planet" (Yancey 1990, 241).

Christian leaders must declare that the end of the human story is not suffering, but joy and peace and eternal fellowship with God and the great crowd of witnesses gathered around the Throne in heaven. This is no escapism. This is the affirmation of hope in this life in the midst of suffering that in the end justice, peace, and righteousness will triumph, and the sufferings of this world are only for a time (Rom. 8:18).

Finally, the church must not only minister to those who suffer unjustly. It is to speak out against all the sin and injustices of its age, and to minister to those who are broken, alienated, poor, and oppressed.

FOLK RELIGIOUS PRACTICES

Folk religions are made up of assortments of disconnected beliefs: of spirits, ancestors, witchcraft, magic, divination, purity, and evil. They are also made up of a bewildering array of religious practices: birth rites, funerals, festivals, temple ceremonies, religious processions, village sacrifices, rain dances, public exorcisms, and pilgrimages. How do these religious behaviors relate to religious beliefs?

Max Weber, Clifford Geertz, and others argue that beliefs give rise to behavior, a position most evangelicals take with their emphasis on preaching and teaching. They assume that when people's beliefs are right, they will behave properly. Emile Durkheim, Karl Marx, and others argue that behavior gives rise to belief. If children are taken to church regularly, they will come to believe the gospel. Some studies show that the correlation between beliefs and behavior is low. People who score low on tests of racism often show the most racist behavior in life. This may be because written exams test explicit beliefs, and do not take into account unconscious beliefs and worldviews. All these explanations take linear views of causality in which one variable is independent and the others are dependent.

We will use a systems approach in analyzing the relationship between beliefs and behavior in folk religions. Beliefs are expressed and reinforced in behavior, and behavior reinforces and transforms beliefs. The bridge between inner and outer worlds is symbols. We will, therefore, first examine the nature of religious symbols, and then their embodiment in myths, rituals, institutions, and religious movements.

SECTION OUTLINE

Section Three examines practices and organization of folk religions, and how these are related to and reinforce folk religious beliefs.

9

THE WORLD OF
SACRED SIGNS

The relationship between folk religious beliefs and behavior is best understood in terms of contemporary theories of signs. Humans alone of all creatures live in a world of their own making—a world of symbols, cultures, and worldviews. Other creatures have languages and communicate to their offspring. Only humans create mental worlds by means of symbols, which enable them to reflect on the world around them, think of other and better worlds, and mold the world to fit their imaginations. They use sign systems, such as languages, gestures, written characters, colors, smells, and architecture, to communicate meaning to one another, and to pass it on from generation to generation. By means of sacred symbols and rituals they search for truth, find their ultimate meanings, experience their deepest feelings, and express their fundamental motivations and allegiances. Symbolization is a universal human process that enables people to range over the whole gamut of human knowledge; past history and future prospect, sciences, arts, and religions. By it people create cultures by which they transform the confusing, threatening, unpredictable world of nature into a world of order, security, and predictability which they can control. In this cultural world, people see themselves as civilized and human, set apart from the beasts of the wild. Hayakawa notes,

> Everywhere we turn, we see the symbolic process at work. Feathers worn on the head or stripes on the sleeve can be made to stand for military rank; cowrie shells or rings of brass or pieces of paper can stand for wealth; crossed sticks can stand for a set of religious beliefs; buttons, elks' teeth, ribbons, special styles of ornamental haircutting or tatooing, can stand for social affiliations. . . . Warriors, medicine men, policemen, doormen, nurses, cardinals, and kings wear costumes that symbolize their occupations. Vikings collected their victims' armor and college students collect membership keys in honorary societies, to symbolize victo-

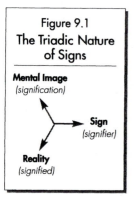

Figure 9.1
The Triadic Nature
of Signs

Mental Image
(signification)

Sign
(signifier)

Reality
(signified)

ries in their respective fields. There are few things that men do or want to do, possess or want to possess, that have not, in addition to their mechanical or biological value, a symbolic value (Hayakawa 1978, 22).

Ernst Cassierer writes,

Man lives in a symbolic universe. Language, myth, art and religion are parts of this universe. They are the varied threads which weave the symbolic net, the tangled web of human experience. All human progress in thought and experience refines upon and strengthens this net. . . . Instead of dealing with things themselves man is in a sense constantly conversing with himself. He has so enveloped himself in linguistic forms, in artistic images, in mythical symbols or religious rites that he cannot see or know anything except by the interposition of this artificial medium (1944, 25).

THE NATURE OF SIGNS

How do signs enable humans to think, create cultures, and communicate their thoughts to one another? To answer this question, it is important to examine the nature and functions of signs.

SIGNS

A sign is anything that stands for (represents, signifies, elicits, recalls, points to, stands in the place of, typifies, denotes, relates to, refers to) something else in the mind of a person or community. Another way of stating this is that a sign is a word, object, action, event, pattern, quality, relation, person, or concrete particular that serves as a vehicle for a conception of some perceived reality.

As noted in Chapter 2, Charles Peirce argues that signs have three parts to them (Figure 9.1; 1955): (1) an exterior form (the *signifier;* e.g., the spoken or written word, the sound of a bell, arrow); (2) a mental concept or image (the *signification*); and (3) the reality the sign refers to (the *signified*).[1] In other words, signs connect the world of exterior realities to inner mental worlds. For example, the word *tree* (the sensory dimension which is part of language) evokes a mental image of a tree

---

1. We reject here the views of Wilhelm von Humboldt and Ferdinand de Saussure, who divided signs into "inner" mental images and the "outer" experienceable forms. Their dualism leaves meaning totally in the mind of a person and has no place for objective external referents, and leads to cognitive relativism, which Peirce's triadic view of signs rejects. They also argue that the bond between the signifier and the signified is arbitrary, and deny any 'universal, transcendent causes to compel the assignment of a particular signifier to a signified' (Saussure 1983).

(subjective dimension) and refers to real trees which people experience and believe exist (objective dimension).[2]

Signs are culturally created categories, but they must also reflect differences that exist in nature itself if they are to be of any value for living in a real world. Many of them have objective referents, so it is possible to test whether they 'fit' or 'do not fit' the real world. This keeps them from being purely arbitrary, culturally shaped categories. For instance, children learn the meaning of words from their experiences and mistakes. Their mother points to a bird and says, "duck," so they say, "duck." She points to another, and again says "duck." They parrot back "duck." Then they see a bird and say, "duck," but mother corrects them and says, "no, that's a goose." In time children learn to differentiate between ducks and geese, not by memorizing definitions in dictionaries, but by ordering their experiences.

People are uniquely free to create symbols, and to manipulate them to form new and complex ideas. They agree to let "X" stand for dollars and "Y" for hours, and manipulate these signs in a formula to calculate how much they earned in one day. They let "X" stand for gallons of gasoline and "Y" for miles, and calculate how far they can go on a tank of gas. This ability to create and manipulate signs enables people to think about the world in which they live and to change it.

Most signs are community conventions. Individuals may develop their own signs, but communication and cultures depend on sets of signs shared by groups of people. Benjamin Whorf, an anthropologist interested in language, wrote:

> We cut nature up, organize it into concepts, and ascribe significance as we do largely because we are parties to an agreement to organize it in this way—an agreement that holds throughout our speech community and is codified in the patterns of our language (Postman and Weingartner 1969, 126).

People learn the meanings of words and other signs from the way these are used in everyday life. They use signs to communicate with one another, to store information and ideas, and to pass on knowledge from one generation to the next. To learn a culture is to learn and understand its signs, and how these shape the way people look at the world. There are many theories of signs which we cannot cover here.[3] Suffice it to say

---

2. For a more detailed analysis of the nature of signs as we view them, see Peirce 1955. According to Peirce, the *object* is the objective reality (real trees), the *representaman* is the signs we use to represent this reality (the spoken or written word *trees*), and the *interpretant* is the mental image these signs stimulate (the mental image and categories of trees).

3. A few include Paul Tillich, Lonergan, Sperber, and de Saussure.

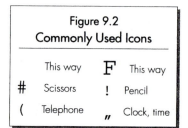

Figure 9.2
Commonly Used Icons

	This way	**F**	This way
#	Scissors	**!**	Pencil
(	Telephone	**„**	Clock, time

that this is a crucial subject for a discussion of religious structures in general and folk religions in particular.

TYPES OF SIGNS

Peirce divides signs into three types: indexes, icons, and symbols (1955, 391). *Indexes* are signs that indicate directly the existence of something else. They are produced by the realities they signify. For example, footprints in the sand show the hunter that a deer has been there, lightning demonstrates the presence of a storm, a heartbeat shows that there is life, and fever and other symptoms warn of the presence of disease. Indexes are natural manifestations and are common to all cultures.

Icons are signs that resemble the realities they represent. Examples include photographs, paintings, sculptures, movies, and graphs. In icons there is generally some similarity between the signifier (arrow, fence, drawing of a tree) and what it signifies (this way, don't cross, tree). The widespread use of icons in computer programs today are a good example (Figure 9.2).

Symbols are more general. They are anything people use individually or corporately to stand for something else. English speakers use words such as 'tree,' 'house,' and 'road' to refer to realities in the real world, and 'ideas,' 'anger,' and 'hope' to represent invisible inner ideas and feelings. They use 'word' as a symbol to represent a whole set of symbols, and 'justification' to speak of a process.

Symbols are mental categories humans create and label to grasp and order the realities in which they live. Without them people cannot think, understand, or even truly experience the world in which they live. With them people can both comprehend and control their world. Cultures are the mental worlds societies construct to live in a confusing world—to give it order and meaning, and symbols are the building blocks they use to construct these worlds. The focus in this chapter is on symbol systems and icons that people use in religious activities.

SYMBOLS AND MEANINGS

Symbols give expression to the three major dimensions of human experiences: the ideas that give meaning to the surrounding world, the feelings that serve as responses to that world, and the values and allegiances that motivate and guide people's actions. Most symbols combine all three, but many emphasize only one of these dimensions.

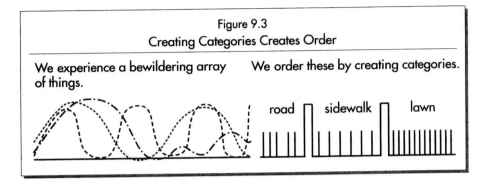

Figure 9.3
Creating Categories Creates Order

We experience a bewildering array of things.   We order these by creating categories.

road   sidewalk   lawn

COGNITIVE MEANINGS

Symbols play a key role in helping people make sense of the world by organizing experiences into mental categories. Nature is infinitely varied—no two trees are exactly alike, no two people look entirely the same. Put simply, there cannot be a separate word for each object or reality in nature. To comprehend the world people must reduce it into a manageable number of categories, so they lump a great many different objects together and call them "trees," even though some are tall and some short, some evergreen and some deciduous, some young and others old. Without creating categories that lump likes together and differentiate them from things that are unlike them, humans cannot begin to grasp the infinitely varied and changing world in which they live.

Creating categories, however, means that people must draw boundaries between different kinds of things. In American homes, walls divide space into different 'rooms.' Furthermore, walls—which should be kept clean—are differentiated from floors—on which people can walk. Moldings make the boundaries clear. Forks, spoons, and knives are placed in different bins, books are ordered by category on shelves, and dark clothing is separated from light in the laundry. Americans sweep the 'dirt' off the sidewalk (the moment it is off it turns into "earth"), pull "weeds" out of the lawn, patch and paint cracks in walls, and cover the cracks down the front of men's dress shirts with ties. Clear categories help people create a sense of order, and therefore meaning in the confusing jumble of their everyday life. Classifications provide people with a sense of continuity and stability over time. An ordered world is one with which they are familiar (Figure 9.3), and gives them a sense of meaning and predictability.

Borders must be maintained or disorder sets in. Dirt appears on the kitchen floor, walls become smudged, and cars show mud spots. When boundaries become fuzzy, people feel a sense of chaos. When boundaries shift, people's fundamental experiences of reality are threatened.

This is why people fight to maintain boundaries, because the lack of boundaries gives them a sense of confusion and meaninglessness.

How do people create boundaries in a world of a bewildering variety of experiences? Order implies restriction. From all possible materials a limited selection must be made and ordered into categories, but there are always things that do not fit into a culture's categories. In Chapter 8 we showed that people often treat ambiguous things as dirt to be hidden—out of sight, and avoided. For example, spittle, urine, feces, and menstrual blood are widely seen as 'dirty.' These are on the boundary between human and not human. In many cultures this list includes hair and nail clippings, milk, and human blood. Dead bodies are widely seen as defiling because they are human and not human at the same time. The concept of pollution is widespread, and helps people maintain order by helping them to avoid confusion at the boundaries between categories.

People also create boundaries by treating ambiguous things as sacred, therefore dangerous and taboo. Temples, idols, religious books, and other sacred objects are treated with care, lest they become polluted and the offenders suffer harm. In the Old Testament, the tabernacle was the place between God and the people of Israel, and therefore holy.

Ambiguities, whether seen as holy or defiling, serve another function. They are unclassified things that can be shaped into new orders. Consequently, they are areas of potential creativity from which new orders can be generated. Chaos may be evil, or it may be unformed potential.

Signs communicate cognitive information in two ways. Many used in everyday life *denote* or stand directly for what they signify. There is a direct association between the signifier and that signified—between the symbol and the 'realities' to which it refers. English speakers see a tree and think of the word *tree*. They see a girl running and speak of "running."

As people use signs, however, they come to associate these with certain experiences and contexts. When they use the signs again later, these secondary associations come to mind giving them *connotative meanings*—the ideas, feelings, values, and beliefs consciously or unconsciously associated with the signs. Connotative meanings bring to mind the encyclopedia of associations people have had with that sign in their lives.

Connotative meanings are often personal and private, and are evoked when the signs are given. Many connotative meanings are public, culturally shaped associations people learn with the signs themselves. For example, the English word "dog" denotes a certain category of animals. Westerners also learn to associate it with ideas such as domestic, friend, and hunting. They extend the association by saying, "he has a dog's life," or "she was treated like a dog." On the other hand, the word "fox" refers to another category of animals that is associated with ideas such as wild, enemy, danger, and object of the hunt. English speakers refer to people as "foxy" and as "outfoxed." Denotative meanings are generally precise, literal, and immediate. Connotative meanings, on the other hand, are often imprecise, associative, and open-ended—allowing for a variety of interpretations.

EXPRESSIVE MEANINGS

Some signs evoke deep sentiments and feelings. Music, dance, and art are often referred to as expressive culture because they are created primarily to express people's affective responses to life. People smile when they receive gifts of flowers or jewelry, and are overwhelmed by grief when they see pictures of loved ones who have died.

In expressive behavior, the experience itself is a central part of the meaning. A child's cry, an adult's laughter, an injured person's moans, an angry person's gestures—all these may be culturally shaped or masked, but the basic patterns are widely distributed. To eat together not only expresses the desire to relate—it is to relate. To bow or prostrate oneself before another is widely understood to mean subservience. To shake spears, throw rocks, or point guns is to threaten violence. In all these signs, the signifier and signified are closely linked in people's minds.

Dance and music are other forms of expressive behavior. The rhythms, beats, melodies, and styles are themselves much of the message. The meanings underlying hard rock concerts are different from those of a symphony orchestra or a funeral dirge. In many societies, percussion sounds, such as firecrackers, drum beats, or gun shots, are used to summon and entertain the spirits. Drugs, frenzied dancing, and mass actions are used to produce ecstatic experiences and higher visions of another reality. Similarly, self-torture is closely tied to experiences of remorse.

EVALUATIVE MEANINGS

Finally, signs enable humans to pass judgments and motivate them to action. They see a red light and stop the car, smell a rose and put their arms around their spouses, hear the choir sing and worship God. Military songs, flags, and religious symbols give people the courage to die for their country or faith. Cheering crowds, bands, uniforms, and mascots drive players to do their best in football and baseball, and the desire to get "A" grades push students to study all night.

MULTIVOCAL SYMBOLS

Symbols are not isolated elements. They belong to sets of symbols in cognitive domains. They derive their meanings not only from the realities

Figure 9.4
Multivocal Nature of English Colors

Domain	Color				
	Red	Yellow	Green	Blue	White
FEELINGS	anger	cowardice	envy	rage	fear, surrender
TRAFFIC SIGNS	stop	slow, yield caution	go	<flashing lights: police>	
POLITICS	Communist		Environmentalist		
CLASS	red neck			blue collar blue blood	white collar
NATURAL SYMBOLS	blood: life/ death	gold: wealth heaven	vegetation: life/fertility	sky: freedom sea	snow: clean, purity

to which they refer, but also from their relationship to other symbols in the domain. For example, "red" refers to a certain color, but it also stands in contrast to "orange," "yellow," and the other colors of the rainbow.

Many symbols belong to more than one cognitive domain. For example, "red" in the set of colors refers to a certain color; in the domain of politics it refers to communism; and in the field of emotions it refers to anger (Figure 9.4). This multivocal nature of symbols weaves webs of meaning that crisscross a culture and link diverse areas into a single whole.

In many societies, the linkage between cognitive domains is far richer than in the West. For example, in India, musical notes are linked to parts of the body, colors, animals and birds, spiritual masters, gods and moods (Figure 9.5). Hearing the base note Sadja (equivalent to the Western note Do) brings to mind the soul, red, the peacock, the sage Dakas, Agni—god of fire, and a feeling of being at home—in a state of trance. To listen to music, therefore, is to evoke religious, aesthetic, and affective meanings. Seeing a peacock evokes memories of a note, melody, color, god, and state of mind.

DOMINANT SYMBOLS

All peoples have a few symbols that take on great importance. These are powerful because they condense deep cognitive, affective, and evaluative themes in a single symbol. They express and communicate the deepest, most intimate experiences of human lives. They generate powerful emotions and moral responses. Victor Turner notes that these dominant symbols

Figure 9.5
Multivocal Nature in Indian Culture

Music Scale Moods	Parts of the Body	Colors	Animals and Birds	Spiritual Masters	Gods
Sadja [Sa = Do] Sa: at home, changeless, invincible, a yogi in trance	Soul	Red of the Lotus	Peacock	Dakas	Agni— god of Fire
Rishabha [Ri = Re] Ri flat: half awake, sluggish, sleepy, morose, sad Ri sharp: perfectly awake indolence of a yawning person	Head	Greenish Blue	Bull	Atri	Brahma— god of Creation
Gandhara [Ga = Mi] Ga Flat: bewildered, helpless, pitiable mood Ga sharp: inquisitive, alert, a questioning child	Arms	Golden Yellow	Goat	Kapila	Chandra— the Moon
Madhyama [Ma = Fa] Ma: grave, noble, powerful, dominates the atmosphere	Chest	Jasmine	Crane	Vasista	Vishnu— Preserver
Panchama [Pa = So] Pa: brilliant, self-composed, better half of Sa	Throat	Krishna Blue	Indian Cuckoo	Bhargava	Narada— Divine Sage
Dhaivata [Dha = La] Da flat: grief, pathos Da sharp: muscular, robust	Hips	Brilliant Yellow	Horse and Frog	Narada	Tumburu— Divine

operate culturally as mnemonics, . . . as "storage bins" of information, not about pragmatic techniques, but about cosmologies, values, and cultural axioms, whereby a society's "deep knowledge" is transmitted from one generation to another (1972, 486).

Most dominant symbols are multivocal. The same symbol has many different meanings, and different levels of significance. For example, the Indian flag stands for: (1) the flag itself (denotation), (2) the nationalistic ideas associated with it, such as 'India,' (3) the Wheel of Knowledge (connotations associated with the wheel at the center of the Indian flag), and (4) national pride and sacrifice.

The multivocal nature of dominant symbols makes them powerful because they act to unify disparate beliefs, feelings, and axiomatic values. They help people resolve contradictions by combining opposites in the same symbol in creative tensions. For example, blood stands for life and death; for purity (washed in blood) and pollution (menstrual blood, blood of murder); of taboo (don't eat blood) and sacred meal (communion). They also bring together diverse experiences and settings, and weave a common thread through them. For instance, people speak of blood covenants, blood sacrifices, blood revenge, blood baths, and blood brothers. These symbols can combine the most disparate elements into a unitary expression.

Dominant symbols are dynamic because they are open-ended and link different analogies and associations in one concrete form. This ambiguity makes them generative, for the network of their associations leads human minds to explore new connections. People link water to baptism, to baptism-by-fire, to initiation, and to death and resurrection.

Unlike ordinary symbols which speak only of surface things, dominant symbols pluck all the strings of the human spirit at once. They aim inward, not outward, and touch the most secret depths of the soul. They can evoke the deepest human feelings and motivate their deepest responses.

FUNCTIONS OF SYMBOLS

Symbols vary greatly in the ways they work. It is important to understand these in order to understand the nature of religious symbols.

COMMUNICATION AND PERFORMANCE

Symbols serve two important functions in society: they communicate information and they transform reality. These two operations are often intertwined in religious life. People bow to images which remind them of their gods, but often come to see these images as the gods themselves. People sing songs not only to communicate their worship to God, but, in fact, to worship him.

COMMUNICATIONAL SYMBOLS

A triadic view of signs explains how human communication is possible. People have inner ideas, feelings, and values. To communicate these, they must encode these in signs that others can experience, whether through sight, sound, touch, taste, or smell. Others receive and decode the signs. For example, John has an idea, feeling, or value he wishes to communicate to Mary. To do so he must encode it into symbolic forms, such as speech, gesture, facial expression, or writing, which Mary can experience (Figure 9.6). Mary then decodes the symbols and creates a mental image of what John communicated. They can check to see if Mary understood John more or less accurately by checking their understandings against the reality to which the symbols refer, and by further communication by means of more symbols. Such checking is easier in communications about the material world ("there are three cows in the pasture") than about spiritual realities ("there is a ghost in the house"). Because people cannot communicate without signs, the world of signs, such as languages, gestures, and icons, becomes increas-

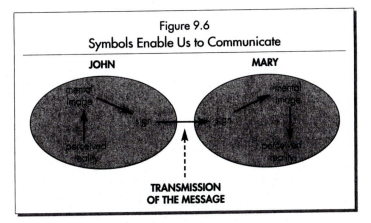

Figure 9.6
Symbols Enable Us to Communicate

JOHN   MARY

TRANSMISSION
OF THE MESSAGE

ingly not only the way they communicate, but also the way they think about things. Sperber and Wilson take this one step further and emphasize the importance of receptors making inferences (or interpreting) about the communicator's intent. When intent and inference match, communication as expected by the initiator takes place. This has crucial implications for applying God's Word to human religious response as we will discuss in the last section of this book.

In communication, the connections between the sign and the reality to which it refers vary greatly. In many symbols the link is arbitrary and loose. In the West, people choose names for children on the basis of personal preference, social convention (certain names for girls, and others for boys), and history (names that have been used in that culture or family in the past). They create new words as labels to refer to new creations, such as radio, television, fax, satellite, and Internet. In time, many of these become socially accepted, and are passed down from generation to generation. By then the link of a symbol to reality is no longer arbitrary. Individuals may try to control or change the meanings of words, or give them their own personal definitions, but their efforts are futile if they cannot get the community to accept their definitions. This social linkage explains why people use different sets of symbols in different social settings. Certain symbols are used in religious contexts, others in economic, social, and political settings.

In other signs the linkage between form and meaning is closer. In many societies a person's name is more than an arbitrary label. Names are given to reflect the person's character ("Brave," "Courageous") or to shape the child's personality. Art, too, is often based on literal or analogical ties between the image and the reality it depicts. It is helpful here to note the distinction between art and history. The religious artist

seeks to communicate a deeper spiritual message, not a historically accurate picture of events. A noted Korean artist painted a series of pictures which depicts Christ as a Korean teacher with the black hat worn
by all traditional Korea teachers. The houses and clothes are Korean in
style. Obviously the artist is not trying to portray historical facts.
Rather, he is trying to depict a deeper truth that Christ identified himself with humanity, all humanity, even Korean humanity, in his life and
death. Western artists have done the same with pictures of Jesus as a
blond, blue-eyed white person.

In some symbols, the sign (signifier) and the reality (signified) to
which it refers are very closely tied. For example, in some societies a
person and her shadow are thought to be integrally related. To harm
her shadow is to harm her. Among the Shilluk of East Africa, the inves-
titure of a new king is a lengthy ritual in which the king-elect sits on the
royal stool, which is the locus of divine and kingly power. The stool does
not just represent this power—it is believed to contain it (Evans-Pritchard 1962, 66–86). In much of the world sacred relics and places, such
as the Shroud of Turin, the tooth of the Buddha in Sri Lanka, and the
Black Stone reputed to have been given to Ishmael by the angel Gabriel
and housed in the Kaaba, are equated with holy persons and sacred
events, and are often credited with curative or miraculous powers. A
modern secular example of this association of signifier and signified is
the way fans keep the memorabilia of famous persons such as Elvis
Presley and Madonna.

In religious signs and rituals there is often a close tie between signi-
fiers and realities. This makes them solid and enduring. Such signs provide the skeleton on which the rest of a culture is hung. As Peter Berger
and Thomas Luckmann point out, "[t]he cultural imperative of stability
and the inherent character of culture as *un*stable together posit the fundamental problem of man's world building activity" (1966, 6).

PERFORMATIVE SYMBOLS

Some symbols not only communicate beliefs, feelings, and values,
they transform reality. One example is legal pronouncements. When
judges say to defendants, "I find you guilty," they are not just communicating information. By their pronouncements they transform persons
innocent before the law into criminals. In other words, they change
those persons' statuses in society and the way others relate to them.
Similarly, when ministers say, "I pronounce you husband and wife,"
they change the brides and grooms into married couples in the eyes of
the state and society. Another example of performative signs is found in
Daniel 6:8–9, where King Darius issued an edict and signed the docu-
ment into law, and even the king could not change it. In many feudal

societies, putting seals on letters or objects turned them into the property of the Crown. Today, making a promise or issuing a command, apologizing and warning are performative acts, not simply communication of ideas. People cannot subject these speech events to tests of truth. In all of them, symbols not only communicate, they also have intrinsic power to cause things to happen.

Boundary markers are performative in nature. Fences and rocks marking fields, lines marking lanes on roads or volleyball courts, and temple walls not only show where boundaries are; they create those boundaries.

In magic, too, there is a close tie among beliefs, behavior, and objects. In oral societies, sounds are often thought to be powerful and sacred. People believe that to say things is to cause them to happen. The right sounds in a ritual cause rain to fall. Other sounds, such as drumming and shouting, drive away the evil spirits. For contagious magic, the object must be from the person against whom the magic is performed—a lock of hair, a fingernail, a piece of cloth, or a footprint. For imitative magic, the object must replicate the person in some basic way. A doll is molded and given the name of the person. What is done to the doll is believed to occur to the person. The same is true in magical chants, where every sound must be correct or the chant is ineffective. In amulets, charms, divining paraphernalia, and spirit repellents the shape itself has magical power.

Many rituals are seen as performative. The church's debate regarding the Lord's Supper has to do with the relationship of symbols and the realities they represent. Catholics and other High Church Christians see the bread and wine as more than loose symbols reminding people of the body and blood of Christ. After the consecration these, in fact, are the body and blood of Christ in some mysterious way that ordinary language and thought cannot express. The forms, after consecration, become the message—the means by which grace is administered to the repentant sinner.

DISCURSIVE AND NONDISCURSIVE SYMBOLS

Symbols work in two different ways: discursive and nondiscursive. The distinction is important in understanding the power of sacred symbols. Most symbols people use in everyday life are discursive. There is an immediate referential link between the mental categories of the people, and the world of their experiences. They see a tree, image it in their mind, and think of the word *tree*. They may think of other trees they have seen and compare those with the one before them. They see a girl running, and tell their friends she was 'jogging.' They are reminded of seeing her yesterday, or of their own efforts at running. For the most

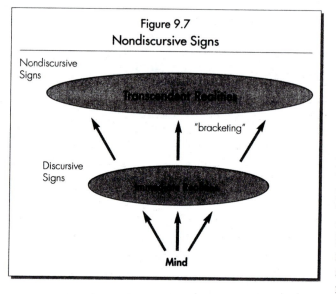

Figure 9.7
Nondiscursive Signs

Nondiscursive Signs

Transcendent Realities

"bracketing"

Discursive Signs

Immediate Realities

Mind

part, discursive statements are about information that can be analyzed and tested to be true or false.

Nondiscursive signs are harder to describe. They do not refer to things directly—they point toward things that cannot be expressed in ordinary words. They go beyond the limits of discursive language to speak indirectly about the "unspeakable." They often refer to ideas, emotions, and motivations that transcend ordinary immediate human experiences. For example, in a lyrical poem Goethe uses "sunshine" and "spring" not to inform the readers about meteorological data, but to communicate deep feelings and values. Other examples of nondiscursive signs include status symbols such as army insignia, national symbols such as banners and anthems, and money. These express and communicate deeper, cultural expressions in the world.

Nondiscursive symbols deal with the ambiguities, uncertainties, and mysteries of life compared with sense experiences, which are immediate and rationally analyzed. They are concerned less with naturalistic realities known through the senses than hidden ones known by looking below the surface of things. For example, in medieval art, Jesus often had a halo around his head to show his inner holiness and deity. Because of their reference to transempirical realities, nondiscursive statements cannot be tested directly to be true or false. They point to realities beyond empirical realities (Figure 9.7). They give expression to emotions and commitments. After singing a song or reading a poem, people do not have more information. They have more experience.

At the heart of nondiscursive symbols is analogy and metaphor. In fact, C. S. Lewis points out (1970, 71), all language, except about objects of sense, is metaphorical through and through. It is the language of imagination. To speak of things beyond immediate experiences humans take ordinary words and use them to point to something beyond themselves. To call God a "Force," like the wind, is as metaphorical as to call him Father or King. The psalmist refers to the Word of God as a "light," "lamp," "law," and "testimony" (Ps. 119).

Nondiscursive signs are often nonverbal. They include smells: incense, roses, coffee, wet grass. Each evokes powerful feelings and memories such as love, nostalgia, and nausea, and appetites such as hunger and thirst. They include taste: chocolate, spices, blood, and ethnic foods, which bring to mind pleasure, pain and ethnic identity. Nondiscursive signs cannot be classified in taxonomies and domains. They can only be listed by causes: perfume, incense, roses, stables, rain, and coffeeshops.

Meaning in nondiscursive symbols does not lie in a literal exegesis of their explicit realities. Rather, their meaning often lies in the acting out of a sign—giving a gift, shaking hands, bowing, standing when a woman enters the room, covering one's mouth when yawning, or standing or raising hands in church. When asked why they do these things, people often cannot give a literal 'meaning' of the action, only some nondescript comment about "good manners," "custom," "showing appreciation," "greeting the person," or "worshiping." A historian may say that shaking hands in the West was originally a sign that one was not armed, and that extending the right hand made it impossible for a person to hit the other, but this account of original meanings (even if such was the case) is far from most people's minds when they shake hands with others today. The meaning of nondiscursive symbols is often not explicit and analytical, but unconscious and publicly shared knowledge.

Nondiscursive symbols lose their meaning when reduced to ordinary language. For example, a young man does not say to his girlfriend, "Honey, I love you. My heart beat is up thirty-five beats a minute, my adrenaline is up 22 percent, and my palms are sweating." He gives her flowers and jewelry, sings songs, and kisses her, all of which convey feelings more powerfully and accurately than simply cognitive information. Von Bertalanffy writes,

> If the meaning of Goethe's *Faust*, or Van Gogh's landscapes, or Bach's *Art of the Fugue* could be transmitted in discursive terms, their authors should and would not have bothered to write poems, paint or compose, but would rather have written scientific treatises (1981, 52).

In discursive communication signs speak of the world outside, in nondiscursive communication people interpret the world around them in terms of categories and realities that transcend everyday experiences. Unlike discursive words, which use categories to make state-

ments about the world, nondiscursive statements use worldly categories to create and establish relationships between categories that refer
to transempirical realities.

METAPHORS

One way to express nondiscursive ideas is to use metaphors, types,
allegories, and other tropes. For example, people speak of God as a
"person," because that is the closest analogy in their experience to enable them to understand him. He transcends gender, yet Christians
sometimes speak of him as Father or Mother. They refer to the church
as a "body" and use the analogies of head, arms, eyes, and heart to refer
to different parts and functions in it. The medieval church was constructed to represent both the cross of Christ and the human body: the
chancel was the head, the transepts the arms, the center the heart, and
the public area the feet. Devotion to the crucifix was directed to the
crucifixion on Golgotha, and thus to Christ for the redemption he
brings.

Metaphors draw on homology, analogy, or contiguity to generate
new insights based on comparisons or oppositions. To express love
Americans speak of flowers, honey, birds, sun, moon, stars, and heart,
and give gifts of perfume, candy, and diamonds. In some societies, metaphors are often extended to different domains of human experience in
complex webs of meaning. The Osage Indians associated the eagle with
lightning, lightning with fire, fire with coal, and coal with the earth. The
eagle therefore was one of the "masters of coal," making it a land animal. The turtle with a serrated tail represented the vault of the sky because it had six or seven serratures that correspond to the six or seven
rays the sun emits when it rises above the horizon. Such connections
are based on resemblances used to link a disparate world into one interconnected whole (Sperber 1974, 26). Metaphors push humans beyond static, easy creeds to dynamic, fluid images that more fully en-
compass the sacred.

EXPRESSIVE CULTURE

Music, art, dance, architecture, pageantry, processions, and other
forms of what anthropologists call expressive culture play a vital role in
nondiscursive communication. They are symbolic languages that communicate not ordinary thought, but intimate feelings. They combine
ideas and feelings in sensory images and give them powerful emotional
reinforcement. Incense, flowers, bells, drums, masks, and images provide concrete symbolic representations of deeper human experiences.
Like any language, these symbols must be learned and appreciated to
understand their power in the lives of ordinary people.

Expressive signs are particularly important in oral societies that encode their beliefs in songs (lyric theology), art, masks, temples, flags, stained glass windows, stations on a pilgrimage, and other visual forms that condense a great deal of information into a single experience and are easily recalled.

BRACKETING

A third type of nondiscursive sign is ordinary symbols that are 'bracketed' to show that they do not point directly to the reality to which they refer, but to realities beyond the immediate senses. English writers use brackets or quotation marks in a sentence to show that they are changing the level of discourse. For example, if they write, "John said that he is going to town," the speaker remains the same throughout, but if they write, "John said, 'I am going to town,'" the bracket marks a change in speakers—there is a shift in the level of discourse from one person to another. Similarly, if people take ordinary symbols, such as words and sentences, and "bracket" them, they are saying, "do not take these symbols at their ordinary face value. Use them to point to something else, something that cannot be fully expressed in words."

There are many ways to bracket symbols. People sing the words, say them in special places such as churches, repeat them in chants and prayers, and embed them in rituals such as weddings and funerals. They decorate their bodies, stand in silence, use drums, and put on masks to communicate deep messages. As noted below, bracketing is central to most sacred symbols.

Icons are a fourth type of nondiscursive sign. We will look at these in more detail when we examine sacred signs.

SACRED SIGNS

At the center of a culture are its sacred symbols. These integrate and give expression to a people's worldview—the mental picture they have of the way things in reality actually are (the cognitive dimension); the tone, character, and aesthetic quality of their life (the affective dimension); and the moral standards that set their ideals and governs their relationships (the evaluative dimensions).

Sacred symbols differ from other symbols because they are representations of that which is beyond the conceptual sphere—they point beyond themselves to the sacred, the world of ultimate reality, a more profound, more mysterious life than that which humans know through everyday experience (Figure 9.8). They communicate meanings about the infinite and transcendent level of reality not accessible through im-

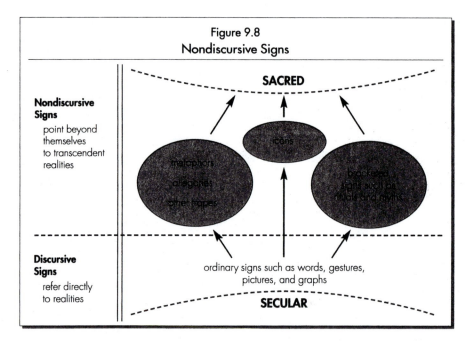

Figure 9.8
Nondiscursive Signs

mediate experience or rational thought, and the 'inner world' of reality not otherwise comprehensible. They resolve the paradoxes of human experience. In so doing they bring ultimate meaning to human existence by delivering people from the immediacy, self-interest, and mundane nature of ordinary life and relate them to the universal and sacred. Human speech is too poor to convey all the thought aroused by such basic problems as the alternation of life and death, and the sublimity of hope. Only sacred symbols do this.

ICONS

Icons are images, pictures, and masks that point to transcendent realities through resemblances that go beyond metaphors, allegories, and other tropes. For example, religious icons embody the presence of spiritual realities in mystical ways. Relics of saints do more than remind worshipers of sacred lives; they embody the sacred power of the saints, which is transferred to those who touch and venerate them. Idols are often seen not only as reminders of the god or even the abodes in which the gods live, but as the gods themselves. Other religious icons are images through which the worshiper sees the transcendent, sacred world that lies beyond surface realities. Common religious icons include water, which stands for cleansing, both materially and spiritually, and blood, which speaks of death and life. In the medieval Western church, the lion was a sign of Christ the Lion of the Tribe of Judah, because he stood for the king of the beasts—strong, compassionate, and noble. The lion was also believed to sleep with its eyes open, and so to represent vigilance. The leopard, in contrast, stood for Satan—cunning and evil.

The Eastern Orthodox Church sees icons as works of art through which the beauty of God and heaven shine, just as saints are people through whom the beauty of the Lord streams. It uses icons not only to help believers think about transcendent truths, but to experience these more directly by seeing through the images to the realities that lie beyond them. This church rejects the dualism of matter and spirit that has characterized the church in the West. For it icons have theological significance for they represent the transformation and, consequently, sanctification of matter.

BRACKETED SACRED SIGNS

People use bracketed signs to speak about the mysteries of religion, and to remind themselves that these are sacred. They wear special clothes and go to special places at special times to show that what is happening is set apart from ordinary life. They begin and end a worship service with prayer. They kneel or stand, and begin prayers with "Our God. . . ," and end them with "Amen" to show that they are speaking to God, not humans. They kneel, bow, or raise hands to indicate worship. They sing, chant, read, and preach their message, using special words and tones of voice to let everyone know that this is not ordinary talk. They use formal liturgies, repeat confessions of faith, recite the Lord's Prayer, and sing the same song again and again.

Two forms of bracketed symbols are myths and rituals. Both take participants out of ordinary life and raise them to the level of transcendent realities. These will be examined in detail in the next two chapters.

DOMINANT RELIGIOUS SYMBOLS

Dominant signs are often religious in nature. For Christians, these include the Star at Christmas, the cross, and the bread and wine at the Lord's Supper. Communion denotes a common meal eaten by Christians in a ritual setting. The bread denotes the body of Christ, its breaking his death, the cup his blood, and the eating together declares oneself to be a follower of Christ who participates in the community of the church. Even dominant secular symbols take on a religious aura (Figure 9.9). The U.S. flag is a sacred symbol in battle, and people give their lives to rescue it from defilement.

Dominant sacred symbols are condensed. They bring together many, often opposite, beliefs and emotions, and in so doing unite disparate meanings in a single symbolic formation—tears of repentance and for-

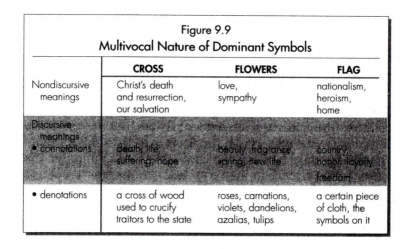

Figure 9.9
Multivocal Nature of Dominant Symbols

	CROSS	FLOWERS	FLAG
Nondiscursive meanings	Christ's death and resurrection, our salvation	love, sympathy	nationalism, heroism, home
Discursive meanings • connotations	death, life, suffering, hope	beauty, fragrance, spring, new life	country, honor, loyalty, freedom
• denotations	a cross of wood used to crucify traitors to the state	roses, carnations, violets, dandelions, azalias, tulips	a certain piece of cloth, the symbols on it

giveness, words of joy and sorrow. They are combined in rich textured rituals. At fiestas people dance, eat, drink, parade, make music, burn incense, and wear bizarre modes of dress—all these actions contribute to an emotional and social mix that gives the people their corporate identity. Every time they celebrate their fiestas, they reaffirm the importance of their group and their place in the universe.

CHRISTIAN RESPONSE

What implications does this analysis of sacred symbols have for the church and its missionary outreach? First, it forces missionaries and Christian leaders to reevaluate their own views of the nature of symbols, particularly of sacred symbols. This century has seen a retreat from religious symbolism in the West. An increasingly secular world is mechanistic, technological, and rationalistic, while denying transcendence and mystery. This spiritual disintegration has all but destroyed the ability of Westerners to respond to sacred symbols. Many reject the elaborate symbolic worship of High Church traditions and stress simple, straightforward, literal language about God. In this discursive literalness, the distance between image and reality is often forgotten, and with it the sense of divine transcendence and mystery, The ability of metaphoric and symbolic speech to communicate the truth is not understood. We use one or two words for God, and assume that God is thereby fully known to us. Our view of God becomes static and narrow. Metaphors, on the other hand, push us beyond the static, easy creeds to dynamic, fluid images that more fully explore the mystery and immensity of the sacred. In church and missions Westerners need to recover the importance of sacred symbols in preserving the transcendent truths of the gospel over the centuries.[4]

UNDERSTANDING SIGNS IN THE BIBLE

Sacred signs play an important role in biblical history, particularly in the Old Testament. We see this in the language the Hebrews use about God. All the stumbling and awkward attempts to describe God literally in words fall short of revealing a God who continues to resist attempts at classification, one who says of himself, "I am who I am" (Exod. 3:14). Lydia Harder points out that the Hebrews used nondiscursive ways to describe him.

> The Hebrew people, well aware that God was beyond speech, were reluctant to speak God's name. Stories, metaphors, and various substitute names were used instead of the name YHWH to describe their relationship to God and still preserve the sense of holiness and transcendence. God could be characterized as the God of war as well as the God of peace, the God who never changes and the God who repents. They sang praises to God as the stable rock of our salvation as well as extolled the dynamic vitality of God as the spring of living water (1988, 1).

The proper name of God was sacred, and not to be spoken lightly. In reverencing it, the people pointed to the transcendence, mystery, and holiness of God. To speak his name in ordinary conversation was to reduce him to finite realities.

The tabernacle and later the temple were dominant multivocal symbols, condensing and reenacting the whole of divine revelation. This was where the people met God in a special way. The sacrifices, washings, special clothes, and incense were sermons communicated by actions. The altar of burnt offering, laver, table of shewbread, golden candlesticks, altar of incense, and ark with its cherubim, tables of the law, and Aaron's rod—all proclaimed profound, multifaceted truths that spoke not only to the minds, but also to the hearts and wills of the people. They demonstrate the importance of metaphors in communicating divine truth. Modern Christians do not understand the rituals and sacrifices of the Old Testament. Consequently, they relegate these to a past age, and fail to learn the central lessons these ceremonies bring to a full understanding of the gospel.

The strength of icons, metaphors, and nondiscursive symbols is also their weakness. We see this, too, in the Bible. It is not a great distance

---

4. As will be seen in Chapter 11, the answer to the decay of powerful sacred symbols into dead tradition is not to eliminate all such symbols; it is to constantly re-create new and living sacred symbols that renew faith and allegiance.

from an icon to an idol, from a metaphor to equating it with reality, with washings and sacrifices as signs to equating them with substance—with purity and worship.

USING SIGNS IN COMMUNICATING THE GOSPEL

Understanding the nature and purpose of signs is important when planting churches. Many societies are oral and encode messages in symbol systems other than the printed page. They use images, masks, dress, art, dramas, stories, rituals, songs, chants, proverbs, riddles, and many other aural and visual signs to symbolize their beliefs. How can we best communicate the gospel to them while utilizing the symbols they already know, rather than first requiring them to learn to read?

EXEGETING SIGNS

To understand the world of signs for a given people requires learning to exegete their symbol systems. The study of their sacred symbols, in particular, provides a window on a people's understanding of ultimate reality. Victor Turner suggested that a study of symbols involves three levels of analysis: exegetical meaning, operational meaning, and positional meaning.

Exegesis is our effort to uncover deep meanings—to make explicit what often lies implicit in human statements and actions. Biblical scholars exegete the underlying meaning of biblical texts, and present their results in commentaries. Anthropologists exegete cultures by studying explanations people give concerning their actions, and present findings in ethnographies. They seek, as much as possible, to understand the people's point of view, and describe symbols and rites in terms that reflect that understanding.

All intercultural communication takes place through signs, and the fact that different cultures do not share the same signs and their denotative and connotative meanings raises many important and difficult questions. How can missionaries communicate Scripture when there is no common words for God, sin, salvation, heaven, or eternal life?[5] Missionaries from the West need to understand the nature of Bible translation. They also need to know the strength of icons, tropes, and bracketed signs in helping people experience sacred realities. Worship cannot be reduced to words, nor to statements about God. It addresses God himself. The church must always resist the temptation to reduce

---

5. This is why it is important for missionaries to study at least basic theories of linguistics, rituals, myths, and other sign systems that specialize in translating signs from one culture to another.

God and divine mysteries to rational propositions, or to equate them with mental images.

Operational meaning is revealed through the ways symbols and activities are used in the context being studied. This approach focuses on the shared and emotive meanings people have about the way a symbol or rite is handled, by whom and when.

Symbols and actions also have positional meaning. They derive their meanings from relationships with other symbols in symbol systems. For instance, blood and milk play central roles in many different rites among the Ndembu of Tanzania. In birth rites they speak of life and nurture, in wedding rites of procreation, and in funerals of death. Taken together, the total meanings of fundamental sacred symbols help people understand the ultimate truth and norms of their society. The study of symbols, their meaning, and their uses in different contexts is essential for missionaries to understand the worldview underlying a culture. This must be learned and explicated to be useful in ministry.

INTERCULTURAL COMMUNICATION

Effective communication requires learning the sign systems people use in everyday life. It begins by learning their language, but it must go far beyond this. Missionaries need to learn the meanings of tones of voice, gestures, space, time, colors, objects, architecture, and behavior if they want to understand the people's world.

In oral societies, people use sounds extensively to communicate to one another. Their worlds are highly immediate, personal, and relational (Ong 1969). Communication is a flux of immediate encounters between humans, full of emotions and interpersonal interests. In their worlds, sounds point to the invisible and speak of mystery. The hunter hears the tiger before he sees it. It should be no surprise, therefore, that people believe in spirits, ancestors, gods, and other beings they cannot see.

In oral societies, the gospel must be presented in concrete terms, by means of dramas, songs, rituals, object lessons, and other ways which are easy for people to remember. One method often overlooked by Protestants are catechisms. Like the early church creeds, these are brief theological summaries that can be readily memorized and recalled. Today many Protestants have smorgasbord theologies, and lack a simple, coherent understanding of the gospel (Bibby 1987). Confessions and catechisms not only provide a comprehensive view of Christian faith, but they also preserve that faith over time. Churches that recite them, even after the members have lost a vital, living faith, can experience revival later as the younger generation raised in the church grasp these truths.

Literacy introduces new symbol systems. Information is stored on paper and in books. This enables people to read about distant places and new ideas. It enables them to organize large bodies of information and run complex organizations. It also freezes ideas into set forms. Oral versions of local stories are told and retold, and in the retelling are slightly changed. Written texts remain the same over time. Moreover, written communication carries little sense of mystery, and leaves little room for what is not seen. In literate societies, the gospel should be communicated through print, but Christian leaders must not overlook the fact that even in these societies, much of the communication is oral.

In communicating the gospel, it is important to make clear to people the meaning of the signs that are used. There is a danger that people learn to use signs without understanding their meanings. There is also a danger that the people misunderstand the prayers and practices of missionaries, and view these as magical formulas to acquire supernatural power or to harm a rival, or as efficacious rites that purify those who participate.

How can missionaries communicate the gospel effectively? First, it is important in many societies to minister publicly in concrete, visible, and tangible ways. Religion in the West is largely seen as a matter of private belief, and is relegated to the home or church. In much of the world, religion is a public activity done so that all can observe. Churches often have no walls, and non-Christians stand outside watching the Christians worship. Believers kneel in prayer in market plazas, railroad stations, and other public places. Moreover, common people often need these concrete expressions to affirm their faith. Common people tend to symbolize their faith in action, drama, dance, painting, carving, and architecture. Because they live in cultures where temples, festivals, and rituals are used to communicate religious meaning, it is important to avoid simply presenting doctrines in abstract terms. Rites of healing, deliverance, and reconciliation need to be done in public as a witness to God's love and power. Western missionaries must deal with their fears and sense of shame in public places.

Public ministry also calls for living symbols, whether spoken words or actions. Kneeling, bowing, laying on of hands, anointing with oil, and other behaviors are not magical ways to ensure God's blessing and healing, but they are public symbols declaring to those around that Christians put their trust in God and seek his help. Prayer before surgeries, seeding a field, opening a new school, and dedicating a church show faith in God to the whole community—Christian and non-Christian alike.

ROLE OF SIGNS IN CONTEXTUALIZING THE GOSPEL

Contextualization of the gospel in other cultures must begin at the level of signs. This is true for Bible translation. It is equally true for Christian behavior and rituals. We must examine carefully the nature of signs in Scripture and in the culture in which we minister to determine which can be used to communicate the gospel without losing its meaning. In any culture, some signs can be used to convey Christian meanings, but others cannot because they are too closely tied to non-Christian meanings. For example, the use of aqua blue in Indian dramas signifies the Hindu god Krishna. It is impossible to use that color on the face of an actor in a Christian drama without drawing in connotations of Hindu mythology. In such cases, to avoid syncretism, we may introduce our own cultural symbols, but this often results in nominalism because the gospel remains foreign, and does not take root in the dominant symbols of the people's lives.

As Protestants we also need to understand the importance of nondiscursive symbols in communicating religious truth. In our fear of idolatry and the elaborate symbolic worship of High Church traditions, we often reject the use of physical imagery, such as sculpture, painting, and architecture, and stress the use of simple, straightforward, literal language about God. By so doing we forget that we cannot reduce God or the gospel simply to words, and that words can become idols just as readily as other signs. To speak of transcendence and mystery, Christians need to use nondiscursive symbols.

A study of signs and sign systems is foundational in understanding folk religions. We will examine their use in myths, rituals, and religious organizations, and our mission response in the following chapters.

10

SACRED MYTHS

Two forms of communication play particularly important roles in religious life in traditional societies, myths, and rituals. We will focus on mythology in this chapter and rituals in the next. Most societies have stories of creation, and of the origins of their people and culture. Other stories explain why things are as they are—how evil and death entered the world, why animals are different from humans, and what causes lightning and thunder. These cosmic stories explain how reality came into existence through events that took place in primordial time, often by the acts of supernatural beings. Still others tell of the end of all things. What are we to make out of these stories? Many of them appear to be convoluted tales of fantastic and esoteric events. This has been a central question in seeking to understand what is obviously an important part of the lives of many people.

NATURE OF MYTHS

In anthropological terms, myths are "a narrative resurrection of primeval reality told in satisfaction of deep religious wants, moral cravings, sacral submissions, assertions, even practical requirements" (Malinowski 1954, 19). In other words, a people's mythology serves as a cultural repository of truth that seeks to validate their belief systems.

In popular, everyday speech the word *myth* carries the idea of a fictitious story which is not true but only imagined. In this sense, the word stands in distinction from 'reality.' The origin of this meaning lies in the Greek rationalists, who attacked the stories of the gods as narrated by Homer, because these gods stole, committed adultery, and deceived one another, just like humans. It was in this setting that the early church fathers defended the historicity of Jesus, and refused to accept the apocryphal Gospels and unwritten sayings as authentic documents. Origen, on the other hand, stressed the fact that biblical history has spiritual meanings that lie beyond history, and argued that the incarnation, resurrection, and ascension of Christ have cosmic as well as historical significance. In other words, the gospel is both historical and transhistorical in nature.

Another common view sees myths as prelogical attempts to explain the world, as primitive philosophies premodern people believed to be true "once upon a time" and used to allay their fears by projecting these onto mysterious beings.

A third misunderstanding of the word sees myths as literary forms used to convey moral truths, but not fundamentally different from legends and fables. Most societies have "folk tales." These are not seen by the people as stories about the true nature of reality, but as humorous stories told to make a moral point or to entertain. For example, Coyote is the humorous prairie-wolf who plays pranks in North American tales. He is a trickster, deceiver, and accomplished rogue. The West has its stories of Paul Bunyan and Luke Skywalker. These folk tales, however, are sharply differentiated by the people from their myths.

A fourth misunderstanding of myth reflects the contemporary secular discrediting of anything religious and sacred—its rejection of belief in God, angels, spirits, miracles, and the like.

All these English usages are unfortunate for they are the opposites of the original meaning of the word, namely, that myths are transcendent stories believed to be true, which serve as paradigms people use to understand the bigger stories in which ordinary lives are embedded. They are master narratives that bring cosmic order, coherence, and sense to the seemingly senseless experiences, emotions, and ideas in the everyday world by telling people what is real, eternal, and enduring.[1] Robert Antoine observes,

> Myths are not lies or second hand "unscientific" approaches, but a *sui generis* and irreplaceable method of grasping truths which otherwise would remain closed to us. "The language of a myth is the memory of the community," of a community which holds its bonds together because it is a "community of faith" (1975, 57).

Care must be taken, however, not to reduce myths to intellectual discourses that answer questions of "why" and "wherefore." They transcend pure rationality and science because they speak of things that people may not directly perceive, and of mysteries and infinite realities they cannot fully comprehend. Myths look beneath the surface world at

---

1. Postmodern critiques charge that all meta narratives are suspect and oppressive because they work on the unconscious. We argue that without authoritative meta narratives, people have no sense of place or purpose in the universe, and are alienated from one another and reality.

what is really going on in this world.[2] They are the language not only of thought, but of the imagination. They speak of things too hard for humans to bear by telling these things to them indirectly, forcing people to discover their meanings by active imagination and thought until the truths 'dawn' on them. Like nondiscursive symbols, myths point people in the direction of things that transcend immediate experience. They speak of eternal truth that transcends time, in contrast to empirical truth that is time- and language-bound.

Myths are archetypes of human existence, told in story form by common folk who are not philosophers, to give meaning to their lives and expression to deep emotional stresses they face. Human stories change, but myths abide and give life. A Western tendency is to try to find ultimate meaning in abstract analysis. By so doing people remove themselves from participating in reality and become detached, outside observers. Narratives, on the other hand, draw people into reality. As C. S. Lewis points out, humans find meaning only as they participate in it.

> [T]he only realities we experience are concrete—this pain, this pleasure, this dog, this man. While we are loving the man, bearing the pain, enjoying the pleasure, we are not intellectually apprehending Pleasure, Pain or Personality. When we begin to do so . . . the concrete realities sink to the level of mere instances or examples: we are no longer dealing with them, but with that which they exemplify. . . . As thinkers we are cut off from what we think about (1970, 65).

As we saw in Chapter 5, humans find meaning in the stories of their lives because narratives give meaning to the past, explain the present, and provide guidance for the future. Myths link their stories to the cosmic story. In telling myths humans come nearest to experiencing concretely the bigger meanings of their lives. In them, people see not truth but reality, because truth is always about something, but reality is what truth is about (Lewis 1970, 66).

People in societies around the world speak of two levels of reality: this world—the world of humans and history, and the world beyond—the world of divine beings and cosmic history. This world is viewed as derivative, contingent, and illusory; the other world, as real and substantial. This world is a stage on which humans play their parts. The

2. The Enlightenment shift to an interest in and control of this world led to abandoning truth in the modern world. The central question was how. Right answers to this question enable humans to control their environment. Questions of what is truly going on beneath the surface materialism of this world are rarely asked in science. The result has led to the trivialization of life and human pursuits. Like in an auto race, technology, speed, competition, and winning are all important, but at the end, everyone ends up where they began. They have gone nowhere.

world beyond is their ultimate abode. The relationship between these two worlds varies in different cultures. In many, myths are divorced from history. Consequently, as we saw in Chapter 5, human history and biography have little meaning. They are constantly changing, and will come to an end.

Many myths chronicle a sacred story that transcend history. These myths are stories told about the gods and events in time before the world began. They deal with sacred underlying *realities,* and are *the* sacred stories. Hence they are believed to be 'true' in the cosmic sense. However, they not only report past events, they are exemplars—models or prototypes that give meaning to human actions, and help them to understand contemporary events. But they are more. They give rise to and intertwine with the history of this world. It is this breaking of the sacred into this world that establishes and gives it meaning. Myths put people in touch with the cosmos.

The heart of Christianity is this inseparable link between the cosmic drama and human history. This link gives the latter meaning and purpose, and ties the present to the past and the future. Christ's incarnation, death, and resurrection are both historical facts and cosmic realities. Lewis notes,

> For this is the marriage of heaven and earth: Perfect Myth and Perfect Fact: claiming not only our love and obedience, but also our wonder and delight, addressed to the savage, the child, and the poet in each one of us no less than to the moralist, the scholar and the philosopher (1970, 67).

FUNCTIONS OF MYTH

Myths fulfill an indispensable need in the lives of most people. They express, enhance, and codify belief; safeguard and enforce morality; assure the efficiency of rituals; and contain practical rules for the guidance of humans. Myths are vital to human civilization. They are not idle tales, but hardworking; active forces. They are not intellectual explanations or artistic imagery, but charters of life and moral wisdom. Myths serve several important functions by giving meaning to human existence.

A COSMIC VALIDATION

First, myths have great power because they make sense out of the universe—they explain reality in ways people can understand. They are grand narratives with plot, structure, purpose, and design that give meaning to everything. They transcend time and reveal the deeper realities of existence by imparting a sense of awe in the face of the mysterious nature of the universe. They explain why things are constituted as they are. They give a larger view of reality, and give it cosmic validation. Everyday knowledge is often made up of bits and pieces of information. Eugene Peterson writes,

> Learning stories isn't the same as learning the multiplication tables. Once we've learned that three times four equals twelve, we've learned it and that's that. It's a fact that doesn't change. The data is stored in our memory for ready access. But stories don't stay put; they grow and deepen. The meaning doesn't exactly change, but it matures. . . . We keep on telling stories, the same old ones, over and over and over again, in a way quite different from saying the multiplication tables over and over again. The stories keep releasing new insight in new situations. As we bring new experience and insight to the story, the story gathers that enrichment in and gives it back to us in fresh forms (1997, 36–37).

Deliverance from Oppression

[myths are often captured in song]

When Israel was in Egypt land
Oppressed so hard they could not stand.
Let my people go.
Go down Moses, way down in Egypt land,
Tell O'l Pharaoh,
Let My People Go!
Oh, let us all from bondage flee,
And let us all in Christ be free!
Let my people go.

Myths transform bits of information into larger pictures or models that give meaning to the parts. They enable people to explore the contradictions in which they live—the tensions between good and evil, love and hate, acceptance and rejection—and show them that there is something beneath the surface of the visible, audible world. They communicate something that is "just as real, maybe even more real, than what we're seeing, and hearing and touching" (Peterson 1997, 38). Myths help make sense of a confusing and often fearsome world. They integrate and validate the reality in which people live. In this sense myths and rituals communicate not only knowledge, but also wisdom—an understanding of the picture as a whole.

A RATIONALE FOR BELIEFS AND VALUES

Second, myths are prototypes for life. They model acceptable and unacceptable behaviors in the society, and so teach people codes of ethics. For example, Exodus is the true history of how God delivered Israel from the hands of Pharaoh and the Egyptians. That story, however, is more than history—it is the archetype Israel used to interpret its later experiences. Parents told the story, and reenacted it in rituals, such as the Passover, to teach their children faithfulness and obedience to Yahweh, who delivers his people from suffering and oppression whenever they repent and turn to follow him. Joshua ordered twelves stones from the Jordan River to be piled up on the river bank as a memorial, and instructed the people that whenever they saw this monument to tell the story of what God had done for Israel (Josh. 4). Whenever Israel was in trouble, the prophets reminded the people that God had delivered them from the bondage of Egypt and given them a new land. The exodus became one of their myths—the true history that helped them understand all their subsequent stories. Israelites lived their lives intentionally by experiencing themselves as characters in that story, and by interpreting events in their lives in terms of the meaning provided by its dramatic and cosmic events. The exodus has also become the central paradigm by which African Americans and other oppressed people understand their suffering existence in the world.

A Source of Identity

Third, myths give people an understanding of their place in the universe—a sense of personal identity. They do so by guiding people, stage by stage, through the course of life. Many of them do so by reactualizing the beginnings of the universe, time, and humans through the retelling and reenacting of the events. Myths, to a degree, shape who people want to be and how they should live. Someone may want to be a 'missionary' and the models for this are the stories of Mary Slessor, Hudson Taylor, E. Stanley Jones, and other successful missionaries. Others want to be 'preachers' whose lives are shaped by the stories of Charles Spurgeon, D. L. Moody, and other great preachers. Myths demonstrate the ideal and exemplary—how humans and things should be. The mythical heroes and heroines provide examples for human lives.

A Source of Community

Fourth, myths tell people the community to which they belong, their place in it, and the moral order of the society. To be a part of a people is to be a part of their story. Rollo May writes,

> Our powerful hunger for myth is a hunger for community. . . . To be a member of one's community is to share in its myths, to feel the same pride that glows within us. . . . The outsider, the foreigner, the stranger is the one who does not share our myths, the one who steers by different stars, worships different gods (1991, 45).

Many myths have to do with the origins of 'our people,' and how a society came to be where it is today. These stories are more than secular histories. They trace the origins of the community to God, ancestors, and other transcendent beings. For example, after Genesis 12 the Old Testament is the story of the people of Israel, an epic narrative made up of many episodes combined to communicate an overarching theme: "You will be my people and I will be your God." These parts are often mythical in themselves, establishing the origins and reasons for the moral values that undergird the people of Israel. The stories tell of predecessors who modeled righteousness or who demonstrated the consequences of sin and unrighteousness. This myth is not just for Israel, however. It is for all human beings whom God created and calls to himself. Scripture is ultimate truth that takes on mythical proportions in the human context. This leads us to look at various types of myth.

TYPES OF MYTHS

There are a bewildering variety of myths, and no simple analysis can do justice to them all. For our purposes we will examine a few types that are found in most societies.

ORIGIN MYTHS

Origin myths, which explain how the world came into existence, are the most universal kind of myth. They often tell of gods and goddesses who created the earth, or gave it existence through their death and dismemberment. Others, such as the Japanese myth of origins, speak of the procreation of the world, which was born out of the union of two gods or *kami*. Origin myths frequently separate the world into different realms—most often, heaven, earth, and underworld—and describe how the oceans, land, mountains, and all of nature came to be. They describe the origin of first humans, and explain how they came to suffer and die. Other origin myths describe how humans acquired fire, bows and arrows, and houses, and how they came to domesticate animals and plants. In doing so, these myths justify the new situation.

THE DANGUN MYTH

In the beginning two animals, a bear and a tiger, wanted to become humans. Hwan Ung, son of Hwan In (God), heard their petitions and came down the mountain. He promised they would become humans if they obeyed his orders. For one hundred days they were to stay in a cave, shunning sunlight, and eating only garlic and mugworts. At the end of that time they would emerge as humans. So the animals went into the cave together, hoping to come out humans.

The tiger paced anxiously every hour while the bear sat quietly and prayed for her human form. Finally, the tiger, unable to endure the wait any more, leaped out from the cave, and remained a tiger ever after. The bear waited in patience, and after a hundred days she emerged from the cave. Her bear body fell away and she emerged a beautiful woman, Ung Nyu.

Hwan Ung fell in love with the beautiful, virtuous bear woman, so he descended to earth and married her. Not long after this Ung Nyu gave birth to a human son whose name was Dangun. He is the progenitor of the Korean people.

[Note: this makes humans half-gods and half-animals, living between two worlds]

SEPARATION MYTHS

Separation myths are widespread. They explain how humans lost their pristine state in paradise, and came to suffer toil and separation from God. According to the Nuer cattle-herders of the southern Sudan, the sky and the earth were originally connected by a rope attached to the Tree of Creation by which humans first entered the world. Every day people climbed down the rope from the sky to obtain their food. When people died on earth, they ascended to the sky via the rope for a short time and returned to earth rejuvenated. The Nuer have different versions explaining how the rope was severed, making death a permanent human condition. In one, a girl descended from the sky with some companions to get food on earth. She met and had sexual relations with a young man. He had originally come from the sky, but he had spent his whole life growing up on earth. When it was time for the girl to return, she refused, declaring her love for the young man. Her companions ascended to the sky and cut the rope, severing forever the means for immortality (her behavior reflects traditional marriage customs—she joins the husband). Consequently, people are now separated from Kwoth, the high God, Ancestor, Creator, and Spirit of the Sky, not because of sin, but because an impetuous young girl and her vindictive companions (Ray 1976, 33).

WHY WE DO NOT LIVE ON FOREVER

Furu [God] made Oruwa, the first man and called him Oruwa. "It is not good for just this man to be in the very big bush by himself," Furu said. So he made a woman, Sikau, as Oruwa's wife. They had three sons, Womau, Fompai and Tuwou, and a girl, Opai.

Womau and Fompai picked shoots off a sago palm and with other ingredients prepared a concoction for the people just made to drink. This would make them live on forever, simply by their shedding their skins at the normal time of death, as snakes do. Another man, Koufai (no one knows where he came from) warned the people that they would die if they drank the mixture. A small harmless snake said, "No, you should all drink it and you will not die." However the people believed Koufai and so threw the concoction away. Various snakes and animals who found and drank the mixture have lived on forever. If only the people had not believed Koufai, we would all live forever.

God, angry with the people for not drinking the mixture, changed their language that night. Next morning the people could not understand each other for they were speaking several languages. Womau and Fompai dispersed the people, sending each language group to a different area.

(A myth of the Wape of New Guinea. Adapted from McGregor 1969, 202–3)

According to another Nuer myth, there was once a couple who had no children. In desperation the wife made an offering to Imana, the high God, who was moved by her plea and gave her a son in a pottery jar on condition that she did not tell anyone of his origins. The wife had a sister who was barren and jealous of the new mother. She finally persuaded her sister to reveal to her the origin of her child. She then went to ask Imana for the same favor of him, and had a son. Realizing the seriousness of her broken vow, Nyinakigwa cried, "I have offended Imana, I have killed my children." The sky opened and the children fell to the world below where there were misery, famine, thirst, and work. The sisters begged Imana for forgiveness, but he promised only to show pity on the children and alleviate their condition in the world below. One day, he promised, their expiation would be complete and they would return to the sky. (Ray 1976, 33–34). Here the loss of paradise is seen as the result of an explicit act of disobedience against the creator's will.

The Dinka of the Sudan believe that in the beginning, Nhialic, the high God, and humans were close friends, and people climbed up to the sky by a rope. There was no death or illness, and a minimum of labor was needed to produce food. Nhialic was good to them, but the sky was close to the earth so humans had to be careful not to strike Nhialic when planting and pounding the millet. One day a woman used a long-handled hoe to plant millet and, raising it upward, she struck the sky. Nhialic was angry and withdrew far above the earth. Thereafter people had to labor for food, and suffer sickness and death (Ray 1976, 54–55). Today the Dinka see God as a stern father disappointed by his creation.

CULTURE HEROES

Many stories tell of mythic figures who live between the world of humans and the gods, and who turned people into full humans by teaching them culture in ancient days. Typically these culture heroes brought fire that turned raw meat into food and melted rocks into metal. They introduced language, agriculture, and techniques for brewing beer and baking bread. They taught people arts, crafts, laws, ceremonies, and social organization. They were the link between the original sacred realm and the mundane world of ordinary human life. Culture heroes also defeated monsters and other evil forces threatening human existence. In the end, however, these culture heroes, like the gods, became offended with human ineptness and left humans to their own devices.

CATASTROPHES

Myths of cosmic cataclysms are widespread. Some occurred in the past, some recur periodically, and some are expected in the future leading to the end, or to a new creation. Stories of a flood are common. Other cosmic catastrophes include earthquakes, conflagrations, falling mountains, and plagues. Often these are caused by the anger of the gods because of the sins of human beings. In many of these myths of calamities, most humans are killed, and only a few survivors remain to repopulate a virgin earth, now purified of previous evils. Judgment is followed by restored order and morality.

In some apocalyptic myths, a judgment will take place in the future, and the world will cease to exist. In the Caroline Islands, Aurepick, the Creator's son, will submerge the island with a cyclone when he sees that the chief no longer has any concern for his subjects. The Nigritos of the Malay Peninsula believe that Karei, an evil god, will destroy the earth and all its inhabitants when people no longer obey him (Eliade 1975, 56–57). In these myths the destruction is final. Other myths, however, tell of a destruction followed by the re-creation of an earthly paradise in which the dead will rise, and death and sickness will be abolished. The Choctaw Indians and the Eskimo of North America believe that the world will be destroyed by fire, but that the spirit of humans will return, reclothed with flesh to inhabit their traditional lands. Underlying all these myths is the belief that the world is degenerating and that destruction and re-creation are needed to restore the cosmic order.

In many eschatological myths creation, degeneration, and destruction are followed by re-creation, degeneration, and destruction in an endless cycle of time. In Judeo-Christian cosmology the final judgment occurs once. Time is not circular, but linear and irreversible. In it human history begins in sacred history and ends in sacred history. The belief in an immanent end of present human history and the coming of heaven was strong during the persecutions of the early church, but receded after Christianity became the official religion of the Roman Empire.

Millennialism is widespread around the world today, often the result of the encounter of traditional religions with Christianity. As we will see in Chapter 13, these include Melanesian Cargo Cults, the Native American Ghost Dances, and many of the African Independent Churches. Frequently these nonwestern millenarian movements look for a day when the local people will obtain all the material goods—the 'cargo'— that all Western peoples seemingly have. This will come, they teach, only through cosmic cataclysms in which God will give them what is justly theirs, and punish the colonialists who are rich because they have stolen the goods God sent to them.

WESTERN SECULAR MYTHS

Considering their importance in giving meaning and purpose to our lives, it should be no surprise that people in present-day secularized societies also have their myths. It is important to understand these for they have shaped not only Western cultures, but also the ways Western missionaries understand their task.

One dominant myth in North America has to do with the New Land. The Renaissance gave Europe a new confidence in human capabilities, and the discovery of North America was seen as God's favor—a Manifest Destiny—in giving humankind a new beginning in a New World (May 1991). Some saw the "new world" as a rebirth of humanity without poverty or injustice or persecution. This myth drove the Puritans and settlers to populate "New England," and build cities such as New York and New Haven. As the East Coast was settled, the new frontier became the West with its explorers (Daniel Boone, Kit Carson, Calamity Jane), hunters, trappers, and frontiersmen, all of whom lived lives of isolation and bragged about it. They were followed by pioneers, cowboys (Buffalo Bill, Bill Cody), and ranchers.

The basis of this myth was faith in a new beginning in which people could tame nature—the Wild West—and create a new utopia in which freedom reigned. The "rugged" individual (Lone Ranger, lonely cowboy) was the one to accomplish the task by relying on himself or herself in battling both nature and the evils of Old World civilization. This battle required violence, but violence was justified if it achieved the right ends. Outlaws and gangsters, such as Jesse James and Bonnie and Clyde, became heroes because they stood against the oppressive institutions of the Old World and the East.

This vision of a New World pushed settlers west. It also gave the country an unquestioning faith in anything new: new brands of medicine, new technologies, new religions, new ways of life, and, more recently, the "New Age." It also led to belief in the self-made person. New experiences, and renewal of the self through therapies and 'do-it-yourself' formulas are assumed to be good.

Change, too, was assumed to be good. The New World is better because it is New. So, too, are the New Deal and the New Frontier in politics. The result is unending progress as people compete and the fittest succeed, and as people re-create themselves in new possibilities. This faith in competition leading to progress underlies modern theories of evolution and capitalism. Combined with rugged individualism, progress led to a stress on self-fulfillment, self-indulgence (seen in TV ads for comfort, cars, and beautiful women), and narcissism. Even love is defined as the fulfillment of a person's emotional needs, not as a commitment to and relationship with others. As de Tocqueville noted early on, "They never stop thinking of the good things they have not got" (cited in May 1991, 114).

In this larger myth are embedded lesser myths. Horatio Alger wrote some of the most important stories in America in the nineteenth century. These tell the story of a poor boy, Luke, who by sheer effort and intelligence became rich and triumphed over a rich oppressor. These stories were widely read; they gave hope to poor Americans slaving in menial jobs, and justified to the rich their wealth. The underlying moral is that the poor must rise on their own industriousness, thrift, diligence, and deferral of self-gratification, and the rich need not take responsibility for them.[3] Today commercial industrialism promises western peoples a paradise on earth.

CHRISTIAN RESPONSES

How should the Christian church respond to myths? It is clear that most Western missionaries are not aware of how deeply myths shape the lives of a majority of the world's people. They think of the gospel primarily in rational, analytical terms. Consequently, their preaching and teaching is often perceived as irrelevant by listeners. Specialists in oral literature have shown that for most of the world's people the best way to communicate the gospel is through some form of story that captures the people's attention and causes them to think about divine "truths." Stories invite people to enter another world that is larger than themselves—the world of God's creation, salvation, and blessing. Missionaries should adapt the biblical stories to this style of communication. In fact, much of Scripture is already in this oral structure that so many understand much better than the bearers of the gospel who come from the West.

---

3. As Rollo May points out (1991), the stories of the Great Gatsby and Peer Gynt trace the collapse of this myth of progress and the self-made person. As Peter Berger points out (1969), secular myths of progress cannot provide a belief system to live by!

MYTHS OF SPIRITUAL WARFARE

One area in which the analysis of myths is important in modern missions is the current debate over the nature of "spiritual warfare."[4] At core this has to do with a missionary's understandings of the cosmic story. Missionaries often see the story of Scripture, but also bring their own cultural myths that have shaped how they interpret biblical references to the confrontation of God and Satan. Examples of spiritual warring are found in most mythologies, and knowing what these are can help believers guard against becoming captive to them when reading Scripture—cultural inferences and God's intentions do not always correlate. We will examine four myths that continue to influence the contemporary debate.

WESTERN DUALISM

Western worldviews are shaped by Cartesian dualism that divides the cosmos into two realities—the supernatural world of God, angels, and demons, and the natural material world of humans, animals, plants, and matter. The dominant myth of the latter is biological evolution. According to this, the evolution of life takes place through an endless battle between strong and weak in which the strong win and breed new strains of life. On this level, there is no moral distinction between good and evil, justice and injustice.[5]

The dominant myth of the supernatural domain is that of a battle between God and Satan, angels and demons, and good and evil. This battle takes place in the heavens, and has little to do with what happens on earth, except as heavenly beings intrude on earth. Angels and evil spirits are not seen as essential realities in ordinary, everyday life. In secular versions of modernity, the reality of the supernatural is denied.

In some Christian circles this meta narrative has led to theological and practical demythologization of the Scriptures and life. Biblical accounts of angels and demons are explained away, and they are not seen as essential realities in ordinary, everyday life. Human systems account for poverty, oppression, suffering, and other evil, and the church is called to confront them. In other circles the battle is seen as a spiritual warfare between God and Satan, the fallout of which is felt by humans on earth.

---

4. The term was originally used by Alan Tippett to refer to the battle that goes in the hearts of seekers when they think of following Christ instead of their old gods. This fear arises because they do not know from experience that Christ is indeed stronger than their old gods. Consequently, after their conversion any misfortune, sickness, or death is seen as the punishment of their old gods for forsaking them.

5. This amoral view of nature becomes a problem when humans evolve, for here we clearly must speak of good and evil, but we have no basis on which to build a sense of morality.

TRADITIONAL RELIGIONS

As we have repeatedly emphasized throughout this book, people around the world have a strong sense of the spiritual and its impact on daily life. Many people see the earth and sky as full of beings (gods, earthly divinities, ancestors, ghosts, evil shades, humans, animals, and nature spirits) relating, deceiving, bullying, and battling one another for power and personal gain. For the most part these beings are neither totally good nor totally evil. They help those who serve or placate them. They harm those who oppose their wishes.

Spiritual warfare in many animistic societies is seen as an ongoing battle between different alliances of beings. For the most part these alliances are based on ethnicity and territory. The gods, spirits, ancestors, and people of one village or tribe are in constant battle with those of surrounding villages and tribes. When the men of one group defeat those of another, they attribute their success to the power of their gods and spirits. When they are defeated, they blame this on the weakness of their gods. We see this in the way the Philistines and other tribes in the Old Testament viewed their battles with the Israelites. The battle between David and Goliath was seen not primarily as a battle between human armies, but as a battle between Yahweh and the gods of the Philistines.

Land plays an important role in traditional views of spiritual warfare. Gods, spirits, and ancestors reside in specific territories, and protect their people who reside on their lands. Their powers do not extend to other areas. When people go on distant trips, they are no longer under the protection of their gods. Nor do traditional gods extend their domains through the conquest of neighboring gods. Gods and people defeated in battle serve the victors. They do not become followers of the more powerful god.

THE INDO-EUROPEAN MYTH

The most widespread myth in Western cultures is the Indo-European myth of a cosmic spiritual battle between good and evil (Larson 1974; Puhvel 1970; see sidebar). With the spread of the Indo-Europeans from inner Asia to Europe, Mesopotamia, and South Asia, this myth in its various forms became the basis for the religions of Babylon, Sumer, Canaan, Greece, India, and Germany, to name a few. During the Middle Ages the formal religious beliefs of Europe were Christianized, but popular entertainment, including sports, movies, fables, politics, and wars, remained based on the Indo-European myth.

Fundamental to the Indo-European myth is the belief that good and evil are two independent eternal entities in eternal conflict. In this dualism, good and evil are represented by two opposing superhuman beings: a good God (Ninurta, Indra, Marduk, Mazda, Rama, and others) and a bad God (Asag, Vritra, Tiamat, Marmaduke, Ravanna, and others). All reality is divided into two camps: good God and bad God, angels and demons, good nations and evil ones, good humans and wicked ones. The line between the two camps is sharp. The good has no evil in it. Good beings may be deceived or forced into doing bad things to gain righteous ends, but, at heart, they are good. Similarly, evil beings, though at times they do good, are fundamentally wicked. Evil beings have no redeeming qualities, and must be destroyed so that good may reign.

THE INDO-EUROPEAN MYTH

From the beginning Ahura Mazda, god of light, life, order and truth, has been battling Ahriman, god of darkness, death, chaos and falsehood. The real world and all of life springs from their struggle. Ahura Mazda creates the world of life and warmth; but Ahriman, to thwart good, creates the world of death. Ahura Mazda creates an earthly paradise where roses flourish, humming birds fly, and cattle graze, but Ahriman creates insects and wild beasts to destroy and harass all living creatures. Ahura Mazda creates a great peaceful, prosperous city, Ahriman introduces lies and deception; Ahura Mazda teaches work and faithfulness, Ahriman sloth, deception and misery; Ahura Mazda introduces just and moral government, Ahriman tyranny and anarchy. Ahriman and his forces seek to darken the light and spoil the beauty of creation by tempting humans into self-indulgence and greed, and fill them with rage and anger.

The life of the universe is the constant struggle of these two forces. Humans are called by Ahura Mazda to kindness, goodness, justice and truth, but Ahriman tempts them to lie, oppress, and murder. People are free to choose whom they will support, and every act and thought is an expression of their allegiance. Their choice has no effect on the ultimate outcome. After 12,000 years of battle, Ahura Mazda will triumph, but until then there is no final victory. (Adapted from Biallas 1989, 210–11)

The battle is for control of the universe. If the wicked king wins, he creates an evil empire in which evil reigns. If the good king conquers evil, he establishes a kingdom of righteousness, justice, peace, love, and harmony. To win, therefore, is everything, but ultimate victory, particularly in the face of apparent defeat, is evidence of who is good and who is evil. The defeated must admit the superiority and therefore worthiness of their conqueror. In folk religions, conversions to new gods often follow dramatic 'power encounters.'

THE CONVERSION OF THE MALDOVIANS TO ISLAM

In old times Maldive islanders believed that the sea off Male, the king's island, was haunted by an evil spirit of great power who threatened to destroy the people, and demanded the regular sacrifice of young virgins to appease his anger. Annually one was tied to a stake by the shore in the evening. The next morning she was found dead. In 1340, Iban Battuta, a Muslim mendicant, came to the island and volunteered to be tied to the stake in place of a young girl. The next morning the terrified islanders arrived, expecting to find a corpse. To their astonishment they found the mendicant alive, reciting verses from the Koran. So the king and his subjects converted to Islam.

Morality in the battle is determined by a morality of "fairness," "equal opportunity," and success. To be fair, the conflict must be between those thought to be more or less equal in might. The outcome must be uncertain. It is "unfair" to pit a professional ball team against a team of amateurs. Equal opportunity means that both sides must be able to use the same means to gain victory. If the evil side uses illegal and wicked means, the good side is justified in using them too. In cowboy films, the sheriff cannot draw first, but when the outlaw does, the sheriff can gun him down without a trial. In a moment the sheriff becomes judge, jury, and executioner. In the end, both sides use violence, deceit, and intimidation to win the battle. Whatever evil means the good hero uses to gain the victory are now justified as necessary and expedient. Success is the proof of right, and enables the victor to establish order—the greatest good. The greatest evil is chaos.

In the Indo-European myth, the battle between good and evil is fought on different levels (Figure 10.1). In the heavens, it is the battle between the gods and demons, in society between righteous and evil kings and people, and in nature between good and bad animals.[6] The real battle is at the highest level, but skirmishes are fought on the lower ones. Humans are but pawns in the battles of the gods.

Underlying the Indo-European myth is the deep belief that relationships in the cosmos are based on competition, that competition is good, and that the good (strong, successful, intelligent) will ultimately win. The results of this unceasing competition are progress (civilization), development (economic), evolution (biology), and prowess (sports) as the stronger, better, and brighter defeat the weaker, badder, and duller.

In this myth, the battle is the center of the story. It is what people want to see. Many fables end with the words, "and they lived happily

6. All three tiers are seen in the *Panchatantra,* the tales told in Indian villages to instruct children regarding the virtues and vices of daily living. Lessons are taught through the use of stories that tell of the intrigues and battles of the gods, of humans, and of animals. Aesop borrowed many of his tales from this book. Today the same worldview is reflected in comics such as Mickey Mouse, Donald Duck, and Road Runner, in which animals live in a world that mirrors that of humans. They, in turn, live in a world that mirrors that of the gods.

ever after." There
is, however, no
story worth telling
during the "happily
ever after." People
pay to see the foot-
ball game, and go
home at the end of
the game claiming
victory or making
excuses for a loss.
The story ends
when the detective
unmasks the vil-

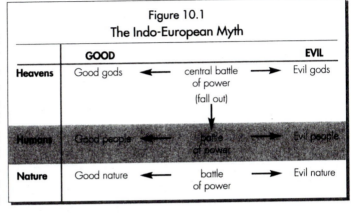

Figure 10.1
The Indo-European Myth

	GOOD		EVIL
Heavens	Good gods	← central battle of power (fall out) →	Evil gods
Humans	Good people	← battle of power →	Evil people
Nature	Good nature	← battle of power →	Evil nature

lain, the cowboys defeat the Indians, Luke Skywalker and Princess Leah thwart the Evil Empire, and Superman destroys the enemies of humankind. Victory in the Indo-European myth is never final, however, nor evil fully defeated. Evil rises again to challenge the good, so good must constantly be on guard against future attacks. Today's Super Bowl does not make a team the unchallenged victors forever. They must defend themselves next season.

This fascination with battle is evident in modern sports: football, basketball, tennis, hockey, chess, and Monopoly. People pay to see a baseball game. When the battle is over, everyone waits for the next one. The Indo-European religions may have died in the West, but as Walter Wink points out (1992), the Indo-European myth dominates modern thought. It is the basis for the theories of evolution and capitalism, and is the dominant theme in Western entertainment. It is told and retold in westerns, detective stories, murder mysteries, and science fiction. It is Superman, Spiderman, Super Chicken, Underdog, Sherlock Holmes, Colombo, the Lone Ranger, and Star Wars. It is the basis of most of the video games in arcades.

In Christian circles the Indo-European myth leads to a view of spiritual warfare as a cosmic battle between God and Satan in which the battle is fought in the heavens, but it ranges over sky and earth. The central issue is power: Can God defeat Satan? Can Christians overcome demons? Humans are seen as passive victims who will turn to Christ if they are delivered from the control of Satan.

BIBLICAL VIEWS OF SPIRITUAL WARFARE

The biblical cosmology differs radically from the modern, animistic, and Indo-European myths (Figure 10.2). In the fallen world the lion eats the lamb (Isa. 11:6), and competition, not cooperation, works best.

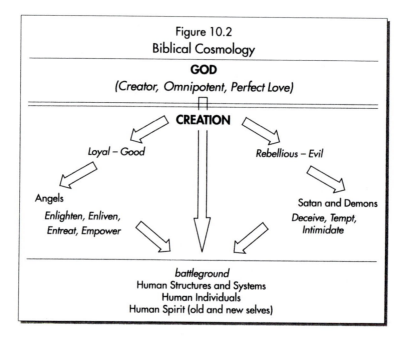

Figure 10.2
Biblical Cosmology

GOD
(Creator, Omnipotent, Perfect Love)

CREATION

Loyal – Good   *Rebellious – Evil*

Angels   Satan and Demons
Enlighten, Enliven,   *Deceive, Tempt,*
Entreat, Empower   *Intimidate*

battleground
Human Structures and Systems
Human Individuals
Human Spirit (old and new selves)

This, however, is not God's way. He cares for the weak and marginal. He calls Christians to love their enemies, and to seek reconciliation and peace. The biblical view represents God's reality which should, ideally, be reflected in the natural realm.

A biblical view of spiritual warfare must begin with God as eternal, righteous, loving, and good. Evil is not eternal or ultimate. God and Satan, good and evil, are not eternal and coexistent. In the beginning was God alone, and God was good. Satan, sinners, and sin appear in creation. Second, creation depends on God for its present existence. God did not create a universe that exists independent of him. Satan and sinners, like all creation, are contingent, and continue to exist through God's sustaining power. Their very existence in their rebellion is testimony to God's mercy and love.

The battle in Scripture between God and Satan is not one of power, to see who wins. God's omnipotence is never questioned. Even the power Satan and his followers use in fighting against God is God-given. The Old Testament writers attribute Israel's victories and its defeats to God. Unlike animistic and Indo-European myths, where success in battle is attributed to the power of the victors' god, Israel's losses are not blamed on Yahweh's defeat at the hands of other gods, but on Yahweh's judgment of his own people because they turned to other gods.

The encounter between God and Satan is a moral encounter. It is the

battle between holiness and evil, justice and injustice, love and hate. As
Eugene Peterson writes,

> There is a spiritual war in progress, an all-out moral battle. There is evil
> and cruelty, unhappiness and illness. There is superstition and ignorance,
> brutality and pain. God is in continuous and energetic battle against all
> of it. God is for life and against death. God is for love and against hate.
> God is for hope and against despair. God is for heaven and against hell.
> There is no neutral ground in the universe. Every square foot of space is
> contested (1997, 122–23).

God is righteous, light, life, and truth. Evil is the perversion of
good—deceitfulness, darkness, and death. It is rebellion, broken relationships, idolatry, alienation, and worship of the self. In this battle the
cross is the ultimate and final victory (1 Cor. 1:18–25). This was not an
apparent loss saved at the last moment by the resurrection. The cross
makes no sense in Indo-European terms. In it Christ should have taken
up the challenge of his tormentors, called in his angelic hosts waiting
poised in heaven, and come down from the cross.

Satan rebelled against God, and all humans, following Adam and
Eve, joined the insurrection. But God did not march in to destroy them
all when they fully deserved punishment. He reached out to win people
back to himself. His desire is not to stand triumphant on the battlefield,
but to gather all his creation around his throne in a kingdom of *shalom*.
At the heart of Scripture is God's love. In the Indo-European myth, rulers oppress the weak, and leaders command their followers. Scripture
speaks of love and commitment to the other regardless of the counter-
response. It gives priority to building community over fulfilling oneself;
to servanthood, not lording it over others (Luke 22:25–27); to loving
one's enemies, not destroying them (Luke 6:27, 35).

The biblical worldview focuses on relationships, not tasks and
achievements. Consequently, it has room for chaos. Unlike the Indo-
European view that all chaos is evil, Scripture has room for creative
chaos as the unformed potential from which spring life and creativity—the unshaped material out of which God created the universe
(Gen. 1:2), and the infant not yet grown to adulthood. It also has room
for the chaos that is inherent in all truly mutual relationships. Marriage requires both husband and wife to give up their own self-interests
for the sake of the other. The birth of a child introduces turmoil into
the routine of the home. Friendships mean letting go of power and
sharing decisions.

What, then, is the battle? On the highest level it is between God and
Satan and their angelic hosts, but it is not one of power. The Scriptures

use the metaphor of a king and a rebellious vassal or steward (Matt. 21:33–43; see Gulick 1990). A faithful steward is appointed to rule over part of the kingdom, but later he rebels and persecutes the righteous in his district. The king does not arbitrarily cast out the rebel. He first demonstrates that the vassal is not worthy to rule by sending messengers calling the rebels to repentance and renewed allegiance. Satan and his followers, through humans and religious and political systems, find these messengers guilty on false charges and condemn them to death. The king sends his perfect son who is also found guilty and executed. The case is appealed to the supreme court in heaven. There the judgment is found to be unjust, and the case is overturned. The lower court itself is found to be evil, and, therefore, no longer legitimate, so it is removed from power and punished. The central issue is not one of power, but of justice and legitimacy.

God's final victory is the cross on which his Son died, not a battlefield strewn with slain foes. It is the victory of righteousness over evil, of love over hate, of God's way over Satan's way. If Christians do not see the cross as God's triumph, they need to examine their understanding of spiritual warfare. On the cross Jesus became Lord and victor over all the powers of evil. His obedience unto death "rendered powerless him who had the power of death that is the devil" (Heb. 2:14). The cross was Satan's undoing (Col. 2:15), but Satan's defeat is not an end in itself. Rather, it removes the obstacles to God's purpose of creating people fit for his kingdom (Gen. 12:1; Exod. 19:3ff.; 1 Peter 2:9).

On the personal level the battle between good and evil in Scripture rages in the hearts of individuals whom God is seeking to win and Satan is trying to keep. It is for the allegiances of human beings who are not passive victims caught in cosmic battles. They are central actors, and the locus of the action. They all were co-conspirators with Satan, and self-worship was the basis of their idolatry. But God in his mercy and love calls them to repentance and to restored fellowship with him in his kingdom. The biblical parable here is the wayward son. The father lavishes his love on his son, but the son rebels and turns on his father. The father is not interested in defeating his son, but in winning him back, so he reaches out in unconditional love. The son wants to provoke the father into hating him, and twists logic to justify his rebellion, but the father takes all the evil his rebellious son heaps on him and continues to love the son. When the son repents, he is restored fully into the family (Matt. 5:44–45; Luke 6:35–36). Satan, on the other hand, is seeking to keep the loyalty of each individual, but his methods are deceit, half truth, temptation, accusation, and fear.

In salvation, people turn from evil and are delivered from the power that Satan formerly had over them. Every person who is "in Christ" shares in Christ's uniqueness, and need not be apprehensive or feel paralyzed with fear concerning Satan and evil spirits (1 John 4:4). Christians are encouraged to pray for deliverance from this deceiver who seeks to woo them back (Luke 8:12). To believe that Satan still has control over Christians is to deny the greatness of their salvation. Satan and his hosts are dreadfully real and represent the powers of darkness arrayed in battle against God's kingdom of light. They seek to keep sinners from converting, and to win back those who have been saved. On the other hand, the hosts of God's angels minister to protect and guide the saints (2 Kings 6:17; Gen. 31:3, 11, 12; Dan. 8:15–16, 9:3, 20–23; Matt. 1:20).

On the corporate level the battle is for human systems. Human beings create societies and cultures. There is much good in these, but there is also much evil in them. Cultural systems can blind people from the truth, and social systems can keep individuals from coming to Christ. Family ties, religious structures, and social systems prevent them from converting on pain of persecution and death.

Missionaries must take spiritual warfare very seriously, but they must be careful not to focus on the battle as a cosmic battle between God and Satan to see who is the victor. To do so is to reduce God to the level of his creation, and to introduce doubt and fear as to the outcome of the battle. Most misfortunes and illnesses are not directly caused by demonic sources. They are part of the fallen estate of humans and the judgment of sin. The greatest hindrance to people coming to Christ is not demon possession, real as it is, but fallen cultural and social systems which lead people to the worship of self—the created rather than the creator (Rom. 1:21–25).

Missionaries should also avoid the equation of Satan and his followers with territories that can be exorcised. To do so is to introduce animistic beliefs into the Christian worldview. It also implies that the people living in these lands are hapless victims of the cosmic battles of the gods, and that once they are delivered they will be ready to believe. This sells human sinfulness short. Even if demons are driven out, humans call them back and renew their individual and corporate rebellion against God.

The focus must be on God and his power, and the fact that being 'in Christ' protects people from the onslaughts of the enemy. When the focus is on demons and the battle, people are in danger of despair and lose sight of the fact that God is and always has been creator and ruler of all. C. S. Lewis notes,

There are two equal and opposite errors into which our race can fall about the devils. One is to disbelieve in their existence. The other is to believe, and to feel an excessive and unhealthy interest in them. They themselves are equally pleased by both errors, and hail a materialist or a magician with the same delight (1961, 3).

A secular approach to spiritual warfare denies its existence. A traditional or an Indo-European approach turns it into animism and magic. Missionaries must reject all three in a biblical understanding of warfare.

IMPORTANCE OF MYTHS IN MINISTRY

The study of myth can help missionaries and church leaders in other important ways. Too often they present truth as theological formulas to be learned, but these are often abstract and detached from life. Even catechisms tend toward a systematic analysis of truth. History and myth, on the other hand, speak directly to people by showing them the stories they are living, and the stories of their people and the universe. The fundamental message of the Bible is the history of God and his actions—of cosmic history. The Western penchant for synchronic, abstract logic often inhibits both the storytelling and the understanding of the story.

THE BIBLE STORY

The good news story of the Bible should be told as a whole. Too often communicators teach specific passages or focus on central doctrines. The Bible comes to human beings in the form of a narrative, and it is this large, somewhat sprawling story that people find meaningful. Peterson writes,

> Within the large, capacious context of the biblical story we learn to think accurately, behave morally, preach passionately, sing joyfully, pray honestly, obey faithfully. But we dare not abandon the story as we do any or all of these things, for the minute we abandon the story, we reduce reality to the dimensions of our minds and feelings and experience. The moment we formulate our doctrines, draw up our moral codes, and throw ourselves into a life of ministry apart from a continuous re-immersion in the story itself, we walk right out of the presence and activity of God and set up our own shop (1994, 5).

Presenting the overall story of the Bible is important in evangelism. This has been demonstrated by the method the New Tribes Mission now uses in reaching non-Christian traditional societies. The missionaries present the basic biblical story in a series of lessons, starting with Genesis and the existence and nature of God, then move through creation, fall, law, and prophets, and finally tell the story of Christ as the fulfillment of history. In doing so they show people their own place in the unfolding cosmic drama outlined in Scripture, and challenge them to make meaningful decisions to follow Christ.

Recent developments using a "storying" approach to presenting the Bible in oral contexts have been very successful. Presenting the story from beginning to end in a chronological and structured way enables primarily oral people to understand biblical principles and symbols in ways that communicate more effectively in their context. Such representations of the gospel can be assimilated and reproduced by people of any age or background, and can be reproduced more simply in another language and culture than any other form of communication (Slack 1990, 1–2).

An awareness of the sweep of biblical history and cosmology is important, too, for mature Christianity. Most Christians in the West have a smorgasbord theology (Bibby 1987). They jump back and forth through the Bible in Sunday school classes and in sermons, learning a few verses here and there to help them in times of trouble, and give them a sense of morality. Such prooftexting results in having no comprehensive apologetic framework to help them critique powerful myths such as Marxism, Hinduism, secularism, and the New Age. Christian maturity must be rooted in an understanding of the sweep of history in Scripture. As believers grow in the faith, they need theological underpinnings that are embedded in and explicate God's story.

Once the broad story is known, missionaries can draw on specific biblical stories which communicate messages appropriate for specific situations. The exodus and the cross have been important messages for people suffering persecution and oppression, such as the African American slaves and the workers of Latin America. Acts provides missionaries with a model for understanding the current mission movement as the church moves out from Jerusalem to Antioch and the ends of the earth, crossing social and cultural boundaries.

Finally, Christians need personal heroes of faith to shape them, and to model life for new believers. Abraham, Sarah, Moses, Deborah, David, Paul, and the other saints in Scripture and church history are important examples for Christians. Missionary biographies have played an important role in motivating individuals and churches to mission. The stories of old leaders can show young leaders the way to serve, and to follow through and implement the lessons they learn in their own ministry.[7]

---

7. Jones (1959) illustrates this use of real-life stories in his book *Conversion*. He points out that no systematic analysis of conversion is complete, for conversions differ from case to case. He then describes dozens of conversions that help the reader understand both the essential unity and the broad diversity of human experiences of God's saving grace.

THE PEOPLE'S STORIES

It is not enough to tell people biblical stories and help them to read these stories for themselves. People need to tell their own stories of how God brought them to faith and is leading them on their spiritual pilgrimage. Too often the gospel seems foreign to them because it is brought by outsiders whose story it is. Missionaries need to make it clear that others brought them the gospel so that they could hear it, and that God was already at work in the people's midst before the gospel arrived. There are many stories in missions of individuals who had dreams that someone would someday bring them good news, and these individuals were often the first to accept the gospel when it came to them. We may not accept all such stories as fact. They include numerous reports of appearances of a Black Virgin Mary in Latin America which show that God spoke to the people directly, not through outsiders (see sidebar). We should, however, help people to see evidences that God was already at work in their midst when the Good News came.

In churches, leaders must encourage Christians to tell and write their own stories. In the church everyone is a speaker and everyone has a message. Everyone must have opportunities to be involved in worship by sharing their testimonies of conversion. Articulating their new faith helps believers reaffirm their new identity and separate themselves from their past. Both are important if their experiences are to have permanence. Testimonials are also important in helping believers give public witness to their non-Christian relatives and neighbors. The result is often persecution, but this, too, reinforces their commitment to their new walk.

We must encourage young churches to write their own histories. Missionaries write of their work, but few collect the oral stories of national workers who labor in great difficulty, often in the most remote places. Throughout mission history it has always been the early converts, local evangelists, and ministers who have done the greatest share of the work, yet their stories are often unheard. To collect and compile these stories helps the people see that God is working through them.

THE VIRGIN OF GUADALUPE

On December 9, 1531, twelve years after the conquest of Mexico City by Hernan Cortex, the Virgin Mary appeared to a humble Indian named Juan Diego. On the way to Mass, near the hill of Tepeyac, he heard a sweet song and saw a white cloud encircled by a rainbow. A beautiful women spoke to him in Nahuatle and said she was the Virgin Mary, mother of the true God, and wanted a church built for her on that hill. Juan told Bishop Juan de Zumarraga, who did not believe him. On his way home, the Virgin appeared to him again and told him to speak to the bishop, but when he did he was rejected again. Mary appeared to him a third time and instructed him to take roses which appeared among the rocks to the bishop. He put them in his cloak, and as he gave them to the bishop they fell on the ground. They discovered the image of Mary on the blanket, and it hangs today above the alter of the Basilica of Our Lady of Guadalupe.

Many miracles happened to those who prayed to the Virgin of Guadalupe, most among the Indian population. In 1544 a terrible epidemic killed thousands until the image was brought to town. Then the pestilence abated. In 1629 she prevented a flood, and in 1810 the Virgin became the patron of Mexico when Father Hidalgo, and later Zapata fought under her flag and defeated the oppressors. Pope Pius X declared her "Queen of Mexico and Empress of the Americas." Today she is the single most powerful element in Mexican Catholicism. Pilgrims drink at the sacred well, eat maize cakes in the plaza, light votive candles, give thanks for special healings and observe Mass. She is the symbol of family, nurture, well being and love.

Myths are important in all societies. The stories and their power need to be understood and appreciated. We also need to understand the rituals and ceremonies that enact these myths as sacred dramas, and we now turn our attention to these.

11

RELIGIOUS RITUALS

The heart of folk religions often appears to be rituals: fiestas, New Year celebrations, fairs, festivals, weddings, funerals, masked dances, sacrifices, pilgrimages, and memorial days. Such rites are central to the lives of people and communities around the world. Furthermore, people spend large sums to perform these rituals at great expense to their own economic development. Why this emphasis on rituals?

Early anthropologists such as Lewis Henry Morgan saw rituals as archaic and irrational, and discounted them as superstition. Protestants often associate rituals with salvation by works and contrast them with salvation by faith. Westerners commonly see rituals as harmless interludes where traditional people get away from the tedium of their ordinary lives, or they discount rites as dead, meaningless performances that keep humans from facing inner spiritual voids. These judgments say more about those who hold these ideas than about the people who practice rituals. They show how little those who live in a secular, antiritual culture understand of the importance of rituals in most people's lives. Rituals play a central role in most societies. They are multilayered forms of communication that have the ability to grip people in ways verbal explanations cannot. They express what words cannot convey—not the trivialities of life, but its immensities. If missionaries hope to win converts and plant vital churches around the world, they need to reexamine the role of rituals in human societies, and their own antiritual biases. Only then are they able to understand the need for living rituals to express and sustain faith in young churches.

Before we look at specific rituals, we need to examine the nature and function of rituals in general.

THE NATURE AND FUNCTION OF RITUAL

Rituals are important in building human communities and maintaining their beliefs. They are structured transactions in which speech and

283

behavior are socially prescribed. They are bracketed social encounters in which the purpose has to do not with the concerns of ordinary life, but with the underlying relationships between the participants. Rituals range from simple rites such as shaking hands, bowing, or embracing when meeting friends, to complex religious ceremonies in which people leave the mundane world to relate to the sacred. Beneath the surface differences, however, rituals share many common characteristics.

RITUAL AS STRUCTURE AND ANTISTRUCTURE

In examining the nature and functions of rituals, it is important to recall the need for structure and order in human life. Total freedom in any society leads to chaos and solipsism. Everyone lives alone in his or her own world. For human relationships to take place there must be some structure, some underlying order. In everyday life this includes such things as a common language, agreed-upon ways of relating, shared beliefs, and a common worldview. In other words, to relate to one another, people must more or less 'play by the rules of the same game.'

What are these 'rules' that maintain order in human communities? The first of these are social rules—the norms that order relationships between people as they form families, groups, communities, societies, and global social systems. The second of these are cultural rules—the norms that order the way people think, feel, and evaluate their world. These standards make possible language, culture, thought, discussion, technological advances, arts, entertainment, and worship. Third, individuals construct their own personal rules—the ways they order their own lives in their societies and cultures. Finally, there are cosmic rules—the moral order in the universe which people believe was created by gods, defined by the ancestors, or instituted by culture heroes when they taught people to be civilized and human. These rules are the basis for religious life. Rituals recreate the social, cultural, personal, and cosmic order necessary for human life by making these rules explicit. In so doing they alleviate social and intellectual turmoil, and restore order to the society and the cosmos by dramatizing and dealing with the situations that precipitated the need for the ritual in the first place.

STRUCTURE AND ANTISTRUCTURE

Everyday life oscillates between order and freedom. Human beings need order, so they create formal roles, rules, and relationships. They clean their houses, dress up, and customarily greet one another. They find it costly and stifling, however, to maintain high order all the time. Moreover, high order kills creativity and makes relationships imper-

---

Figure 11.1
Informal and Formal Structures in Baseball

SANDLOT	BIG LEAGUE
Informal	Formal
Anyone can participate	Highly paid professionals, T.V. and spectators who pay to see the game
Teams chosen informally	Competition for players recruited by drawings and high salaries
No role specialization, players rotate	Specialized roles
Fuzzy boundaries, unkempt field	Clear boundaries, immaculately clean field
Ad hoc rules negotiated by players	Fixed rules enforced by umpires
Goal: have fun	Goal: entertain and make money
Victory leads to celebration	Victory leads to honor and money
Spirit: 'just a game'	Spirit: war—winning is everything

---

sonal. So they loosen up a bit to give themselves room to breathe and to enjoy some freedom. But if they go too far, they slide toward chaos in which freedom becomes license, relationships become anonymous (everyone simply sits in a circle and vibes together), and social systems collapse. Consequently, people periodically seek to reaffirm some order to maintain social and cultural systems. The primary means of accomplishing this is through formal rituals.

'Formal' here means highly structured patterns of social behavior. In all societies there are occasions when high order is very visible and precise. Examples include High Mass in a Catholic church, a formal wedding, a courtroom when the judge is present, the crowning of the king of England, and the funeral of an American president. These are ritual occasions.

Human life, however, can never be all high order. Most of the time actions are more informal. There is an underlying implicit order, but some flexibility is allowed in observing the rules. For example, Sunday night meetings are generally more informal than Sunday morning services. People do not dress as 'properly,' and talk with one another when they enter the sanctuary. There may be no bulletin, or even a specific order of service. Flexibility and personal expression are encouraged. Still, other areas of life have little order. Vacations on the beach and Saturday morning chores at home are ad hoc affairs. A crowd can become a stampeding mob, an army a rabble of deserters. Humans order many areas of their lives along a continuum from high order to informality to chaos.

Formal, semiformal, and nonformal occasions can be organized along a continuum that is fluid and changing (Figure 11.1). Cultures, societies, and individuals oscillate between the two—sometimes de-

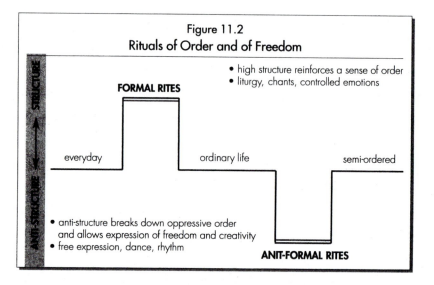

Figure 11.2
Rituals of Order and of Freedom

STRUCTURE

ANTI-STRUCTURE

FORMAL RITES

• high structure reinforces a sense of order
• liturgy, chants, controlled emotions

everyday   ordinary life   semi-ordered

• anti-structure breaks down oppressive order
and allows expression of freedom and creativity
• free expression, dance, rhythm

ANTI-FORMAL RITES

manding high order to restore structures, and sometimes allowing low order to undermine oppressive structures and foster personal relationships and creativity; sometimes declaring boldly what people believe and sometimes discovering new truths; and sometimes needing order in personal lives and sometimes 'more space.'

Victor Turner discusses this oscillation as the tension between structure and antistructure. Structure views society as a system of jural, political, and economic positions, offices, statuses, and roles that are differentiated and culturally ordered (Turner 1969, 177). Structure, in the extreme, tends to become rigid and impersonal. Antistructure consists of idiosyncratic individuals who regard each other as autonomous equals sharing a common humanity, and see one another as persons, not as segmented into statuses and roles. Carried too far, antistructure makes organized human activities and societies impossible.

Rituals can roughly be divided into two types: those that reinforce the need for structure by formally enacting high order, and those that express the need for freedom and creativity by tearing down the order and allowing free expression and opportunity to construct new orders (Figure 11.2). People need both. They need a sense of order in a chaotic world, so, regularly they have highly structured rites that renew this in their personal and corporate lives. High order, however, can become oppressive and deadening. Consequently, people periodically need rites that break down the existing orders and enable them to give free expression to their joys, fears, frustrations, and longings. These rites are characterized by antistructure: by abandonment to personal emotions, creativity, and expression. In this sense, rituals mediate between everyday life and ideal forms.

SURFACE AND DEEP STRUCTURES

In everyday life people converse with one another, shop in the market, drive cars, cook meals, and read magazines. This infinite diversity on the surface is possible only because there are underlying categories and rules that enable them to generate an infinitely varied set of behaviors and still know what is going on. For example, when people speak, they generate with ease millions of sentences they have never heard before, but understand what each of these means because of the rules underlying their language. Similarly, people know the rules for paying for merchandise in shops, the services of doctors, and tolls on bridges. They know the difference among stamps, tickets, coupons, and money, and the rules for driving on the road with cars, trucks, bicycles, and ox carts. These categories, rules, and assumptions represent the deep order underlying people's lives.

DEEP SOCIAL STRUCTURES

Ordinarily humans focus on the tasks at hand, such as teaching a class or building a house. These tasks are normally embedded in systems of relationships with other people. One person is the teacher, the others the students; one is the boss, the others the workers. Knowledge of these statuses and the behavior expected of each is implicitly shared by those involved. In daily interactions there is a danger that these mutual understandings become frayed, and they need to be made clear before work can resume. One way to do this is through rituals, for rituals focus not on surface activities but on underlying relationships. This can be seen in the brief ritual two North American co-workers enact when they meet each other for the first time in the morning. Normally this involves four or five stylized comments:

PERSON A	PERSON B
"Hi, how are you?"	"Fine, and you?"
"Okay. It sure is a nice day!"	"Ya, we need this kind more often."
"Sure do. Got to go now, see you later."	"Ya, see you later."
"So long."	"So long."

On the surface, this exchange seems trite and hackneyed. It might be all right for one time, but the same thing when people meet each other the first time every day? Moreover, it appears to be dishonest. People ask us, "How are you?" But if we start telling them our troubles, they try to get away as soon as they can with some grace. If they are not really asking about health or economic conditions, why do they ask? To understand the transaction, it must be seen in context. It occurs the first time people meet each other each day, and has to do not with the tasks at hand, but with affirming the underlying relationship between them. When people say, "Hi. How are you?" they are really asking, "Is our relationship still okay?" To say we are "fine," and to ask about the "well-being" of the other is to reaffirm that the relationship is good. If they meet us later the same day, they simply say "Hi," or otherwise acknowledge our presence, and pass on.

The importance of greetings in setting the stage for the day's relationships between persons becomes obvious when one person does not reply to a greeting. If someone simply walks by us, we wonder, "What's the matter? Doesn't he like me?" Similarly, when a person is gone for a month's vacation or extended absence, the simple four-stroke greeting is not enough when we next meet. We must extend the ritual to seven or eight strokes: "Hi, How are you after your long trip?"—"Did you enjoy your vacation?"—"You did what!?"—"Well, it is good to see you back."—"I've got to run now, but we can talk more about it later."—"Ya, I'd love to see the pictures you took."—"Got to go now, see you later." We need to acknowledge that they were away, welcome them back, and reincorporate them into the normal cycle of life.

More complex rites reestablish or transform complex networks of relationships. At a wedding, not only are a bride and a groom involved, but also parents, family members, friends, and community. Each enacts his or her socially defined role in highly explicit ways—the bride wears a gown, the groom a tuxedo, the bridesmaids gowns, and the best men matched suits. All behave as expected, and in doing so, reaffirm their particular roles and recognize the roles of the others. If another man tries to step into the groom's place, the ritual breaks down until social order is restored.

All rituals speak about the deep social structure underlying the relationships between those involved. Over time this social order is blurred, and people need to bring it to the surface, examine it, and renew it by affirming its existence, or transform it into a new order.

DEEP CULTURAL STRUCTURES

Just as there are deep social structures that make everyday transactions possible, so there are deep cultural structures that enable people to think, feel, and judge the world around them. On the cognitive level, these structures make up their deep beliefs and worldview—the categories they use to organize their experiences, the logic with which they think, and the realities they are convinced are real. These are the cultural lenses that people look through, not what they look at.

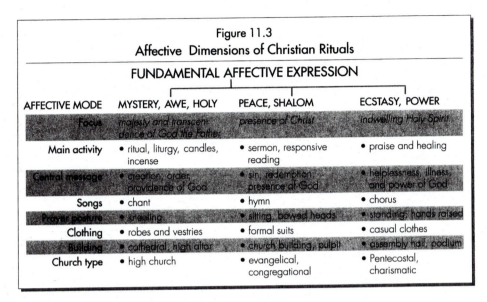

Figure 11.3
Affective Dimensions of Christian Rituals

FUNDAMENTAL AFFECTIVE EXPRESSION

AFFECTIVE MODE	MYSTERY, AWE, HOLY	PEACE, SHALOM	ECSTASY, POWER
Focus	majesty and transcendence of God the Father	presence of Christ	indwelling Holy Spirit
Main activity	• ritual, liturgy, candles, incense	• sermon, responsive reading	• praise and healing
Central message	• creation, order, providence of God	• sin, redemption, presence of God	• helplessness, illness, and power of God
Songs	• chant	• hymn	• chorus
Prayer posture	• kneeling	• sitting, bowed heads	• standing, hands raised
Clothing	• robes and vestries	• formal suits	• casual clothes
Building	• cathedral, high altar	• church building, pulpit	• assembly hall, podium
Church type	• high church	• evangelical, congregational	• Pentecostal, charismatic

On the affective level, deep cultural structures help people experience life and sense what is beautiful and ugly, pleasant and unpleasant, and aesthetically desirable and undesirable. These feelings are given expression in rituals. For example, American Protestant churches that agree on doctrine often disagree sharply on what constitutes a truly worshipful 'experience' (Figure 11.3). Some feel that true worship is based on feelings of awe and wonder in an encounter with God, who is transcendent and above all comprehension, others desire the ecstasy and thrill of the Holy Spirit at work in them, and still others the feeling of deep inner peace and tranquility from an awareness of Christ who is with them.

On the evaluative level, deep cultural structures lay the foundations for judgments and morality—for what is right and wrong, just and unjust, good and evil.

Rituals bring to the surface—to the explicit attention of the participants—the largely invisible foundations on which their society, culture, and personalities are built. They also show people how their structures should be. They provide people with a model of what it means to be fully human, fully male or female, or fully a person of God. For example, in an American church wedding, the bride is dressed in white and the groom in formal attire. They treat each other with the greatest love and respect, and pledge to live only for the other. They are courteous to their new in-laws. A few months later at home alone, things are often quite different. The new husband and wife argue, ignore each other, and want their own way. Why then the poetic talk of love and self-sac-rifice in the marriage ceremony? Here the ritual not only publicly estab-lishes a new relationship between them—that of a married couple, it also states the society's ideals for marriage—what a marriage should re-ally look like. The fact that no one lives up to the ideals all the time does not make it irrelevant. Without deep values and ideals, no truly human society is possible.

DEEP PERSONAL STRUCTURES

Each individual develops a sense of core identity—who they are, why they are here, and what they want out of life. This personal deep struc-ture is an essential part of personality, and shapes much of who a per-son is. As we will see later, much of that sense of personal identity is cre-ated by rituals such as birth, initiation, marriage and death rites, and other rituals such as graduation, promotions, and retirement banquets.

DEEP COSMIC STRUCTURES

Deep structures constitute the core of culture, providing people with their understanding of the ultimate cosmic frame of reality. Humans give expression to their deep beliefs, feelings, and morality in their rit-uals.

Rituals also give expression to and reinforce the social structures, communicate information about the culture's cherished beliefs, feel-ings, and values, and provide a sense of personal and corporate identity to those involved either as participants or as audiences. In so doing, they integrate these into one powerful experience of reality. It is this in-tegration of all dimensions of life in ritual enactments that makes ritu-als so powerful in both renewing and transforming societies, cultures, and individual persons in short periods of time.

MULTIVOCALITY

Rituals, like dominant symbols, acquire power not only because they integrate social, cultural, individual, and spiritual realities at a deep level, but also because they are multivocal in nature. They combine many diverse and contradictory meanings in a single set of symbols. For example, during initiation rites the novices both die to their old lives, and are reborn to their new lives in the same rite. Similarly, New Year days bring to memory the successes and failures of the past year, and the potentials of the new one. For Christians, the communion ser-vice has many layers of meaning: it reminds them of the atoning death of Christ for sins, the need to confess sin today and be forgiven, the gathering of the local church as a community of believers, the global celebration of the church as the universal body of Christ, the day when Christ will gather all believers around his table in heaven, and much more. The result is a symbolic density that carries great power and potential for bringing together diverse and contradictory ideas.

Because such rites condense so much meaning in a single event, they are storehouses of corporate memories. In reenacting these memories, people recall their deep history. This multivocality also fosters creative reflection as people unpack the many connotations and the linkages between them. For instance, for Christians, Christmas generates many different ideas which taken together make the celebration rich and rewarding. With their condensed meanings, rituals have great power to move people and to motivate them to renew their ultimate allegiances. They also have the power to transform humans totally in a very short period of time.

Rituals are not detached events. They are part of larger orders made up of other rituals and of ordinary life. Events in regular sequences acquire a meaning from relation with others in the series. For example, for Christians, Sunday is not just a day of worship and rest, it is also the day before Monday and the day after Saturday. To understand its importance, we must be aware of its place in the larger cycle of the week. Similarly, Sundays fit into the larger ritual calendar of the year that includes Advent, Easter, and Christ's ascension. The cycle of ordinary Sundays is also broken by great religious days such as Thanksgiving and Memorial Day. Taken together rituals tell the whole story of a people's fundamental beliefs.

RITUALS AS THEATER

Rituals are more than collections of symbols. They are public performances that organize symbols in stylized ways to restore a sense of meaning by means of theater. They present reality as a drama with a plot. They prescribe ways of speaking and acting which are repeated regularly and thereby bring order to the world. They do this by revealing the underlying structure of things, by focusing their attention on that structure, and by involving people in dramatic performances that reenact and restore the ideal order of things as authorized by tradition, the society, and the gods. People perform rituals, and, in so doing, they re-create an awareness of their ultimate stories.

FRAMES

Rituals are dramatic frames that set certain places, times, and activities apart from ordinary life and help people concentrate their attention on desired themes. They have beginnings and ends, and shut out intruding thoughts. They mark off a different kind of reality from ordinary life. For example, funerals, fiestas, football games, and church services are times set apart from everyday life. Frames also create in people a special kind of expectancy, a mood of receptivity to new things. They are a form of bracketing that signals that symbols should not be understood in their ordinary sense, but in reference to the transcendent realities to which they point. They show the whole picture of life in a single snapshot that encapsulates corporate and individual memories.

DRAMAS

Rituals are powerful enactments or dramas in which members of a community play society formally, and, in so doing, express and renew their deep ideas, feelings, and values. The analogy of a drama is appropriate. In rituals, individuals assume different formal roles, but in the acting they are mysteriously drawn into the roles they play—for a moment they are Moses, King David, Ruth, or Macbeth. Their performance coordinates their brain and body, and transforms them into new beings. Moreover, dramas are narratives with plots, structure, purpose, and design. They give meaning in terms of a story that has meaning because it moves to a climax or conclusion that reflects on real life.

Rituals have two important dimensions: what they "say" and what they "do." They are more than stylized ways of communicating para-messages about the nature of things. They are also seen as performative activities that create those realities. Eating together is fellowship, and it rebuilds relationships which have withered away by neglect. Dancing in a circle is to be in community, not only the desire for it. Rites are believed to cure illnesses, increase fertility, defeat enemies, change people's social status, remove impurity, and reveal the future. By them people communicate with the gods, settle moral conflicts, manipulate sacred power, make children adults, and renew the flow of time. Many people are skeptical about the skills and knowledge of particular doctors, priests, medicines, and the correct performance of particular rites, but their belief in the efficacy of the system of ritual as a means to accomplish change is not assailed.

Rituals are theater interweaving several levels of drama into a coherent, comprehensible whole. They speak to people at different levels of human experience. We will examine four of these levels to see how rituals are multivocal in nature.

SOCIAL DRAMAS

Rituals are social dramas. In them individuals as actors play prescribed roles, and, in doing so, restore or transform the social order. Some rituals reaffirm or clean up the existing social order. For example, in many North American Protestant churches, on Sunday morning the pastor gets up to preach. The congregation knows he is the pastor because of his apparel and demeanor. The choir director leads the choir dressed in robes, ushers wearing tags that say 'Usher' lead people in, and the laity find their places in the pews. Lay persons do not try to sit on the stage, nor does the pastor try to sneak out the back. In this sense, every time rituals are performed, they both reflect and re-create the social order that makes relationships possible. A society is a structure of statuses and roles which are often differentiated and hierarchical in nature. In the course of ordinary life, these structures become fuzzy and ambiguous, and the original order needs to be restored. Rituals reaffirm the roles, relationships, power structure, and economic responsibilities of the society. At times, however, social structures need to change to conform to the changing world. Rituals are also used to mark transitions, and to change people into new beings—children into adults, singles into married couples, and humans into ancestors.

Ultimately, rituals bind the community together, and give it a sense of common identity by giving it a common fellowship and history. For example, it is interesting that American missionaries often celebrate the Fourth of July abroad as a way of reaffirming their American identity. Somehow if they do not do so, they feel less 'American.'

Cultural Dramas

Rituals also serve as cultural performances. They renew and reshape people's inner worlds. On the cognitive level rituals make visible the worldview underlying cultural understandings of reality, and communicate fundamental beliefs. They are mnemonic devices—forms of corporate memory maintained by reenacting the past, and brought into the present and future. For example, in Deuteronomy the Israelites were instructed to pile up twelve stones after they crossed the Jordan River. Whenever people saw these stones, they were to remember and retell the story of God's great deliverance. With no living rituals people are in danger of cultural amnesia, and becoming people without a history and without meaning.

On the affective level, rituals give expression to people's deepest feelings—of sorrow, tenderness, loyalty, and respect—and help them deal with fears and anxieties. They help resolve conflicts by establishing formal obligatory relationships that stress harmony and order. When Western people want to express love, they have dates, celebrate wedding anniversaries, and go on special vacations.

On the evaluative level, people express in rituals what moves them most. Rituals reveal the values of the group, such as generosity, respect for elders, importance of kinship, and hospitality and greetings, giving them the weight of social and divine authority, and motivate people and groups to action. Monica Wilson writes (1954, 241),

Rituals reveal values at their deepest level . . . men express in ritual what moves them most, and since the form of expression is conventionalized and obligatory, it is the values of the group that are revealed. I see in the study of rituals the key to an understanding of the essential constitution of human societies.

But rituals are more than inner states of mind. By involving bodies as well as minds, they provide experiential knowledge that people would not otherwise know or be able to communicate. Rituals bind together minds, hearts, and bodies in one act of knowing. As we sing the familiar words of old hymns that have shaped our thoughts in the past, our hearts rise up within us and our souls worship God. There are many things humans cannot experience without rituals.

Rituals are semantically 'open' in that new meanings, public and private, may be added. On different occasions one or another of these meanings may be paramount, but the multisemic nature of ceremonies means that the other ideas are latently hidden. The interplay of these multiple meanings makes rituals dynamic and creative.

Personal Dramas

Rituals also give expression to an individual's deepest personal beliefs and values. They give release and control to emotions at such times as death, separation, marriage, birth, conversion, and baptism. In short, they integrate personal experiences in intense moments of affirmation and transformation. A person's most profound experiences of worship, mystery, peace, and ecstasy occur in the context of rituals, as do many life-changing decisions, such as conversion.

But rituals do more than express and transform personal ideas, feelings, and values. Socially they restructure personal roles in community, and psychologically they help people adjust to new states. As we will see, most major changes in life are marked by rituals of transition.

Cosmic Dramas

The most important rituals are sacred ceremonies that link life experiences to the sacred, to the transcendent. Sacred dramas are where gods, spirits, and ancestors meet people in special ways. People who are not religious often turn to sacred rituals at times of death and disaster to give meaning and to reaffirm that life ultimately makes sense.

Many sacred rites are reenactments of cosmic myths, which tell of events in cosmological time, such as the time when the event first took place. In many traditional religions the world cannot be repaired, it can only be re-created by a ritual return to the source of the outpouring of energy, life, and fecundity that occurred in the primordial past at the creation of the world. Without these rites of new birth, the world falls back into darkness and chaos. Many people believe that the original protagonists of the underlying myth reappear and join with the living to restore life to the earth. Time in such rituals is not the present, but a return to the time when the event first took place.

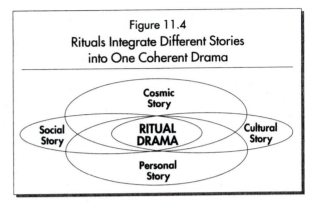

Figure 11.4
Rituals Integrate Different Stories into One Coherent Drama

Synchronically, rituals provide a sense of cosmic order. Humans need some idea about the order behind the experiential world around them—a map of how things are related to each other. Sacred rituals transcend ordinary understanding by pointing to underlying realities that transport people above everyday realities. They constitute the absolute values and paradigms for all human activities. Mircea Eliade writes,

> It is the experience of the sacred—that is, an encounter with a transhuman reality—which gives birth to the idea that something *really exists*, that hence there are absolute values capable of guiding man and giving a meaning to human existence. It is, then, through the experience of the sacred that the ideas of *reality, truth,* and *significance* first dawn, to be later elaborated and systematized by metaphysical speculations (1975, 139).

The repetition of the same rites gives people a sense of unchanging realities in the daily flux of life. There is a stable order on which they can depend in a world of change and chaos.

Diachronically, sacred rites give meaning to humans by telling their stories, and linking those stories to the cosmic story (Figure 11.4). Secular rituals combine social, cultural, and personal stories into a single drama. Sacred rituals embed these in the grand cosmic drama, namely, the dramatic reenactments of the key cosmic events involving the gods, spirits, ancestors, humans, and nature. In reenacting the stories of the past, participants see beyond mundane, transitory experiences of everyday life into the mystery of supernatural realities. In so doing, sacred rituals make life meaningful by reminding people of their ultimate "story." As we saw in Chapter 3, many people have three stories: the cosmic story, the history of a particular people (tribe, group, nation), and a personal story (biography). Biographies have meaning when they are part of the history of a people. The people's story takes on meaning only

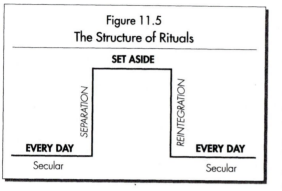

Figure 11.5
The Structure of Rituals

if it is a part of a cosmic story. In sacred rituals people reenact the cosmic story, and in so doing, affirm that they are part of that story, that the gods and ancestors are always present, even though they as humans in their finite temporality cannot grasp this present-ness except by "re-presenting" the action of God over and over again in their rituals.

This view that sacred rituals are directly linked to cosmic realities leads to a sacramental view of rituals that ties human events to the cosmic order of things. Catholic and other high churches that have a sacramental view of marriage believe that when a pastor says, "I now pronounce you husband and wife," he is not only changing the personal, social, and cultural systems, he is announcing a change that has taken place in the heavens. These two are now married in God's sight. Divorce, therefore, is not only a violation of social norms, it is a transgression against God and the cosmic order of things. It creates not only social, cultural, and personal chaos, but also spiritual disorder.

THE STRUCTURE OF RITUALS

Rituals are highly structured sociocultural events. Arnold van Gennep points out that most rituals have three stages: separation from ordinary life, ritual activity, and return to everyday life (1960, 26–28; Figure 11.5).

SEPARATION

Rituals begin with a symbolic separation from ordinary life. People often go to special places at special times, wear special clothes, paint themselves, put on masks, talk in formal language, and do a multitude of other things to show that they are now in different state of life. This separation is often marked by rites of purification and depiction of the loss of old identities through symbolic death. For example, those entering initiation rites are often segregated from normal community life, stripped of their clothing, and made to eat simple food or fast. At funerals, those closely related to the dead often wear special clothes and have their heads shaved. Such symbolic behavior signifies their detachment from their roles in society.

Separation often takes the form of behavior that stands in contrast to ordinary life. On Sunday mornings North American Christians used to dress up to show that they were entering the presence of God, and therefore needed to be clean and pure. Meeting God, for them, was no ordinary event. Today, in urban settings, where much of work is high order and formal, people want to meet God on personal, informal terms. Rural people visiting city churches are frequently aghast at the lack of respect and the uncleanness of city Christians. Urban people find the high order of rural churches stuffy and traditional.

Separation often involves purification—a washing away of sins and a confession of misdoings. These are symbolized by washing with water, shedding of blood, and separation from the world. Entering rituals impurely is often seen as dangerous and possibly even deadly. Separation is frequently seen as a death to the old world and ways of life. For instance, in Bantu initiations into adulthood, Buddhist admissions into a monastery, and Christian baptisms the person must die to the old before he or she can be reborn a new being.

The main function of separation is to distinguish those involved in the ritual from the rest of the community, and at the same time to associate them with a new identity and group. The ritual is everything. An individual can claim significance only by virtue of belonging to the group. Moving out of the village, hiding in a hut, shaving of the head, anointing with oil, mutilation of the sex organ, song-and-dance, degrees of uncleanness and ritual cutting, and collecting firewood set individuals apart from the community, and prepare them for ritual transformations.

TRANSFORMATION

After people have separated themselves from their ordinary lives, they focus their attention on the central activity of the ritual. As we will see, this activity involves the renewal, transformation, or re-creation of the cosmic, cultural, social, and personal orders. In this state the initiates have two important experiences: liminality (being in transition) and communitas (close interaction with others in the same experience). We will explore these concepts in some detail.

LIMINALITY

People at the center of a ritual are liminal beings (V. Turner 1969). They lose their status in normal society, and enter a state of transition— a time during which they are in the crack between two identities: neither here nor there, no longer the old but not yet the new. Liminality is a moment out of time and out of secular social structures, a limbo of status-lessness. It involves the whole person in relation to other humans. Ordinary life is concerned with rationality and order. The liminal state is often seen as sacred, powerful, holy, and set apart time in which the old structures, rules of order, and identities are suspended.

Liminality is symbolized in different ways. One is transvestism. Among the Maraquet, young girls in initiation rites must wear men's clothing to show they are neither male nor female in the time of transition. Obscenity and abuse are used to show that normal social restraints are removed. Painting the body and nakedness are also signs of liminality. These are protests against the established order, but, at the same time, they are intended to preserve and strengthen that order.

COMMUNITAS

During the time of transition when old statuses are gone, there is a special kind of camaraderie, a new bond among those involved, an I–Thou relationship, in which people meet each other in their primal humanity. The humble and lowly meet the sacred and powerful as equals. Victor Turner refers to this as communitas—the deep sense of oneness with other humans that runs deeper than surface social differences of gender, class, ethnicity, and office. Communitas presents society as an undifferentiated, homogenous whole, in which individuals confront one another at the level of their inner most,[1] not as divided into statuses and roles. It is the feeling Christians have when they experience spiritual revivals—when all gather at the foot of the Cross as sinners, and all earthly differences disappear. In rituals, the only differentiation is between the leaders in charge of the ritual, and the people involved, and these differences may be minimized or maximized as cultural values and the intent of the ritual dictate.

Ordinary life is lived in community with its structures, hierarchies, rules, and norms. In rituals, people break out of the growing tyranny of community, and enter the world of communitas, where equality, fellowship, and deep feelings of unity are experienced and expressed. In it the participants are liberated from the roles and duties of everyday life, and free to contemplate the greater meanings of life. When rituals end, however, people must return to community life. Life is a dialectical process that involves an alternating exposure to structure and communitas, to steady social states and social transitions, and to the experiences of equality and inequality.

Victor Turner (1969) defines three types of communitas: normative, existential, and ideological. 'Normative' communitas characterizes rituals that reaffirm the existing order and reestablish the norms of everyday life. One way rituals do so is by using highly structured activities that restate the existing order. Another way is using role reversals. The high-ranked persons become low, and the low high. The master be-

---

1. Loewen (1975) uses this concept of the 'inner most' in an excellent series of articles to make us aware of that deep inner self we all guard against trivial exposures.

comes the servant, and the servant the master. For example, in one South Indian ritual, women have power over men. They order men around, and pelt them with cow dung. The result is obvious—chaos and disorder. Then the ritual reaffirms the dominance of men, showing that it is they who maintain harmony in the cosmos. Role reversals reinforce the normal structure by stressing the absurdity and ludicrous nature of the reversal. They bring social structure and communitas into right mutual relationship once again by reinforcing existing roles, recognizing prestige, and giving of gifts. But they also give people a place to vent their frustrations at being low.

The second type of communitas is 'existential' or 'spontaneous.' Here the focus is on transformation. The old order is destroyed so that a new order may emerge. Consequently, rituals of this type are characterized by antistructure, which occurs when normal structures are removed in some way. Antistructure, as discussed earlier, does not oppose structure; it occurs outside of regular structure and opens the door to creativity. Transformative communitas plays an important role in music, poetry, and art which break the rules of ordinary life to demonstrate new ways of looking at reality. The unstructured spontaneity, and experience of common humanity on a person-to-person level also creates the potential for forging new social configurations. But such a state is fearful, for those involved are not sure where they are going.

Turner labels the third kind of communitas 'ideological.' This refers to the utopian models of society that seek to institutionalize existential communitas in everyday life. Examples of this are monastic communities and secret societies, where separation from the world and existential equality become the norms of everyday life.

REINCORPORATION

During the transition period individuals or groups are given a renewed sense of their identity in the society and the cosmos. At the end they are returned to secular life, and incorporated in their new statuses back in the larger community. This often involves a ritual of homecoming in which the initiands are welcomed into a new status through symbols of a new birth into a new identity. Those reentering society often bathe, put on new clothes, and anoint their heads. They receive gifts, and songs and dances are performed to honor them. They are now expected to behave in accordance with their new positions, norms, and ethical standards. Gennep refers to this final step of returning to ordinary life as 'reincorporation' or 'reaggregation.' Returning from ritual experiences, people bring the sense of the sacred back with them into ordinary life, and sacralize what too often has become purely secular. Monday mornings Christians remember with warmth the worship of Sunday, and bring a sense of God's presence with them into the workplace.

Eating and drinking together are widespread rites of reincorporation. The sharing of meals confirms the bond of fellowship. Other common symbols of reincorporation are being tied together, covered by the same garment, kissing one another, holding hands, embracing, pronouncing oaths, and exchanging gifts of cloth, weapons, gold or silver coins, garlands, pipes, rings, blood, and sacred objects such as candles and icons. These activities symbolize a mutual transference of personality. Among the Zaramo and Wasagala two individuals become 'blood brothers' by sitting face to face, the legs of one crossing those of the other, while a third person brandishes a sword above them, pronouncing a curse against the breaker of the fraternal bond as they exchange blood (Gennep 1960, 31–32). Among the Shammar, an Arab tribe, if a man seizes the end of a string or thread held by his enemy, he immediately becomes that person's honored guest, and must be cared for and protected (Layard 1861, 317).

Everyday greetings are rituals reaffirming the incorporation of individuals into the community. People clasp hands, rub noses, embrace, and separate themselves from the outside world by removing their shoes, coats, or headdresses. They unite by eating or drinking together, and perform rites before household gods. In so doing they identify themselves in one way or another with those they meet.

The protocol of receiving strangers often involves extensive rituals of incorporation. This is especially true in Indonesia, Polynesia, and certain parts of Africa. A stranger is often lodged in the 'men's house,' and adopted as a member in one of the clans or families. He is then expected to carry out all the functions of a full member of the tribe, including the giving of gifts and participation in military and political activities. These rites of incorporation sometimes include sexual rites, such as wife exchange. When central Australians wanted to establish trade relationships with other tribes, they sent two men and two women bearing cockatoo feathers and nose bones as messengers. After the messengers and the men of the camp discussed the business at hand, the male messengers left, leaving the two women behind. If the men of the camp accepted the negotiations, they had sexual relations with the women; if not, they did not touch the women (Gennep 1960, 34).

FUNCTIONS OF RITUALS

Rituals serve important functions in a society. They help people remember who they are, re-create a world order, give people a sense of identity and belonging, relate them to the transcendent, and indoctrinate insiders and outsiders alike to the true values and perceived realities of a society.

First, rituals are festivals of remembrance. In them people express and renew their deepest beliefs. Sin, here, is to forget the divine nature of reality—it is religious amnesia. In rituals people reenact the sacred stories of the past, and so preserve their corporate memory. For example, in the Old Testament the people of Israel retold the story of their deliverance from Egypt in annual Passover rites, and in their annual pilgrimages to the tabernacle and later the temple. Today Jews all over the world remember the holocaust by means of memorials. With no rituals of memory, humans are all in danger of cultural amnesia, and becoming people without a history and without meaning.

Second, rituals re-create the world order. They not only communicate information. They transform reality. Rituals turn single men into husbands, make barren women fertile, bind the living to the ancestors and the land by the shedding of blood, and cause rain to fall. The enactment of rituals reestablishes order and alleviates cosmic chaos, social confusion, and cognitive dissonance. Religious rituals sacralize the secular. People enter the sacred event bearing the mundane cares of everyday life. They leave with a renewed sense of their sacred importance.

Third, in rituals a group experiences itself most intensely as a unified community, and members recognize themselves as belonging to one another. The performance communicates to all the participants the strength that lies in solidarity and collective existence. If an individual can claim any significance, it is only by virtue of belonging to the collective, and this is determined by being allowed to participate in the rituals of the group. Moreover, it is during ritual performances that individuals take and are allowed to take their place in the society. This provides them with their own self-identities.

Fourth, rituals often act as a form of social catharsis. In them conflicts are expressed, powerful emotions such as hate, fear, grief, and affection are evoked, and resolutions are sought. Because rituals are times of high formal social control, they seal off and channel human responses, and the potential for violence is avoided. People can castigate and damn one another in ritual settings, knowing that the public will prevent physical damage, and that the ritual itself is designed not only to give vent to pent-up emotions, but also to work out socially accepted solutions to the strife and bridge schismatic rifts in the community.

Fifth, because religious rituals take place in sacred time and space, they enable people to experience and relate directly to the gods, spirits, ancestors, and supernatural forces. For example, the Hopi elders believe they cause rain by dancing the Rain Dance. The shaman brushing the patient with a wisp of grass believes he is thereby driving off evil spirits. The tribesman pouring out water on the ground to assuage its thirst is making sure the earth will be pleased and bring forth crops. The Ashanti relate to Ogun by offering him sacrifices. They prepare themselves morally and physically by abstaining from cursing, fighting, sexual intercourse, and certain foods, all of which defile them and make them unfit to speak to Ogun. They sing songs to attract his attention, and the priest casts kola nuts to determine his attitudes. If Ogun is angry, they offer him snails and palm oil to calm him, and if he is hungry, he is given pigeons and dogs to satisfy his appetite. They burn the sacrifices at the stone pillar where he meets them, and share kola nuts to show Ogun that they are united in their worship of him. Hidden grudges and angers are set right to renew their social solidarity. The result is a deep experience of relating to Ogun.

Finally, rituals are a form of indoctrination. In them, the community celebrates the events that saved, established, or renewed it, thereby linking itself to its past and the successive generations who have gone on before. The people reperform the rites as their ancestors performed them, and teach these rites to their children who pass them to their children. In doing so they give expression in conventionalized and obligatory ways to their deepest beliefs and allegiances. For example, during their imitation rites, Maraquet girls in Kenya are taught their roles as wives, and learn the lore and practices of the society. The teaching itself often reflects the ambiguity of gender relations. Both the socially dominant male perspective and the female points of view are presented. Girls are reminded to be faithful and obedient to their husbands, but enjoined not to agree too quickly to have sexual intercourse in order to show their own power. Older women test the initiates, and give them advice regarding the realities they will face. On the other hand, rituals reeducate regular participants who recall their past experiences. The most secret parts of a ritual are only revealed to the old by other old people. The elderly use their knowledge to exercise power and control over the initiates and younger adults. This reinforces a hierarchy based on age and is the basis for solidarity and maintenance of tradition which women/men associate with themselves as a group (Kibor 1998).

TYPES OF RITUALS

Rituals can be divided into three major types: rites of transformation (to create new order and move individuals and groups through life), rites of intensification (to reinforce existing order), and rites of crisis (to enable people to survive emergency situations). Each of these serves an important function in the life of communities and individuals (Figure 11.6).

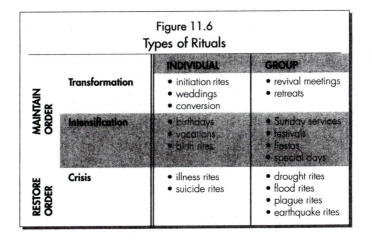

Figure 11.6
Types of Rituals

		INDIVIDUAL	GROUP
MAINTAIN ORDER	**Transformation**	• initiation rites • weddings • conversion	• revival meetings • retreats
	Intensification	• birthdays • vacations • birth rites	• Sunday services • festivals • fiestas • special days
RESTORE ORDER	**Crisis**	• illness rites • suicide rites	• drought rites • flood rites • plague rites • earthquake rites

RITES OF TRANSFORMATION

The first major type of rituals are transformation rites. Gennep (1960, 20) compares these rites to doorways and corridors in a house through which people must pass to go from one room to another. In modern societies the walls are thinner and the doors wider and more open to movement. In traditional societies, rooms are carefully isolated, and the passage from one to another must be made through formalities and ceremonies that involve stopping, waiting, crossing the threshold, and entering the new room. Rites of transition help people create a new order when the old order is no longer adequate. Transformative rites are performed to order the cycle of the seasons, to mark the transitions in life of individuals and groups, and to revive religious conviction. Examples of rites of transformation include pilgrimages, retreats, evangelistic crusades, camps, and revival meetings. They also include rites associated with conversion, birth, marriage, graduation, retirement, and death.

CHARACTERISTICS OF RITES OF TRANSFORMATION

Rites of transformation focus not on restoring an already established order, but on creating a new one in which individuals and communities are radically changed. They do so by creating an expectation of something new, and by involving participants in intense experiences of liminality, spiritual encounter, and communitas that generate spiritual, artistic, and cultural creativity. This creativity destroys the old paradigm for living, but it also invites the creation of new ones. People look at life differently. This type of ritual makes lasting worldview changes possible in short, intense periods of time. We now examine some of the characteristics of these rites (Figure 11.7).

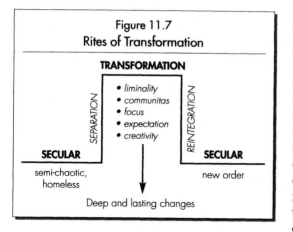

Figure 11.7
Rites of Transformation

TRANSFORMATION

SEPARATION

- liminality
- communitas
- focus
- expectation
- creativity

REINTEGRATION

SECULAR

semi-chaotic, homeless

SECULAR

new order

Deep and lasting changes

ANTISTRUCTURE

Rites of transformation are characterized by antistructure. Transformation requires tearing down of the old to make way for the new. Transformation rites are like remodeling a house. First the walls must be broken down and windows torn out. The result is chaos—or antistructure. During the process people are sustained by the faith that a new order will emerge which is better than the old. As this takes place, their faith is confirmed.

The tearing down of old structures is often symbolically expressed by a separation from ordinary life. Participants often go to a new place, hear a new person (a prophet), and expect something new. Previous categories and classifications are dissolved, and participants are seen as 'dead' to their old roles, and neophytes are symbolically treated as embryos, or newborn infants. Nothing demarcates them structurally from their fellows. During the ritual they may go naked, dress in dirty rags, or lie on the earth to show that they have no identity at all. Or they might dress or behave like the opposite sex, or in ways that normally are seen as immoral or indecent. Chiefs and kings may be beaten or insulted to show their loss of status. These rites are characterized by spontaneity, not regulation, and by antistructure, not high structure.

Antistructure is reflected in the order of the services, which are often highly unpredictable. New songs are sung, there is no defined liturgy, and the unexpected takes place. The audience follows the instructions of the leaders. An example of this is evangelistic crusades, which rarely have bulletins, liturgies, and rigid orders.

LIMINALITY

Another characteristic of transformational rites is liminality—the feeling of being in limbo, rootless, not being tied to anything, neither this nor that. As we have seen, this is an ambiguous condition in which the old is gone, but the new has not yet set in—a feeling of timelessness in, yet beyond space. In this condition between one reality and another, all the normal reference points that give order and meaning to life are gone. Neophytes are seen as sexless or bisexual, and considered unclean or polluting. They are neither here nor there—"betwixt and between" the positions assigned them in ordinary life by law and custom. They are nobodies, secluded in a building or in the forest, separated from normal life, and laden down with many taboos and restrictions. They possess nothing, to demonstrate they have no status, property, insignia, or rank. They must remain silent and submissive to the elders who have complete authority over them. They are the shapeless mass out of which new beings will be created.

It is widely believed the formlessness of antistructure and liminality has power and is, therefore, both full of potential and danger. The danger lies in the fact that people are neither in one state nor the next. This expresses itself in two ways—people in transition are vulnerable to the attack of spirits, witches, magic, and other forms of evil, as discussed in Chapter 6, but they, too, are often seen as dangerous to others because of their great power (Douglas 1966, 96). These dangers are controlled by taboos and rituals designed to protect the novices, and to protect the public from their powers. Rituals are also used to make sure that the power at work in the novices does not kill them, but transforms them into their new statuses. In this process of transformation, death and rebirth are symbolically tied together. Initiates die to old life and are reborn to the new, and the symbols of pollution and purification mark the gravity of the event.

Transformation rites recognize the potency of disorder found in dreams, faints, frenzies, and drugs, and use these to find powers and truths not reached by conscious effort. Special powers are believed to come to those who abandon rational control for a time and explore the disordered regions of the mind beyond the confines of society. For example, Andaman Islanders leave their bands and wander in the forest like madmen, and when they return they have the power to heal (Douglas 1966, 94). The same is true for the Ehanzu of Tanzania.

EXISTENTIAL COMMUNITAS

Rites of transformation are further characterized by existential communitas—a feeling of camaraderie and intense community that marks a sharp break from ordinary life. The everyday world consists of normal structures where people have established statuses, and where relationships and events are predictable. All know their place in the community, from chiefs to peons, from high school teachers to day laborers. Families, associations, and institutions bind people into a social order. Communitas introduces new relationships, and new ways of relating to one another. During the ritual people look at one another and at life differently. For example, in Christian revival meetings and on pilgrimages, ordinary statuses such as "doctor," "lawyer," and "construction worker" become meaningless. All participants are equals.

One consequence of this existential communitas is an intense sense of comradeship and egalitarianism among the participants. Ordinary social differences are lost in the common search. The result is a sense of spontaneous communitas that often leads to lifelong bonds of intense mutual identification between them.

The one social distinction in existential communitas is that between leaders and initiates. The ritual elders have absolute authority over the latter, to shape and remake them into new persons. They represent the Sacred—God, ancestors, spirits, powers—as it breaks into human lives in the moments of the ritual. The initiates are expected to be passive and humble, to obey instructors implicitly, to accept without complaint arbitrary punishments and hardships on pain of ostracism or death, and so to learn bravery and inner fortitude. This is seen in military boot-camps in which novices are transformed into soldiers. Such rites do not bring the leaders into an existential identification with the novices. For the leaders this is part of their normal activities.

Those who experience existential communitas often try to institutionalize it, but this fails, for existential communitas cannot be captured by social structures. For example, Peter wanted to set up residence on the Mount of Transfiguration, but had he done so, he would soon have been fetching water, gathering firewood, cooking meals, and doing laundry—and in the process he would have lost the transcendent nature of the moment. Monks try to institutionalize existential communitas by living in monasteries set apart from ordinary life, and by disciplines such as prayer, poverty, obedience, common life, and celibacy (their new family is the monastic order). The result is what Turner calls ideological communitas. In time, even in monasteries, life becomes routinized and institutionalized in subtle ways, and the sense of spontaneity, freedom, and equality is lost.

INSTRUCTION AND TESTING

A further characteristic of rites of transformation is instruction and testing in which novices are ritually made into new beings by the elders, ancestors, and spirits. They are led to ask ultimate questions. They learn the sacred lore, values, and behavior of their new life. In short, they learn their culture—that which sets them apart from other peoples and animals. Such instruction carries with it moral lessons regarding the deep values of the society. In initiation rites, adolescent boys and girls learn what it means to be men and women, and how the sexes should relate to one another. These are not just ordinary teachings, but ontological truths and values that reshape their very being. They enter the rite as a tabula rasa—a blank slate on which is inscribed the knowledge and wisdom of the group as those pertain to their new status. In the process girls become 'women,' and boys 'men.' In transformative rites brides and grooms learn how to live together in harmonious families, graduates are instructed on how to take their places in the world of work and business, and recruits learn how to be soldiers. During installation rites elders may chide the chief for being mean, selfish, greedy, and using witchcraft—all of which are against the common good. In admission to secret societies the elders teach the novices the secret knowledge of their association and the mysteries of the ancients.

TRANSFORMATION AND REINTEGRATION

Rites of transformation are characterized by transformation. They provide initiates with a new religious frame of reference that gives them new identities, and new meaning to their world. The power of these pedagogical rituals lies in the anticipation and openness to the new that they create in the novices and in the public. At their best, they can change a person or society by providing, in one transforming experience, a new and vital vision and faith.

Transformative rites are rich with symbols of transition—of being in the womb, invisible, in darkness, in a wilderness, in an eclipse of the sun or moon, or of dying. They symbolize separation from ordinary social life. Novices are often removed from the community and placed in isolation—outcasts with no place in the society, associated with dirt, obscenity, and lawlessness, and dead to their old way of life, which is now seen as a time of ignorance. But this death is not the end, it is the seed that is planted and that will sprout again.

The result of this death is formlessness—the state between death and rebirth. The unborn are in positions of ambiguity—are they male or female, human or spirits? Among the Lele both mother and unborn child are vulnerable and dangerous to others, so the mother does not go near sick people (Douglas 1966, 95). The Nyakyusa believe that the fetus voraciously eats grain in storage bins, so a pregnant woman must not speak to people reaping grain without first making a ritual gesture to cancel the danger.

After the transformation the initiates are reincorporated into their society as new persons with new identities. Their return is depicted symbolically as a rebirth or resurrection which shows that the novices have attained another mode of existence inaccessible to those who have not undergone the initiatory ordeals. Their return is fraught with danger, and may be hedged around by further rites of reincorporation. They have experienced power in their transformation and are often seen as hot, dangerous, and needing insulation and time to cool down, or they can be harmful to others.

TYPES OF RITES OF TRANSFORMATION

All societies have rituals that mark important transitions in the life of individuals and communities. These fall roughly into three types. The most widespread are life-cycle rites, often referred to as 'rites of passage.' These mark a person's progression from childhood to young adulthood, to marriage, to retirement, and, finally, through death, to the status of an ancestor. They may include ceremonies of social puberty, betrothal, pregnancy, retirement, and other transitions in people's lives. The second type includes induction rites for entering associations with limited membership. The third category includes pilgrimages and other rites in which supplicants leave their homes in search of new religious realities.

LIFE-CYCLE RITES

Life-cycle rites have been immortalized by Gennep (1960). As we saw in Chapter 5, all societies have rituals that mark the transition between different stages and statuses of a person's life, and, in so doing, give meaning to it. It is important here to note that these transitions are generally marked by public rituals that differ greatly in detail from society to society, but serve similar sociocultural and religious functions.

Birth rites are public admission of new members into the society. Birth rites transform infants into human beings, give them a social identity, and recognize the changes that take place in the lives of others. Until these rites are performed, the new life is not seen as a human being.

Initiation rites mark the transition from childhood to adulthood. In many societies they are obligatory for all young men and women. They are often tied to puberty and sexual maturity, but they are primarily social, not biological events. They vary with the gender of the individual and can range all the way from late childhood to postadolescence. The Samo, for example, rarely initiate males before they are in their late teens or early 20s, whereas females are often initiated considerably younger.

Marriage rites mark the transition from single adults to married couples. They are often related to the biological processes of mating and procreation, but the two are not the same. Premarital sex is common, particularly in the Pacific Islands, but this does not mean the people have no moral standards. There adolescent mating is a personal matter, but marriage is a change in social status legitimizing the sexual union between two persons, and assigning them new relationships to each other, their offspring, their relatives, and society in general.

Funerals are public recognition that a member of the community has left the land of the living to become one of the ancestors, or to enter another reality. They arrange for the disposal of the body and the preparation of the spirit for its new existence, they channel expressions of grief and provide comfort and support to living relatives and friends, and they reorder the social relationships of the living that death has disrupted. They often transform the deceased into ancestors, and assign them new and honored roles in the community. Funerals display the importance of the deceased person. Children and the aged are often buried with little ceremony. Mature adults receive full rites. Great persons, such as chiefs, kings, queens, and presidents, receive elaborate and costly funerals because they are representatives of what it means to be fully human.

INDUCTION RITES

A second type of transformation rite marks the induction of new members into associations with limited membership. These include the men's and women's secret societies of West Africa, and the mystery cults common in the Near Eastern world during the time of Christ. They also include rites such as baptism by means of which people enter the church. Other rites admit shamans and medicine men into their vocations through intense ecstatic personal experiences with the spirit world, and modern medical doctors into their profession after schooling and proficiency examinations.

PILGRIMAGES

So far we have looked at rites of transition as public or personal ceremonial events. We must not overlook the importance of pilgrimages as rituals of penitence, fulfillment of vows, and exploration. During the Middle Ages, Christians from Europe made long treks to cathedrals in Rome, Tours, and Santiago, and to shrines in Antioch and the Holy Land.[2] Today Catholics go to the Virgins of Guadalupe, Majugorje, and Lourdes; Muslims make pilgrimages to Mecca; Buddhists, to the great temples in Thailand, Myanmar, and China; and Hindus, to the great Hindu shrines of Sri Sailam, Badrinath, Varanasi, Kidarnath, and dozens of other sacred sites. It has become fashionable for Indian villagers to take tours to five or six such shrines on tour buses to earn merit, fulfill vows, and sightsee. In Taiwan, common people make pilgrimages to famous temples, such as that dedicated to Ma-tsu in Paikang (Goddess of the Southern Sea), to reaffirm their loyalties to the temple, to pro-

2. For an excellent discussion of this, see Sumption 1975 and V. Turner 1978. Pilgrimages are most common in peasant societies where, for the great majority, rural existence is monotonously regular and ruled by overpowering conventions. To go more than a few miles from home for most is a great and dangerous adventure. In modern societies secular tourism has become something of a weak substitute for pilgrimages.

cure divine healing and guidance, and to enjoy a time of withdrawal from the burdensome problems of everyday life.

Pilgrimages begin with a physical separation from the familiar terrain of home and daily life. Commonly this separation is associated with suffering hardships and mortifying the flesh. Pilgrims walk barefooted on rocky trails, crawl on their knees, or prostrate themselves on the ground every two or three yards. They often eat nothing but dried bread and water, wear only simple clothes, and carry little or no money, sharing with other pilgrims what little they have, and depending on the free hospitality of others. Alms given them brings special merit to the givers. The pilgrims face the perils of fast rivers, thieves and wild beasts.

FROM THE SERMON *VENERANDA DIES*

(Tenth-century Europe)

The pilgrim may bring with him no money at all, except perhaps to distribute it to the poor on the road. Those who sell their property before leaving must give every penny of it to the poor, for if they spend it on their own journey they are departing from the path of the Lord. In times past the faithful had but one heart and one soul, and they held all property in common, owning nothing of their own; just so, the pilgrims of today must hold everything in common and travel together with one heart and one soul. . . . Goods shared in common are worth much more than goods owned by individuals. Thus it is that the pilgrim who dies on the road with money in his pocket is permanently excluded from the kingdom of heaven. For what benefit can a man possibly derive from a pilgrimage undertaken in a spirit of sin?

From: *Liber Sancti Jacobi*, vol. 1.
(Sumpton 1975, 124–25).

On route, most pilgrims experience existential communitas. They distribute what they have, join for protection against external dangers, and share shelters at night. All the normal status differences are leveled. Class and ethnic distinctions are abandoned on pilgrimages. All are primal humans gathered in a single venture seeking a new life.

Pilgrims go for many purposes: as penitents seeking forgiveness of sin and assurance of entry into heaven; as supplicants wanting healing from diseases; as expectants seeking miracles and blessings; and as devotees showing their total devotion. Numerous stories abound of the miraculous experiences they have on their journeys and the transformations they undergo on the way. To die on pilgrimage is often seen as the supreme self-sacrifice and a sure way to enter paradise.

On their return, pilgrims are reincorporated in their societies, but as new people—as those with special merit, wisdom, and powers. Many bring back talismans and relics as amulets that bring healing and success to those who touch them.

Pilgrimages are frequently associated with markets. Westerners tend to think of markets as places for buying and selling goods, visiting with friends and acquaintances, exchanging news, and making new relation-

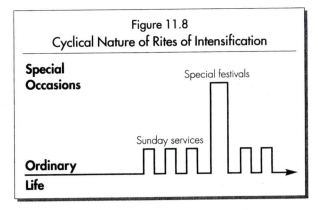

Figure 11.8
Cyclical Nature of Rites of Intensification

ships. In much of the world, however, markets are associated with religious shrines. Markets among the Ibo, Tiv, and Hausa of Nigeria were often founded as religious sites, and regular rituals were conducted on market days to ensure peace and to obtain the protection of the spirits. The Aztecs held their markets in temple squares, and today Indian markets in Central America are also centers of worship. Peasants come to sell their goods, and to seek the favors of the saints (Wolf 1962, 82–83).

RITES OF INTENSIFICATION

The second type of rituals are rites of intensification. These are sometimes called rites of restoration or renewal. They publicly reaffirm the existing social and religious order, which become blurred and forgotten in ordinary life. In a sense, they are like house cleaning. As people live in their homes, these become dirty. Dust settles on the shelves, food is spilled on the floor, clothes are left lying on the chairs, and rugs are soiled. Periodically the family stops and cleans things up. Rites of restoration act as social and religious house cleaning rituals, restoring meaning to a world that is falling into chaos and meaninglessness. They do so by providing participants with a high sense of order and purpose in the context of the ritual.

Rites of intensification are generally cyclical. Minor ones, such as Hindu temple ceremonies to awaken, feed, and care for the gods, take place daily. Others, like Muslim Friday services, are weekly events. More major ones are monthly, yearly, or once each number of years. For example, each week Christians attend Sunday services. In time, however, these become routine and ordinary, so Christians organize special rites, such as Christmas, Easter, or other important festivals as 'high' rites of intensification (Figure 11.8). Other examples of rites of intensification include New Year's rites, harvest rituals, annual fiestas, birthdays, anniversary rites, and annual conferences.

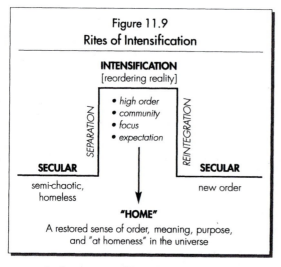

Figure 11.9
Rites of Intensification

INTENSIFICATION
[reordering reality]

- high order
- community
- focus
- expectation

SEPARATION

REINTEGRATION

SECULAR
semi-chaotic,
homeless

SECULAR
new order

"HOME"
A restored sense of order, meaning, purpose,
and "at homeness" in the universe

CHARACTERISTICS OF RITES OF INTENSIFICATION

Effective rites of intensification can produce a strong sense of renewal in a short period of time. They generate strong emotions that provide participants with a feeling of familiarity—of 'being at home.' They give people a feeling that their lives have order and meaning, and an understanding of their world. Many, such as festivals, give opportunities for expressions of the joy of feeling oneself incorporated into a community. Others, such as coffee breaks, weekends, Sunday services, and vacations in the West, make the routine and burden of daily life more meaningful. We will look at the characteristics that enable these rites to function (Figure 11.9).

STRUCTURAL REAFFIRMATION

Restoration rites are characterized by remembrance and reaffirmation of the existing structures. The same rites are repeated week after week, year after year, at regular times dictated by the calendar. They often mark changes in the seasons, from scarcity to plenty or plenty to scarcity. Consequently, they are referred to as 'cyclical rites.' This cyclicalness gives people a sense of stability and unchanging reality, for the constant repetition of the same events again and again gives a feeling that time has stopped, and that we are only reliving the past. These are times when people remember and reaffirm reality as it has been passed down (cf. Deut. 16; Josh. 4).

HIGH ORDER

Rites of intensification are characterized by high order and predictability. They generally consist of a specific set of events, repeated the same way time after time, and performed as faithfully as possible to previous rituals. For example, High Church liturgies are printed and use common elements such as the Lord's Prayer, Apostles' Creed, standard worship readings, prayer books, and chants. Much of what will be said and done in the service is spelled out beforehand in detail. That is why there is the urge to appeal to tradition, where custom becomes an immovable law.

This high order gives participants a sense of a meaningful universe, and a guide to their life in it. An awareness of the sacred and transcendent is achieved by bracketing the symbols used in the ceremony, as discussed in Chapter 9. This begins by placing them in ritual contexts, and often includes such things as praying, kneeling, bowing, chanting, using icons, and singing songs again and again. Repetition adds to their impact, because it focuses not on cognitive meanings but on generating deep emotions. Other forms of bracketing include wearing special clothing, using special times and places, and assuming particular postures. Rites of renewal reinforce the authority and structure found in tradition and the present society, but because they are also characterized by liminality, they can create strong reassurances that the order which has begun to crumble in everyday life will be restored and all will be well again

Normative Communitas

Rites of intensification are characterized by normative communitas. This is a state in which the fundamental social order is accentuated. Roles are accentuated by using special clothing, titles, and other social symbols. There is often a clear hierarchy—for example, of men over women, leaders over laity, and the high-ranked people over the poor and marginalized. In Western college graduation services, students wear robes and sit in the front of the auditorium. Professors, administrators, and president, dressed in more splendid gowns and wearing insignia and medals appropriate to their rank, enter in order of their rank—the lowest enter first as heralds of the highest, who come last and sit in the middle on the stage. Roles are reinforced by public recognition of prestige, awarding titles and degrees, and the giving of gifts. Leadership is in the hands of 'priests'—leaders with institutionally recognized rights and powers to control the rite. The ritual order is strictly regulated by tradition. In normative communitas the community unites in rituals to mobilize and renew the social structure of ordinary life, and the status and power needed for social control to maintain order and control. All this ritual enactment serves to intensify and reinforce the existing social and power structures of the community.

Sometimes this reinforcement is achieved by reversing normal statuses and roles for a time to show that such changes lead only to chaos. Outrageous ways of acting, ludicrous humor, masked figures, and transvestites all show that such antisocial behavior leads to the collapse of normal life. Then the normal social statuses are reinstated and social and cosmic order is restored. Such reversals reinforce the belief that society is a structure of statuses and roles, and that the existing social differences and inequities are morally and religious justified (V. Turner 1969, 177). Nothing underlines regularity so well as absurdity or paradox, or emotionally satisfies as much as extravagant or temporarily permitted illicit behavior.

RENEWAL

Rites of renewal also provide focus in the ritual on its central theme and a rise in expectations. People set aside the cares of everyday life and give their attention to the ritual. They come expecting to reaffirm their beliefs and sense of community, and feel cheated if these expectations are not met. This concentration on the ritual can result in a strong reaffirmation and integration of beliefs, feelings, and morals on the part of the participants. People return to their ordinary lives with a restored sense of order, meaning, and purpose.

The danger in rituals of intensification is that, over time, they can become dead traditions. People forget the reasons for the rites, and perform these simply because these are central to their tradition. On the positive side, rituals can preserve beliefs during times of secularism—beliefs long forgotten can reemerge as people rediscover them. For example, people in nominal Christian churches with liturgies that include the reading of Scripture can rediscover, many years later, the power of the Bible to transform their lives. Nominal churches that have no such liturgical traditions often experience no such renewal of faith.

TYPES OF RITES OF INTENSIFICATION

Rites of intensifications vary greatly. Only a few types can be examined here.

FESTIVALS AND FIESTAS

Community festivals, fiestas, and fairs are found in most societies. Each takes practices from its greater religious tradition, and adapts these to express the particular beliefs and social structure of the local community. Festivals are organized by the community leaders, and are times when people can publicly display their status and wealth. They often include eating communal meals to reaffirm the corporate identity of those who participate, and celebrate the prosperity of the community during the past year. Central to many of these sacred gatherings are processions in which the gods, ancestors, and dignitaries are paraded through their territory on palanquins to entertain them, and to symbolize the loyalty of their people.

Festivals, fiestas, and parades are public demonstrations of power and celebration. Roberto da Matta compares Independence Day, religious processions, and Carnival in Brazil. At a military parade, the authorities and the common people are stationary; the mobile components are the soldiers, who symbolize the power of authority. Mediation between the people and the authorities is effected by symbols of power: the marching soldiers who are armed with weapons. In religious processions, the ecclesiastic, civil, and military authorities carry the image of the saint, surrounded by a disorderly crowd of all social types. The latter are "penitents fulfilling promises, disabled people seeking relief from their infirmities, and ordinary people merely demonstrating their devotion to the saint" (1991, 44). In Carnival the people themselves march in disguise, seeking laughter, music, happiness, and sexual pleasures—things they experience little in the hardships of everyday life. There is a great leveling, as people of all walks of life participate in a religious rite that strips everyone of their social roles as members of a family, neighborhood, race, and social class. The costumes break down the hierarchy and inequality of everyday Brazilian life. The masked 'bandit' dances with the 'sheriff,' a 'skeleton' with a young pretty girl. Ritual clowns ease the intensity of solemn rites with their buffoonery and hilarity, but it is precisely their deviance from the norms of social behavior that reinforces those norms. The Carnival parade mediates between antagonistic fields by uniting the happy and sad, the healthy and sick, innocents and sinners, and authorities and people in their common humanity. It reinforces their identity as Brazilians (Matta 1991, 44).

Indian villagers celebrate a great many festivals each year. The most prominent mark the changes in seasons and years, or celebrate the rites of passage in the lives of the gods. Hindus observe such all-India festivals as Dasara, Divali, Holi, Shiva Ratria, and Vinayaka Chauti. On Ugadi, a regional festival, craftsmen worship their tools, barbers their knives, washermen their washing stones and firepots, weavers their looms, and drivers garland their trucks and buses. Castes, too, have their own festivals. On Chiluka Dvdashi Brahmins and merchants decorate cows and offer them brown sugar in worship. On Nagula Panchami the same castes fast and offer foods to cobras living in anthills, and on Kartika Purnami they venerate the Tulsi tree.

In many villages the most important festival is a religious fair *(jatra)* which celebrates the marriage of the gods. Some draw more than a hundred thousand people, who camp in surrounding fields, visiting and offering private worship during the days. On successive nights the god is taken on procession through the streets, meets his bride, is married, and is paraded through the village on a great chariot or juggernaut. Muslims in the villages have their own festivals with processions, fire walking, and offerings of food commemorating Muslim holidays, and remembering local Muslim saints *(durgas)*.

MEMORIAL SERVICES

Another common form of intensification rite is memorial services. These are times when people remember their common history. In traditional societies this often involves commemorating famous ancestors who led the people to their land and defeated fierce enemies. In state societies memorial ceremonies retell the stories of national heroes. For example, in the United States these would include the Fourth of July, George Washington's birthday, and the anniversary of Martin Luther King's death.

SOCIAL SATIRES

Many cultures have social rites that satirize oppressive social orders. For example, the traditional Korean Masked Dance is a form of entertainment in which the common folk ridicule the shortcomings of the upper-class society, mock the philandering of the monks, and make fun of the tribulations of husband-wife-concubine relationships. The injustices and foibles of human beings are exposed in public and cheered by the audience that participates freely in the satire. For the moment, the oppressed are honored and the powerful ridiculed. Such ceremonies enable the people to vent their grievances publicly against the prevailing social conflicts and taboos using dramatic forms. In so doing, they are able to vent some of their deep hostilities, enabling them to live in unjust situations without total desperation (King 1983).

RITES OF CRISIS

Crisis rites are performed when danger or crisis, such as famine, drought, flood, or epidemic, threatens to disrupt the normal social and cultural orders, and when divine judgment punishes humans for breaking the moral order. These rites may involve individuals, families, or the community as a whole. Plagued by disease, droughts, unexpected deaths, repeated accidents, solar eclipses, or strange events, people often turn to divination to determine the cause, and rituals for a remedy. These often involve sacrifices to placate the gods, ancestors, or spirits. Decoys may also be used to lead them astray, or somehow distract them so they do not pay such close attention.

CHARACTERISTICS OF CRISIS RITES

Crisis rites share several common characteristics (Figure 11.10). First, they re-create order out of chaos. The people's world is falling apart, and rituals are needed to restore structure and meaning to it. This may involve placating or driving off the spirits and powers which are the causes of disaster. It may require the supplication of God to re-create order as he did in the beginning.

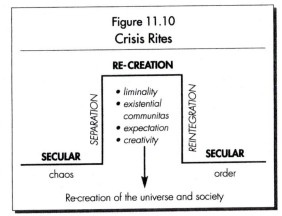

Second, crisis rites are characterized by liminality and existential communitas. There is no structure to renew. Structure itself must be created out of disorder. This can be achieved when everything is up for reexamination, and all possible structuring can be considered. Crisis rites have a powerful integrative effect on communities. They unite different segments in concerted action to preserve the whole. Strong villages are those that can unite to forestall disaster; weak ones can only bear their plagues in silence. The result of effective crisis rites is to restore to the community and individual a sense of cosmic, social, and personal order. The world becomes a world again.

TYPES OF CRISIS RITES

Crisis rites are not regularly scheduled rites. They arise out of the crisis created by an emergency, and are determined by the nature of the disaster they address.

CRISIS AND PROTECTION RITES

Many crises that strike individuals and communities have to do with illnesses, and epidemics, droughts, floods, earthquakes, and wars. When massive disasters spread through the land large corporate rites of healing and protection are often organized to counter the danger and to restore order. For example, in South India, when whole villages are caught up in epidemics, droughts, floods, and other disasters, Village Strength Rites are conducted at the village navel stone to placate the spirits of the earth causing the crisis—Maisamma in the case of smallpox, Poshamma in the case of cholera, and so on. In these sacrifices, everyone, high caste and low, Hindu, Muslim, and Christian, is expected to contribute to the purchase of the animal, or the offering is thought to be inefficacious. The headman of the Leatherworker Caste kills the animal with a sword, and the villagers process around the village ritual boundaries, burying bloody rice balls and cracking coconuts to generate power for the community. Any household that refuses to contribute jeopardizes the village as a whole. When evil spirits pass through the land, animals are sacrificed and buried in the major roadways entering the village. In Nagaland, rites are used to build magical walls on the village boundaries to keep supernatural forces and raiders away, and to generate power to overcome foes. Many other rites serve to ward off evil, protect people from the attack of spirits, and stop epidemics. These vary greatly from society to society, but accomplish the same purpose—enabling people to rise above their immediate circumstances and survive crisis.

Healing and deliverance rites are performed to cure individuals and communities that are sick or possessed. For example, the Korean *kut* is a ritual in which shamans invoke spirit-powers to deal with physical, psychological, and social disorders, and natural disasters. The ceremony begins with highly structured dances, fixed rules, and intelligible words to invite the spirits to attend. It then moves into a stage of antistructure in which the shaman, now spirit-possessed and in a state of semiconscious intoxication, uses unintelligible syllables, frenzied dance, jerky, bodily gestures, and shouts to entertain the spirits and to communicate their messages to the living. Here the living negotiate relationships with the dead. The final rites are again highly structured. They send the spirits away, and return the participants to normal life. Like many regeneration rites, the *kut* combines structure and antistructure to restore order to everyday life.

RE-CREATION RITES

One particular type of crisis rite is that of the re-creation of the universe at the end of each year. In some societies, New Year's rites are better treated as major crisis rites. As we have seen, in many traditional societies the world cannot be repaired. It must be re-created by a ritual reenactment of the original creation. If this is not done, the world will fall into chaos and darkness. For example, for the Polynesians, in the beginning there were only darkness and water. Then Io, the Supreme God, said, "Let the waters be separated, the heavens be formed, and the earth be!" These cosmogonic words are seen as a formula for creation, charged with sacred power. Used in proper rituals, they re-create the world each year, make barren women fertile and assure success in battle.

CHRISTIAN RESPONSE

How should Christian leaders and missionaries respond to the rich, colorful, dramatic, disgusting, confusing, yet beautiful rituals encountered so often around the world? Before responding, it is important to examine the role of rituals in the Bible. In the Old Testament, God dealt with a largely oral society by instituting elaborate rituals to teach the people his ways and to give them a method to store his message. By means of the tabernacle, priestly robes, blood sacrifices, washings, taboos, offerings of bread and incense, marchings, shouting, chanting, singing, and a hundred other ways the people expressed their faith in God. Moreover, God instituted all three types of rites to provide a full range of occasions for the people to meet him and reaffirm their loyalty to him: intensification rites (daily and weekly rites in the tabernacle, Lev. 1–7; Sabbath observances, Exod. 31; festivals of Passover, First Fruits, Weeks, Trumpets, and Booths, Lev. 23; and the annual Day of Atonement, Lev. 16; the Sabbatical Year, Lev. 25; and the Year of Jubilee, Lev. 25), transformation rites (life-cycle rites, Lev. 12; ordination of the priests, Lev. 8–9; and dedication of the tabernacle, Num. 7), and crisis rites (rituals associated with leprosy, Lev. 13–14; body discharges, Lev. 15; and making of vows, Lev. 27).

CHRISTIAN RITES OF TRANSFORMATION

Rituals play a central role in creating and renewing religious beliefs in most societies, and it is important for missionaries to be aware of the need to embody the gospel in living ritual forms. Over time rituals can become meaningless routines, but the answer to dead rituals is not no rituals. It is to constantly create and renew rituals in the lives of individuals and churches.

First, it is important that churches create Christian rites of transformation that mark and reinforce changes that take place in the lives of individuals and congregations. These fall into several broad types.

CONVERSION AND REVIVAL RITES

Leading people to faith in Christ is central to the mission task. These conversions are, in part, public acts and need to be expressed through public rites of transformation. There are many secret believers, but the church should encourage new converts to make their new stand known in order to confirm them at this turning point in their lives and incorporate them into the community of believers. Concrete witness, such as public testimonies and baptisms, are important if their experiences are to have permanence. These rituals bring moral support and encouragement from the church, and help the converts show themselves and others how their lives find new meaning in Christ. The sense of belonging is as important as doctrinal beliefs in establishing new believers. Public testimonies also strengthen the church as members share their struggles to live the new life. But these rituals often lead to persecution and ostricism for they are public declarations of conversion to a new faith.

Revival is also important in the life of believers and churches, and is often fostered by vital rites of transformation. Sunday services and festival days keep churches together and help believers to be faithful, but they do not deal with the tendency over time for services and believers to become routinized and stale. Revival meetings, camps, and special occasions set aside for renewal help churches to hear afresh what God is saying to them. Churches on the American frontier had revival meetings in which traveling evangelists called Christians to repentance and nonbelievers to faith.

Renewal must be personal. Retreats and pilgrimages can be transforming experiences in the lives of believers whose spiritual lives have grown stagnant. But renewal must also be corporate, involving the congregation as a whole. Individuals and families may find renewal through camps and retreats, but when they return to the routines of church life they soon lose their newfound zeal. What is needed are rites of corporate renewal in which churches as whole bodies unite in special times for confessing sin and gaining a new vision of their calling, and in reaching out to the lost around them. In many parts of the world, such rites of revival are central to the lives of the churches.

CHRISTIAN LIFE CYCLE-RITES

Missionaries and church leaders must help new churches develop meaningful rituals marking the transitions of life and give expression to Christian faith and allegiance corporately and publicly. They need to help young churches develop rituals for setting people apart for special ministries and to mark transitions in their lives such as ordinations, promotions, and retirements. Dedication of buildings and inaugurating new programs, such as mission outreaches, are times both for corporate celebration and commitment, and for public testimony to the world.

A special word needs to be said about life-cycle rites. Because these play such an important role in the religious lives of most people, it is important that churches develop Christian rites that convey biblical truths about the meaning of life. Birth ceremonies, weddings, and funerals are times of public display where non-Christians can window-shop the gospel.

Initiation rites are particularly important. Western missionaries have often condemned initiation rites as pagan. In part this rejection was based on the fact that many elements in initiation rites are, indeed, unchristian in nature. In part, however, it was due to the fact that Western societies have no initiation rites, and Western missionaries do not know what to do with them. They recognize pagan marriages and funerals as valid rites that need to be transformed. In contrast, they try to stamp out initiation rites. Churches in cultures where there are initiation rites must provide substitute rituals that enable Christians to become adults in a social sense. These rites must be different from baptism, however; otherwise everyone, non-Christians included, will want to be baptized in order to become adults in the society.

It is particularly important to develop strong Christian funerals. They make death tangible and real, and bring closure to life on earth. They help the bereaved to own their pain and deal with the staggering weight of grief and loss. They bring to the fore the central questions of bafflement and pain, and provide meaning to life and death by proclaiming the good news of eternal life in Christ.

CHRISTIAN RITES OF INTENSIFICATION

It is important for churches to create living rites of intensification to maintain and constantly renew the spiritual life of their members. As A. H. M. Zahniser points out (1997), this has important implications in discipling new believers. Rites of intensification, such as weekly worship services, Easter and Christmas celebrations, Bible study groups, and prayer retreats, help strength the faith of believers through corporate participation.

Zahniser points out that rituals can be an effective way of discipling new believers. Many Protestant churches think of discipling in terms of formal verbal instruction. Rituals can play an important role in teaching people religious beliefs, reinforcing these beliefs with deep emotions, and motivating them to make lasting personal commitments. Baptism and the Lord's Supper are vital to the life of every church. So, too, should be the dedication of infants, marriages, and funerals. Some churches also have Christian initiation rites in which the parents, relatives, and church gather to transform adolescents into adults. Such rites are particularly important substitutions in societies that have pagan initiation rites. It is important, in such Christian rituals, not only to perform the rites, but also to use the occasion to instruct new believers, and remind the old ones, regarding the meaning of the ceremony. Liturgical calendars are another way to tie worship services to the whole of the gospel. This was true in the Old Testament and the annual cycle of festivals.

Christian rituals, such as festivals, baptisms, and funerals, are times when churches can publicly testify to their faith to their neighbors, display their hope and joy, and celebrate their unity. In many parts of the world people see Christianity as a drab, colorless, intellectual religion with no exhilaration or thrill. In some countries, Christians celebrate Christmas, Good Friday, and Easter by parading through the streets of their communities, affirming their hope and declaring their identity with the church. In doing so they dramatize their witness to non-Christian neighbors.

Large public gatherings of Christians, such as mass crusades, are also testimonies to the world of Christ's presence. Moreover, they encourage ordinary believers who live all their lives in small communities and know only a few hundred other Christians, and who are amazed when they see so many other believers from around the world. In the Old Testament, Israelites from all over the land gathered three times a year in Jerusalem to worship and fellowship. These assemblies played a powerful role in maintaining the unity of Israel.

Western churches, too, need to learn the power of rituals in discipling and renewing Christians (Zahniser 1997). Douglas notes that one of the characteristics of modernity is the divorce of external forms and internal meanings in rituals. A modern Christian says, "I go to church in order to worship." Getting out of bed (rather than sleeping in), dressing in clean clothes, and going to church are not part of worship. They only bring us to a place where worship (perceived as an inner personal experience) can occur. Invocations, prayers, offerings, and songs are included in services, but they are commonly considered only preparatory for the sermon about truth. For people in high ritual societies, every act involved in preparation, performance, and clean up are essential to the meaning of the rite.

CHRISTIAN RITES OF CRISES

Finally, missionaries need to encourage new Christians to develop rituals that will relieve or protect them from crisis. As we saw in Chapter 6, it is important for Christians to experience and proclaim that God is deeply concerned about the crises of life, and, in many societies, they can best do so by means of public rituals of healing, deliverance, opposition to oppression and violence, and delivery in times of famine, flood, and destruction. It is also important that churches minister as communities of *shalom* in times of crisis, and to demonstrate that, in Christ, people can be spiritually and physically restored, and also receive eternal salvation. An example of this is the Samo. Every Samo is a shaman by virtue of knowing how to perform crisis rituals for themselves or others in the household. When the idea was transferred by Samo Christians to an understanding of the "priesthood of all believers," they began to encourage each other through spontaneous prayer, encouragement, and even all night song fests resembling pre-Christian all night dances (Shaw 1981).

The contemporary Western church needs to rediscover the importance of living rituals in the life of its members. Worship in modern churches is often reduced to discursive communication about God, and not meeting him in moments of sacred encounter. We need to encourage people to develop rituals that remind them they are citizens of God's kingdom, and that as strangers on earth, pilgrims, and travelers with no place to rest their heads, they will one day be united with their Creator in a new and holy place.

12

RELIGIOUS LEADERS AND INSTITUTIONS

All corporate activities require social organization. This may be minimal, as in the case of many folk religious actions, or it may be extensive, as in high religions with their bureaucracies, buildings, schools, libraries, and large budgets. We will examine briefly some of the ways in which groups of people structure religious activities, and how these structures shape and limit the religious life of the people. We will examine first the nature of religious leadership, and then the social structures that emerge as people organize corporate religious life.

RELIGIOUS LEADERS

In all religions there are leaders: shamans, diviners, healers, magicians, astrologers, palmists, prophets, priests, preachers, evangelists, mystics, saints, gurus, and sadhus. These operate in different contexts and different ways, but they all serve to mediate between humans and the sacred. It is critical for missionaries to understand their roles in their particular contexts.

One way to group religious leaders is to differentiate between those concerned with this-worldly matters and those concerned with other-worldly affairs. The former includes healers, exorcists, doctors, sorcerers, magicians, astrologers, and the like. The latter include priests, prophets, saints, evangelists, mystics, monks, ascetics, dervishes, sannyasins, and bikkus. This structure closely reflects the contrast between leaders in folk and formal religions, and is the focus of the discussion that follows.

LEADERS IN TRADITIONAL RELIGIONS

Most leaders in folk religions are part-time practitioners—men and women who maintain their lives as do others in their societies, but who

323

are known to have special gifts of healing, divination, fortune telling, or bringing fertility to the soil or success to the hunt. Specialists in folk religions fall into a few broad types. Here we will focus on shamans, healers, and diviners.

SHAMANS

Shamans are the most common of folk religious practitioners. They are men or women who are religious specialists believed to exercise control over spirits which they use primarily for good.[1] They are not magicians who seek to control events through formulas and rites. Rather, they rely on their mastery of the spirit world, ecstasy, and healing to assist fellow human beings. They enter the upper or under worlds at will through trances via openings such as smoke holes in a house and holes in the ground. There they find the causes of diseases or misfortune, whether these are due to witchcraft, curses, violations of taboos, or other spirit causes. Once the cause has been diagnosed, they prescribe specific treatment. They battle evil spirits who have lured away the souls of living humans. They find, identify, and return souls that are lost or have wandered away from a body during sleep. They remove foreign objects that have entered a person, causing illness. They summon spirits and question them to find out what they want. They often are intermediaries between the living and the dead. A shaman may speak the words of the deceased, and the mourners crowd around, arguing with the dead or weeping at their accusations.

Shamans are also called to send off the souls of people at death. These often wish to stay in the house with the family, but, as noted earlier, their presence can cause difficulties. Shamans are able to go into a trance and speak with the soul of the newly departed, who may plead to be allowed to stay. In some cases, the shaman may catch the spirits and send them off to the underworld, but the homesick souls may escape, and the shaman must rush back to the house to catch them again. These encounters with the spirit world validate the shaman's power and authority in the eyes of the people.

Shamans carry out their work in seances, generally held in a tent, house, or igloo. The people gather round, the lamps are extinguished, and the shaman, dressed in special clothes, begins beating a drum and singing softly, often using animal sounds. The tension builds as the shaman goes into a trance and enters the spirit world. At times, dancing, chanting, fasting, and drugs are used to gain altered states of conscious-

---

1. The word *shaman* comes from the Tungus of Siberia. The role of shaman as medium and diviner is found throughout northeast Asia, the Arctic Circle, and the Americas. In some forms it is also found in Southeast Asia, Oceania, India, Tibet, and China.

ness. Then the shaman announces to the audience that the spirits are approaching, and enacts the ensuing battle, speaking in different voices. At the end the spirits communicate a message and the drumming ceases. The shaman is left lying exhausted, asserting a lack of memory of what has happened.

Being a shaman brings power and honor, but is also a dangerous activity. To acquire the special powers often requires a mortal combat or special spiritual encounter in which the novice may experience a near-death experience. Some people become shamans by choice, others through inheritance. Most do so through traumatic experiences which they interpret as calls to that vocation: they become desperately ill and experience miraculous healings, or they are forced to accept the role by spirits that torture them until they agree. Novices undergo long training involving physical and spiritual testing under the tutelage of an older shaman before they begin their own practices. They are thought to be empowered by the spirits of wild animals such as stallions, wolves, eagles, reindeer, jaguars, or bulls, or by mythical creatures like dragons. Shamans must feed and placate their animal spirits, or these will gnaw at their vital organs. If their shadow spirits are killed, it is believed shamans will die.

HEALERS

Most societies have people other than shamans reputed to heal the sick. Many are thought to do so through natural means. For example, midwives and doctors are often used at childbirth to assist the mother during delivery. The Maya have bone-setters who are seen as sacred specialists. They have a gift *(fortuna)* which they discover in a dream in which they are told they will soon see a small bone-like object, and are instructed to pick it up. If they resist picking up such an object when they are awake, they suffer ill health themselves. Those who pick it up become bone-setters. They learn how to set bones, not from other practitioners, but through dreams, and they charge no fees for their services because it is a hallowed duty.

Local doctors use medicines abstracted from herbs, bark, leaves, and other sources. Among these are the *vaids* who dispense Ayurvedic medicines in India, the Muslim *hakim* who uses Unani medicine, allopathic doctors, homeopathic doctors, chiropractors, and the like. Many medicines are prescribed for specific illnesses. Others are used to prevent married people from separating, help people to get rich, cause others to become crazy or sad at heart, evoke illicit love, and create insomnia. These medical practitioners (erroneously called "medicine men" or "witch doctors") often treat both the body and the spirit of the patient. Most make no distinction between them. These practitioners widely act as counselors and psychologists to the mentally disturbed.

DIVINERS

Another common religious specialist is the diviner, the 'keeper of secrets.' His or her task is to disclose the causes of misfortune and death by scrutinizing the past to identify the responsible spiritual and human agents. In many societies all human problems, such as barrenness, illness, failure in hunting, and even death, are attributed to moral conflicts in the human community. Nothing is perceived to "just happen." There is always a cause. The diviner must discern the acts of immorality that have provoked the vengeance of the ancestors, or uncover the destructive hand of witches. They are not only physicians attending to the physical ills of their clients, but also moral counselors, holding up misdeeds and community conflicts to public scrutiny.Diviners usually interrogate their clients to identify the important circumstances of the situation. They learn the symptoms of the disease, 'map' the kinship and social relationship of others involved, and examine the surrounding circumstances. Each relationship carries specific moral responsibilities, as well as potential lines of conflict. On the basis of these interrogations diviners claim to know the hidden causes for the misfortune. They often enter a mild trance, and use symbolic tools, such as a winnowing basket containing sticks, stones, or bones, which they toss, to diagnose the case. They interpret the meaning of the objects as these fall, naming the identity and motive of the witch, ancestor, or person who has caused the illness. It may be a wife jealous of her husband's philandering, an ancestor who has been neglected, or a rival seeking revenge.

In some societies, diviners also foretell the future, enabling people to choose a successful course of action, or avoid misfortune. They cast palm nuts, sticks, bones, or stones, and read the future from the way these fall. Most questions regarding the future have to do with illness, long life, success in love or business, barrenness, the proper location of a new house, money, fights, and other problems of everyday life. The diviner generally offers several solutions by reciting different poems, fortunes, or interpretations, related to the case at hand, and the client must choose the one appropriate to the situation. The process provides clients with a framework to reflect on their own problem, and legitimizes their decisions and courses of action. If the outcome is not favorable, the diviner is rarely blamed, for failure is attributed to other intervening powers, or the client's destiny which does not permit a better result (Ray 1976, 103–11).

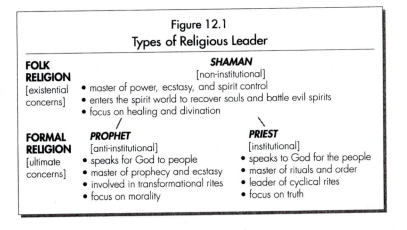

Figure 12.1
Types of Religious Leader

FOLK RELIGION [existential concerns]	**SHAMAN** [non-institutional] • master of power, ecstasy, and spirit control • enters the spirit world to recover souls and battle evil spirits • focus on healing and divination	
FORMAL RELIGION [ultimate concerns]	**PROPHET** [anti-institutional] • speaks for God to people • master of prophecy and ecstasy • involved in transformational rites • focus on morality	**PRIEST** [institutional] • speaks to God for the people • master of rituals and order • leader of cyclical rites • focus on truth

LEADERS IN FORMAL RELIGIONS

The emergence of organized religions (sometimes referred to as 'high religions') gave rise to formal religious specialist roles. These can be grouped broadly into two ideal types: prophets and priests (Figure 12.1).[2]

PROPHETS

Prophets are men and women who see themselves as spokespersons for God, calling people to repentance and transformation. They receive their authority from God or the ancestors, and their calling is often legitimated through dramatic experiences such as visions, dreams, and miraculous healings. Most are marginal people, 'edge men,' who strive with a passionate sincerity to rid themselves of the clichés associated with the institutions and role-playing of formal religious organizations. They are commonly associated with liminality and communitas, and with rites of transformation and crisis. Their identity is often reflected in their rough dress, simple food, transiency, residence on the periphery of the society, and their rejection of formal learning as a means to gain power and truth. The prophets of the Old Testament and John the Baptist are examples.

Prophets are different from diviners. The latter do not act on their own initiative, but on the initiative of their clients. They are consultants, not leaders. Prophets, on the other hand, go to the people directly and challenge them to action. For example, among the Nuer of

---

2. Ideal types are broad analytical categories that enable us to organize a field of analysis. They do not refer directly to specific realities, and few if any cases fit them totally. Their purpose is to develop high-level generalizations that enable us to see the big picture.

Figure 12.2
Prophets and Priests

	PROPHETS	PRIESTS
FOUND	when old structures are inadequate for new situations; times of social turbulence, political turmoil, and spiritual crisis	during times of relative social stability and prosperity
APPOINTMENT	through inner certitutde of a divine call to a particular task and human obedience	through the religious system; election, training, installation, appointment, promotion
FOCUS	on broad issues; idealistic, and a concern with past and future	proper procedures, rituals; realistic, concerned with the present
LEADERSHIP	charismatic	bureaucratic
LIFESTYLE	frugal, simple, emphasizes communal living	adapted to the community, preserves individual privacy
BEHAVIOR	emotionally expressive, eccentric	calm, temperate, programmed
ATTITUDE TO SIN	intolerant, iconoclastic	allows for human failures and imperfections
COMMUNICATION WITH GOD	seeks direct access to God through personal revelation	seeks knowledge of God through public revelation
SPIRITUALITY DEFINED	inner piety and social involvement	living in harmony with sacred tradition
NORMS	God speaks to the specific time and situation	timeless laws and universal principles
AUTHORITY	personal charisma and spiritual	office and work
ROLE AND FUNCTION	moral and ethical preacher, fore-teller, exhorter of people to turn back to God	teacher of orthodox doctrine, guardian of tradition, minister at the altar in worship
TRAINING	apprenticeship on the job	formal training prior to ministry
RELATION TO SOCIETY	outside to judge and call to repentance	inside to maintain the religious culture
RELATION TO CHURCH	reformer, critic, detached, no territorial ties, no place in hierarchy	guardian of tradition and creeds, tied to specific congregations, empowered, appointed and legitimatized by hierarchy
SELF-IDENTITY	outsider	member of the religious organization
CHANGE AGENT	social and spiritual reform, gives up forms, acts on existential truth, calls for dynamic changes	liturgical renewal, legislative reforms without schism, restrains change, makes moderate reforms

East Africa, prophets in the past organized cattle raids against their neighbors, the Dinka, performed rituals to stem widespread epidemics, settled blood feuds between clans, and introduced new deities from neighboring societies. They lived alone in the bush, fasted, and wore long, unkempt hair to communicate the fact that they were "outsiders" belonging to a separate, sacred reality. They were seen as superhuman bearers of the divine, completely possessed by the spirits (Ray 1976, 111–12). When the British imposed their rule over the region, some of these prophets mobilized large numbers of the people to resist them.

PRIESTS

Priests are leaders in the religious establishment (Figure 12.2). They represent the people to God, and sustain the life of their religious community by exercising ritual and symbolic authority. They get their authority and power from their office, which they acquire through institutional processes such as appointment, election, and inheritance. They are often trained in schools, and have mastered the performance of religious rituals. They focus on proper procedures, doing things in an orderly manner, keeping the laws, and following the rules. They are keepers of tradition and corporate memory.

TEACHERS

Every society has some sort of religious instruction, ways to inculcate religious beliefs and values into the minds and hearts of adherents. Instruction may be informal, as in many traditional societies where family members instruct as the need arises, or formal where individuals intentionally study a particular religion or doctrinal belief. In either case, the focus is on enabling people in this world to understand what is happening in the other world, or the transempirical realm. In this sense, religious instructors, teachers, gurus, or other culturally designated individuals are also part of the group of religious practitioners we are discussing here.

A TYPOLOGY OF RELIGIOUS LEADERS

Utilizing the analytical model that undergirds this book, religious leaders can be placed along two continuums: their interaction (or lack thereof) with formal institutions, and the direction of their contact with spiritual power—either speaking on behalf of the people to spiritual powers, or on behalf of these powers to ordinary people. By contrasting these two continuums, we are able to develop a grid (Figure 12.3) where each quadrant characterizes a different type of religious leader. The behavior of these leaders varies greatly from one society to

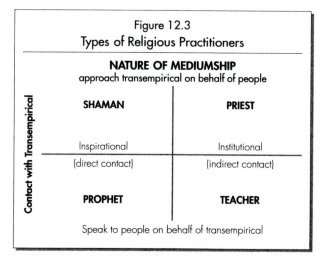

Figure 12.3
Types of Religious Practitioners

NATURE OF MEDIUMSHIP
approach transempirical on behalf of people

SHAMAN	**PRIEST**
Inspirational	Institutional
(direct contact)	(indirect contact)
PROPHET	**TEACHER**

Contact with Transempirical

Speak to people on behalf of transempirical

another, but the attributes set up by the grid are helpful in enabling an outsider, such as a missionary, to determine the basic nature of the practitioners they observe in particular contexts.

In folk religions there is often a tension among these four types of practitioners—the local lay healer, the outsider who comes bearing a message from God, the official who shepherds the people and represents them to God, and the one who gives them instruction. On one level, the conflict is between folk practitioners (such as shamans, magicians, and religious healers) who deal with the existential problems of everyday life and are not part of religious organizations, and formal leaders who deal with questions of ultimate truth and are part of established institutions. This contrast is evident in the tensions between the Muslim clergy, and Sufi saints, and between Hindu Brahmin priests and village exorcists and magicians.

On the institutional level, the conflict is between priests and prophets, and how religious information is passed on to others. Priests seek to build institutions. For them the old is safe, tested, and enduring, and the new is threatening, dangerous, and ephemeral. Institutions are necessary to preserve orthodoxy. Prophets see institutions as dead tradition. For them the old is legalistic, human-centered, ingrown, and dead. The new is living, vital, and God-centered. This conflict is seen in the Old Testament between the prophets and the priests. Today, in Christianity it is the tension that often exists between pastors, and itinerant evangelists and revivalists.

The distinctions among prophet, priest, teacher, and shaman are not sharp ones. The same person may function in several capacities in different contexts, in one as a prophet, and in another a priest or teacher. Pastors are priests in their own congregations, but prophets when they are invited by another church to preach in revival meetings and challenge its traditional ways of doing things. Nevertheless, the distinction helps explain some of the dynamics in religious communities.

RELIGIOUS ORGANIZATIONS

All corporate religious activity involves some social organization, but as societies become more complex, specialized and formalized structures emerge. The first specialists to emerge in human history were religious leaders, the shamans. In time, the formal roles of priest and prophet developed, and organized religion became the responsibility of a select group of religious teachers.

The rise of specialization and formalization has led to the formation of complex religious institutions such as temples, mosques, churches, schools, monasteries, and ecclesiastical systems. These are subcultural 'frames' that act like social entities. They have members with different roles, property, and cultural beliefs and norms. For some people, a religious institution is their place of work, and the place where they get their primary sense of identity. Others come to the institutions for religious activities, but have their identity in other institutions, such as schools, banks, and shops.

TYPES OF ORGANIZATIONS

Max Weber (1946), Howard Becker (1957), and Ernst Troeltsch (1931) differentiate among different types of religious institutions. They order these along a continuum from institutions that separate themselves from the surrounding social structures, on the one hand, to those that participate in them, on the other. Because these scholars analyzed mainly Western Christian institutions, they used the term 'sects' for religious communities that see themselves as countercultural alternatives living in a hostile society, and 'churches' for those that seek to be a part of the society and to shape it. Unfortunately, the term 'sect' came to have negative connotations, while 'church' was seen as the desirable norm. Weber noted that sects usually have charismatic-type leaders and voluntary membership, while churches have a professional priesthood and compulsory membership. Later, the terms 'cult' and 'ecclesia' were used to add breadth to the analysis (Figure 12.4). We will draw on Weber, Troeltsch, and Becker to form a model for analyzing sects (including cults) and churches (including ecclesias).

CHARACTERISTICS OF SECT AND CHURCH

As used here, the terms *sect* and *church* are neutral terms describing the relationship religious organizations have to their cultural surroundings. The differences between them can be summarized in terms of several key factors which refer both to the nature of the organization and the degree of its involvement in a society.

Figure 12.4
Types of Religious Organization

	CULT	SECT	CHURCH	ECCLESIA
	NOT OF THE WORLD ◄ - - - - - - - - - ► *IN THE WORLD*			

Attitude:	Withdrawal from the world • radicalism • tension with the world • all members set apart	Identification with the world • conservatism • accommodation to the world • only monastic orders separate
Membership:	Exclusive, by voluntary choice • total commitment by all	Inclusive, by birth and choice • priests more committed than laity
Community:	Limited, high, exclusive • store information in memory • verbal	Extended, low, inclusive • use print, radio, T.V., media • media communication
Controls:	Informal • uncompromising ethics • often value nonviolence • often oppose the state	Formal • adaptive ethics • militant to the degree society is • use the state
Appeal:	Lower classes • oppressed groups	Higher classes • dominant groups
Organization:	Egalitarian • priesthood of all believers • men and women leaders • charismatic leaders	Hierarchical • set aside priesthood • male dominance • priestly leaders
Boundary Maintenance:	High • mental isolation • discourage new ideas	Low • mental accessibility • encourage critical thinking
Nature:	Moral community • culturally marginal	Social institution • culturally central
Gospel:	Community governed by law • subjective holiness • word and rules	Grace administered to the masses • objective grace • rites, sacraments

—————————— *ROUTINIZATION OF CHARISMA* ——————►

Sects see themselves as in the world but not of it. They often oppose the state and surrounding culture. They tend to have high boundaries which set their adherents apart from the world, and expect their members to be different in significant ways from the people around them. Consequently, they often have a clear sense of identity and community solidarity. Churches, on the other hand, seek to be in the world in order to transform it, and are willing to accommodate to the state and society. They admit members more freely, and with fewer demands.

Another factor is membership. Sects are voluntary associations based on personal choice, which often requires a strong commitment to the 'cause' the sect represents. Consequently, they are often viewed as 'radical' by members of the broader society. Churches often depend on recruitment by birth for growth.

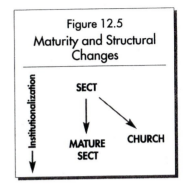

Figure 12.5
Maturity and Structural Changes

A third factor is commitment. For sects, commitment to their cause must be total. Members must be willing to give sacrificially of their time and resources for the sake of the community. In contrast, churches often require more commitment on the part of the priests and other full-time officials than of the lay people who have a wide range of commitments beyond the church.

A fourth factor is institutionalization. Sects are often new religious movements with weak institutional structures. They stress individual expression, egalitarianism, and new activities. Churches are often bureaucratic institutions in which hierarchy, tradition, and corporate rites are the norm. Because they are often large and living in the world, they may lack intimate fellowship among the members.

THE BIRTH OF NEW RELIGIOUS MOVEMENTS

Most new religions are born as folk movements among the oppressed and lower-class peoples, who see in them new avenues of hope. At this stage, these movements must define their identity in the context of the larger community of which they are a part, and they generally do so by attacking the old religions as dead, and by claiming to be the true religion. In time, such movements, if they survive, become institutionalized. As they gain numbers, power, and acceptance in the larger society, they seek to gain recognition by other religious bodies and to temper their sectarian separatism. In the process they often become churches. Other sects build institutional structures, but remain countercultural movements (Figure 12.5). We will return to this subject and examine it in greater detail in Chapter 13.

INSTITUTIONALIZATION

Religious groups, such as churches, are corporate bodies of human beings, which means they must take on social forms. Without these organizational structures, there can be no relationships among believers and no corporate worship. There is also little transmission of religious faith from one person to another, or from one generation to another.

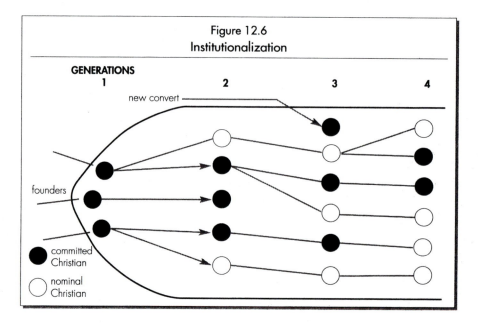

Figure 12.6
Institutionalization

A religious community builds social structures to express and preserve its faith, but, in time, these structures alter the relationships in the community through the process called 'institutionalization.' Eugene Peterson writes,

> [As new ministers we] take on responsibilities in the wonderful new world of worship and work. We advance in the ranks, and before we know it we're telling others what to do and how to do it. All this is good and right. And then we cross a line—we get bossy and cranky on behalf of God. We begin by finding in God a way to live rightly and well, and then along the way we take over God's work for him and take charge of it making sure others live rightly and well. We get the idea that we're important, self-important, because we're around the Important (1997, 151).

Christian leaders need to understand these process of institutionalization, and their positive and negative effects on religious movements, including Christian congregations, if they are to guard against becoming captives and tyrants in the institutions that structure religious life.

GENERATIONS IN AN INSTITUTION

Social institutions undergo changes from the time of their birth to their full-grown state. One way to look at these changes is to look at the successive generations of people in them (Figure 12.6). The first generation is made up of the "founding fathers and mothers." These are drawn together by a vision of something new for which they are willing to pay a high price. They may have to leave their old religious communities to join the new movement, resisting the pressures of friends and relatives to draw them back. They

Figure 12.7
The Processes of Institutionalization

HIGH COST - - - - - - - - - - - - - ➤	FOLLOW THE CROWD
STRONG FELLOWSHIP - - - - - - - ➤	IMPERSONAL
INFORMAL ROLES - - - - - - - - - ➤	FORMAL ROLES
AD HOC PROCESSES - - - - - - - - ➤	RATIONALIZED RULES
CHARISMATIC LEADER - - - - - - - ➤	ADMINISTRATOR
UNITY BASED ON TRUST - - - - - - ➤	UNITY BASED ON CREED AND ORGANIZATION

also face high risk, for there is no assurance that the new organization they found will survive. Cut off from their old world, they are bound together by strong ties of fellowship and oneness of purpose. New converts, who come later, are like these first-generation members, for they, too, often pay a high price to leave an old community to join the new one.

The second generation is made up of the children of the founders. Here a major structural change takes place. While the founders paid a high price to leave their old institutions and form the new one, their children grow up in the new structure. The cost they pay is not so high, but neither is their commitment. Most, however, acquire secondhand the vision that motivated their parents.

By the third, fourth, and fifth generations, the new movement has become "the establishment." These generations grow up in the institutional religious structures. In Christian churches the children go to Sunday school and youth meetings with their friends. In Christian schools and hospitals, people work their way through the ranks to positions of leadership. To remain in the institution is, for them, the path of least resistance and cost. The strength of these later generations is their stability and continuity over time. The life of the church, like any religious institution, depends on one generation passing on the faith to the next. The weakness is the threat of nominalism. The spiritual vision of the founders is dimmed as it is routinized in institutional life. What began as a movement becomes a bureaucratic organization.

PROCESSES OF INSTITUTIONALIZATION

Over the generations, an institution normally grows and matures, and with maturation come the problems of middle age—loss of vision and hardening of the categories. This institutionalization of human organization is characterized by a number of related processes (Figure 12.7). We have already noted the high cost of starting a new movement and the camaraderie among new members. Later, these shift to an attitude of maintaining the status quo in an often increasingly impersonal environment.

In the process of institutionalization, informal relationships give way to formally defined social roles. At the beginning there is often no official leader, no secretary, no treasurer. Different members volunteer to do the work. If the organization grows, roles are formalized. Instead of deciding each week who will lead, the group decides that one person will be their regular leader. But this transforms their relationships to the leader, who is no longer John or Mary, but more formally Rev. Smith.

Similarly, ad hoc arrangements are replaced by rules in which relationships are standardized. At the outset, many things are handled by casual decisions. In a new church the leader may ask someone at the last moment to lead the singing or read the Scriptures. Later, such arrangements must be made well in advance so that the names can be put into a bulletin. At first, there is no fixed order of service. Changes in the program can be made during the service. Later, the liturgical order becomes fixed, and, in time, may even be considered sacred.

Formal rules are a function of size. They are necessary for large institutions to operate smoothly. They are also functions of culture. Western cultures, with their obsession for uniformity, efficiency, rationality, and order, tend to organize institutions along the lines of bureaucracies in which tasks and relationships are divided and allocated to different people. The result is a mechanical approach to human organization, in which people become standardized parts in a human 'factory.' The goals are production and gain. In many parts of the world institutions are built on the model of kinship groups or small, local communities, and remain more negotiational over the generations. Formal rules are also a function of class. The higher educated elite are often more concerned with formal organization, long-range planning, and control. The common folk and the poor are more interested in existential experiences and meeting everyday needs, and have little concern for formal rules and structures. This is one reason why charismatic-style churches appeal more to commoners than to upper-class people.

Founders of new movements tend to be dynamic prophet-leaders who command a following by means of their personal charisma. Such leaders can rarely lead a mature, established organization, because they act too much on personal impulse, outside established procedures. They must be succeeded by priestly leaders if their movement is to endure. If they are replaced by other charismatic leaders, those leaders will re-create the organization in line with their own vision. Formalized roles and relationships call for administrators who identify with the people, and are selected by institutional processes. This transition from a charismatic founder to a bureaucratic leader is crucial for the survival of any organization.

Finally, unity in the group based on trust and fellowship gives way to unity based on explicit roles and creeds. In the intimacy of early gatherings, everyone knows everyone personally. Differences in belief are bridged by mutual trust. As the institution grows and becomes more impersonal, the bonds holding members together must be more formally defined. The result is a growing sense that relationships in the group are becoming impersonal.

Figure 12.8
Dangers of Institutionalization

VISION ----------------➤	ROUTINE
GOAL ORIENTATION --------➤	SELF-MAINTAINANCE
FLEXIBILITY ---------------➤	INFLEXIBILITY
FOCUS ON PEOPLE ---------➤	FOCUS ON PROGRAM
FELLOWSHIP AND	
PARTICIPATION ------------➤	ALIENATION
PEOPLE CONTROL	THE INSTITUTION
THE INSTITUTION ---------➤	CONTROLS PEOPLE

BENEFITS AND DANGERS OF INSTITUTIONALIZATION

Some measure of institutionalization is essential for any corporate religious action. Informal activities consume a great deal of time and energy to simply maintain themselves. New decisions must be made for each event, no matter how small. Institutionalization reduces the constant effort necessary to operate the organization by standardizing the decision-making process. Institutions are also necessary to mobilize large numbers of people and resources to carry out otherwise impossible tasks. They also support specialists who articulate the religious beliefs of the movement, and train leaders for various activities

Institutionalization also has its dangers (Figure 12.8). What begins as an organization to help the people often becomes a bureaucracy of religious elite who dominate the common folk and keep them bound with legalism and tradition. In the process the original vision is often lost, and religious roles become jobs that people use to compete for status and money. For example, to evangelize a neighboring community, a church forms a committee. To keep its minutes, a secretary is appointed and an office set up. In the end, the secretary, pressured to type letters and file reports, sees little connection between those tasks and the evangelization of the neighborhood, and works largely for pay.

Another danger is that vision gives way to self-maintenance. Religious organizations are often started to serve people in need, but as time passes, more and more of their effort and resources are spent on running and improving the institutional structures.

A third danger is that flexibility gives way to inflexibility. In the early stages of an institution's life, decisions are made on an ad hoc basis. Rules and procedures are established to reduce the number of decisions that must be made, but these also reduce flexibility in decision making.

Too many exceptions to administrative rules make them useless, so pressures build to ensure conformity.

A final danger is the shift in focus from people to programs. Young institutions are generally more people-oriented. There is a strong emphasis on fellowship and meeting one another's needs. As institutions grow, more and more emphasis is placed on building programs and maintaining institutional structures. In a showdown, institutional needs take priority over human needs, and the institution gradually controls more of the people it sought to help. The focus has subtly shifted from meeting others' needs to meeting its own needs.

CHRISTIAN RESPONSE

What implications does this analysis of leadership and institutions have for the task of the Christian church and its mission to the world? Westerners are masters at building formal bureaucratic organizations to 'get the job done.' They organize committees, draw up constitutions and by-laws, set up accounting procedures, and expect converts to know what is going on, and how to fit in. Often, however, converts are common folk who have no experience in running formal bureaucracies, or of filling specialized religious roles. Moreover, they live in cultures that organize social activities on the basis of kinship and community practices. Consequently, the Western-style organizations missions have frequently built often have not worked. Unfortunately, local people have often been blamed when, in fact, the problem is with a penchant to build mechanistic bureaucracies based on specialization, formal procedures, and hierarchy of control.[3] People in event-oriented societies are expected to show up at the set time for services, keep quiet in church, and obey the rules—exceptions, excuses, and tardiness are not appreciated. Common folk, however, tend to create loosely structured, ad hoc arrangements for group activities. Events are often organized or canceled on the spur of the moment, and everyone is involved, often with no clear lines of command and little apparent order. Most missionaries and ministers find it hard to live this way, so they continually seek to impose their organizational order on the young churches.

Another problem concerns the nature of leadership. Westerners think in terms of full-time trained specialists who are paid for their work. They find it hard to think of self-supporting lay leaders in charge of the church, and doing the preaching and teaching. For the most part, Western formal ways of organizing the church have failed because they

---

3. For an excellent discussion of Western bureaucratic organizations, see Berger et al. 1973 and Ellul 1964.

do not fit the way common folk organize their activities. Ironically, Western missions have often been more willing to contextualize the gospel than church polity. We now offer suggestions emerging out of the study of leaders and institutions to encourage new churches and their leaders to make an effective impact for Christ in their cultural context.

LEADERS

How should leadership be organized in young churches around the world? Westerners place great emphasis on training leaders for formal roles in bureaucratic institutions. The prevailing view is that leaders must be able to read, and that some formal education is necessary to prepare pastors, evangelists, Bible teachers, administrators, and other church leaders. Consequently, Western missionaries often feel that they must remain in charge of the work until young leaders complete degrees. This takes years, so young churches remain dependent on outside leaders far too long, and bright young natural leaders leave to start independent churches or drift into other vocations. The notions of ministries as paid specialized professions, and of the nature of ordination must be challenged before they are exported around the world.

MOBILIZING NATURAL LEADERS

All societies have leaders and ways of preparing them. These culturally relevant approaches to training leaders need to be studied and adapted to the context of the church in that place. Many depend on the emergence of 'natural leaders'—those people who naturally take on leadership responsibilities in the events of everyday life. These are often elders who have learned wisdom from experience. They may also have special gifts, charisma, a vision, and a drive that lead others to trust their decisions. The most rapidly growing churches are those that identify and empower such natural leaders among the new converts. Generally these lack schooling and many cannot read, but they can motivate and organize the common people to carry on the work of the church, and to evangelize their neighbors.

Building the church on natural leaders is not new. Paul spent a few years in one city and planted a church. He then turned it over to local converts and kept in touch with them by mail as they needed help. The same pattern is used by the rapidly growing independent churches, which we will examine in the next chapter. Their founders are generally dynamic, prophet-type leaders, who command the attention of others. Among them are Simon Kimbangu, founder of the Church of Jesus Christ, Kimbongu; Isaiah Shemba, prophet of the Zulu Nazareth Church; Josiah Oshitelu, founder of the Church of the Lord Aladura (all

of Africa), Bhakta Singh of the Bhakta Singh Fellowship (India), and
Watchman Nee of the Little Flower church (China).

TRAINING LEADERS

Young churches need not only natural leaders who plant churches,
they also need trained leaders who are Bible scholars, Bible translators,
theologians, and specialists in other ministries. As churches grow, they
often associate with one another, and with the church worldwide. How
should leaders be trained for these more formal and often academic
roles?

In the past missionaries have usually started schools patterned on
those in which they studied in the West. Speaking of Africa Pius
Wakatama writes,

> Most missions establish Bible schools to train prospective clergy and to
> give a good biblical background to laymen. They are generally patterned
> after Bible schools in America which concentrate only on teaching the
> Bible and related studies. . . . The result is that we now have many trained
> young people from Bible schools who are unemployed. Unlike the well-
> to-do churches of America, African churches do not have such positions
> as assistant pastor, youth pastor, youth minister, minister of music, min-
> ister of Christian education and so on. . . . [T]hey feel cheated. Their
> diplomas do not help them to secure jobs or to be helpful and needed
> members of their communities (1976, 51–52).

In training leaders, particularly for rural churches, it is important to
select those who are recognized leaders in their communities. Such
pastors need wisdom more than knowledge, and faithfulness and holy
lives more than special skills. Moreover, in training these leaders, it is
important that they not be educated beyond the level of their ministry.
Most church planting has always been done by lay leaders and pastors
with little formal training, living on the level with the people they serve.

In preparing leaders at this level, it is important to use indigenous
methods of training. Often this involves a method of apprenticeship, in
which young leaders are discipled by older, experienced ones. Young
leaders may also be asked by their churches to occupy different positions and demonstrate their aptitudes for ministry. In such settings,
they benefit most from informal biblical education.

Bible schools and seminaries are needed to train leaders for some
urban churches, for preparing biblical materials for use in the
churches, and for doing theological reflection in that context. Today, as
churches around the world form global communities, it is important
that they have leaders who can participate in international organizations. It is important that African, Indian, Chinese, and Latin American

theologians join in dialogue with North American and European theologians, and that mission leaders from these lands partner in reaching out to new peoples. Leaders at this level need education in the best Bible schools and seminaries the world has to offer, but it is also important that they break out of their own cultural patterns and become global in their thinking.

PROPHETS AND PRIESTS

Knowing how prophets and priests function can help mission leaders understand the dynamics of a living church. Evangelists, revival preachers, and visionaries are its prophets. They help the church see the big picture, listen for the voice of God, and be open to renewal and transformation. When traditionalism and institutionalism clog the arteries of the church, prophets open up new ways of living as God's people in the world.

Prophets alone, however, cannot maintain the life of the church. It needs stability and continuity over time, not a radical revolution every year. Moreover, prophets are often impatient with ordinary Christians and ignore them. Prophets demand so high a commitment that few can follow them. It is priests, in the form of pastors, teachers, counselors, and administrators, who maintain the life of the church in the long run. They instruct the people, minister to the weak and faltering, and revive the defeated. They pastor the sick and bereaved. They conduct the rites of intensification that renew spiritual life weekly, and in so doing maintain the life of the community.

The church needs both prophets and priests. Throughout the Old Testament we hear much of the prophets God sent to bring renewal to Israel. Casual readers tend to overlook the fact that day to day, week to week, and year to year, it was the priests in the hundreds of villages and towns who conducted sacrifices, organized worship services, nurtured the weak, cared for the aged, and taught what it meant to be God's people in their particular times and places. They initiated the newborn, married the young, and buried the dead, and, in so doing, reenacted God's presence in the midst of his people. When the people forgot God, he raised up prophets to remind them of himself. That renewal, however, had to be institutionalized in the life of the people for it to continue.[4] The prophets were often public figures, but their lives were often hard. Priests were a part of commu-

---

4. Elijah started a School of the Prophets, but, in a sense, that is an oxymoron. Schooling by its very nature moves in time to training priests. We see this in the West with the gradual movement from Bible institutes to Bible colleges, and finally to academically oriented Christian colleges.

nity life, and their lives often trudging and tedious. Together, however, prophets and priests kept the Word of the Lord alive among the remnant in Israel.

MISSIONARIES AND EXECUTIVES

A study of the relationship between prophet and priest clarifies the tension often found in missions between missionaries and home administrators. The former are more like prophets, concerned with the big story and with action. They are on the front lines. The latter are more like priests, concerned with details, and proper and realistic procedures—reflecting the established order. Missionaries chafe at waiting a year or two for funds for particular projects, so they contact friends and home churches to get the job done. Administrators oppose working outside normal channels because each exception threatens the order they have established.

In missions, too, each needs the other. Prophets often start great programs, but to maintain these, the programs must be routinized and turned over to priestly leaders. In time institutionalized religion becomes rigid and needs renewal, and this comes through the mouth of prophets. As churches grow, however, some attention to structure and polity is essential.

CHURCH ORGANIZATION

How can a study of religious institutions help us to understand the young churches missionaries help plant? We will look at a few lessons we can learn by way of illustration.

FOREIGN INSTITUTIONS

One characteristic of Western Christian missions has been the development of complex formal social institutions, such as churches, denominational organizations, schools, hospitals, and youth associations. Most Western missionaries belong to the educated elite in their churches, and have learned how to organize programs and build institutions to carry out the work of formal religion. It should not be a surprise, therefore, that they spent a great deal of time and effort in building institutions to carry out their work. Most missionaries today find themselves spending much of their time and effort in building and maintaining these institutions.

The introduction of formal organizations has often had a destructive effect on the level of local churches. It has destroyed the spontaneity of everyday religious life, and eliminated most lay people from participation, because they lack education, specialized skills, and knowledge to participate in the formal roles of a highly organized church. Institutionalization has also led to the professionalization of leadership and alienation of the laity. The churches that do grow spontaneously in most parts of the world are those that are loosely organized, flexible, and naturally reproducing themselves.

A further problem is that Western-style organizations are costly. They require buildings, equipment, budgets, and salaried personnel. For the most part, these resources come from abroad. The local churches cannot afford them. Consequently, when missions withdraw, the churches are left with heavy financial burdens to simply maintain them. Church leaders cannot afford to let these die, for this brings disgrace on them and costs many Christians their jobs. But there are often not enough funds in the churches to maintain the institutions as outsiders established and maintained them. This has created a huge liability for local churches all over the world. One common solution has been for leaders to raise funds from the outside, but this creates a dependency and helplessness that sap the churches of vital outreach ministries.[5]

INDIGENOUS CHURCHES

By the mid-nineteenth century it became clear in the modern mission movement that in many parts of the world the church was more like a 'potted plant' maintained by outside care than a 'tree growing and reproducing in native soil.' This led to a strong cry for planting indigenous churches. Henry Venn and Rufus Anderson outlined three essentials for such churches: they should be self-supporting, self-governing, and self-propagating. In institutional terms, this means that churches should have economic, political, and social autonomy. To this they could have added self-theologizing or theological autonomy. Together these can lead to self-expression. Unfortunately, such is often not the case.

Despite great emphasis on the Three Selves, churches for decades remained dependent on outside resources. In part, this was due to the fact that missionaries often decided when the people were mature enough to govern themselves, and that churches did not want to give up financial aid. Furthermore, in many cases the missions set up local organizations to govern the churches, but these organizations were largely Western in character. The result is that today young churches around the world are struggling to operate denominational structures they cannot afford and that do not fit their cultural patterns of organization. Moreover, given their experiences with mission agencies, young

---

5. Charles Forman's discussion of the history of financial dependence in Pacific Island churches clearly demonstrates this problem as well as suggesting solutions (Forman 1985).

churches believe it is their task to maintain the church, and the task of outside missionaries to reach other peoples.

In planting indigenous churches, it is important from the outset to help churches take responsibility for their life, and to avoid creating economic or political dependency. This requires a major shift in the way missionaries and leaders think of their work. Too often in the past, they came as spiritual parents. They were the centers of activity, and their beliefs and practices dictated the norms that converts should emulate. This approach leads to young churches dependent on outside leadership and resources, and Christians who are often accused of being foreigners.

Planting churches that are autonomous from the beginning requires an incarnational view of mission in which the people are seen as active participants in organizing and planting churches, and missionaries as catalysts helping them to study and apply Scripture for themselves. Monte Cox points out (1997b) that this shift from a paternalistic to an incarnational view of missions has major consequences in the way missionaries view their work (Figure 12.9).[6] First, missionaries need to be generalists, who call on specialists to help deal with specific needs. Overspecialization has fragmented Christian ministries and undermined the central vision of ministering to whole people. Second, the goal of missions is the transformation of people in every area of their lives. This process begins with conversion but must lead to new lives and new communities that point to the reign of Christ on earth. Third, ministries must be owned and operated by the local churches. Only then will they take responsibility for the gospel in their setting. Grassroots leadership must be developed to avoid the cumbersome hierarchies of large institutions, and indigenous organizational structures should be used as much as possible. Fourth, ministries must be appropriate to the need. Modern leaders see money and large-scale programs as the answer to particular needs. Spontaneous church growth takes place when people matter more than programs, and they are allowed to operate in ways and with technologies familiar to them. Finally, mission should lead to sustainability without dependence. To achieve this, leaders must tap the local resources and develop local participation and leadership. It is important to empower local Christians, and help them develop the capacities to carry on their work with-

6. The points listed here adapt and summarize Cox's analysis of the shift that is taking place in Christian relief and development agencies as they reassess the failures of Western programs in the past. The same principles that argue for a long-range focus on transformation rather than relief applies in the church to the move from paternalistic to incarnational ministries. In education the shift is from pedagogy to androgogy, in which students are seen as active participants in their education.

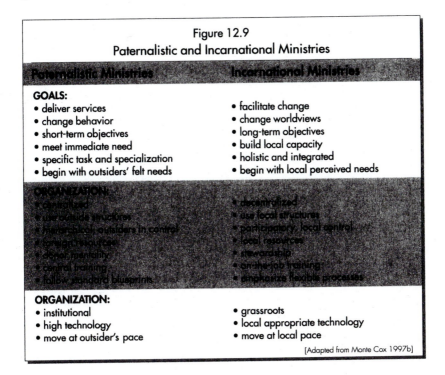

Figure 12.9
Paternalistic and Incarnational Ministries

Paternalistic Ministries	Incarnational Ministries
GOALS:	
• deliver services	• facilitate change
• change behavior	• change worldviews
• short-term objectives	• long-term objectives
• meet immediate need	• build local capacity
• specific task and specialization	• holistic and integrated
• begin with outsiders' felt needs	• begin with local perceived needs
ORGANIZATION:	
• centralized	• decentralized
• use outside structures	• use local structures
• hierarchical, outsiders in control	• participatory, local control
• foreign resources	• local resources
• donor mentality	• stewardship
• central training	• on-the-job training
• follow standard blueprints	• emphasize flexible processes
ORGANIZATION:	
• institutional	• grassroots
• high technology	• local appropriate technology
• move at outsider's pace	• move at local pace
	[Adapted from Monte Cox 1997b]

out outside control. Community involvement is more important than money for sustainability.

Missionaries and church leaders face other problems when they hand over institutions built under the paternalistic model of ministry to local churches. This involves not only a change in leadership, but in the whole institutional structure, including funding, accountability, and ownership. National leaders are often caught in the middle of the tensions that rise in such radical changes.

INSTITUTIONAL RENEWAL

Any long-range vision for missions must include not only the planting of new churches, but also the renewal of old ones. The former without the latter eventually leads to nations full of dead and dying churches. The birth of new congregations is no guarantee that they will remain spiritually alive. In many parts of the world today, lands once evangelized are now populated by nominal Christians.

Many missionaries and church leaders have tried to establish "steady-state" churches—churches that remain forever strong in faith and ministry. But there is no spiritual "steady state," neither in churches nor in individuals. Over time, the institutionalization of religious life leads to nominalism and traditionalism. In view of this almost inevitable situation, is there no hope for organized churches? Some reject the construction of institutions, hoping to retain a relatively unstructured way of life, but antistructural movements have never been successful. They are unable to build stable, enduring churches, or to organize people into communities of common purpose and mutual support.

The answer to institutional rigidity in the church is to understand how the benefits of institutions can be applied to ecclesiastical structures so they can operate effectively in a particular context. By watching this process at work, leaders can try to keep organizational structures flexible and relevant, and to make organizations the servants of the church and not its masters. They can also foster institutional regeneration in which churches, as corporate bodies, are renewed periodically. This can be done, in part, by rituals of renewal in which members of the organization together seek God's guidance and revival. Festivals, religious fairs, and revival meetings have played powerful roles in reviving and reshaping churches around the world. To that end we turn now to examine the nature of religious movements, and to apply our findings to the life of the church.

13

RELIGIOUS MOVEMENTS

Religious systems, like other areas of culture, are constantly changing in response to internal social pressures, environmental changes, and foreign ideas and control. While change is a constant factor in all religions, many important religious movements are characterized by revolutionary shifts in worldviews. A study of these dramatic changes can help us understand the dynamics of folk religions and the nature of split-level Christianity.

One significant factor in change in the past four centuries has been the spread of Western culture and colonial power over much of the world. The impact of this cultural collision has led to numerous religious movements among the common people in traditional societies. Faced with foreign ideas, and overrun by the political and technological power of another culture, people respond in different ways, ranging from complete acceptance to total rejection of the new ways.

One common response to cultural confrontation has been the emergence of revitalization movements that restructure old religious belief systems to answer the needs of the people in their new context. In the last century, the Ghost Dance, Peyote, and Shawnee Prophet and other nativistic movements were born in North America. In this century, thousands of Cargo cults have arisen in New Guinea and Oceania (Worsley 1968; Strelen 1978), and more than six thousand messianic and independent church movements have been reported in Africa alone (Barrett 1968). In Japan New and New New Religious sects (McFarland 1967) and in South America spiritist movements have exploded in recent years. How can we understand these religious movements, and what implications do they have for Christian missions?

NEW EMERGING RELIGIOUS MOVEMENTS

Most religious movements emerge out of severe cultural crises generated by major physical disasters, or by collision with more powerful cultures such as the colonial expansion of the West. When cognitive dissonance reaches a point at which many people feel acutely uncomfortable, and widespread personal and social disorganization arises, a prophet often appears who promises a new satisfying way of life. He or she begins to proselytize, condemning the existing situation and claiming to revitalize the society by giving the people a new workable identity based on a mixture of ancient beliefs, imported and reinterpreted ideas, and new understandings. An aura of euphoria, fellowship, and altruistic endeavor often surrounds these movements in their early stages, but they frequently face militant opposition, ostracism, and persecution. Most of the new religions born in this century have emerged out of the clash between traditional small-scale societies and the powerful civilizations of India, China, and the West.

REVITALIZATION

In a seminal article, Anthony F. C. Wallace (1956) charts the course many of these new religious movements take. At their core, he notes, is a deliberate, organized effort by members of a society to construct a more satisfying worldview. Often these movements are started by "prophets," or charismatic leaders, who claim to have a special revelation and call people to follow them. These movements rise quickly, totally absorbing their adherents and giving them a whole new lifestyle. At the center is usually an expectation of the imminent coming of a new world with no sickness, poverty, or oppression. Frequently there is a prophecy of the destruction of their oppressors.

Using the organic analogy presented in Chapter 3, societies can be seen as operating to maintain the life of their members, and to reduce stresses that threaten to damage or disrupt this social life in much the same way that biological processes work to maintain life and reduce stress in living creatures. The ability of people to maintain their society depends on their ability to understand how it operates and how it relates to the environment. When they are under severe stress, and their worldview cannot reduce this to manageable levels, they may choose to keep their worldview and learn to live with the stress, or they may be willing to face the anxiety of changing their beliefs in order to reduce the stress they face.

Wallace defines five stages through which revitalization movements pass (Wallace 1956). There are marked differences among such movements in terms of specific beliefs, and each is colored by local cultural differences, but the basic structure of such movements is essentially the same (Figure 13.1).

1. *Steady state.* A people's culture provides the majority with more or less satisfying ways of meeting their needs and reducing their stress to

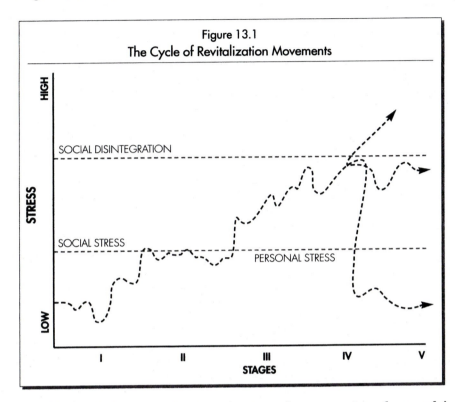

Figure 13.1
The Cycle of Revitalization Movements

a livable level. Changes take place that introduce stress into the people's everyday lives, but so long as these do not seriously interfere with their ability to meet their basic needs, they do not feel the need for radical change. Individuals experience intolerable stress from time to time, but most have support systems that enable them to reduce it to manageable levels. For most people, their culture is in a steady state.

2. *Increased individual stress.* Marked change is often induced in a society by prolonged droughts, epidemics, political subordination, or cultural conquest. Or there may be internal cultural tensions, as some areas of life undergo change while others lag behind. Such changes often generate in individuals increasingly severe stress, which they are unable to reduce through their normal coping mechanisms. If the old cultural ways no longer deal with their anxieties, individuals often look for alternative cultural solutions to their problems. But this increases their stress, because people are afraid that acceptance of new practices will undermine all their existing beliefs and customs, and that the new ways will be no better than the old, There is anxiety in leaving the security of old and familiar ways of life, however imperfect it is, and striking out on a new and uncertain course.

3. *Cultural distortion.* Faced with prolonged stress and no satisfactory cultural way of dealing with it, people respond in different ways. Rigid individuals prefer to live with stress rather than change their ways. More flexible people change some of their beliefs in attempts to reduce the tensions. Some turn to alcoholism, become depressed or experience malaise, or drop out of society altogether. Others turn to violence or reject the social norms. The result is an increase in conflicts between various groups in the society, between different sets of beliefs and values. This leads to a further increase in stress. In the end, people are disillusioned with their worldview and lose a sense of meaning in life.

4. *Revitalization.* If this process of deterioration is not halted, the society will die out, or be defeated and absorbed by another society. Frequently, however, a revitalization movement, often religious in nature, brings in a new set of beliefs and ways of coping with life in a more satisfactory way, thus restoring meaning to existence and renewal to the culture.

Revitalization often begins with a prophet who, in a vision, sees a new world that provides a fresh explanation to life and its possibilities. The prophet has often experienced an abrupt and dramatic change of personality, leading to significant changes in lifestyle, such as the dropping of deep-seated habits like alcoholism. The leader's message of a new worldview generally calls for the destruction of the old world and the emergence of a new utopian society. The prophet is the final authority in defining the message. People are converted and join the movement as followers. A few cluster around the prophet as disciples, and later become leaders who interpret the message and institutionalize the movement. Generally there is opposition from outside, and the leader must devise strategies to face the resistance.

For individuals, revitalization leads to a more active and purposeful life. As increasing numbers of people join the movement, a social revitalization takes place. Relationships are renewed and group action enthusiastically pursued. If the new activities help to reduce stress and restore meaning to the society, they soon become part of the social order.

5. *New steady state.* If these religious movements succeed, they lead to a new steady state in which people once again can cope with stress and find meaning in their existence. Then begin the processes of institutionalization discussed in Chapter 12. Administrative leadership is set up, membership defined, organization patterns established, funds raised, and buildings constructed. When this takes place, these new religious movements face the question of their relationship to the world around them. Some become politicized and end up as nativistic movements, seeking to reestablish the people's power in the political arena.

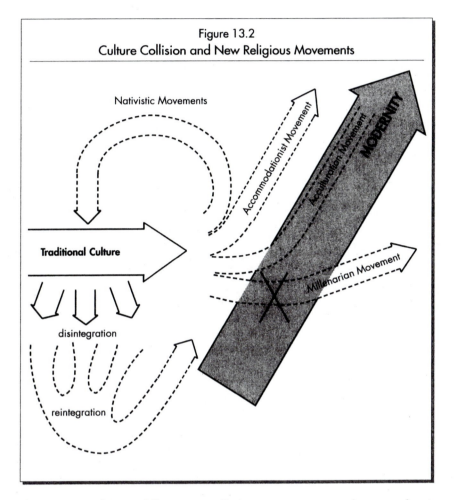

Figure 13.2
Culture Collision and New Religious Movements

Nativistic Movements

Accommodationist Movement

Acculturation Movement

MODERNITY

Traditional Culture

Millenarian Movement

disintegration

reintegration

Others reject this and become religious movements that emphasize spiritual realities and reject any political involvement.

While many new religious movements fail, others succeed in achieving a cultural transformation and a new steady state. Christianity, Islam, the Reformation, communism, and Buddhism were born in revitalization movements. As Wallace points out, probably few people have lived who have not been involved at some time or other in the revitalization process.

TYPES OF MOVEMENTS

Harold Turner (1981) provides a useful taxonomy for understanding new religious movements based on the solutions they offer to the crises they face (Figure 13.2). *Nativistic* movements seek to solve crises and improve the temporal lot of the people by returning to traditional roots and reviving certain aspects of the people's religious past. The present is seen as evil and must be destroyed in order that the people may go back to a former golden age. A classic example of a nativisitic movement is the Ghost Dance that spread among some Native American tribes which were facing economic deprivation and disease at the end of the nineteenth century. In 1870, Taivo, a Paiute, had a vision from the "Great Spirit" that a massive earthquake would destroy everyone, including the settlers who were taking away their land, but that after three days, all Indians who joined the dance would be resurrected. When this did not occur, the movement died. It was revived twenty years later when Wovoka, a prophet, who had learned some Christian theology, had a vision of heaven and the happy reunion of the living and dead in an unending utopia. The Great Spirit told him that if the people danced the Ghost Dance, the old earth would be wiped out by an earthquake or flood, and a new one would appear. The movement spread among the Plains Indians as a resistance to the encroachment of European culture, but it came to a sad ending when those who resisted the settlers died at Wounded Knee. Similar movements are found among the Australian aboriginals, and in Kenya, where the Mau Mau movement mustered traditional rituals to overthrow European rule after World War II.

In *accommodation* movements, sometimes called importation movements, people respond to crisis and culture clash by seeking neither to lose their identity by assimilation into a foreign culture, nor to revive their past. Rather, they desire a new identity in which there is a selective combination of old values and imported riches. The Cargo Cults of New Guinea are examples of accommodation movements. Reported as early as 1893, they have proliferated in great numbers to the present. An important theme in present-day cults is that "cargo," the Tok Pisin word for trade goods such as steel axes, canned goods, rifles, and jeeps, will arrive by ship or plane and be given to the New Guinea people by their ancestors. In preparation to receive these goods, villagers cleared landing strips, erected bamboo control towers, and built cargo sheds. Men stood ready with tin-can microphones to guide the planes to safe landings. To counteract the influence of such exaggeration the Australian government arranged for cult leaders to be taken to see modern Australian factories and stores, in hopes they would give up their beliefs. Many returned, however, more convinced that the ancestors had, in fact, sent them goods, but that the colonial 'masters' had intercepted these on the way.

In an interesting variant, the people of the island of New Hanover tried to elect Lyndon Johnson as their president in 1964 so that they would receive the cargo. Bos Malik, their leader, told them they would have to buy Johnson, so they refused to pay taxes to the Australian administrators and collected more than $82,000. When an armed force was sent to suppress the tax revolt, Malik promised that the liner *Queen Mary* would arrive with the cargo, and American troops would drive out the Australian oppressors. Obviously, no American troops appeared, and the revolt was crushed.

Messianic movements frequently emerge among people who have had some exposure to the Christian message, and have heard of a messiah that will come to deliver them from their current plight. A prophet (or messiah) is established as leader and often becomes a political figure representing "his people" against perceived oppression. These commonly occur when uprooted, desperate masses in towns and countryside, living on the margins of society, rise up in rebellion. The movements value equality, abolition of rank, minimization of sex differences, having property in common, and simplicity of speech and manners. They tend to maximize religious experience, and oppose bureaucratic institutions. In short, they seek to create a liminal community. Over time, the impetus for these movements becomes exhausted, and they become institutions among other institutions, often more fanatical and militant than the rest for the reason that their members feel themselves to be the unique bearers of universal human values. Millenarian movements, which focus on the coming golden age when everything will be perfect (as that culture envisions it), are an extension of messianic movements.

The emergence of new religions is a worldwide phenomenon. We will examine only a few areas of the world to illustrate their growth and diversity.

RELIGIOUS MOVEMENTS IN TRADITIONAL SOCIETIES

Not long ago, Christians believed that the religions of tribal peoples, which they saw as little more than superstition, would be replaced by Christianity. This has not been the case. Traditional religions often persist as undercurrents after people become Christians. The result is a split-level religious scene in which orthodox Christian beliefs coexist in uneasy tension with traditional beliefs. Christians attend church on Sunday, but during the week turn to the shaman, magician, and diviner for help in the problems of everyday life.

A second phenomenon is the emergence of new religious movements wherever tribal religions confront high religions, such as Christianity, Islam, and Hinduism. These independent movements belong neither to traditional religion, nor to the engulfing high religion, both of which are often hostile toward them. Most are local indigenous religious re-

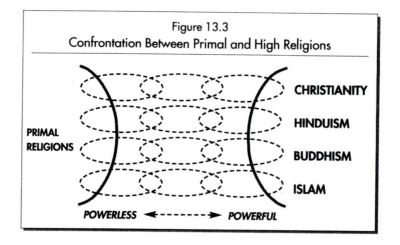

Figure 13.3
Confrontation Between Primal and High Religions

CHRISTIANITY

HINDUISM

PRIMAL
RELIGIONS

BUDDHISM

ISLAM

POWERLESS ◄ - - - - - - ► POWERFUL

sponses created by the common people which incorporate elements from both the tribal and high religions in various ways. Roughly, these movements range along a continuum between the primal and the high religion involved in the encounter (Figure 13.3).

Many independent movements have emerged out of the encounter between Christianity and tribal religions. One example is the Ratana Church of New Zealand, founded by Wiremu Ratana among the Maori during the traumatic worldwide epidemic of influenza in 1918. Today the church has nearly thirty thousand adherents. In Africa Simon Kimbangu founded the largest independent church in Africa, drawing on different religious traditions to shape his ideas. Earlier both of these leaders were members of Christian communities, but they broke from these to start new movements using forms and symbols deeply rooted in their local cultures.

The founders of other independent movements often had more remote contacts with Christianity, and their teachings are garbled understandings of the gospel. A striking example is found among the Western Guaymi Indians of Panama. In 1961 a young prophetess named Delia Atencio proclaimed a new message, calling her people to resist the incursions of Spanish influence.

> Delia Atencio . . . had visions of the Virgin Mary and her "husband," Jesus Christ, coming up out of the Fonseca River with a secret message for the Guaymi. God had given them five years in which to obey him, by withdrawing from the disturbing Latin (Western) contacts and goods; by following a strict moral code including rejection of polygamy, alcohol, traditional festivals, and fighting; by working hard and following the new religious forms she taught them. . . . If they did all this faithfully, God

would suddenly bring a new paradisiacal life to the Guaymi with happiness and prosperity. They called her "Mama Chi," and her movement spread to over twenty thousand Guaymi before her death in 1964 (H. Turner 1981, 47).

Another example of traditional revitalization movements is the Cargo Cults of Melanesia, which we noted earlier. For more than one hundred years, missionaries and traders in the area have reported revitalization movements based on local myths, which said that someday culture heroes or ancestors will return to earth and bring the people prosperity. These include the "Taro Cult" of New Guinea, the "Vailala Madness" of Papua, and the "Tuka Cult" of the Fiji Islands. Peter Worsley notes that these movements have the same central themes:

> [T]he world is about to end in a terrible cataclysm. Thereafter God, the ancestors, or some local culture hero will appear and inaugurate a blissful paradise on earth. Death, old age, illness, and evil will be unknown. The riches of the white man will accrue to the Melanesians (1997, 343).

The Cargo Cults emerged out of the encounter of traditional societies of stone and wood technologies with the people of European origin who were perceived as radically different and infinitely more powerful. Above all, these strangers had cargo, goods which the Melanesians attributed to the white skins' superior magic. When European missionaries arrived with all these things, the people sent delegations to ask for more people with cargo. When oil companies drilled wells, the people remembered that their ancestors would return through a hole in the ground (Walls 1996, 136).

NEW RELIGIONS IN LATIN AMERICA

Many new religions have emerged in Latin America in this century, most of them spiritist in nature. Among them are Umbanda, Candombl, Macumba, Xango, and Kardecisim. "Spiritism" here means the evoking of spirits of the dead to receive news from them, to consult them (necromancy), or to bring them under the control of humans for good or evil. It is rooted in a worldview that affirms that spirits exist as live and active powers in nature, and that they are interested in communicating and interacting with human beings. Many spiritists affirm that the souls survive after death, and that some of these, called "mediums," make contact with people still living and transmit knowledge to them from the spirit world that enhances their lives.

One root of Latin American spiritism was the religious beliefs of the African slaves brought to the New World. Many became Catholics, but in private they retained their beliefs in spirits, magic, ancestors, and

---

Figure 13.4
Orixás and Catholic Saints

In Umbanda the African Orixás are identified with Catholic saints.

Oxalá	• the creator, corresponds to	Jesus
Iemanjá	• mother of all *orixás*, is	Virgin Mary
Ogun	• god of iron, corresponds to	Saint George
Oxossi	• god of the forest, is	Saint Sebastian
Xangó	• god of the storm, is	Saint Jerome
Oxum	• is seen as	Saint Catherine
Omulu	• is seen as	Saint Lazarus

divination. They gave Christian names to their spirits, and linked two religious systems (Figure 13.4). A second root was the widespread veneration of saints by the Spanish Catholic settlers. A third were Native American religious beliefs, which influenced Umbanda in particular.

Umbanda, Candombl, Macumba, and Xango are sometimes referred to as 'low spiritism,' because they initially appealed to the common folk. Umbanda was founded in 1908 by a medium near Rio de Janeiro, and organized into the Spiritist Union of Umbanda at its First Congress, held in Brazil in 1941. Kardecism, on the other hand, appeals to the intellectual elite of Brazil. Allan Kardec, a teacher in France, became interested in the strange paranormal phenomena which occurred with the Fox sisters in March 1848, in Hydesville, Pennsylvania. He declared that spiritism is not a form of the occult. He wrote,

> Spiritism is the new science which by irrefutable proof comes to reveal to humankind the existence and nature of the spirit world and its relation to the material world. It shows us this world no longer as supernatural but, on the contrary, as one of the living and unceasing active forces of nature, as the source of infinite phenomena heretofore uncomprehended and therefore rejected as the domain of the fantastic and marvelous. . . . Spiritism is the key which helps us to explain everything easily (Kroker 1987, 1).

Kardec outlined the basic laws of spiritism in a book called *Livro dos Espritos* (Book of the Spirits, 1857), in which he maintained that his methods enabled humans to communicate with the spirits.

Spiritism is growing rapidly in much of Latin America today. Many people are attracted to Kardecism because of its simplicity and its claims to scientific authority. Popular forms of spiritism appeal particularly to the millions migrating to the big cities, where they are often lost and confused. Spiritist teachings and small groups provide support and self-confidence for the uprooted, offering them, in their oppressive subexistence, a new hope for a better life. Young people are attracted because it is easy for them to become leaders since little formal training is required. Most spiritist movements do not require members to leave their traditional churches, and allow people to mix their beliefs.

One of the greatest reasons for the growth of these new spiritist religions is that they give answers to the everyday problems of human life by making available to followers the possibility of communicating with the spirits. The living can communicate with dead loved ones. The sick and demon possessed are promised healing and deliverance. The poor are assured material blessings.

The relationship of Latin American spiritism to Christianity is complex. A great many Catholics practice both Christian and spiritist rites, often with little censure by local Catholic priests.[1] A few priests have strongly opposed this two-tier approach to religion, but many are willing to work with spiritistic healers, many of whom heal and do great works in Jesus' name.

The attitude of traditional evangelical churches toward spiritism has been a mixture of indifference and fear. Missionaries and church leaders rarely deal with matters related to Umbanda, Macumba, and Kardecisim, because of their own modern dualistic worldview and their fear rooted in a lack of knowledge of these movements. Few people go to Protestant pastors for help, because they do not deal with problems of magic and spirits (Kroker 1987, 4). Charismatic leaders reject spiritism, but they often use worship forms and practices that resemble those found in spiritism.

NEW AND NEW-NEW JAPANESE RELIGIONS

In this century more than 23,000 new religions have emerged in Japan, attracting more than 57 million followers. Some, such as Sokka-Gakkai, Rissho Koseikai, and Seicho No Ie, emerged after World War I, during a period of severe economic deprivation and military totalitarianism. After World War II, many new religions such as Tensho Kotai Jingu-kyo and Ananai-kyo and New-New religions (*shin-shinshukyo*, post 1960) such as Kurozumikyo and Tensho Kotaijingu-kyo have arisen (Haracre 1986). An estimated ten or twenty new new religions are now founded in Tokyo alone each year.

Since 1549 Christianity has grown to about 1.6 percent of the Japanese population. The new and new-new Japanese religions now have an estimated membership of more than 20 percent of the people. What explains their rapid growth, and what do they offer that attracts so many followers?

Neill McFarland (1967) argues that following World War I Japan faced an invasion of modernity, a severe economic depression, and a major earthquake in 1923—all of which contributed to a cultural iden-

---

1. David Barrett's *The World Christian Encyclopedia* reports that more than sixty million Brazilians are practitioners of both Catholicism and spiritism (1982, 188).

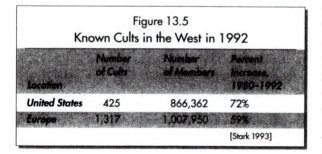

Figure 13.5
Known Cults in the West in 1992

Location	Number of Cults	Number of Members	Percent Increase, 1980–1992
United States	425	866,362	72%
Europe	1,317	1,007,950	59%

[Stark 1993]

tity crisis. The defeat in World War II, the public declaration by the emperor that he was not a god, the desperate social, economic, and spiritual conditions from 1945 to 1955, and the ongoing invasion of modernity with its secularism and materialism compounded the identity crisis. Buddhism and State Shintoism failed to provide meaningful understandings of life, so the people are presently turning to new religions that combine Buddhist, Shintoism, Christian, and modern themes in new ways. These promise the people hope in a confusing and changing world—health, wealth, success and happiness, and a restoration of good family life by affirming ancestor veneration. The appeal of these religions is that they offer answers to the central questions of folk religion. Moreover, they offer a strong sense of community in small intimate groups (*hoza* circles) in which people can share their troubles and blessings, and in mass ceremonies which affirm their new corporate identity.

WESTERN CULTS AND NEW RELIGIONS

Cults and other new religious movements are increasingly widespread in the West (Figure 13.5). So, too, is faith in magic, good luck charms, and astrology. The 1991 International Social Survey Program found that one-third of West Germans, and 27 percent of the Irish believe in fortune tellers. Some forty thousand individuals in France list themselves as professional astrologers, and ninety thousand are registered as fortune tellers and witches in Germany. Forty-two percent of the British claim to believe in fortune telling, 30 percent in astrology, and 24 percent in good luck charms (Stark 1993, 395–96). Since the collapse of the Soviet Union, many cults have extended their mission outreach to Russia and East Germany. Clearly, the emergence of new religious movements in our day is not limited to non-western lands.

CHRISTIAN RESPONSE

How should Christian missions respond to recent religious movements? It is important to remember that Christianity also began as such a movement. Similarly many of the new religious movements emerge on the fringes of mission churches, often in remote areas where only rumors of the gospel are heard. Movements have also characterized peo-

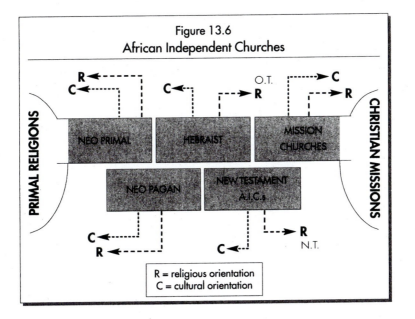

Figure 13.6
African Independent Churches

ple who felt denominational churches were too Western and foreign. We will examine several areas in which an appropriate Christian response is needed.

AFRICAN INDEPENDENT CHURCHES

A great many independent religious movements in the world today are found in sub-Saharan Africa. Due to the great mission work of the nineteenth and twentieth centuries, Christianity spread rapidly throughout that continent, giving rise to churches tied to Western denominations. Alongside these have emerged some ten thousand African Independent Churches (AICs)[2]—more than three thousand with a combined membership of three million in South Africa alone. They are a significant factor in the rapid growth of Christianity in that part of the world.

Harold Turner provides a useful taxonomy for evaluating these indigenous movements (1981; see Figure 13.6). Some of these movements are neo-primal. They are renewal movements in the old religion that seek to reshape it in response to the encounter with Christianity and Western culture. Generally they are strongly opposed to Christianity, but they

2. The phrase 'independent churches' is widely used for those new movements that are recognizably Christian but stand in contrast to the 'mission' or 'older' churches planted by missions from the outside. Some refer to these as "African Instituted Churches," or "African Indigenous Churches" (Lasisi 1998).

often replace the traditional gods and spirits with a supreme God who makes moral demands on people. Examples of these movements are the Dina ya Msambwa Religion of the Ancestors in Kenya and Godianism in Nigeria. Both worship the "God of Africa" who, they say, revealed himself in Egypt several millennia ago. Other movements are neo-pagan because they seek to combine tribal and Christian beliefs and rites. Among these is the Bwiti cult of Gabon and the Dima cult in Ivory Coast.

Turner calls another set of independent movements Hebraists. These make a clear and conscious break with vital aspects of the old religion, but do not place Christ at the center of their teaching. Consequently, they cannot be regarded as clearly Christian. They emphasize the Old Testament, and adopt practices found in it, such as polygamy, blood sacrifices, ephods, prophets, and kings. Many see themselves as Israelites, descendants of the ten lost tribes. Examples include the Israelites of South Africa, and the People of Judah in Uganda.

Finally, there are the AICs which focus on Christ and the New Testament and see themselves as Christians. Often they do not emerge out of a conscious desire to set up a new church, but as movements within old ones. These include the Kimbanguists of Central Africa, the Zionists throughout the southern part of Africa, the Church of the Lord (Aladura) of West Africa, and the Ethiopian independent churches. Many AICs are radical Biblicists. A major factor leading to their emergence was the translation of the Bible into African languages. Once they could read the Bible for themselves Africans discovered that Abraham and David were polygamists, and that the Ten Commandments ordered parents to be honored. These themes resonated with their own cultural traditions and often called the missionaries, who brought the Word, into question.

Most AICs are started by young prophetic type leaders who had no opportunities for leadership in their traditional religions (because of the old patriarchal leaders) or in mission churches (because they are 'natives'). They often claim to have been commissioned by God through a vision, dream, or near-death experience to bring a new religion to their people. On their return to earth, they gather disciples and form tight-knit communities of believers, which provide members with a strong sense of community.

THE CHURCH OF JESUS CHRIST ACCORDING TO KIMBANGU

In 1918, during a devastating flue epidemic, Simon Kimbangu, a young Baptist catechist, heard a voice telling him, "I am Christ, my servants are unfaithful. I have chosen you to witness to your brethren and to convert them." He fled to Kinshasa to escape the call, but returned home to farm. In 1921 he prayed for a sick woman and she was healed. Rumors of his powers spread and soon his village became known as "Jerusalem." Kimbangu held services and Bible readings during which he trembled like the traditional healers. He laid hands on patients who came, and instructed them to hold fast to Jesus Christ. He claimed to only to be a servant of Christ to his people, and many became his followers. Other prophets arose who urged the people not to pay taxes and to stop working for the Belgian colonial government. The result was a nationalist movement that Kimbangu neither intended nor controlled. He was arrested and sentenced to death, but the sentence was later commuted to life imprisonment. He died in 1951, but the movement grew and today numbers in the millions. To Africans Kimbangu is a symbol that just as God acted in the past by raising prophets, so he has acted among them and raised up a prophet for the salvation of Africans. (Adapted from Ray 1976, 194–99)

Most AICs totally reject many of the old customs, such as reliance on ancestors, shamans, medicine bags, magical objects, and traditional rites. Old divinities are rejected as demons, and a new ethic is rigorously enforced, demanding love, peace, sexual discipline, industriousness, and the avoidance of alcohol and tobacco. Church order is often carefully defined, with members wearing different uniforms marking rank and function. They express their worship in traditional African ways, such as singing, dancing, eating together, and praying publicly for those who are sick. Services are long (often running all day Sunday), and include drumming, dancing, prophesying, healing, protection from evil spirits, and the promise of a new order of freedom and prosperity. These independent religious movements give people a new sense of identity, hope, and dignity in the midst of the confusion, frustration, and powerlessness they face in their encounters with dominant colonial societies. Their worldview encourages individuals to take responsibility for their own future instead of blaming their misfortunes on others, such as witches or sorcerers.

Why are these churches growing so fast? Their appeal is their focus on working within an African worldview. They appeal to revelation through prophecy, dreams, and visions, which provide people with a sense of a direct contact with the "Word of God."[3] Healing, too, plays an important role in independent churches. When asked, many members say that they come to the church because they were healed by the prophet or people in the church (Daneel 1970, 12). But it is not healing alone. Most mission churches also profess and practice divine healing. Moreover, AICs are often deeply involved in Western-style medical ministries. The difference is how the two groups view the nature of healing.

3. Dreams also play an important role in the mainline churches. Many of their ministers first recognized their vocation in a dream.

Independent churches attribute sickness to spirits, evil forces, witch-craft, and curses, which point to moral and social offenses and obliga-tions not met, as discussed in Chapter 8. Health, for them, involves more than physical well-being. It involves treating not only the illness, but also the patient by restoring harmonious relationships and spiritual well-being in the community. In contrast, mission churches often see healing as either a spiritual matter having to do with one's relationship with God, or a medical therapy having to do with natural causes. At mission hospitals the patient is asked to take pills, but these are often not seen as instruments of God's power. The Christ Apostolic Church split from the Apostolic Mission because they believed the quinine mis-sionaries used to protect against malaria was the missionaries' fetish (Walls 1996, 99). Harold Turner puts it well, "In Africa the prime con-cern is with spiritual satisfaction and power" (1967, 70). This is why many members of mission churches go to independent churches when they become sick. This is also why independent churches often reject Western-style medical treatments because these are not seen as the power of God, but the craft of humans.

Independent churches raise difficult questions of contextualization. The prophets of the independent churches often act very much like local diviners. Like the Shona traditional healer *(nganga)* in Zimbabwe, the Zionist prophet divines the cause of illness and attributes it to bro-ken social relationships: a living enemy who wrongfully has caused the illness with spirit help, the spirit of a deceased person, or a spirit laying legitimate claim to restitution and plaguing the living to gain justice. Both the traditional diviner and the Christian prophet claim divine rev-elation as the source of the diagnosis, and the diagnoses often look vir-tually identical. Both may attribute an illness to "the spirit of an old woman whom grandfather chased away years ago and who died alone in the bush." Both use rituals in the process: the diviner reads divina-tory bones or contacts the spirits by his extra-perception; the prophet lays on hands, anoints with oil, and uses particular words in prayers to give them exceptional power. Some Zionist communities use sanctified needles, soap, strips of cloth, and the prophet's staff as symbolic medi-cines. Despite these similarities, the answers the two give are radically different. The traditional diviner seeks remedies that placate the spirits, but the prophet affirms the power of the Christian God which surpasses all other powers. The latter uses objects as visual concretizations of Di-vine Power, and have no medical effect in themselves (Daneel 1970, 30–49). The focus is in whom they place primary allegiance, giving glory to God rather than to the spirits or symbols of power.

The AICs offer a gospel, not so much of correct doctrine, but of power to deal with the needs of daily living—of security, fertility, health for all, guidance, and good relationships. They respond to the fact that Africans do not explain life without reference to religion and the spirit world. Religion here is power—power against threats of death and to have life in abundance, and religion that is not experienced as power is unsatisfying for Africans.

The AICs represent a serious attempt to bring the gospel into the African culture by expressing it in images familiar to African people and in responding concretely to their needs and aspirations. Taylor notes that these movements are a reaction against a Christ who was presented to Africans "as the answer to questions a white man would ask, the solution to the needs that Western man would feel, the Saviour of the European worldview" (1958, 24). In contrast, Africans seek a Christ who is known as a brother, and who answers their questions. These movements take the African worldview seriously by making it clear in their faith and practice that salvation must include the offer of protection against magic, sorcery, and witchcraft. It is noteworthy that most AICs uncompromisingly oppose participation in the traditional rites related to veneration of the ancestors or divination through traditional diviners. However, the role of prophecy becomes very significant in bridging the gap between the gospel and their African cultures (Moyo 1996, 31). The prophetic leader is seen as an African leader who is not to be confused with the diviner, but gains respect by meeting those needs which were met by the diviner. AICs recognize that since religion permeates the entire traditional African way of life and cannot be isolated, Christianity must bring Christ into all of African culture, if it is to succeed.

Although many revitalization movements are the unintended offspring of Christian missions, churches and missions tended to reject them as unchristian. In recent years, bridges of fellowship and recognition of Christian foundations have been extended to many of the Independent churches. Some of the AICs now belong to the World Council of Churches. Few Western missions, however, have been willing to work with Hebraist churches.[4]

Today the distinction between 'mission' and 'independent' churches in Africa is becoming blurred. Most African churches are now independent, address African questions, and have appropriated more African forms of worship and teachings. Many independent churches, on the other hand, are as mission-related as the older churches. Moreover, in

---

4. One mission actively working with Hebraist communities is the Africa Inter Mennonite Mission (AIMM), a cooperative venture of various Mennonite mission boards, which seeks to influence these movements by setting up Bible training programs for the leaders of these communities.

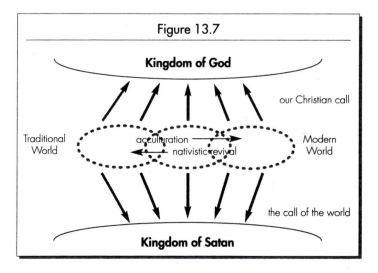

their interaction with the global church, many are becoming increasingly orthodox in their theologies. Consequently, the differences between the two are virtually indistinguishable (Walls 1996, 114).

There is a danger in ordering independent churches along a continuum from traditional to Western worlds. It equates Christianity with Western modernity, and traditional cultures with paganism. It is important to distinguish between these two dimensions (Figure 13.7). People have a right to choose or reject modernity. The missiological task is to call both those who keep their traditional cultures and those who adopt modern practice to model within their communities what it means to be the people of God living in the kingdom of God, and to critique their cultures in the light of Scripture (Van Engen 1996).

PEOPLE MOVEMENTS

New religious movements often give rise to mass or people movements in which whole families and communities turn to Christ. In the past, many missionaries rejected these movements as misguided, and encouraged seekers to make individual decisions of faith. This response often killed the movements. Missionaries, who came from societies in which people were taught to make personal decisions and take responsibility for themselves, did not understand the processes of decision making in highly group oriented societies in which elders make all major decisions, including arranging marriages and religious loyalties. Not everyone agrees with the elders, but they go along with the decisions to maintain the unity of the group. How should missionaries and leaders respond to these movements of whole peoples to Christ?

It is important to allow the dynamics of group decisions to take their course. The initial decision is not so much a decision by all to follow Christ as it is to explore Christianity further. Churches and missions need to send pastors to instruct the people, and encourage them to discuss their decision because, in a sense, the gospel is on trial. After some time, those who reaffirm their desire to become Christians should be baptized.[5] This second decision is critical for their growth. Others will choose to return to their old gods. Having affirmed the unity of the group by joining in its first decision, they are now free to reject the new religion.

People movements are important in group-oriented societies. Converts who come to Christ one by one are often ostracized by the group, and they have little witness among their kin and neighbors. When a number of families become Christians together, the village cannot reject them without destroying the community. The new Christians also have a community of fellowship and support in one another. There are also problems with group movements. If there is little or no follow-up to the initial response, the movement dies, or the Christianity that emerges is shallow. When there is proper follow-up, people movements can lead to strong, growing churches, even in hostile environments.

FORMAL RELIGION AND FOLK RELIGIOUS MOVEMENTS

Another type of revitalization movement is renewal in established religions and churches. Revivals of new religious vision and fervor often occur on the margins of the institutional structures, and are led by prophets and folk leaders. Priestly elites often feel threatened, and seek to stamp them out, or to excommunicate their followers because these movements do not fit the bureaucratic order or theological orthodoxy established by the institutional leaders.

Tensions between folk religious movements and formal establishments are difficult to resolve. The latter have the power of organization, money, and, at times, legal support. The former has the support of the people. If such movements are squashed, there may be no renewal of vitality in the church. If they are absorbed uncritically, they can distort its theological stance. In churches it is important that the leaders keep in close touch with their laity, and guide them not by command and control, but by modeling and patient instruction (2 Tim. 2:14–16; 4:2). The separation between leaders and lay people has devastating consequences for the life and outreach of the church.

---

5. See Donovan 1978, for an example of this type of thinking among the Masai in Kenya.

CHRISTIAN RESPONSES TO FOLK RELIGION

Having sought to understand folk religions phenomenologically in terms of the key questions they seek to answer and the practices that result, it is time to turn to the remaining steps in the process of critical contextualization. The ontological critique of the beliefs and practices of folk religions is based both on testing the reality of the events described by the people, and on a biblical evaluation of the truthfulness of their claims. Chapter 14 deals with general theological principles for developing a Christian folk religion, and notes some of the pitfalls to be avoided. Chapter 15 provides guidelines for the third step, the evaluation of the old beliefs and practices in the light of biblical truth. It also examines the fourth step, namely, missiology—the process by which new converts and churches learn to apply and internalize their biblical findings in everyday life, and move from old ways to new biblically based ones. For believers, this leads to Christian maturity. For churches it is an ongoing process of living as God's people in a fallen and ever-changing world. A full elaboration of ministry in the life of the church is beyond the scope of this book.

SECTION OUTLINE

Section Four provides guidelines for completing the second, third, and fourth steps in the process of critical contextualization.

Chapter 14: Examines theological principles for developing a Christian response to the questions and needs expressed in folk religions.

Chapter 15: Provides guidelines for evaluating folk religious beliefs and practices in the light of Scripture, and for leading people and churches from their old ways to a new life in Christ.

14

THEOLOGICAL RESPONSES TO FOLK RELIGION

How should Christians respond to split-level Christianity and the bewildering variety of folk religions around the world? How can churches deal with the resurgence of witchcraft in Africa, spiritism in Latin America, Cargo Cults in Melanesia, new religions in Japan, and New Age and neo-paganism in North America? To ignore them and hope that they disappear as Christians grow in faith is to open the door for a syncretism that threatens the heart of the gospel. To try to stamp them out and replace them with imported beliefs and practices leads to split-level Christianity.

The answer we outlined in Chapter 1 is to deal with old beliefs and practices, and to provide biblical answers to the questions people face in their everyday lives. The first step in this process of critical contextualization is to examine phenomenologically the people's beliefs and practices to understand these as the people do. Section One developed a model for studying folk religions, and Section Two used this to examine four key questions most folk religions seek to answer. Preliminary Christian responses were given to each of these questions. Section Three looked at the public expressions of folk religions—their symbols, myths, rituals, organization, and movements.

So far, much attention has been given to the phenomenological study of religions for several reasons. First, this is the step most neglected by missionaries in the past. Many study Scripture and theology, but do not study the people. The effective communication of the gospel cannot take place, however, without a deep understanding of the language and culture of a people. Too often missionaries focus their attention on the message they bring, and ignore the context in which they communicate it. Consequently, the gospel remains incomprehensible, fragmented, foreign, and irrelevant. Second, missionaries need to understand the religious beliefs and practices of the people to provide biblical answers to the questions they face, and to contextualize the gospel and the church in the local setting. Good contextualization requires wise judgments, not an uncritical acceptance or rejection of old ways. Wise judgments, however, require a deep knowledge of local realities. Without such understanding missionaries often jump to false or premature judgments. Third, many of the key issues facing young churches emerge out of real-life situations that are always in particular contexts. Each culture presents a different set of questions that must be addressed theologically. For one it is polygamy, ancestors, and the spirit world, for another it is social oppression, injustice, ideologies, and massive social systems that stand in opposition to God. Missionaries must address not only the issues that emerge out of the study of Scripture but also those that emerge in the daily life of the church.

The second step in the process of critical contextualization is to test the people's beliefs and practices in the light of biblical truth and tests of reality. This calls for a deep knowledge of the Bible and theological frameworks for understanding Scripture that serve as the criteria by which human social and cultural systems are evaluated and judged. Because folk religions are so diverse, no single set of theological answers will solve all the problems that arise. Specific theological responses must be developed for each of them. There are, however, general theological principles that can be used to deal with the many theological questions that confront Christian churches as they emerge from folk religious contexts.

GENERAL THEOLOGICAL PRINCIPLES

Theological principles that apply particularly to the questions raised in folk religions must be grounded in a larger theology of God, creation, sin, salvation, and Christ's return. There is always the danger in dealing with the pressing needs of everyday life to focus on one or another doctrine, and to lose sight of the gospel as a whole. What we need are biblically balanced answers to the existential questions addressed by folk religions.

A THEOLOGY OF THE INVISIBLE

Given the fact that the modern mission movement originated in the West, and the West increasingly depends on the world of sight, it is imperative that Christians recover an awareness of the invisible in this world. Peterson writes,

> [M]ost of the reality with which we deal is invisible. Most of what makes up human existence is inaccessible to our five senses: emotions, thoughts,

dreams, love, hope, character, purpose, belief. Even what makes up most of the basic physical existence is out of the range of our unassisted senses: molecules and atoms, neutrons and protons, the air we breathe, the ancestors we derive from, the angels who protect us. We live immersed in these immense invisibles. And more than anything else, we are dealing with God "whom no one has seen at any time" (1994, 89–90).

Until the invisible world becomes a living reality in the lives of Christians, they will not be able to deal with the questions folk religions raise.

A theology of the invisible must take seriously a trinitarian understanding of God (as presented in Chapter 5), who is continually involved in his creation by his providence, presence, and power. It must take angels seriously, for they are God's ministers on earth, and it must take Satan and demons seriously, for they are fallen angels seeking to keep people from turning to God in repentance and faith.

A THEOLOGY OF WORSHIP AND SUBMISSION

At their core, folk religions are human efforts to control life. This is reflected in the first sin, when Satan tempted Adam and Eve, not to worship him, but to worship themselves. They could, he said, become their own gods. Self-centeredness and self-possession remain the greatest human temptation and the central concern for most folk religious beliefs and practices. People make sacrifices to gods and spirits to bargain for healing and prosperity. They turn to ancestors and divination in attempts to control their own well-being.

The desire for control also leads to a magical approach to problems, for magic enables humans to control their world, the gods, ancestors, and other beings in the middle zone. Even Christians are tempted to seek to control God by sacred formulas when their prayers do not bring the desired results.

The gospel rejects an ego-centered religion and a magical mentality. The center of its message is God and what he does. It calls humans to submit themselves to God, and to live not by control but by faith in his plan (Isa. 8:19–22; Jer. 27:9–10; Gal. 5:20; Rev. 21:8). This change from self-centeredness to God-centeredness is one of the most difficult for humans to make. The problem is compounded when people with middle-zone worldviews are asked to develop a theology that emphasizes God's volition and human response rather than searching for and trying to manipulate God.

A HOLISTIC THEOLOGY

Christians need to present God's work in the whole of creation. This begins with a theology of cosmic history: of God, the heavens, and eter-

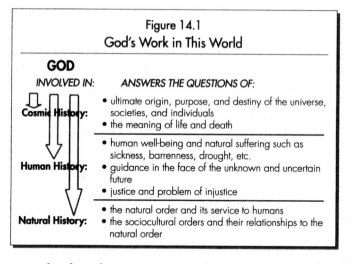

Figure 14.1
God's Work in This World

GOD

INVOLVED IN:	ANSWERS THE QUESTIONS OF:
Cosmic History:	• ultimate origin, purpose, and destiny of the universe, societies, and individuals • the meaning of life and death
Human History:	• human well-being and natural suffering such as sickness, barrenness, drought, etc. • guidance in the face of the unknown and uncertain future • justice and problem of injustice
Natural History:	• the natural order and its service to humans • the sociocultural orders and their relationships to the natural order

nity (Figure 14.1). This answers the ultimate questions raised by high religions regarding the ultimate origins, purpose, and destiny of all creation. It must include a theology of human history: of humans created in the image of God, the fall, God's redemptive acts in the Old Testament, Christ's death and resurrection in the New Testament, and the work of the Holy Spirit in the church. This answers questions related to redemptive history. It must also include a theology of God's work in the lives of individuals: of the meaning of life, desire for a good life, need for guidance, and longing for justice, and explanations of death, disasters, the unknown and evil in poverty, injustice, racism, and oppression. This answers the existential questions of everyday human lives.

A whole theology must also include nature: its design, its voice praising its Creator, its suffering at the hand of evil, and the new creation in which it will be fully restored (Rom. 8:22; 2 Peter 3:11–13). Nature is the place where humans meet God and converse with him. Modern-day Christians are ready to see God's hand in cosmic history, and, at times, in human history, but they see nature as an autonomous reality operating according to impersonal laws. Only as they see God at the center of nature will they root out the secularism that plagues the contemporary world. This is an important process in churches in the West as well as traditional mission contexts. The rapid shift to post modernity, with its focus on self-fulfillment and ultimate narcissism forces a reevaluation (i.e., a need for an application of critical contextualization) of the Western, well-entrenched, and institutionalized church.

It is not easy for modern Christians to recover a holistic theology. Implicit in English and other Western languages is a Neo-Platonic dualism that separates supernatural from natural, God from nature, and religion from science. This dualism is not found in Hebrew thought. Rather, the word used for this world and its order is *bara*, "what is created," which includes angels, humans, animals, plants, and matter. The word implies that these originate in and are continuously dependent on

God for their very existence. Events in human lives cannot be divided into ordinary and miraculous. This affirmation of God's presence in all things is essential in answering the questions raised by folk religions.

A THEOLOGY OF THE KINGDOM OF GOD

A whole gospel is founded on a theology of the kngdom of God—in God's rule and work in the world. After the fall, sickness, suffering, starvation, and death became a part of the world. Christ's response was to come as a human, and to establish and proclaim his kingdom as the new work of God on earth. The message of salvation includes good news to the poor, release to the captives, sight for the blind, and liberty to the oppressed (Luke 4:18–19). But how does this kingdom relate to human experiences as people live in the kingdoms of this world with famine, oppression, poverty, suffering, disease, and death?

Down through history prophets have claimed that the kingdom of God has already come in its fullness for God's people. Christians, they say, need not be sick or poor or failures or sinners—or even die. In Paul's day some claimed that the resurrection had already taken place (2 Tim. 2:18). Despite such preaching, sincere, devout, praying Christians remain poor and broken. In fact, they become sick and die.

The kingdom of God has come to earth in the person of Christ. It is found wherever God's people are obedient to the King. It has also come to humans in signs—those times when God shows them through extraordinary experiences what the kingdom is like. But signs are not the reality to which they point. Signs of the kingdom are all around, but the kingdom will come in its fullness only with Christ's return (Rev. 12:10). Until then, Christians live between two worlds. They are people of this sinful world: they are tempted and sin, they are weak and fail, and the processes of disease, degeneration, and death are at work in them from the moment of birth. But they are also people of the kingdom: although they sin, in God's sight they are sinless; although they face death, they have eternal life; although they see a decaying world around them, they also see the signs of a heavenly kingdom in the transformed lives of God's people.

A THEOLOGY OF POWER AND THE CROSS

Most folk religions seek power as the key to prosperity, health, success, and control over life. In response, Christians need a biblical theology of power. They face two dangers. On the one hand, they may avoid every kind of bold and sensational act for fear it is magic, even when God asks it of them. The church then is poor in the manifestations of God's power. On the other hand, through zeal to demonstrate God's power Christians can run after the sensational, even when God does not will it. Neither miracles nor the cross can be taken out of the gospel without distorting it.

The Scriptures have much to say about power. God is the God Almighty (*El Shaddai*, Gen. 17:1), who created and sustains all things by his power (Gen. 1), who defeated Satan and his hosts (John 16:33), and who will bring all things into subjection to himself (Eph. 1:22). Moreover, by his might he saves those who turn to him and gives them power to become like him and bear witness to his greatness. All this must be affirmed.

Scripture also has much to say about the ways in which power is to be used. Unfortunately, many Christians think of power the way the world around them does. They see it as active—it manifests itself by demonstrations of might that overcome the resistance of the opposition. Consequently, they seek to show the world God's superiority by means of power encounters that demonstrate his ability to heal and cast out demons, confident that when non-Christians see these, they will believe. Scripture and history show that demonstrations of God's power lead some to believe, but many to rise in opposition, persecuting and often killing God's servants. They include Satan and his hosts, and humans who oppose God and his kingdom of righteousness both individually and corporately through human institutions such as those that crucified Christ and persecuted the early church.

God's use of power is demonstrated supremely on the cross. There Satan used his full might to destroy Christ, or to provoke him to use his divinity wrongly. Either would have meant defeat for Christ—the first because Satan would have overcome him and the second because it would have destroyed God's plan of salvation. Godly power is always rooted in love, not pride; redemption, not revenge; and concern for the other, not the self. It is humble, not proud, and inviting, not rejecting. Its symbol is the cross, not the sword. This is why the world sees God's power as weakness (1 Cor. 1:23–27).

Christians and churches are in desperate need of showing God's power in transformed lives and in a Christlike confrontation of evil wherever they find it, whether demonic, systemic, or personal. They must also guard against distortions of a biblical view of power, divorcing it from truth, and temptations to use power for their own glory. They are stewards, called to be faithful in using the power God gives them for his glory.

A THEOLOGY OF DISCERNMENT

In dealing with folk religions, Christians need a theology of discernment. People seek signs to assure them that God is present, but apart from the fruits of the Spirit, there are no self-authenticating phenomena. Miraculous healings, speaking in tongues, exorcisms, prophecies, resurrections, and other extraordinary experiences are reported in all major religions. Bab Farid, a Pakistani Muslim saint, is said to have cured incurable diseases, raised a dying man to life, converted dried dates into gold nuggets, and covered vast distances in a moment (Gilchrist 1987, 32). Hundreds of thousands of people flock each year to the Hindu temple of Venkateswara at Tirupathi, South India, to fulfill vows they made when they prayed to him for healing. Upwards of 15,000 people claim healing each year at Lourdes, and many more at the Virgin of Guadalupe near Mexico City. Scripture points out that Satan counterfeits God's work, and warns God's people to guard against being led astray (Matt. 7:15–16; 1 Tim. 4:1, 7; 2 Tim. 3:1–4:5; 2 Thess. 2:9–10). They are to test the spirits to see whether or not these come from God (1 Cor. 12:3; 1 Thess. 5:20–21; 1 John 4:1–6). In this, their attitude should not be one of skepticism, but of openness to hearing the voice of God when he truly speaks to them.

What are the signs that enable Christians to discern the work of God and differentiate it from the work of self or Satan? It is too simple to say that what God's people do is of God (cf. Matt. 7:21–23) or that what non-Christians do is of Satan (cf. Num. 22–24). Human experiences must themselves be tested, for they are not self-authenticating.

The Bible provides several clear tests of God's work. First, does it give the glory to God rather than to humans (John 7:18; 8:50; 12:27–28; 17:4)? Around the world today people are drawn to strong personalities, and tend to deify them. This is particularly true in folk religions. Second, does it recognizes the lordship of Christ (1 John 2:3–5; 5:3; James 2:14–19)? The test here is not one of orthodoxy, but of submission to Christ in humility and obedience. Third, is the evidence of God's power through the Holy Spirit emphasized, or the manifestations of the flesh? Fourth, does it conform to scriptural teaching? Are those involved willing to submit their lives and teachings to the test of Scripture? Fifth, are the leaders and people accountable to others in the church? The interpretation of Scripture is not a personal matter, but a concern of the church as a hermeneutical community. Sixth, do those involved manifest the fruits of the Spirit (Gal. 5:22–25)? Is there love or self-centeredness, patience or short tempers, gentleness or arrogance? Seventh, does the teaching and practice lead believers toward spiritual maturity (1 Cor. 12–14)? Some things are characteristic of spiritual immaturity which should be left behind as Christians grow spiritually. Eighth, does it lead Christians to seek the unity of the body of Christ, or is it divisive (John 17:11; 1 John 2:9–11; 5:1–2)? This does not mean that divisions will not occur. It does mean that teachings that lead believers to a sense of spiritual superiority have led them astray.

DISCERNING THE WORK OF GOD

Jonathan Edwards was involved in a great revival in which there were many experiences, both positive and negative. In the process he developed a number of criteria for discerning the work of God.

I. SIGNS THAT ARE NOT NECESSARILY EVIDENCES OF THE WORK OF GOD
  • great religious experiences in themselves.
  • religious experiences that have a great effect on the body.
  • fluent, fervent, and abundant spiritual speaking.
  • experiences beyond a person's control.
  • religious experiences that bring texts of Scripture to mind.
  • the appearance of love in a religious experience.
  • multiplied religious experiences, accompanying one another.
  • religious experiences that bring joy followed by conviction.
  • spiritual experiences that lead a person to spend much time in religious activities and zealous participation in public worship.
  • experiences that cause men and women to praise and glorify God with their mouths.
  • religious experiences that produce confidence of being in a good spiritual state.
  • religious experiences that are outwardly pleasing and acceptable to the truly godly.

II. SIGNS THAT ARE EVIDENCE OF THE WORK OF GOD IN A PERSON'S LIFE
  • true believers exhibit divine affections.
  • they love divine things—the ground for gracious affections.
  • they have an appreciation for the loveliness of moral excellence of divine things, a deep sense of personal sin, and a longing for holiness.
  • they do not downplay godly rationality—the sense of the heart.
  • they have a spiritual conviction of the reality and certainty of divine things.
  • they have a humility that is spiritual and thoroughly godly.
  • in them spiritual discoveries alter the very nature of their soul; their lives are transformed into Christ's likeness.
  • they have a spirit of gentleness that leads to a spirit of love, meekness, quietness, forgiveness, and mercy.
  • they have gracious affections that soften the heart followed with a Christian tenderness of spirit.
  • there is a symmetry, proportion and balance in their lives.
  • they strive for spiritual attainment, whereas false ones rest assured in themselves and their achievements.
  • their conduct demonstrates the outward evidence of the inward changes that have taken place.

(Edwards 1959)

A THEOLOGY OF SUFFERING AND DEATH

Christians need a theology of sickness, injury, suffering, and death. These consequences of sin cannot be divorced from each other. The processes of aging and death are at work in humans from the moment of their conception. The side effects of this are sickness and bodily suffering.

God often does heal people by natural and by extraordinary means, but for Christians, their full deliverance is only after death, when they receive their new bodies. The hope and joy Christians manifest in godly dying and at funerals is a powerful testimony to others of power of the gospel.

Today there is little recognition that it may be God's will for a Christian to be sick, suffer, or undergo trials and difficulties in life, or that God can use these for their good. God can use sickness and suffering to draw people to himself, and to teach them patience and maturity (Job 42:5–6; James 1:2–4). These are also the consequence of persecution for Christ's sake. Paul adds that in suffering Christians, in small measure, share in the suffering of Christ.

Many Christians do not recognize that illnesses are often the body's warning to them to stop living unhealthy lifestyles. There is little acknowledgment that Christians and non-Christians share in the common lot of fallen humanity, which includes famines, plagues, and illness. This does not mean that God is uninterested in the lot of Christians. It does mean that he loves both the saved and the lost, that he is working out his purposes in a fallen world, and that one day he will bring in a new and perfect creation.

A THEOLOGY OF THE CHURCH AS CARING COMMUNITY

In dealing with the longings expressed in folk religions, it is important for churches to be caring communities in which the fallen, sick, oppressed, and needy find refuge, and in which the hostilities and jealousies of life that give rise to witchcraft are handled and forgiven. They must also be places where believers gather to pray for God's blessings, and his deliverance from public crises such as droughts, plagues, and wars. Churches must also be communities that read the Scriptures together and hear what God is saying to them in their particular contexts.

THEOLOGICAL PITFALLS

In dealing with folk religious beliefs and practices, there are dangers to avoid. This fact should not keep Christian leaders from engaging in the critique of folk religions and theological development in specific contexts. It does mean that they should be aware of problems that may arise. Here we seek to caution new churches and those who assist them about certain areas that frequently give rise to syncretism and heresy.

SYNCRETISM

The danger in responding to folk religions is not so much heresy as it is syncretism—combining elements of Christianity with folk beliefs and practices in such a way that the gospel loses its integrity and message. The problem here is not with old religious beliefs, but with the underlying assumptions on which they are built. The gospel must not only change beliefs, but also transform worldviews, otherwise the new beliefs will be reinterpreted in terms of the old worldviews. The result is Christo-paganism.

One important area needing transformation is that of the magical mentality that dominates most folk religions. If this is not challenged, Christianity will be seen as a new and superior magic. This magical tendency is not restricted to traditional religionists. It is just below the surface in all fallen human beings. Magic makes them gods because it gives them control over nature, supernatural powers, and even God, through the practice of the proper rites. This was the experience of Simon (Acts 8:9–24) the magician who, seeing the miracles of Philip, Peter, and John, wanted to buy their kind of power with money. Peter severely rebuked him for his old magical worldview. Simon repented, but he had learned a hard lesson—the gospel cannot be reinterpreted in other worldviews. It brings with it its own worldview that supersedes all others.

Magic is the opposite of Christianity. In magic humans are in control. In Christianity they are called to submit unconditionally to God and his will. The difference between the two is not in practice. It is in attitude. Magic is formulaic and mechanistic. Christianity is based on worship and relationships. Prayer is magic if supplicants believe they must say the right things in right tone of voice accompanied by certain right actions to be assured of the right answers. It is worship when they kneel before God and cast their cares on him. The difference is often subtle. Christians can begin to pray seeking God's help, but, when the answer is delayed, unconsciously begin to become coercive in their attitudes. They can read Scripture to learn and grow, or to gain merit that earns them their desires. Some carry Bibles in their pockets, confident that these, like amulets, will protect them from harm.

Engaging worldviews is not only the task of new Christians in non-Christian contexts. The danger of becoming captive to non-Christian worldviews is as great or greater among followers of Christ who live in the West where Christian assumptions still often dominate. They are in danger of reinterpreting the gospel in terms of their own cultural categories—of equating it with Western civilization, material prosperity, individualism, human rights, and freedom.

HUMAN-CENTEREDNESS

One of the most difficult worldview themes to deal with is the androcentrism of religions created by humans. People see themselves as the center of the world, and everything revolves around them and their lives. Their religions provide them ways to get what they desire by bribing or begging the gods, spirits, and ancestors, and by controlling supernatural powers. The modern worldview shares in this androcentrism.

Christianity challenges this androcentrism, and calls believers to a theocentric view of reality. New believers come to Christ with their own interests in mind—their salvation, their health, their well-being, their freedom from oppression. God begins with them where they are, and the church must do the same. This is not the problem. The danger is institutionalizing immaturity. God calls Christians to spiritual growth in which their focus on themselves gives way to a love for God and others. While ministering to seekers at their point of need, the primary focus should be on moving to mature expressions of worship and ministry. Unfortunately, many Christians have bought into the emphasis on personal health and prosperity as ultimate ends, and focus on themselves rather than on the millions around the world who are lost and dying because of poverty, oppression, and violence.

It is a small step from self-centeredness to self-deification, the first and most fundamental of human sin. Satan did not tempt Adam and Eve to worship him, but to worship themselves—their own freedom, their rights, and their potential of becoming gods. Self-possession, not demon possession, is the greatest danger facing human beings. It is hard for Christians to move from feeling they need to be in control of their lives to entrusting themselves completely to God's mercy and submitting to his will.

The results of self-centeredness in the church can be devastating. It leads to authoritarian leadership, competition, divisions, and spiritual pride. Even those renewed in spiritual movements often look down on those not involved, and have a judgmental attitude toward those who disagree with them. Christ-centeredness leads to humility, a desire for the unity of the church, and a willingness to hear as well as speak (Rom. 15:1–2; 1 Cor. 10:12).

EXPERIENCE-BASED THEOLOGY

Folk religions are existential and experience-based. The result is a pragmatic concern for power rather than truth. Different methods are tried simultaneously to solve human dilemmas, with little concern that these often contradict one another. In such settings it is easy for Christians to base their theology on experience. The test of truth is success. The sign of spiritual life and vital worship is feelings of excitement, health, and prosperity. As Jonathan Edwards pointed out, experiences are not self-authenticating. They must themselves be tested for their reality and cause. Christians need to avoid reading their experiences and theologies into Scripture and focusing on these rather than on Scripture itself.

A corollary of experience-based theologies is confusing reports with reality. In folk religions there are many stories of spirits, visions, miraculous events, magical powers, witchcraft, fulfilled prophecies, guidance through divination, and the successes of amulets and rituals to protect people from calamities. It is important to take these seriously, for they reflect the reality as the people see it and upon which they act. It is equally important not to equate all phenomenological reports with ontological reality. Careful, sensitive investigation of these reports is needed, and independent verification sought when possible. Christians must also test the sources of these events when they prove to be real. Not all that is attributed to God is his doing.

REINFORCING SECULARISM

Contradictory as it may seem, by overemphasizing miracles Christians can reinforce secularism. By looking for supernatural events as manifestations of God's presence, they imply that God is not directly at work in natural phenomena which are studied by science. But as the knowledge of science grows, God is increasingly pushed to the margins of life. Moreover, as miracles become routine, they no longer appear to be extraordinary, and people look for new and more spectacular miracles to reassure themselves that God is with them. The net effect of these dynamics is the secularization of everyday life. The answer lies neither in seeking miracles, nor in denying them. It is to reject the dichotomy of miracle and natural together, and to see the naturalness of God's extraordinary healings and the miraculous nature of his ordinary ones. The church must avoid making miracles the signs of God's presence, and the center of its attention and ministry.

GENERATING FALSE GUILT

Christians rejoice when God works in extraordinary ways to heal the sick, deliver the bewitched, and bring justice to the oppressed. What about those whom God chooses not to deliver? Too often they experience a false sense of guilt and despair, and are in the greatest need of ministry. To attribute sickness and death to a lack of faith or to spiritual defeat is too simple an answer (Job; John 9:2; 2 Cor. 12:7–9). Even more than a theology of healing, the church needs a theology of suffering and death—one that does not see these as failures, but as part of God's greater redemptive work.

IMBALANCE

In discernment it is important to be biblically balanced (Matt. 23:23–24). It is easy to emphasize one truth at the expense of others. It is easy to begin with Christ as the center of a Christian's life, but in the business of life to unwittingly move the center to one of the expressions of the gospel, such as healing, justice, peace, or deliverance. In time, Christ becomes peripheral, the justifier of what is now the Christian's real concern. Balance is maintained only if Christ, not a particular cause, remains the true center of believers' lives (Figure 14.2).

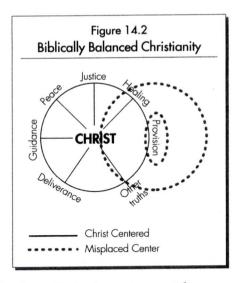

Figure 14.2
Biblically Balanced Christianity

———— Christ Centered
•••••• Misplaced Center

EXALTING THE LEADER

In folk religions leaders are often charismatic authoritarian prophets, who develop personality cults. People who do not understand what is going on in life are attracted to a big leader who claims to know the way. Such leaders often appear in young churches, but this creates problems. It encourages most Christians to be followers, who have an uncritical trust in their leaders. They attribute healings, prophecies, and miracles to the leader. The leaders are tempted to take credit for the work, and encourage the adoration of their followers, and not be accountable to others. Leadership, healing, guidance, exorcisms, and other ministries in the church belong to the congregation. Some members may have particular gifts, but they use these as members of the body.

Having examined some of the theological principles that must be considered in the second step in critical contextualization, it is time to turn to the final two steps, namely, an evaluation of old beliefs and practice in the light of biblical truth, and the transformation of individuals and communities through discipling and spiritual growth.

15

MISSIOLOGICAL RESPONSES

We come now to the final steps in a critical response to folk religions and split-level Christianity: an evaluation of traditional beliefs and practices in the light of biblical truth, and a transformation of believers and churches from unbiblical ways to authentic Christian life and witness in their particular contexts.

BIBLICAL EVALUATION

The third step in the process of critical contextualization as outlined in Chapter 1 is to evaluate old beliefs and practices in the light of biblical truth. It is important to recall that our aim is not to destroy folk religions and to replace them with formal Christianity. It is to develop a vibrant Christian folk religion that is rooted in the gospel. The life of the church is found in a laity for whom the gospel is a reality that reconciles them to God and one another, and touches every area of their lives.

It is important to note, too, that there is no standard formula for dealing with folk religions. They vary greatly from culture to culture, and a different response must be made to each of them. There is not one kind of witchcraft. Practices loosely labeled witchcraft are found around the world. Similarly, there are many varieties of ancestor veneration, ways of seeking guidance, and beliefs in spirits and possession.

Given this diversity of religious expressions, it is important to provide young churches with broad theological principles for dealing with the specific beliefs and practices they face. It is even more important to teach them how to do theology and contextualization in their own context. Only as churches take this task upon themselves will they become mature and learn to live as Christians in their particular sociocultural contexts. Only then will they learn to preach the gospel in ways that are understood by the people, and respond to needs without compromising the church's prophetic call. Answers to the questions raised by folk religions must be hammered out in the context of the local beliefs and practices, and constantly be reformulated as times and cultures change. This is best done by local Christians who understand and live in these settings.

Do local believers have the right to read and interpret the Scriptures? Theoretically, most evangelicals would admit that they do. In practice, many missionaries are threatened when national leaders begin to develop their own theologies, and when common folk interpret Scripture for themselves. This is understandable. First, whenever the laity does theology, a great many answers are given, some of which do not appear to be orthodox. What boundaries are there to theology, and what checks are there to correct falsehoods? Second, for evangelicals, theology lies at the heart of their being and their missionary endeavors. When truth is defined in terms of a specific theological formulation, to tamper with that formulation is to undermine the whole task. The priesthood of all believers is good theology, but in practice does it not open the doors to all kinds of heresies? In the end, the priesthood is often limited to missionaries, theologians, and other church leaders.

Today young churches around the world are formulating their own theologies. Severe tensions often develop between daughter and parent churches, but the young churches can no longer turn back. If they are to make the gospel relevant to their own people, they must do theology in their cultural settings. Attempts to export theologies developed in the West and to preserve them unchanged have, to a great extent, failed.

If believers are free to do theology, what are the theological absolutes? Evangelicals hold the Scripture to be true, for it is God's revelation, but how can Christians preserve that truth if they allow all believers to read and interpret the Scriptures in their own cultural settings? The answer lies, in part, in a meta theology—a biblically based way of doing theology that sets limits to theological diversity. What follows are some principles for a biblically based meta theology.

THEOLOGY ROOTED IN SCRIPTURE

The first principle of a biblically based meta theology is that theological reflection must be rooted in the acceptance of Scripture as divine revelation. The Bible is not a record of humans searching for God, but of God revealing himself to them in the particular contexts of history, culture, and society. It is the source not only for finding answers to human questions, but of defining the worldview through which they should look at reality.

GUIDED BY THE HOLY SPIRIT

Second, believers must seek the guidance of the Holy Spirit in interpreting Scripture. They must study it on their knees, in a spirit of humility, willing to listen and learn rather than with dogmatic self-assurance. Christians must recognize that their theology is an understanding of Scripture, not Scripture itself. Consequently, they must hold their theological convictions strongly, to the point of being willing to die for them, but must not equate these with Scripture. They must admit that their understanding of truth is partial, biased, and possibly wrong, and test their convictions by returning to Scripture. They must recognize that the same Holy Spirit that they seek to guide them in their study of the Bible is at work in other believers. They must also allow others the greatest privilege they allow themselves, namely, to make mistakes.

DONE BY THE CHURCH AS A HERMENEUTICAL COMMUNITY

Third, Christians must be open to the checks of the Christian community. Interpretation and application of Scripture in everyday life are not just personal matters. Ultimately the church as a whole must act as a hermeneutical community.

In the process of doing theology believers need one another to help them detect their personal biases, of which they themselves are often unaware, just as they need others to help them see the sins they do not want to admit to themselves. They must also test their beliefs in the community of the church. Serious debate over theological issues is not a sign of the lack of commitment to Scripture on the part of the protagonists. Committed Christians will always disagree on difficult issues. They must enter discussions with a commitment to truth as Scripture reveals it, and a willingness to listen to the interpretations of others without immediately branding them as heretics. This appeal to the community of believers as the basis for interpreting Scripture does not reduce interpretations to social consensus. Rather, the community that accepts the authority of Scripture and seeks the guidance of the Holy Spirit is able to check the personal biases of individual interpretations of the Bible. Individuals must be open to correction and growth in their understanding of biblical truths.

On the global level, when people from different cultures study Scripture together, they can help one another check cultural biases. It is almost impossible for individual Christians to see the cultural grids they bring with them to the study of the Bible. These are better seen by sisters and brothers with other worldviews. For this reason, missionaries and church leaders from outside play important roles in helping local churches to do theology, not by dictating the answers, but by acting as catalysts helping the people to understand Scripture better, and to gently remind them of their cultural biases. It is more important that young Christians learn to take their questions to Scripture, than that they get all their answers right.

EVALUATING THE CONTEXT

One of the hermeneutical tasks of the church is to evaluate and respond to the sociocultural and historical contexts in which it finds itself. Here it must undertake the process of critical contextualization for itself. Missionaries and church leaders can help local churches work their way through the process by encouraging the congregations to gather information on the old ways when problems arise. At this stage, the leaders' task is to understand the traditional ways, not judge them, for if they are critical the people will not talk freely for fear of being condemned. The old ways simply go underground. Moreover, it is important to remember that the people are the experts in analyzing their own culture.

Missionaries and church leaders should also help churches study the biblical truths about the matter. For example, in dealing with demon possession, they teach people the Christian doctrines of spirits, angels, and demons. Here the leaders play a major role, for this is the area of their expertise. Lay Christians should be involved in the study, however, because they must learn how to interpret the Bible for themselves. It is important that the leaders be sensitive to the problems of cross-cultural understandings in interpreting Bible passages into the local language.

After studying Scripture, the church must test its old ways in the light of the new. The gospel is a call to change, but if the leaders make the decisions about change, they become police enforcing their decisions. If the people make the decisions, they will corporately enforce them. To involve people in the process of critiquing their own culture in light of new truth draws upon their strength. They know their old culture better than do outsiders, and are in a better position to accurately judge it after they have been biblically instructed. To include them in the decision-making process also helps them grow spiritually by teaching them discernment.

Christians may respond to old beliefs and practices in different ways. They will keep many old cultural ways, just as Christians in the West do, but they will reject other customs as unchristian. Outsiders may not understand the reasons for this repudiation, but the people know the deep hidden meanings of their old ways. Sometimes missionaries and pastors need to question practices people have overlooked because these seem so natural to them. Christians will transform some old practices by giving these explicit Christian meanings. They may use their word for high God for the God of the Bible; give new words to old melodies; and use traditional stories and proverbs to teach biblical truths. Christians should also create new symbols and rites to communicate Christian beliefs in forms indigenous to their own culture. One sign of spiritual life in a church is its ability to do theology and create indigenous Christian music, art, and rites. The church should also adopt imported rites that speak of its new identity as part of the church universal. When people become Christians, they acquire a second history and spiritual heritage. Baptism, the Lord's Supper, church creeds, and hymns not only provide them ways to express their new faith, but also symbolize their ties to the historical and global church.

After critically evaluating their old ways, people, led by their pastors, need to create new beliefs and practices that are both Christian and native. They are no longer pagans, but they should not imitate Western Christians. This process of critical contextualization takes the Bible as the rule of faith and life seriously. It recognizes the work of the Holy Spirit in the lives of all believers open to God's leading. It also strengthens the church by making it a hermeneutical community in which everyone seeks to understand God's message to his people in the context of their everyday lives. The process is summarized well in the Willowbank Report of the Lausanne Committee for World Evangelization.

> It is the need for this dynamic interplay between text and interpreters which we wish to emphasize. Today's readers cannot come to the text in a personal vacuum, and should not try to. Instead, they should come with an awareness of concerns stemming from their cultural background, personal situation, and the responsibility to others. These concerns will influence the questions which are put to the Scriptures. What is received back, however, will not be answers only, but more questions. As we address Scripture, Scripture addresses us. We find that our culturally conditioned presuppositions are being challenged and our questions corrected. In fact, we are compelled to reformulate our previous questions and to ask fresh ones. . . . This process is a kind of upward spiral in which Scripture remains always central and normative. We wish to emphasize that the task of understanding Scriptures belongs not just to individuals but to the whole Christian community, seen as both a contemporary and historical fellowship (LCWE 1978, 11).

Contextualization must be an ongoing process in the life of the church. On the one hand, the world is constantly changing, raising new questions that must be addressed. On the other hand, all human understandings and obedience to the gospel are partial. Through continued study and response, all Christians should grow in spiritual maturity.

MINISTRIES OF TRANSFORMATION

The final step in critical contextualization is ministries that transform individuals and churches, and help individuals and congregations to move from where they are to where God wants them to be. Christian faith is not simply an intellectual exercise in search of truth, nor is it primarily positive feelings of worship to Christ. It must go beyond knowledge of biblical truths to their application in the lives people live. It is the process of hearing and applying the unchanging truths of the gospel to life issues in specific contexts. It is to follow Christ as Lord in every area of life.

How does this transformation of lives and communities take place? Missionaries and church leaders cannot expect people simply to abandon their old ways and adopt new ones. People can only move from where they are by a process of transformation. This is true for individuals as well as social and cultural systems. The leaders must begin where the people are, and lead them step by step toward God's ways. This process is often slow and halting, as believers move forward and slide back. It is often piecemeal. Believers deal first with one area of their lives and then another, often overlooking what to outsiders are important areas needing transformation. In all this, leaders must be patient and redemptive, and not give up.

On one level, transformation is personal. In Christ, people become new creatures. As Paul points out, their lives should reflect the presence and power of the Holy Spirit, making them holy and Christlike in character. The transformation begins with conversion, but it must continue throughout life as believers grow in holiness and Christian maturity. People come with their sins and scars, and leaders must begin with them where they are and gently lead them to Christian maturity. Evangelism and discipling are both essential to the life of the church. The first without the second leads to weak, immature churches poorly grounded in faith. The second without the first leads to ingrown, pharisaical churches that die in their self-centeredness.

On another level, transformation must also occur in social and cultural systems. Corporate transformation must begin in the church. It is the outpost of God's reign on earth and should manifest the social order of the kingdom of God, which is based on love, reconciliation, servanthood, and submission to Christ. The explicit beliefs and underlying worldview of the church must also be transformed to fit those in Scripture. If new converts learn Christian teaching, but continue to think in terms of the underlying categories and assumptions of their old worldview, the gospel will be subverted. The social organization of the church must be transformed. A church that holds to orthodox teachings but operates like the world denies the reality of the gospel. The vital continuity and expansion of Christianity require both a true gospel and a transformed church. The gospel gives life to the church, and the church proclaims the gospel. Either without the other soon dies.

Ministries of transformation must focus on people, not programs. They are not tasks to be accomplished by means of human engineering and action. They begin with learning to understand people, identifying with them, and building relationships of love and trust. They involve communicating the gospel in ways the people understand, and helping them to critique their old religious ways and think biblically in their everyday lives. Those who expect in this book to find strategies for quick solutions to the problems raised by folk religions will be disappointed. Ministry is built on principles, not formulas.

Transformative ministries have to do with the particular. The gospel is truth for people living in specific places and times, and caught in their own dilemmas. In dealing with folk religions it is important to remember that they are incredibly diverse. There are many kinds of witchcraft, divination, spirit possession, and magic, and each requires a biblical response that deals with its particular nature. Specific missiological answers must be formulated in specific contexts by the leaders and missionaries involved. This book does not provide ready answers to the many different beliefs and practices of folk religions around the world. It seeks to provide a conceptual framework whereby Christians can think biblically about folk religions they encounter.

Ministry is an ongoing process, not a job to complete. People hear the gospel through their existing categories, assumptions, and beliefs. Conversion begins when they turn to Christ as Lord, but it must lead to the transformation of their beliefs, worldviews, and lives. This movement toward a mature, truly biblical understanding of reality is a long and difficult one because it calls Christians to new and radical ways of thinking and living in their societies and cultures. It must take place as new fields of ministry are opened, and new generations are born. It must continue as the world around the church changes. Each generation of Christians in each location must discover for itself the message of the gospel for themselves and their times and places.

EVANGELISTIC MINISTRY

Central to the church's ministries of transformation is evangelism—calling people to leave their old gods and to follow Jesus Christ. There can be no greater transformation for humans than the work that God does in their lives when they turn to him in faith.

Many people turn to faith through ministries on the 'middle' or existential level. They are often in crisis, facing the problems of everyday life, and are open to hearing new answers. Ministries of healing lead many to faith in Christ. Similarly, ministries of compassion to the poor and starving, of deliverance to the oppressed and broken, and of love to the lonely and abandoned open the doors for sharing the gospel with nonbelievers who are seeking help. Weddings, funerals, festivals and other rituals are occasions when the church can portray the hope and joy of Christian faith to the community. Giving public testimonies of what God has done in the lives of his people is often more powerful in moving seekers to consider Christ than abstract discourses on theology.

Churches need to develop ministries to the oppressed—the poor, battered, jobless, lonely, orphaned, widowed, aged, disabled, and displaced. They are around and in the church, often unseen. One measure of the godliness of a church is the way it treats the marginalized. The world takes care of the successful, the powerful, and the wealthy. The church exists for others. It is entrusted with the care of those lost on the margins. These ministries may take many forms. Special times of prayer can be set aside for those in need. The church also needs a ministry of hope and assurance to those God chooses not to deliver in dramatic ways.

PASTORAL MINISTRY

The transformation of believers is a lifelong process involving pastoral ministries of discipleship and renewal. Missionaries and leaders need hearts of compassion which seek to help people to grow in faith, and not drive them away, to share in their struggles and not judge them from a position of superiority. They must deal with the everyday needs of their people. They need to minister to the sick and dying, help those seeking guidance, and respond to those who believe they are bewitched or possessed. People need the spiritual healing that comes from being loved even more than they need physical well-being.

The transformation of churches is also an ongoing process. As the world around them changes, they must constantly seek anew to understand what it means to be the sign of God's kingdom in their context. With regard to the existential concerns of folk religions, the church must challenge the values that underlie most folk religions—the obsession with the self, the present, and the good life on earth. It must guard against popular and pragmatic methods that offer immediate solutions, but subvert the gospel. The health of the church in the next century will depend, in large measure, not only on maintaining theological orthodoxy, but also in giving biblical answers to the existential questions people face in their everyday lives.

TEACHING MINISTRY

A third transformative ministry in the church is teaching. Older, more mature Christians should be examples and teachers at heart. They must begin where young believers are in their faith, but they should instruct, encourage, and rebuke, and do so with a firm but gentle spirit.

They should settle disputes and strive for unity and harmony in the congregation, balancing the needs of the members as individuals with the needs of the congregation as a whole. They must model Christian responses to old religious ways, such as divination, witchcraft, and magic.

Paul was an example of balanced teaching. When a movement of ecstasy swept through the church in Corinth, causing some members to exalt speaking in tongues, healing, and other visible manifestations of God's work, Paul took a strong stand, seeking to maintain order and unity in the church. He did not reject the spiritually young for their excesses and their pursuit of the spectacular. Rather, he instructed them in love and firmness to work as one body, to subordinate their personal desires to the well-being of the church, and to guard lest their behavior bring offense to the gospel in the world around them.

PROPHETIC MINISTRY

Every church has a prophetic calling. It must proclaim the good news that creation will one day be restored to perfection; that sickness, loneliness, pain, and death will cease; and that all God's people will spend eternity in his presence with unbounded joy and wholeness. This, truly, is the good life. The church must examine the sociocultural context in which God has placed it, and speak out against sin, injustice, oppression, and hatred. The criteria for making judgments are not the values of the world, nor the majority vote of all those who call themselves Christian. It is the Word of God, understood and applied by communities of committed believers, and proclaimed to the society in which they live. Particular responsibility is placed on leaders to help their congregations in this ministry (1 Tim. 3:2–7; Titus 1:6–9).

Finally, churches must deal with the challenges raised by folk religions. If they do not, their public witness will be compromised by the private practices of their members. Only when all areas of life are brought under the lordship of Christ will churches have a vibrant life and winsome witness in the world.

RESPONDING TO POPULAR RELIGIOUS BELIEFS AND PRACTICES

We began this book by seeking to both acknowledge and deal with a problem that has plagued Christian mission, almost from its inception—the problem of split-level Christianity. Through the development of a model we have called "critical contextualization" we sought to both present the problems and work toward solutions. Our thesis has been that understanding the religious manifestations of the folk (common people in any socioreligious context) can itself be a means to lead appropriate ministry meeting people's felt needs and issues.

The structure of this book models our approach through the application of two models, critical contextualization as a process that enables churches to grow in Christian maturity, and a three-tiered framework for the analysis of religious phenomenology using organic and mechanical analogies. Having established these models in Section One, we have tried to demonstrate their applicability for missionaries and church leaders who find themselves dealing with the beliefs and practices of people to whom they minister. Increasingly in our pluralist world, these issues are no longer pertinent for missionaries, but regularly confront the churches in what used to be largely homogeneous communities in Western Europe and North America. Split-level Christianity is a phenomenon that impacts every corner of the world today. Presenting the underlying principles as they relate to beliefs in Section Two and religious practices in Section Three will, we hope, enable Christians to effectively relate to their neighbors next door or half way around the world.

Having understood the models and interacted with the beliefs and practices of the people, we present, in Section Four, a concern for reaching and discipling the lost. Our focus is both theological and missional as we integrate the elements of the models with the reality of God's kingdom both on earth and in heaven—empirical and transempirical. This has been our purpose and our passion, and, like all who read this book, we struggle daily with the application of these principles to the reality of our own lives and ministries. Critical contextualization remains an ongoing process that will not end until we all stand around the throne of God and join that great throng of believers from every language, tribe, and nation, and worship the Lamb who was slain for the salvation of all people. To him alone be wisdom, honor, power, and glory for ever and ever, amen! (Rev. 7:9, 11).

REFERENCES

Adelowo, E. Dada. 1987. Divination as an aspect of healing processes in the major religions of Nigeria. *African Theological Journal* 16:70–95.

Antoine, Robert. 1975. *Rama and the Bards: Epic Memory in the Ramayana.* Calcutta: Thompson.

Attagara, Kingkeo. 1968. *The Folk Religion of Ban Nai.* Bangkok: Kurusapha Press.

Augsberger, David. 1986. *Pastoral Counseling Across Cultures.* Philadelphia: The Westminster Press.

Baago, Raj. 1968. *The Movement Around Subba Rao: A Study of the Hindu-Christian Movement Around K. Subba Rao in Andhra Pradesh.* Madras: The Christian Literature Society.

Barrett, David. 1968. *Schism and Renewal in Africa: An Analysis of Six Thousand Contemporary Religious Movements.* Nairobi: Oxford University Press.

Barrett, David. 1982. *World Christian Encyclopedia: A Comparative Survey of Churches and Religions in the Modern World A.D. 1900–2000.* Nairobi, Kenya: Oxford University Press.

Becker, Ernest. *Denial of Death.* New York: Free Press. 1973.

Becker, Howard. 1957. Current sacred-secular theory. In *Modern Sociological Theory.* Howard Becker and Alvin Boxkoff, eds. New York: Dryden Press.

Bediako, Kwame. 1995. *Christiantiy in Africa: The Renewal of a Non-Western Religion.* Maryknoll, N.Y.: Orbis Books.

Berger, Peter. 1969. *The Sacred Canopy: Elements of a Sociological Theory of Religion.* Garden City: Doubleday and Company, Anchor Books.

Berger, Peter L., Brigitte Berger, and Hansfried Kellner. 1973. *The Homeless Mind: Modernization and Consciousness.* New York: Random House.

Berger, Peter, and Thomas Luckmann. 1966. *The Social Construction of Reality: A Treatise in the Sociology of Knowledge.* Garden City: Doubleday and Company.

Biallas, Leonard J. 1989. *Myths, Gods, Heros and Saviors.* Mystic, Conn.: Twenty-third Publications.

Bibby, Reginald. 1987. *Fragmented Gods.* Toronto: Irwin.

Bird, Frederick, 1980. The nature and function of ritual forms: A sociological discussion. *Studies in Religion* 9 (Fall): 387–402.

Bloom, Allan. 1987. *The Closing of the American Mind: Education and the Crisis of Reason.* New York: Simon and Schuster.

Bosch, David. 1991. *Transforming Mission: Paradigm Shifts in Theology of Mission.* Maryknoll, N.Y.: Orbis Books.

Broster, D. K. 1947. *The Flight of the Heron.* London: W. Heinemann.

Bulatao, Jaime C. 1992. *Phenomena and Their Interpretation: Landmark Essays 1957–1989.* Manila: Ateneo de Manila.

Bunn, John T. 1973. Glossolalia in historical perspective. In *Speaking in Tongues—Let's Talk about It.* Watson E. Mills, ed. Waco, Tex.: Word Books.

Burnett, David. 1988. *Unearthly Powers: A Christian Perspective on Primal and Folk Religion.* Eastbourne, England: MARC.

Carpenter, Mary Yeo. 1996. Familism and ancestor veneration: A look at Chinese funeral rites. *Missiology* 24: 503–17.

Carroll R., and M. Daniel. 1995. The Bible and the religious identity of the Maya of Guatemala at the conquest and today: Considerations and challenges for the nonindigenous. In J. Rogerson, M. Davies, and M. Carroll R., eds. *The Bible in Ethics.* Sheffield, England: Sheffield Academic Press.

Cassierer, Ernst. 1944. *An Essay on Man.* New Haven, Conn.: Yale University Press.

Clendenin, Daniel B. 1995. From the verbal to the visual: Orthodox icons and the sanctification of sight. *Christian Scholar's Review* 30:30–46.

Codrington, Robert. 1969. *The Melanesians: Studies in Their Anthropology and Folklore.* Oxford: Clarendon. Originally published in 1891.

Cox, Monte B. 1994. *Missiological Implications of Kalenjin Traditional Concepts of Deity, Sin and Salvation.* M.A. thesis. Harding Graduate School of Religion.

———. 1997a. The symbolic anthropology of Mary Douglas: A primer for missionaries. Unpublished paper. Trinity Evangelical Divinity School.

———. 1997b. Wanted: Missionary generalists for holistic ministry. Unpublished paper. Trinity Evangelical Divinity School.

Curley, Richard T. 1983. Dreams of power: Social process in a West African religious movement. *Africa* 28:20–37.

Daneel, M. L. 1970. *Zionism and Faith-Healing in Rhodesia.* The Hague.

deYoung, John E. 1966. *Village Life in Modern Thailand.* Berkeley: University of California Press.

Donovan, Vincent. 1978. *Christianity Rediscovered.* Maryknoll, N.Y.: Orbis Books.

Douglas, Mary. 1963. Techniques of sorcery control in Central Africa. In *Witchcraft and Sorcery in East Africa.* John Middleton and E. H. Winter, eds. London: Routledge and Kegan Paul.

———. 1966. *Purity and Danger: An Analysis of the Concepts of Pollution and Taboo.* London: Routledge and Kegan Paul.

Dye, T. Wayne. 1976. Toward a cultural definition of sin. *Missiology* 4:26–41.

Edwards, Jonathan. 1959. *Religious Affections.* New Haven, Conn.: Yale University Press.

Eliade, Mircea. 1959. *The Sacred and the Profane: The Significance of Religious Myth, Symbolism and Ritual within Life and Culture.* New York: Harcourt, Brace, Jovanovich.

———. 1965. *Rites and Symbols of Initiation.* Translated by Willard R. Trask. New York: Harper and Row.

———. 1975. *Myth and Reality.* New York: Harper and Row.

————. 1976. *Occultism, Witchcraft and Cultural Fashions.* Chicago: University of Chicago Press.

Ellul, Jacques. 1964. *The Technological Society.* New York: Random House.

Etuk, Udo. 1984. New trends in traditional divination. *African Theological Journal* 13:83–91.

Evans-Pritchard, E. E. 1937. *Witchcraft, Oracles and Magic Among the Azande.* Oxford: Oxford University Press.

————. 1962. *Essays in Social Anthropology.* London: Faber.

Forde, Daryll. 1954. *African Worlds: Studies in Cosmological Ideas and Social Values of African People.* London: Oxford University Press.

Forman, Charles. 1985. Playing catch-up ball: The history of financial dependency in Pacific Island churches. In C. Miller, ed. *Missions and Missionaries in the Pacific.* New York: The Edwin Mellen Press.

Fountain, Daniel E. 1989. *Health, the Bible and the Church.* Wheaton, Ill.: The Billy Graham Center.

Frazer, Sir James George. 1922. *The Golden Bough: A Study in Magic and Religion.* Abridged edition. London: Macmillan. Original 12 vols. published 1911–15.

Frazer, Sir James E. 1966 (orig. 1933–36). *The Fear of the Dead in Primitive Religion.* 3 vols. New York: Biblo and Tannen.

Geertz, Clifford. 1965. The impact of the concept of culture on the concept of man. *New Views of the Nature of Man.* John R. Platt, ed. Chicago: University of Chicago Press. 93–118.

————. 1979. Religion as a cultural system. In *Reader in Comparative Religion,* 4th ed. William A. Lessa and Evon Z. Vogt, eds. New York: Harper and Row. 78–89.

Gelner, Ernest. 1992 *Postmodernism, Reason and Religion.* London: Routledge.

Gennep, Arnold L. Van. 1960. *The Rites of Passage.* London: Routledge and Kegan Paul.

Gilchrist, E. 1987. Bab Farid. *Outreach to Islam.* III: 31–33.

Gittins, Anthony J. 1993. *Bread for the Journey: The Mission of Transformation and the Transformation of Mission.* Maryknoll, N.Y.: Orbis Books.

Gmelch, George. 1989. Baseball magic. In *Magic, Witchcraft and Religion: An Anthropological Study of the Supernatural.* 2nd ed. Arthur C. Lehmann and James E. Myers, eds. Mountain View, Calif.: Mayfield Publishing.

Guilick. 1990. Chapel message. Fuller Theological Seminary.

Haracre, Helen. 1986. *Kurozumikyo and the New Religions of Japan.* Princeton, N.J.: Princeton University Press.

Harder, Lydia 1988. Our God-talk: Images, idols, metaphors and masks. *Women's Concern Report.* Report No. 76. January–February. pp. 1–3.

Harrell, Stevan. 1979. The concept of soul in Chinese folk religion. *Journal of Asian Studies* 3:519–28.

Harvey, David. 1990. *The Condition of Postmodernity: An Enquiry into the Origins of Culture Change.* Cambridge, Mass.: Blackwell Publishers.

Hauerwas, Stanley, and W. H. Willimon. 1989. *Resident Aliens.* Nashville: Abingdon.

Hayakawa, S. I. 1978. *Language in Thought and Action.* 2nd ed. New York: Harcourt Brace Jovanovich.

Hayashi, Minoru. 1996. Term paper at Trinity Evangelical Divnity School.

Hayes, Stephen. 1995. Christian response to witchcraft and sorcery. *Missionalia* 23:239–53.

Headland, Thomas N., Kenneth L. Pike, and Marvin Harris, eds. 1990. *Emics and Etics: The Insider Outsider Debate.* Nebury Park, Calif.: Sage Publications.

Henry, Rodney. 1971. *Filipino Spirit World: A Challenge to the Church.* Manila: OMF Publishers.

Hiebert, Paul G. 1993. 1993. Evangelism, church and kingdom. In *The Good News of the Kingdom.* Charles Van Engen, Dean S. Gilliland, and Paul Pierson, eds. Maryknoll, N.Y.: Orbis Books. 151–61.

———. 1994. *Anthropological Reflections on Missiological Issues.* Grand Rapids: Baker Book House.

———. 1999. *The Missiological Implications of Epistemological Shifts.* Vally Forge, Pa.: Trinity Press International.

Hill, Harriet. 1996. Witchcraft and the gospel: Insights from Africa. *Missiology: An International Review* 24:323–44

Hill, Harriet, and Jon Arensen. 1995. *The Best of Ethno-Info.* Nairobi, Kenya: Summer Institute of Linguistics.

Hobson, Steve. 1996. Filipino Worldview Conversion. Paper written for Trinity Evangelical Divinity School.

Horton, Robin. 1962. The Kalabari world-view: An outline and interpretation. *Africa: Journal of the International African Institute* 32:3:197–219.

———. 1964. Ritual man in Africa. *Africa* 34: 85–104.

———. 1967. African traditional thought and western science I & II. *Africa* 37:50–155.

Hyman, Ray, and Evon Z. Vogt. 1967. Water witching: Magical ritual in the contemporary United States. *Psychology Today.* May.

Idowu, E. Bolaji. 1970. Faiths in interaction. *Orita: Ibadan Journal of Religious Studies* 4:85–102.

———. 1975. *African Traditional Religion.* Maryknoll, N.Y.: Orbis Books.

Jeffrey, David L. 1980. Medieval monsters. In *Manlike Monsters on Trial.* Marjorie Halpin and Michael Ames, eds. Vancouver: University of British Columbia Press.

Jones, E. Stanley. 1959. *Conversion.* New York: Abingdon Press.

———. 1970. *The Reconstruction of the Church—On What Pattern?* Nashville: Abingdon Press.

Kähler, Martin. 1971. *Schriften zür Christologie und Mission.* Munich: Chr. Kaiser Verlag.

Kakar, Sudhir. 1982. *Shamans, Mystics, and Doctors: A Psychological Inquiring into India and Its Healing Traditions.* New York: Knopf.

Kato, Byang. 1975. *Theological Pitfalls in Africa.* Nairobi: Evangel Publishing House.

Kavanaugh, John F. 1991. *Following Christ in a Consumer Society—Still: The Spirituality of Cultural Resistance.* Maryknoll, N.Y.: Orbis Books.

Keyes, Charles F. 1990. Buddhist practical morality in a changing agrarian world: A case study in northeastern Thailand. In *Ethics, Wealth and Salvation.* R. Sizemore and D. Swearer, eds. Columbia: University of South Carolina Press.

Keysser, Christian. Trans. Alfred Allin and John Kuder. 1980. *A People Reborn.* Pasadena: William Carey Library.

Kibor, Jacob. 1998. *Persistence of Female Circumcision Among the Marakwet of Kenya: A Biblical Response to a Rite of Passage.* Ph.D. dissertation, Trinity Evangelical Divinity School.

Kim, John T. 1996. *Protestant Church Growth in Korea.* Belleville, Ontario, Canada: Essence Publishing.

King, Eleanor. 1983. Reflections on Korean Dance. In *Korean Art 4: Korean Dance, Theater and Cinema.* The Korean Natonal Commission for UNESCO. Seoul: The si-sa-yong-o-sa.

Kirwen, Michael. 1987. *The Missionary and the Diviner: Contending Theologies of Christian and African Religions.* Maryknoll, N.Y.: Orbis Books.

Kleinman, Arthur. 1980. *Patients and Healers in the Context of Culture.* Berkeley: University of California Press.

Kramer, Gerald P., and George Wu. 1970. *Introduction to Tainwanese Folk Religions.* Taipei: Privately printed.

Kranft, B. M. 1985. *Good Company and Violence: Sorcery and Social Action in a Lowland New Guinea Society.* Berkeley: University of California Press.

Kraus, C. Norman. 1974. *The Community of the Spirit.* Grand Rapids: Eerdmans.

———. 1987. *Jesus Christ Our Lord: Christology from a Disciple's Perspective.* Scottdale, Pa.: Herald Press.

Kroker, Vlademar. 1987. Spiritism in Brazil. *Missions Focus* 15:1–6.

Kuhn, T. S. 1970. *The Structure of Scientific Revolutions.* 2nd ed. Chicago: University of Chicago Press.

Larson, Gerald J., ed. 1974. *Myth in Indo-European Antiquity.* Berkeley: University of California Press.

Lasisi, Lawrence A. 1998. Bridges to Yoruba Muslims from African Indigenous Churches: Contextualizing the Gospel for Muslims in Southwestern Nigeria. Pasadena, Calif.: School of World Mission, Ph.D. proposal. Fuller Theological Seminary.

Laudan, Larry. 1977. *Progress and Its Problems: Towards a Theory of Scientific Growth.* Berkeley: University of California Press.

———. 1996. *Beyond Positivism and Relativism: Theory Method and Evidence.* Boulder, Colo.: Westview Press.

Lausanne Committee for World Evangelization. 1978. *The Willowbank Report: Report on a Consultation on Gospel and Culture.* Wheaton: Lausanne Occasional Papers No. 2.

Layard, A. H. 1861. *Nineveh and Babylon.* London: Murray.

Lessa, William A. 1966. *Ulithi, a Micronesian Design for Living.* New York: Holt, Rinehart and Winston.

LeVine, Robert. 1973. *Culture, Behavior and Personality.* Chicago: Aldine Publishing.

Lewis, C. S. 1961. *The Screwtape Letters*. New York: Macmillan.

———. 1970. *God in the Dock: Essays on Theology and Ethics*. Grand Rapids: Eerdmans.

Lewis, I. M. 1986. *Religion in Context: Cults and Charisma*. Cambridge: Cambridge University Press.

Lim, Guek Eng. 1984. Christianity encounters ancestor worship in Taiwan. *Evangelical Review of Theology*:225–35.

Loewen, Jacob. 1975. *Culture and Human Values: Christian Intervention in Anthropological Perspective*. Pasadena, Calif.: William Carey Library.

Lowery-Palmer, Alma. 1980. *Yoruba World View and Compliance*. Ph.D. dissertation. University of California Riverside. University Microfilm Institute.

Magesa, Laurenti. 1997. *African Religion: The Moral Traditions of Abundant Life*. Maryknoll, N.Y.: Orbis Books.

Malinowski, Bronislaw. 1954. *Magic, Science and Religion and Other Essays*. Garden City, N.Y.: Doubleday.

Marett, Robert R. 1909. *The Threshold of Religion*. 2nd ed. London: Methuen.

Masson, Denis, 1995. What makes them tick? African versus Western thinking processes. In *The Best of Ethno-Info*. Harriet Hill and Jon Arensen, eds. Nairobi: Summer Institute of Linguistics.

Matta, Roberto da. 1991. *Carnivals, Rogues and Heros: An Interpretation of the Brazilian Dilemma*. Notre Dame, Ind.: University of Notre Dame.

Mauss, Marcel. 1967. *The Gift: Forms and Functions of Exchange in Archaic Societies*. New York: W. W. Norton.

May, L. Carlyle. 1956. A survey of glossolalia and related phenomena in non-Christian religions. *American Anthropologist* 58:75–96. Reprinted in *Speaking in Tongues: A Guide to Research on Glossolalia*. Watson E. Mills, ed. Grand Rapids: Eerdmans.

May, Rollo. 1991. *The Cry for Myth*. New York: Delta Publishing.

Mbiti, John S. 1969. *African Religions and Philosophy*. Nairobi: Heinemann.

McFarland, H. Neill. 1967. *The Rush Hour of the Gods: A Study of New Religious Movements in Japan*. New York: Macmillan.

McGregor, Don E. 1969. Learning from Wape mythology. *Practical Anthropology* 16:201–15.

McIlwain, Trevor. 1991. *Building on Firm Foundations*. 10 vols. Sanford, Fla.: New Tribes Mission.

Mendosa, Eugene. 1989. Characteristics of Sisala diviners. In *Magic, Witchcraft and Religion: An Anthropological Study of the Supernatural*. Arthur C. Lehmann and James E. Myers, eds. Mountain View, Calif.: Mayfield Publishing. 247–53

Middleton, John. 1960. *Lugbara Religion*. London: Oxford University Press.

Mikulencak, Ruby 1987. Science and magic collide in African magic. *Evangelical Missions Quarterly* 23:358–363.

Miller, Char, ed. 1985. *Missions and Missionaries in the Pacific*. New York: The Edwin Mellen Press.

Moody, Edward J. 1989. Urban witches. In *Magic, Witchcraft and Religion: An Anthropological Study of the Supernatural*. Arthur C. Lehmann and James E. Myers, eds. Mountain View, Calif.: Mayfield Publishing. 247–53

Moyo, Ambrose. 1996. *Zimbabwe: The Risk of Incarnation*. Geneva: WCC Publications.

Mulder, J. A. Neils. 1979. *Everyday Life in Thailand: An Interpretation*. Bangkok: D. K. Books.

Mukund, Mulumba. 1988. *Witchcraft Among the Kasaian People of Zaire: Challenge and Response*. Ph.D. dissertation. Fuller Theological Seminary.

Namunu, Simeon. n.d. Spirits in Melanesia and the Spirit in Christianity. Pasadena, Calif.: School of World Mission.Unpublished paper.

Neill, Stephen. 1961. *Christian Faith and Other Faiths*. London: Oxford University Press.

Newbigin, Leslie. 1958. *One Body, One Gospel, One World*. London and New York: International Missionary Council.

Offiong, Daniel A. 1991. *Witchcraft, Sorcery, Magic and Social Order among the Ibibio of Nigeria*. Enugu, Nigeria: Fourth Dimension Publishing.

Oleska, Michael. 1987. *Alaskan Missionary Spirituality*. New York: Paulist Press.

Olthuis, James H. 1985. On worldviews. *Christian Scholar's Review* 14:153–64.

Ong, W. J. 1969. World as view and world as event. *American Anthropologist* 71:634–47.

Opler, Morris E. 1945. Themes as dynamic forces in culture. *American Journal of Sociology* 51:198–206.

Parrinder, G. *Witchcraft: European and African*. London: Faber and Faber. 1958.

Parsons, Talcott, and Edward Shils, eds. 1952. *Toward a General Theory of Action*. Cambridge, Mass.: Harvard University Press.

Pattison, E. Mansell. 1989. Psychosocial interpretations of exorcism. In *Magic, Witchcraft and Religion: An Anthropological Study of the Supernatural*. Arthur C. Lehmann and James E. Myers, eds. Mountain View, Calif.: Mayfield Publishing, 264–77.

Peirce, Charles. S. 1955. [Original 1940] *Philosophical Writings of Peirce*. Justus Buchler, ed. New York: Dover Publications.

Pepper, Stephen. 1949 *World Hypotheses*. Berkeley: University of California Press.

Peterson, Eugene. 1994. *Subversive Spirituality*. Grand Rapids: Eerdmans.

———. 1996. *Living the Message: Daily Reflections with Eugene H. Peterson*. San Franscisco: HarperSanFrancisco.

———. 1997. *Leap Over a Wall: Earthly Spirituality for Everyday Christians*. San Francisco: HarperSanFrancisco.

Pike, K. L. 1954. *Language in Relation to a Unified Theory of the Structure of Human Behavior*. The Hague: Mouton.

Pobee, John. 1982. Political theology in the African context. *African Theological Journal* 11:168–72.

———. 1996. *West Africa: Christ Would be an African Too*. Geneva: WCC Publications.

Price, Raymond. 1964. Indigenous Yoruba psychiatry. In *Magic, Faith and Healing*. Ari Kiev, ed. New York: The Free Press.

Puhvel, Jen, ed. 1970. *Myth and Law among the Indo-Europeans: Indo-European Comparative Mythology*. Berkeley: University of California Press.

Rao, Raja. 1967. *Kanthapura*. New York: New Directions Publishing.

Rattray, R. S. 1923. *Ashanti*. London: Oxford University Press.

———. 1954. *Religion and Arts in Ashanti*. London: Oxford University Press.

Ray, Benjamin. 1976. *African Religions: Symbol, Ritual and Community*. Englewood Cliffs, N.J.: Prentice-Hall.

Richardson, Don. 1978. *Peace Child*. Glendale, Calif.: Regal.

———. 1981. *Eternity in Their Hearts*. Ventura, Calif.: Regal Books.

Ritchie, Mark A. 1996. *Spirit of the Rainforest: A Yanamam Shaman's Story*. Chicago: Island Lake Press.

Ro, Bong Rin, ed. 1985. *Christian Alternatives to Ancestor Practices*. Taichung, Taiwan: Asia Theological Association.

Robarchek, C. A. 1989. Primitive warfare and the ratiomorphic image of mankind. *American Anthropologist* 91:903–20.

Robertson Smith, W. 1889. *The Religion of The Semites*. Edinburgh: Black.

Rosenau, Pauline. 1992. *Post-Modernism and the Social Sciences: Insights, Inroads and Intrusions*. Princeton, N.J.: Princeton University Press.

Rubingh, Eugene. 1974. The African shape of the gospel. *Impact*. (March): 3–5.

Saussure, Ferdinand de. 1983. [1916] *Course in General Linguistics*. Trans. Roy Harris. Chicago: Open Court Classics.

Schreiter, Robert. 1987. *New Catholicity: Theology Between the Global and Local*. Maryknoll, N.Y.: Orbis Books.

Scotchmer, David. 1989. Symbols of salvation: A local Mayan Protestant theology. *Missiology* 8:449–54.

Shaw, R. Daniel. 1981. Every person a shaman: The use of supernatural power among the Samo. *Missiology* 9:159–165.

———. 1990. *Kandila: Samo Ceremonialism and Interpersonal Relationships*. Ann Arbor: University of Michigan Press.

———. 1996. *From Longhouse to Viullage: Samo Social Change*. Fort Worth: Harcourt Brace.

Shorter, Aylward. 1985. *Jersus and the Witchdoctor: An Approach to Healing and Wholeness*. Maryknoll, N.Y.: Orbis Books.

Slack, Jim. 1990. *Evangelism among People who Learn Best by Oral Tradition: The Storying or Chronological Bible Communication Method*. Foreign Mission Board, Southern Baptist Convention.

Sperber, Dan. 1974. *Rethinking Symbolism*. Trans. Alice Morton. Cambridge: Cambridge University Press.

Staples, Russell. 1982. Western medicine and the primal world-view. *International Bulletin of Missiological Research* 6:70–71.

Stark, Rodney. 1993. Europe's receptivity to new religious movements: Round two. *Journal for the Scientific Study of Religion* 32:389–97.

Stephen, M. 1987. Contrasting images of power. In *Sorcerer and Witch in Melanesia*. M. Stephen, ed. New Brunswick: Rutgers University Press 249–304.

Stevens, David. 1997. The earth is more to God than scenery for humans. *Gospel Herald* July 22, 1–3, 8.

Stott, John. 1991. *Life in Christ*. Grand Rapids: Baker Book House.

Strelan. John G. 1978. *Search for Salvation: Studies in the History and Theology of the Cargo Cults*. Adelaide: Lutheran Publishing House.

Sumption, Jonathan. 1975. *Pilgrimage: An Image of Mediaeval Religion*. Totowa, N.J.: Rowman and Littlefield.

Sundkler, Bengt. 1961. *Bantu Prophets in South Africa*. London: Oxford University Press.

Taber, Charles. 1991. *The World Is Too Much With Us: "Culture" in Modern Protestant Missions*. Macon, Ga.: Mercer University Press.

Tambiah, S. J. 1970. *Buddhism and the Spirit Cults in Northeast Thailand*. Cambridge: Cambridge University Press.

————. 1973. The form and meaning of magical acts: A point of view. In *Modes of Thought*. R. Horton and R. Finnegan, eds. London: Faber and Faber Ltd. 199–229.

Taylor, J. V. 1958. *The Growth of the Church in Buganda*. London: Greenwood.

————. 1963. *The Primal Vision: Christian Presence amid African Religion*. London: SCM Press.

Tempels, Placide. 1959. *Bantu Philosophy*. Paris: Presence Africaine.

Tippett, Alan. 1967. *Solomon Islands Christianity*. New York: Friendship.

Troeltsch, Ernst. 1931. *The Social Teaching of the Christian Churches*. 2 vols. New York: Macmillan.

Truzzi, Marcello. 1989. The occult revival as popular culture. In *Magic, Witchcraft and Religion: An Anthropological Study of the Supernatural*. Arthur C. Lehmann and James E. Myers, eds. Mountain View, Calif.: Mayfield Publishing. 403–11.

Turner, Harold. 1967. *African Independent Church*. 2 vols. Oxford: Clarendon Press.

————. 1981. Religious movements in primal (or tribal) societies. *Mission Focus* 9:45–54.

Turner, Victor. 1969. *The Ritual Process*. Harmondsworth: Penguin Books.

————. 1974. *Dramas, Fields and Metaphors: Symbolic Action in Human Society*. Ithaca, N.Y.: Cornell University Press.

————. 1978. *Image and Pilgrimage in Christian Cultures: Anthropological Perspective*. New York: Columbia University Press.

Tylor, E. B. 1913 (orig. 1873). *Primitive Culture: Researches into the Development of Mythology, Philosophy, Religion, Language, Art and Custom*. New York: Brentano's.

Van Engen, Charles. 1996. *Mission on the Way*. Grand Rapids: Baker Book House.

Van Rheenen, Gailyn. 1991. *Communicating Christ in Animistic Contexts*. Grand Rapids: Baker Book House.

Verger, Pierre. 1969. Trance and convention in Nago-Yoruba Spirit Mediumship. *In Spirit Mediumship and Society in Africa*. John Beattie and John Middleton, eds. London: Routledge and Kegan Paul Ltd.

von Bertalanffy, Ludwig. 1981. *A Systems View of Man*. Paul A. LaViolette, ed. Boulder, Colo.: Westview Press.

Wagley, Charles, and Eduardo Galvao. 1949. *The Tenetehara Indians of Brazil.* New York: Columbia University Press.

Wakatama, Pius. 1976. *Independence for the Third World Church, An African Perspective on Missionary Work.* Downers Grove, Ill.: InterVarsity Press.

Wallace, Anthony F. C. 1956. Revitalization movements. *American Anthropologist* 58:264–81.

Walls, Andrew F. 1996. *The Missionary Movement in Christian History: Studies in the Transmission of Faith.* Maryknoll, N.Y.: Orbis Books.

Warneck, John. 1954. *The Living Christ and Dying Heathenis: The Experiences of a Missionary in Animistic Heathanism.* Grand Rapids: Baker Book House.

Warner, Paula. 1990. African healer vs. missionary physician. *Evangelical Missions Quarterly* 26: 396–404.

Weber, Max. 1946. The Protestant sects and the spirit of capitalism. In *From Max Weber: Essays in Sociology.* New York: Oxford University Press.

Wesley, John. 1952. *Plain Account of Christian Perfection.* London: Epworth.

Westermark, Eduard A. 1926. *Ritual and Belief in Morocco.*

Whiting, John W. M., and Irvin L. Child. 1953. *Child Training and Personality: A Cross-Cultural Study.* New Haven, Conn.: Yale University Press.

Wiens, Delbert. 1995. *Stephen's Sermons and the Structure of Luke–Acts.* N. Richland Hills, Tex.: BIBAL Press.

Williamson, Sidney G. 1965. *Akamba Religion and the Christian Faith.* Accra: Ghana Universities Press.

Wilson, Monica. 1954. Nyakyusa ritual and symbolism. *American Anthropologist* 56, no. 2.

Wink, Walter. 1992. *Engaging the Powers: Discernment and Resisting World Domination.* Minneapolis: Fortress Press.

Wolf, Eric R. 1962. *Sons of the Shaking Earth.* Chicago: University of Chicago Press.

Worsley, Peter M. 1968. *The Trumpet Shall Sound: A Study of "Cargo Cults" in Melanesia.* 2nd ed. New York: Schocken Books.

———. 1997. Cargo cults. In *Magic, Witchcraft, and Religion.* 4th edition. Arthur Lehmann and James Myers, eds. Mountain View, Calif.: Mayfield Publishing. 342–46.

Yamamori, Tetsunao, and Charles Taber, eds. *1975. Christopaganism or Indigenous Christianity?* South Pasadena, Calif.: William Carey Library

Yancy, Philip. 1983. Finding the will of God: No magic formulas. *Christianity Today.* September 16, 24–27.

———. 1990. *Where is God When it Hurts?* Rev. ed. New York: Harper Paperbacks.

Young, Joshua U. 1986. *Black and African Theologies: Siblings or Distant Cousins?* Maryknoll, N.Y.: Orbis Books.

Zahniser, A. H. Mathias. 1997. *Symbol and Ceremony: Making Disciples Across Cultures.* Monrovia, Calif.: MARC.

The Economist, 1995. Witchcraft in South Africa. December 9, 85–86.

———. 1995. Chinese offices: Geomancing the stone. *The Economist.* November 25, 90–91.

———. 1995. South Africa: Traditional Healers. *The Economist.* November 25, 86–87.

INDEX

Note: Folios in italics refer to illustrative material.

Paul G. Hiebert (Ph.D., University of Minnesota) is professor of mission and anthropology at Trinity Evangelical Divinity School and the author of several books, including *Anthropological Insights for Missionaries*.

Daniel Shaw (Ph.D., University of Papua New Guinea), professor of anthropology and translation at Fuller Theological Seminary, has written several essays on anthropology.

Tite Tiénou (Ph.D., Fuller Theological Seminary) is professor of theology of mission at Trinity Evangelical Divinity School and the author of *The Theological Task of the Church in Africa*.